Champagne & Shambles

The Arkwrights & the Country House in Crisis

Catherine Beale

Foreword by Ronald Blythe

The History Press

In memory of my mother
Sybil Jane Owens
(née Price, of Abercray, Trecastle, Brecon)
1943–89

Front cover: Hampton Court (Courtesy of Hampton Court)

First published 2006
This edition first published in 2009

The History Press
The Mill, Brimscombe Port
Stroud, Gloucestershire, GL5 2QG
www.thehistorypress.co.uk

Reprinted 2010

British Library Cataloguing in Publication Data.
A catalogue record for this book is available from the British Library.

ISBN 978 0 7524 5435 1

Typesetting and origination by The History Press
Printed in Great Britain

Contents

	List of Plates	iv
	Foreword	vi
	Arkwright Family Tree	viii
	Map of Herefordshire	ix
	Introduction	1
One	The Heir to the Seat	13
Two	The Season and its Harvest	27
Three	Master of the Estate	38
Four	Mastering the Family	54
Five	Foxley Hunting	69
Six	Sons and Mothers	83
Seven	Hodge Finds his Voice	100
Eight	Down Corn, Up Horn	114
Nine	Algiers to Aberystwyth	128
Ten	Sized up, Seized up and Silenced	139
Eleven	Arkwrights Act	149
Twelve	Parasites and Mousetraps	163
Thirteen	Land Loss at Home, Victory Abroad	175
Fourteen	Lord Looted	193
Fifteen	Letting and Going	203
	Epilogue	214
	Notes	227
	Sources and Bibliography	280
	Index	285
	Acknowledgements	301

List of Plates

1. Hampton Court, Herefordshire, north front, *c.* 1880. *(By kind permission of the descendants of Mary Arkwright)*
2. Johnny's twenty-first birthday celebrations, 2–4 August 1854. *(By kind permission of the descendants of Sir John Arkwright)*
3. Willersley Castle, Cromford, Derbyshire, 1888. *(By kind permission of the descendants of Mary Arkwright)*
4. John Arkwright (1785–1858), grandson of Sir Richard Arkwright. *(By kind permission of the descendants of Sir John Arkwright)*
5. Caroline Arkwright and Berkeley Scudamore Stanhope. *(By kind permission of Herefordshire Archive Service)*
6. Johnny in the bachelor days after his father's death. *(By kind permission of Herefordshire Archive Service)*
7. Edward Colley, the agent of the Hampton Court estate. *(By kind permission of Herefordshire Archive Service)*
8. Bonham Caldwall, a trustee of the estate. *(By kind permission of the descendants of Mary Arkwright)*
9. Johnny's uncle Chandos Wren Hoskyns. *(By kind permission of Rev. John Hoskyns)*
10. Johnny with his violin at Aix-la-Chapelle in 1863. *(By kind permission of the descendants of Mary Arkwright)*
11. Johnny and the Three Graces – Fanny, Emily and Alice – with Charlie. *(By kind permission of the descendants of Mary Arkwright)*
12. Sarah Arkwright, 'Tally'. *(By kind permission of Herefordshire Archive Service)*
13. The Herefordshire Hunt's opening meet at Hampton Court in 1866 or 1867. *(By kind permission of Julian Armytage, print dealer)*

14. Johnny's third brother, Henry. *(By kind permission of Herefordshire Archive Service)*
15. Lucy and puppy Greta, *c.* 1869. *(By kind permission of the descendants of Sir John Arkwright)*
16. Johnny's nearest brother in age, Richard. *(By kind permission of the descendants of Mary Arkwright)*
17. Johnny and young Jack in the gardens at Hampton Court. *(By kind permission of the descendants of Richard Chester-Master)*
18. Johnny's splendidly illustrated letter to Geraldine (Pinkie) from Algeria in 1881. *(By kind permission of Herefordshire Archive Service)*
19. Johnny and Robert Eckley, his bailiff, with three prize-winning Hereford bulls. *(By kind permission of the descendants of Sir John Arkwright)*
20. An advertisement for the fruit trays, which Johnny invented. *(By kind permission of the Royal Agricultural Society of England)*
21. Articles found with Henry's body in the glacier on Mont Blanc in 1897. *(By kind permission of the descendants of Mary Arkwright)*
22. Hampton Court, south front, *c.* 1900. *(By kind permission of the owners of Hampton Court)*
23. John Stanhope Arkwright, Jack. *(By kind permission of Herefordshire Libraries)*
24. Richard Chester-Master (back row, right), ADC to Milner. *(By kind permission of Hugh Hardinge)*
25. Geraldine and Richard Chester-Master on their wedding day. *(By kind permission of the descendants of Richard Chester-Master)*
26. Johnny as Lord Lieutenant. *(By kind permission of Herefordshire Libraries)*
27. Sutton Scarsdale, Derbyshire, *c.* 1902. *(By kind permission of the descendants of Sir John Arkwright)*
28. Sutton Scarsdale, *c.* 1998.
29. Tally's home, Harewood, being blown up by the Royal Monmouth Royal Engineers as explosives practice on 22 March 1959. *(Photograph reproduced courtesy of the* Hereford Times*)*
30. Mark Hall, Essex, home of John's brother, Rev. Joseph Arkwright. *(By kind permission of Herefordshire Archive Service)*

Foreword

This is a fascinating story, unique in my experience of rural social history. It gives the facts and figures of what was popularly called the 'coming-down time', that protracted collapse of nineteenth-century land values which continues to shape village life to this day. And not only our countryside, but our politics too. Weather also had a hand in it, years of rain which washed away the late Victorian harvests and were felt to be by some as a divine indictment of agriculture itself. This steady draining of profits from what had immemorially been the basis of real wealth – the fields and forests – and which had for centuries successfully ordered country dwellers into aristocrats, yeomen and peasants, was, as this marvellously documented book reveals, seen at first as an impossibility. Just as the biblical promise of seed-time and harvest never ceasing was believed, so was land ownership seen, even when it was slipping away, as the sure foundation of British society.

Throughout the 'coming-down time' historians, great novelists, and worried diarists all described this dramatic breaking-down of what for generations had been the only true source of wealth and position, the land itself. Its owners had covered it with magnificent parks and palace-like houses. The farmhouses and their work buildings looked profitable and were often beautiful, and at the time when the fissures began to threaten this classic scene many landowners started to care in a new fashion for the labourers and their families, building schools and estate cottages. All this has been much written about by the social historian.

Yet the overall accounts of the 'coming-down time' rarely reveal what was actually occurring at the top as prices fell, farmers struggled and men fled. As Catherine Beale shows, nothing was happening at the top. Taking the Arkwrights of Hampton Court, Herefordshire as a typical landowning Victorian family, she exposes not only their dwindling fortune but their unchanging attitudes. Moreover, she makes us like them, not romantically as we nowadays stare up at the portraits in some country house open to the public, or watch its old life in a film, but as individuals. Johnny Arkwright, a rich young man descended from the famous Sir Richard Arkwright, who invented a spinning machine which brought him a fortune, did not as some might think go on living beyond his means as his landed interests foundered, as it were. He simply went on living the only life he understood. *Champagne and Shambles* might suggest a picture of high living and the devil take tomorrow, but it is devoid of that recklessness which became a cliché in the fiction of the times. Rather we are shown a landowning family which, like so many others, was strangely ignorant of the swift disappearance of its universe – and this in spite of the fact that between the 1870s and 1890s prices had fallen from £54 to £19 an acre. Entire villages were abandoned by the labourers and just before the First World War farms in East Anglia were practically given way. The War, and previous imperial wars, slaughtered the inheritors, and another Arkwright, Sir John, mourned the loss with his plaintive hymn, 'O Valiant Hearts', still sung in country churches on Remembrance Day.

Catherine Beale's achievement is to have written an enthralling biographical economy in which a single landowning family is made to tell the full story of agriculture and the social life around it from the early nineteenth century almost up to the present. In it she has avoided all the stereotypical images of the landowning classes and given us vulnerable human beings who are seen as helpless in one of history's great shake-ups. Alongside this scholarly portrait she sketches our current flirtation with the country house from Brideshead to Gosford Park. It is a sympathetic read and an enlightening one. The many thousands for whom these places are now a reminder of a civilisation should read it – alongside the guidebook. It will alter all their views.

Ronald Blythe

Arkwright Family Tree

(Simplified)

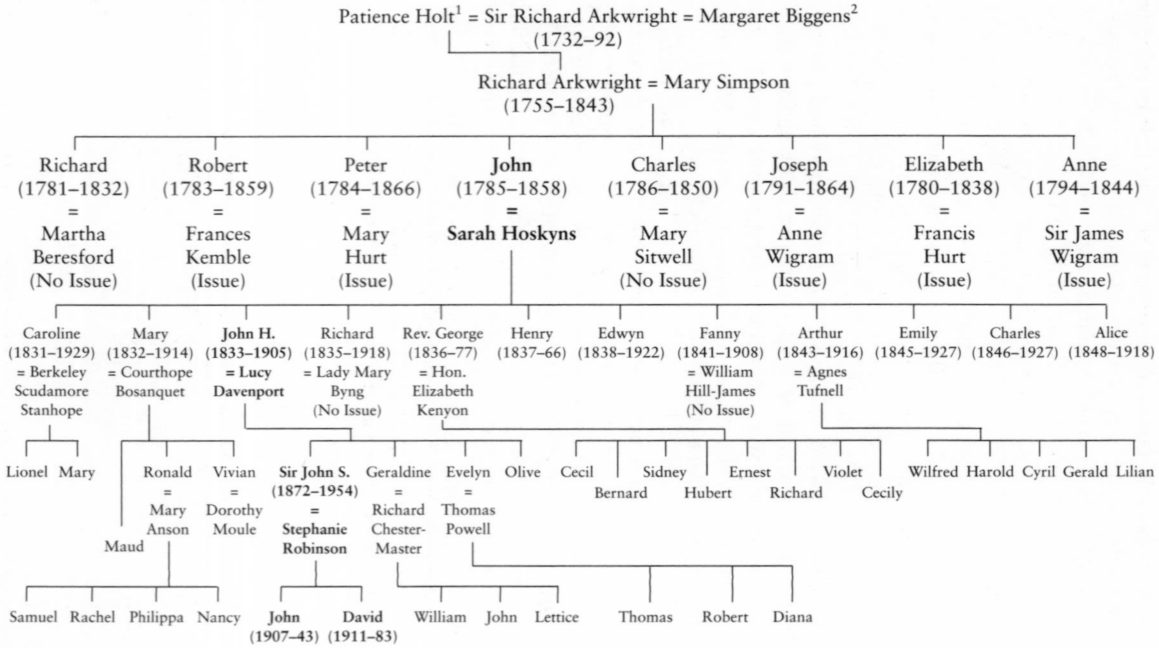

Patience Holt[1] = Sir Richard Arkwright = Margaret Biggens[2]
(1732–92)
Richard Arkwright = Mary Simpson
(1755–1843)
Richard (1781–1832) = Martha Beresford (No Issue)
Robert (1783–1859) = Frances Kemble (Issue)
Peter (1784–1866) = Mary Hurt (Issue)
John (1785–1858) = Sarah Hoskyns
Charles (1786–1850) = Mary Sitwell (No Issue)
Joseph (1791–1864) = Anne Wigram (Issue)
Elizabeth (1780–1838) = Francis Hurt (Issue)
Anne (1794–1844) = Sir James Wigram (Issue)
Caroline (1831–1929) = Berkeley Scudamore Stanhope
Mary (1832–1914) = Courthope Bosanquet
John H. (1833–1905) = Lucy Davenport
Richard (1835–1918) = Lady Mary Byng (No Issue)
Rev. George (1836–77) = Hon. Elizabeth Kenyon
Henry (1837–66)
Edwyn (1838–1922)
Fanny (1841–1908) = William Hill-James (No Issue)
Arthur (1843–1916) = Agnes Tufnell
Emily (1845–1927)
Charles (1846–1927)
Alice (1848–1918)
Lionel
Mary
Maud
Ronald = Mary Anson
Vivian = Dorothy Moule
Sir John S. (1872–1954) = Stephanie Robinson
Geraldine = Richard Chester-Master
Evelyn = Thomas Powell
Olive
Cecil
Bernard
Sidney
Hubert
Ernest
Richard
Violet
Cecily
Wilfred
Harold
Cyril
Gerald
Lilian
Samuel
Rachel
Philippa
Nancy
John (1907–43)
David (1911–83)
William
John
Lettice
Thomas
Robert
Diana

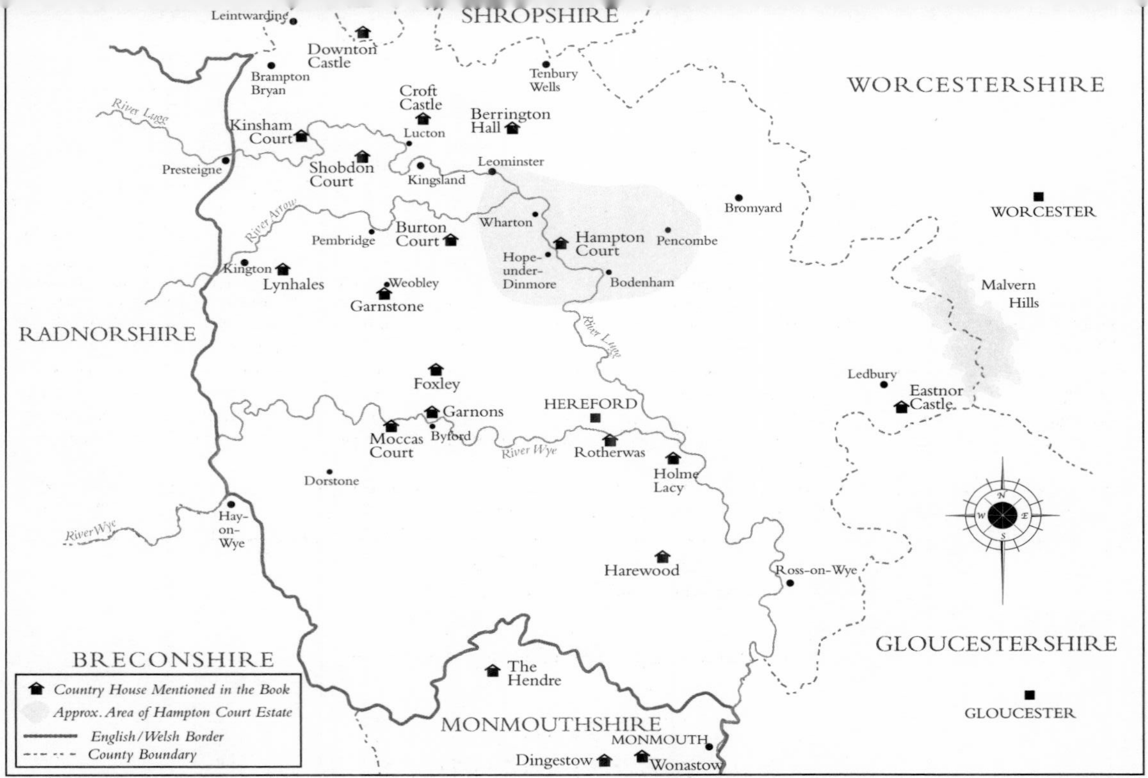

Map of Herefordshire (not to scale).

Introduction

'I am in an awful state of depression which nothing but champagne can remove', wrote Johnny Arkwright in January 1870.[1] Six months after the death of his mother, Johnny, then 36 years old, was struggling to find £25,000 (over a million pounds today)[2] to pay his brothers their inheritance – a sum equivalent to two and a half times his gross annual income. He was privately facing an emotional and financial crisis, but things were about to get a great deal worse.

Johnny's words could have served as the chorus for his entire social class between 1870 and the First World War – the years of champagne and shambles. In January 1870, John Hungerford Arkwright (1833–1905) was the largest landowner in the most agricultural county in England.[3] He was the grandson of 'the richest commoner in Europe',[4] and had inherited a fairytale fifteenth-century crenellated house and the 10,250-acre estate that surrounded it. As one of England's top 365 landowners, he was among the élite class of the most powerful nation on earth.

However, revolution was brewing, a quiet revolution such as only the British could mount, a revolution led by due democratic process and supported by the mob of market forces. Britain's greatest patrician families were about to be engulfed by events beyond their control, by an avalanche of change that would sweep them aside as it – quite literally in 1,200 cases in the twentieth century – demolished their homes.[5]

The downfall of the landed class in Britain is a subject that has been treated in diverse ways in the past. Lord Tennyson's 1886 poem 'Locksley Hall Sixty Years After' boils with anger at the breakdown already under way. Oscar Wilde made ascerbic but amusing observations on the eradication of those whom he regarded as 'unspeakable', in his play *The Importance of Being Earnest* (1895). Among the most humorous treatments of the subject is Noël Coward's 1936 song 'The Stately Homes of England', and Evelyn Waugh fictionalised the Marchmains' plight in his elegaic 1945 novel *Brideshead Revisited*.

In non-fiction, F.M.L. Thompson has undertaken much work on agriculture and landed estates.[6] The recollections of some of the villagers in Ronald Blythe's *Akenfield* (1969) reach back to rural life during this period of upheaval. The most comprehensive account of this process, however, has been given by David Cannadine in his 1990 work, *The Decline and Fall of the British Aristocracy*.[7] Cannadine identifies the patrician élite and compares its members with their counterparts in Europe. He shows how and why their broad acres lost their value, how the aristocracy's political power was eroded and how its control in the shires was superseded by professional local government. The aristocracy, Cannadine further illustrates, had ceased to represent the richest class in society by the dawn of the twentieth century, and it had contemporaneously ceased to rule.

Cannadine's scholarly, comprehensive, and refreshingly irreverent account considers the fall of the landed class as a whole between 1880 and 1930, and dips into a breathtakingly broad range of sources. This book is narrower in breadth, but humanises this social change by plunging more deeply into the predicament of one family over the sixty-year period 1854–1914. In doing so, it attempts to show how the events of their undoing in the second half of the nineteenth century appeared to the landed class at the time; how the balance of power between the bank manager and the patrician client shifted as land values plummeted; how the squire could no longer be sure of getting the right man in at the local parliamentary election; and how the landowner came to be expected to take his seat alongside his tenants in the church hall for Parish Council meetings.

In order to demonstrate this, I have used the extensive collection of private and estate papers preserved by the Arkwright family, and now by Herefordshire Archive Service. 'Keep all your letters,' Johnny advised his son Jack, in 1885, while he was at Eton, just as his own father had advised him.[8] As a result, the Arkwright Collection consists of dozens of boxes each containing up to a hundred yellowing letters, occasionally with pressed-flower enclosures. These passed between husband and wife, and parents and children, revealing the feelings of their correspondent about contemporary change. The broken-backed leather ledgers of tenants' rents and labourers' wages show changing estate management in the attempt to evade ruin. School reports, and elaborate photograph albums lend charm and depth. Close examination of these papers combined with the study of more general works revealed the Arkwrights' story to be a remarkably accurate illustration of the revolution against which they were struggling. I hope that this account will complement the work of Cannadine and his colleagues.

This is a book, therefore, that takes the historical and makes it personal. As a 24-year-old, Johnny Arkwright of Hampton Court, Herefordshire, seemed to inherit the earth, yet he had to mortgage part of his estate in his seventies. Johnny's grandfather Richard Arkwright (1755–1843) bought the quadrangular manor house, contents and 6,220 acres in 1810 from the 5th Earl of Essex. To acquire the estate, Richard paid £226,535 (equivalent to approximately £6.2 million today), a sum equivalent to roughly 30 per cent of the total annual investment in the cotton industry at the time.[9] Richard was the only son of the industrialist Sir Richard Arkwright (1732–92) who perfected a mechanical method of spinning cotton yarn. His patent for the spinning frame, and that for his later carding machine, made him a fortune.

Sir Richard Arkwright's most enduring legacy, however, was the factory system.[10] In 1771, he erected a spinning mill at Cromford in Derbyshire, and to this was added a carding mill in 1776. To supply his workforce, as Arkwright's biographer R.S. Fitton noted, he built 'habitations most comfortable', a chapel for 300 people, a Sunday school, the Black Greyhound Inn and schools for the children.[11] The significance of Cromford was acknowledged in 2001 when the Derwent Valley was designated a World Heritage Site.

Richard Arkwright the younger, the only son, had made a spinning fortune of his own before he inherited his father's fortune in 1792. Through judicious investment and scrupulous attention to detail, Richard increased his wealth. By the time of his death in 1843, he was worth £3.25 million (almost £181 million today).[12] It was estimated in the year 2000 that Richard Arkwright was joint 180th richest man since 1066.[13]

From 1792, Richard Arkwright began to invest in landed estates, not so much because he wanted to set up his sons (though that was the result) but rather because, during the blockades of the Napoleonic Wars, agriculture was producing a good return. He purchased five major estates for a total of £391,000: Normanton Turville in Leicestershire (in 1792), Hampton Court in Herefordshire (1808–10), Mark Hall in Essex (1819), Sutton Scarsdale in Derbyshire (1824) and Dunstall in Staffordshire (1826).[14] Of these, Hampton Court was the largest. On Richard's death, each of his sons took to the estate on which he was living – Robert inherited Sutton Scarsdale, Peter Willersley, John Hampton Court, Charles Dunstall, and Rev. Joseph Mark Hall and Normanton Turville (to which he had taken after the death of their eldest brother in 1832).

Richard never intended to live at Hampton Court. He sent his Matlock land agent George Nuttall to Herefordshire to apply industrial principles to agriculture; the weir near the bridge over the River Lugg was mended, and the river water powered saw- and stone-mills. Brick kilns and eventually a small railway were built at the estate works near the home farm, and professional book-keeping skills were employed in the estate office.

The fourth of Richard's six sons, the Eton- and Cambridge-educated John, asked to reside at Hampton Court in 1814. John had by then seen four of his five brothers marry, and being still single but wishing to settle, he confessed to his father that 'of all the situations I know, there is none which suits my tastes so well as Hampton Court . . . I should like a small farm, grazing or breeding, with liberty to preserve, Shoot and Fish'.[15] His wish was granted, and from then until Richard Arkwright's death in April 1843, John acted as a go-between for his father and the agent at Hampton Court, asking for and having to justify expenditure on the house or estate, and having occasionally to persuade his father to soften some decisions which, being founded on good industrial principles, were not consistent with what was expected of the owner of a landed estate. In the depression that followed the Napoleonic Wars, Richard wanted to cut back on estate expenditure but John had to make him see that it was his responsibility instead to embark on large projects to employ more men. In addition, John persuaded his father to remit up to 33 per cent (in 1823) of the rents in difficult years.[16]

In 1830, amid a flurry of gossip, John married Sarah (Tally), the daughter of impecunious local baronet Sir Hungerford Hoskyns of Harewood Park near Ross-on-Wye. Tally was twenty-three years younger than John, which some deemed '*unfortunate*; persons who know her say her manners are artificial & that she has a very high spirit . . . but love is blind, they say, & Miss H is young & pretty looking'.[17] They produced seven sons and five daughters in the following eighteen years.

By the 1830s, Hampton Court had not housed any children for around 120 years. Tally could no doubt see opportunities for improvements in the domestic arrangements, so, from 1835, John undertook major work on the house to accommodate the family more comfortably. The medieval Great Hall and Great Parlour were reproportioned to produce a dining room and library, and a new drawing room was added at the south-west corner of the house. Nurseries and a schoolroom were also incorporated in the south front.

John's choice of architect, Charles Hanbury Tracy, seemed promising.[18] Hanbury Tracy's predilection for the Oxford collegiate style, visible at his own home, Toddington in Gloucestershire, appeared well suited to

Hampton Court's original architecture.[19] However, disagreements between Hanbury Tracy and Tally over the location of the nurseries resulted in over a decade of alterations and altercations. John grew alarmed at the scale and cost of the work, and Hanbury Tracy was scornful of John's entertainment of the wishes of his wife.[20] John derived infinitely more pleasure from corresponding with, and welcoming on a visit, Joseph Paxton, whom John commissioned to design the new conservatory that was added to the south-west corner in 1845–6.[21] In all, the work cost over £30,000, took twelve years, and produced 'a Herefordshire Windsor',[22] but by the end of his life, John wished that he had never touched a stone.

On his father's death, in addition to Hampton Court, John inherited £50,000 and an equal share in the residue of his father's estate, amounting to £263,745 17*s* (almost £14.7 million today).[23] He spent the rest of his life in Herefordshire acquiring farms and enlarging the estate by 65 per cent, sitting as a Justice of the Peace, taking his turn as High Sheriff, patronising local causes like funding schools and rebuilding churches, hosting bow meetings, and helping to identify suitable parliamentary candidates for the nearby Leominster constituency. For this, he became accepted by the land-owning class in the county and deservedly popular. John was noted as a liberal host, but was rarely ostentatious with his fortune.

To Johnny, John Arkwright therefore bequeathed a modernised house and an estate of 10,250 acres, but, crucially, only a share of his wealth, which John divided between his dozen children.[24] Johnny and his brothers were all educated at Eton and Harrow, and Oxford or Cambridge, and his sisters married well, where they married at all. By the time of Johnny's inheritance in 1858, he and his siblings had been entirely assimilated into the landed class of his day. They were Herefordshire born and bred, and Johnny had been schooled, had cricketed, shot, fished and hunted with the scions of the other great houses in Herefordshire and the neighbouring counties. They knew their (elevated) place in society, and society knew it too.

Johnny would never be subjected to the cutting observation of one local landowner who had referred to Richard Arkwright as late as 1833 as 'a tradesman'.[25] Despite such persistent snobbery, the combination of his father's manufactured inheritance and his mother's landed ancestry makes Johnny a good example of the patrician type, having the money to indulge in patronage of all kinds and the confidence to take an assured place in contemporary society.

Not being titled, Johnny was not strictly a member of the aristocracy, but two of his brothers and one of his sisters married into aristocratic families.

He certainly mixed socially with the aristocracy, in the shires, in London, on committees and on the hunting field. Johnny fits, almost exactly, the model of the patrician landowner as identified by Cannadine, and Hampton Court is a microcosm of the situation nationwide. Johnny was Eton and Oxford educated, lived in the country but was often up in town serving on voluntary committees of local and national importance. He did not labour, but was leisured, and took a wife from his own class. He was at once the pinnacle of the county scene and the bedrock of London society, alert to the subtleties of honour, precedence and protocol and with a strong sense of keeping up his position. He was a liberal landlord and host, and had a safe seat in the saddle. Finally, he 'accepted, implicitly and absolutely, an unequal and hierarchical society, in which [his] place was undisputedly at the top'.[26]

Johnny Arkwright was the second of three John Arkwrights who lived at Hampton Court, but the only one for whom all the seasons of life turned within the 7-mile compass of the pleasure grounds. His father moved there in his thirties, and his son lived there until his fortieth year. It should be noted that I refer throughout to these three men by the names that the family itself used to differentiate between them: John (John Arkwright, 1785–1858), Johnny (John Hungerford Arkwright, 1833–1905) and Jack (John Stanhope Arkwright, 1872–1954).

The decade of working on the Arkwright collection has been leavened by Johnny's irrepressible personality. Through his letters he comes vividly alive, with appealingly human frailties. As a rumbustious child he rampaged about the estate on his pony and was noted at Eton for 'a disposition to noisiness in the House'.[27] He was wildly popular at Oxford where he was given to sinking punts. Hopelessly enamoured of his fiancée, Johnny chose to read love letters in church rather than listen to a boring sermon of 'maudlin verbage'.[28] He couldn't get his bride to their wedding night destination quickly enough, and later said of their propensity to reproduce that 'rabbits are nothing to it!'[29] He frequently confounds the notions of the stern Victorian *pater familias*, particularly in the delight he took in playing with his children.

Johnny was a quintessential county man, promoting Herefordshire's interest on the national stage, and encouraging causes locally, from personally rehearsing the church choir to chairing the Executive Committee for Hereford's Three Choirs Festival. He was a leading agriculturalist, teaching his tenants to graft fruit in his orchards and sitting with the future king on the Council of the Royal Agricultural Society of England. To many he represented 'the epitome of the English squire'.[30] Behind the public front, though, there slunk personal insecurities, producing occasional bouts of the blues. When things began to go seriously wrong for him, Johnny became uncharacteristically bad-tempered and touchy, and even ungracious regarding the wedding of his second daughter.

Johnny Arkwright was therefore no saint, nor was the life that he led one of unbounded ease. The times were not static, and to label the sixty-three years of the Queen's reign 'Victorian' implies a homogeneity that is misleading. The period should not be thought of as all house parties and London seasons. Perhaps the lives of Johnny's kind more closely resembled that cycle up to 1870, but thereafter, they were fighting for survival. In the years before the First World War, the gloves were off, and the sight of the patricians when they took their last stand over Irish Home Rule, for example, was not an edifying one.

I make these points not in any way to deride the landed class. Rather, I hope to toss a lifeline of realism into the soup of nostalgia in which they risk drowning. Since the Victoria and Albert Museum's 1974 exhibition '*The Destruction of the Country House*', the heritage industry has established a strong position in the economy. English Heritage's annual report of 2003 indicates that domestic tourism generates £61 billion of expenditure and provides employment for 7.4 per cent of people in Britain, frequently in rural areas where it is badly needed.[31] The movement has furthermore helped to ensure that no significant houses have been deliberately destroyed since the 1974 exhibition.[32]

The popularity of visiting country houses has enabled some to remain in private hands – Longleat, Beaulieu, Woburn, Blenheim, Chatsworth, Alnwick and Arundel, for example. It has also no doubt contributed to the current interest in history, and it is difficult to imagine that the success of the National Trust's 2002 campaign to save Tyntesfield for the nation would have been possible before the heritage movement took hold.

We British and our visitors alike derive immense pleasure from viewing historic houses, though the precise number of visits made annually is hard to ascertain. The National Trust's 300 or so country properties (some with houses, some just gardens) received 12.6 million visitors in the year to the end of February 2003. The 1,500 privately owned properties that form the Historic Houses Association receive over 14.1 million visitors per year. Visit Britain's annual survey of houses and castles in 2002 received 605 responses from such properties, whose visitors that year totalled 30.5 million.[33]

The experience of touring one of these properties can captivate the visitor. The skilful display of tables set for dinner, writing materials on desks and kitchen dressers laden with copper pans can suggest that life was one of a perpetual carefree house party – all croquet and crinolines, port and partridge shooting. Yet if the invitation to nostalgia is declined, it is striking that (usually) the occupants are missing today, and the properties are owned indirectly by the visitors themselves through what has been described as '*de facto* nationalization'.[34] Over the period covered by this book, such places were inhabited by real people facing frightening times as their way of life came under threat, then crumbled and finally disintegrated. I cannot be alone in having wondered where exactly life went so wrong for Johnny's class, and how his generation reacted at having to let such a rich inheritance go. Noël Coward put it succinctly when he asked, 'What availed the sceptred race', and whether 'the playing fields of Eton' made them 'frightfully brave'?[35]

In Johnny Arkwright's experience, we can find many of the answers. His Hampton Court estate is located in Herefordshire – 'of all the counties of England . . . the most blessed'.[36] The county neighbours Worcestershire to the east, in which Madresfield Court, the house on which Waugh based Brideshead, is located. To the west lies the principality of Wales. Herefordshire is one of those English counties that borders on (or 'marches with') Wales, to which are given the collective name of the Welsh Marches. To the north of Herefordshire lies Shropshire, location for P.G. Wodehouse's Blandings Castle, home of Lord Emsworth, and to the south, Gloucestershire.

Hampton Court should not be confused with its namesake Hampton Court Palace on the River Thames near London. Cardinal Wolsey began his Tudor palace around eighty years after Hampton Court, Herefordshire, was built by Sir Rowland Leinthall, under licence from Henry VI from 1434. The history of the two houses occasionally became entwined, most closely towards the end of the seventeenth century,[37] but there is no deliberate connection between the two.

Even without his father's cash fortune, the extent of Johnny's estate by the 1870s put him in the top 365 landowners in Britain, above some of his titled superiors. Cannadine identifies three ranks of landowners in the 1870s: approximately 6,000 families who owned 1,000–10,000 acres producing an income of £1,000–10,000 per annum; a second group of around 750 families, of which Johnny's was one, that had estates ranging from 10,000–30,000 acres whose owners were all 'economically, great men'; and at the top, 250 territorial magnates who each had more than 30,000 acres.[38] By this calculation, at 363rd in the landowning ranking, Johnny was towards the top of the second group. However calculated, he was definitely one of the 'big people'.[39]

With such a remarkable inheritance, why did Johnny need to seek a special Act of Parliament in 1887 to enable him to remain at Hampton Court, and why did he have to spend Easter 1900 deciding which farms on the estate to mortgage? The answer was all around him. Land ceased to be the bedrock of wealth and status in British society during the second half of the nineteenth century. Since at least the Dissolution of the Monasteries in 1536 – and arguably since the Norman Conquest of 1066 – land had been inextricably linked with wealth, status and political power. The social and political élite had been territorial, its position underpinned by the acres that it owned. As Anthony Trollope had observed in 1867: 'land gives so much more than the rent . . . position and influence and political power, to say nothing about the game'.[40]

The removal of guaranteed prices for grain effected by the Repeal of the Corn Laws in 1846 was bitterly resented by the landowning class. To appease them, special loans were made available from the 1850s, which many took up to drain their land and (after 1864) to improve farm buildings, in order to increase productivity and secure tenants, the landlord's source of income. With a 25-year repayment period, many landowners still owed large sums when, from the 1870s, they came under assault from a variety of sources. Prolonged periods of appalling weather over the next three decades ruined crops and rotted livestock, and encouraged the import first of cheap grain and then, with the development of refrigerated shipping, cheap meat, which ruined tenant farmers. Rental incomes dried up, leaving landowners unable to meet loan repayments. As farms were sold to try to meet obligations, the value of land began to slide, deepening the crisis by the late 1890s.

As competition from imports implies, the world was shrinking as the global economy was born in the last quarter of the nineteenth century. English magnates, formerly kings of their own county realms, began to be judged in the context of the wealth élite of other countries. Newly made industrial fortunes, particularly those in the United States of America, dwarfed those of many English landowners.

During past agricultural depressions, like that prevailing in the 1820s and 1830s, when landowners had sold their estates, their acres had been bought by wealthy merchants, stock-jobbers and industrialists like the Arkwrights themselves. Now, however, new money was invested not in economically vulnerable land with its attendant responsibilities (and, from

1894, death duties) but in new, more liquid holdings, such as stocks and shares, contributing to the fall from fashion of landownership. The landed were disinherited of their status as the most glamorous social group. As Oscar Wilde quipped in 1895: 'Land has ceased to be either a profit or a pleasure. It gives one position, and prevents one from keeping it up.' [41]

By the turn of the twentieth century, the Tory Party, traditionally sympathetic to landowners when in government, was no longer able to justify defending the landed interest when the balance of political power had come to reside in urban constituencies as a consequence of electoral reform. With the reallocation of parliamentary seats under successive Reform Acts, the rural voice became the minority in the House of Commons and many landed sons declined the opportunity to sit in an increasingly professional Parliament. Politically, as a class, landowners began to retreat. At the same time, from the 1880s political pressure groups with a specifically anti-landlordist agenda toured the country encouraging dissent in the atmosphere of growing democratic confidence. David Lloyd George, the influential Welsh Member of Parliament, found the courage to question the status quo and squandered no opportunity to lampoon the landed.

It is this process of shifting ground that is illustrated by this book. In just one generation – Johnny's generation – land turned from being a boon into a burden. He and his contemporaries felt the full force of the avalanche of changes in landowning fortunes in the second half of the nineteenth century. The position, power and prestige that had been theirs by birthright for centuries disappeared west across the Atlantic Ocean. Their pictures, silver, jewels, and occasionally parts of their houses, were not far behind.

Although his times were difficult, Johnny remains a lively companion throughout, appreciating the ridiculous in his own predicament. I have, wherever possible, taken his point of view, and his opinions should not be mistaken for my own. The style that I have adopted is intended to make this a book read for pleasure, although I hope that the inclusion of footnotes will enable others to use the Arkwright Collection. A numbered reference in the notes is, however – because of the way the collection is indexed – that of a box that might contain a hundred letters, so anyone wishing to follow leads will still have much patient digging to do.

Those seeking Johnny Arkwright today will be pleased to note that, with the exception of several of the country houses, many of the places mentioned in the text are not just identifiable, but in many cases have barely changed. Herefordshire was, by the mid-nineteenth century, one of the few counties in England in which industry and manufacturing had not gained a hold – glove-making and carriage manufacture were Hereford's strengths. Despite intermittent attempts, canals had not developed here, and Hereford had no railway until 1853.[42]

Today Herefordshire's economy remains richly agricultural, with 9,603 people employed in agriculture, or around 5.5 per cent of a population that has grown, since 1841, by 53.5 per cent to 174,900.[43] Herefordshire's agricultural workers make up almost 8 per cent of the total number in the United Kingdom. There is still good pasture land for grazing both sheep and the fine beef cattle for which the county is renowned. The strong red soil is well suited to farming potatoes, which has proliferated since Johnny's day, as has strawberry growing with its attendant, controversial polytunnels.[44] Diversity of produce still reigns. Cider apple and perry pear orchards, though fewer, still froth with blossom in the spring, and hop poles strain and stride across the fields. Woodland is still plentiful and oaks grow so freely in the county's generous soil that they have long been known as 'the weeds of Herefordshire'.[45] The architectural wealth of half-timbered oak-framed black and white houses stands as testament to this fact. Hereford city's main employers reflect the agricultural tradition – cider-makers Bulmer's and poultry processors Sun Valley. Herefordshire does, though, feel poised on the cusp of significant change. The years 1991–9 saw a growth in the county's population of 7,000, or 4.4 per cent, entirely due to net inward migration, mainly from other parts of the West Midlands and the south-east – a rate of growth greater than that experienced by the rest of England and Wales. This has applied pressure on the infrastructure, particularly roads. Hereford city's need of a bypass is a frequent topic of letters to the *Hereford Times*. Light pollution is also encroaching on the starlit night skies.

Hampton Court itself remains the picture-postcard castellated house that it was when Johnny lived here. The house has barely altered, and the surrounding landscape has hardly changed. The oaks still lean in the deer park across the road, the skating rink is opposite the gate, and the waters of the Lugg that Johnny fished still roll silently past the south meadows. Sadly, there is no herd of Hereford cattle today in the bull pens at Green Farm, but they are occasionally to be found grazing the surrounding river-meadows.

The contents of the house (some of which had been there since the sixteenth century) were broken up during a three-day sale in 1972. The house and grounds have since changed hands more times than in the previous five and a half centuries put together. After American Robert Van Kampen bought the property in 1994, Hampton Court underwent the most necessary and extensive programme of repairs since John's alterations. Under the care of the estate's manager, Edward Waghorn, the soft red sandstone was replaced where it had worn, and the 122-room house was almost entirely reroofed, redecorated and rewired.

Outside, exciting new gardens, sensitive to the location and classically structured, yet vibrant in texture and colour, were created by David Wheeler and Simon Dorrell, and brought to life by local craftspeople. The glasshouses were recommissioned, and a small army of gardeners was once again employed. Hampton Court's gardens (but not the house) opened to the public in 2000, and are accessible year-round, attracting about 50,000 visitors per annum.

Sadly, Robert Van Kampen died in 1999 and Hampton Court was sold again in 2008. The new owner, Graham Ferguson Lacey, has delighted visitors by opening the 'Castle' to the public, so that you can now see the dining room and Coningsby Hall where the Arkwright girls' marriages were celebrated, or sit in the chapel that was the focal point for the household on so many occasions.

The highly-popular gardens remain open, and there are plans to develop them further. The passage of tens of thousands of feet has, in places, worn the grass, revealing the layout of paths and beds as Johnny knew them. If you are tempted to nostalgia when seeing these spectres of summers past, remember that despite the warm welcome you will receive today, in his time the hoi polloi were allowed in only on high days and holidays. If Johnny is watching from a window, he is no doubt roaring his disapproval, wondering what the world has come to, and reaching for the champagne.

ONE

The Heir to the Seat

William Daggs tapped the barometer in the hallway, and was relieved to note that it rose towards 'fair'. Change was in the air. 'A good thing too,' he might have reflected as he pressed his hat into place and stepped over the threshold into the puddled street beyond. The date of 12 July 1854 was an auspicious day. It marked the coming of age of Johnny Arkwright, the heir to the largest estate in Leominster's neighbourhood.[1] As secretary to the committee organising the estate's celebrations, Daggs hoped for neither lows nor storms.[2]

Daggs strode across Corn Square, gripping the Arkwright banner under his arm and raising his hat in acknowledgement of salutations. He turned between the stooping houses of Draper's Lane, running the day's schedule through his head, until he emerged before the piebald town hall. He was relieved to note that many of the Arkwright tenants in Leominster had already gathered, giving the town an air of market day rather than a holiday. Some were milling between the oak pillars, while others congregated under the Regency arcade at the end of Draper's Lane. Carriages filled Broad Street ahead, while well-wishers on foot and on horseback blockaded the road towards the Priory to the right and Burgess Street to the left.

Daggs at once set about checking that the five wagons from the parishes in which Arkwright owned property had arrived, bearing their oxen and bread. The Hope Ox was a magnificent display, bedecked in flowers, evergreens and gold. He next checked that the brass band that would head the procession was comfortably accommodated in its carriage. The Oddfellows had assembled, bristling with flags on staffs. Blue rosettes had been distributed and streamers fluttered in the northerly breeze that was chasing away the clouds. After mounting his horse, Daggs snapped his fob watch shut at nine o'clock precisely and led off the procession of around 2,000 people for what he had predicted would be 'one of the most happy and joyous gatherings which this county ever produced'.[3]

Five miles away, at Hampton Court, Johnny Arkwright was feeling uncharacteristically self-conscious as his father rose stiffly to his feet to lead the household in morning service in the chapel. After readings, hymns and prayers with a particular note of thanksgiving, the servants were released to their duties. As soon as he could, Johnny returned to the furtive reworking of the speech that he had begun in his rooms at Christ Church, Oxford. His father had noted his unease, but, while offering reassurance, observed to himself that the occasion might help Johnny to appreciate the responsibilities of his station in life.

The notice for the celebrations in the *Hereford Journal* had asserted that 'With the admirable example of such beloved and excellent parents before him, we cannot doubt the future honourable conduct of Mr Arkwright.' John Arkwright knew, though, that his son was instead likely to write to him in the following less than honourable terms:

> You were riding when I departed so I missed the opportunity of telling you a fact in my finances. I borrowed 10£ of my mother because I had no money. And still am owing. The last 100 you gave me went as follows –
>
> 40 College bills
> 20 reading coach
> 10 lodgings
>
> the rest in cricket boating and club subscriptions and wine bills – I have really but just found out what money is, and how far it goes, and can, I know, for the future keep out of debt if I get out now. Will you advance, till I get an income of my own, as I had rather do that than receive more from you which I have no right to, and of course rob my brothers of . . . PS you might think at this time that I had lost about the Derby, but I *had not a single bet*.[4]

At 69 years of age, John knew that the responsibility for the 10,250-acre estate would pull Johnny up soon enough, and his natural inclination was to allow the boy his head while he might; and yet, he needed to instil in him some sound good sense before it was too late. Still, the lad's twenty-first birthday was not the occasion to do so.

Daggs's procession stretched for nearly a mile. Once through the toll gate to the south of Leominster, it passed Broadward, crossed over the Arrow river and was in estate territory. All along the route, cottages showed their 'bit of enthusiasm' with arches over the paths, or flowers at the door. Every by-road and footpath brought new additions to the party. The cavalcade wound its way past Ford's new railway station, and got its first glimpse of the River Lugg that would run alongside the cheerful throng to Hampton Court. At Wharton, Daggs was joined by his father-in-law, Edward Hodges, the senior tenant on the estate. From the bold, square house they proceeded over the railway bridge at Marlbrook.

At Hope-under-Dinmore they negotiated the toll-gate and turned on to the England's Gate road, relieved, no doubt, not to have to climb Dinmore Hill ahead. After crossing the Lugg bridge that John had built in 1826,[5] the happy crowd caught sight at last, between the trees, of the crenellated silhouette of Hampton Court. The band played 'Roast Beef of Old England' as the procession turned up the drive that led straight to the oak gates beneath the entrance tower, where the family awaited them on a specially constructed dais. At 10 o'clock, with all assembled, Edward Hodges presented to John Arkwright the committee's address of congratulation on the coming of age of his heir.

> Your tenants especially take this opportunity of expressing their gratitude for the unvarying kindness, forbearance, and liberality with which they have been treated. Your noble conduct in this respect, surpassed by no landlord in Herefordshire, has enabled them to bear up against many adverse circumstances, and has endeared your name to all their families.

John responded with thanks. 'I am exceedingly proud,' he said, 'at having become by adoption a Herefordshire man, for my feelings and affections are bound up in the county. [Cheers.] My son has the advantage over me that he was born a Herefordshire man, and I hope he will turn out to be a credit to the soil which gave him birth.'[6]

The wagons then fanned out over the estate to Bodenham, Pencombe, Hope, Wharton, Stoke Prior and Docklow, distributing bread, beef and money to John's tenants and labourers. With the formalities over, the well-wishers were free to roam the grounds before dinner. For many, this was a rare opportunity to get beyond the north front of Hampton Court, to walk past the chapel at the east end of the house, round the drawing room on the corner and emerge into the sun of the south front. It was a revelation. From the road, the house wore a gloomy aspect, appearing to lie too close to the foot of Dinmore, the trees on the hill surely rendering the court damp and dark. And yet, as the visitors discovered, between the south walls of the house and the waters of the Lugg that curved around Dinmore, were extensive lawns of perfect seclusion. The sun seemed to be trapped between the hill and the house, a pool of unrelenting light and warmth.

Around 500 people had purchased tickets for the banquet at 3 o'clock in a marquee on Dinmore Hill. Afterwards, Johnny rose nervously to his feet. He thanked the tenantry and especially the organising committee, and assured them that the day would never be erased from his memory. In proposing the toast to the tenantry, 'he regretted to say he knew so little of them and of the science of agriculture . . . but at some future time, he had no doubt, he should take more interest in eradicating the thistles, docks, and other such enemies of the farmer'.

A quadrille band had been engaged for the evening, when the dancing was opened by John and Mrs Hodges. Johnny's mother Tally had the pleasure of dancing with Mr Hodges. At the end of the day, Johnny retired with his parents for some private celebrations. Despite the presence of his five sisters, no doubt Johnny's absent brothers were in their minds. He was certainly in theirs. George, the third son, dined with his tutor Rev. Harbin, at the home of Tally's sister at Cucklington in Wiltshire. George reported to his father 'John's health was drunk by the assembled gentlemen. Harbin's wish was "good health, double first class and leaving of hunting". The last two are doubtful.'[7]

Johnny's brothers were not to miss out altogether. Further celebrations were planned for early August, when they would be at home. In contrast to 12 July's festivities, these were to last for three days and involve not just the immediate but the wider family. John Arkwright, though always a liberal host, was rarely ostentatious with his wealth. The August party was an exception, and a monumental three days of celebration were planned between Wednesday 2 and Friday 4 August.

While Johnny worried about his oratorical shortcomings, his mother concerned herself with her eldest daughters. Prior to the birth of an heir, John and Tally had produced two daughters, Caroline in 1831 and Mary the following year. Known as Carey-Mary in family shorthand, these girls expected much of the forthcoming celebrations, and would be on display to the leading county families. Caroline, though not beautiful, was a bonny girl blessed with endless patience sorely tried by her rumbustious younger brothers. In contrast Mary was asthmatic and the weakest of the Arkwrights' dozen children. Owing to the attention that she had received, Mary was more precious than her older sister. The contrasts between them, though, and their relative isolation as a pair at the head of the four brothers that followed them in age, made them close companions in anticipation and excitement.

It was not only the younger generation who looked forward to the beginning of August. John's three surviving brothers and their families would be attending, Robert from Sutton Scarsdale in Derbyshire, Peter from the Arkwright family home Willersley, at Cromford in Derbyshire, and Rev. Joseph from Mark Hall in Essex. Robert's eldest son, George, was one of the present Members of Parliament for Leominster. Peter had seven surviving sons and five daughters; they would be staying over Dinmore Hill at Bodenham, where Peter's third son, Henry, was vicar of the parish that was in John's gift. Joseph had five sons and six surviving daughters. His wife Anne wrote excitedly in July to inform John that she, Anne and Charles were to travel to Hampton Court together, while Arthur would make his way separately with Godfrey from Sutton Scarsdale.

Wednesday 2 August finally came round and the guests for the opening ball arrived from 9 p.m. Among them were the Countess of Oxford, Lady Emily Foley of Stoke Edith, Viscount and Lady Hereford of Tregoyd, Hon. and Rev. Lord Saye and Sele, and Sir Joseph Bailey of Glanusk. By 10 p.m., 'a galaxy of beauty and fashion had assembled. . . . The sight was most imposing – the superb dresses and costly ornaments worn by the fair daughters of Herefordshire, their graceful and beautiful figures moving in a fairy circle.'[8] Dancing in the Coningsby Hall began at 10 p.m. and continued until the ball supper was announced at 11.30 p.m. To feed the 200 guests, London caterers Mr Holt of Radley's Hotel, New Bridge Street in Blackfriars,[9] and Mr Jacquet of Clare-Court, were employed alongside Mr Merrett of Hereford. They came with ten male cooks, confectioners and a large number of carvers, waiters and runners. John's guests dined on patés, galantines de volaille, hams, tongues, gateau royale and compote de fruit. The guests resumed dancing, and ice creams, cakes, tea and coffee, wine, cool drinks and fruits sustained them until daylight.

On Thursday morning, the youngsters amused themselves with archery on the lawns to the south-west of the house where John habitually hosted county bow meetings. Meanwhile, the large marquees of the Leominster and Hereford Horticultural Societies were joined together for luncheon. The scene was captured by J.H. Brown of Gloucester, who had been commissioned to produce 'a painting of a good size of the Festivities at your beautiful residence – comprising the tents, visitors, trees & mansion'.[10]

Four hundred guests arrived at around 3 p.m. and, with John in the chair, the meal began shortly after 4 p.m., having been held up by the late arrival, to knowing glances, of the newly-wed Lord and Lady Bateman of Shobdon Court.[11] After a sumptuous lunch, the speeches were made.[12] Lord Bateman explained 'our delay in coming amongst you . . . we stayed here very late last night. [Laughter.] That was one thing. And to-day we had at Shobdon

. . . such heavy rain, that on our way hither we got a "complete ducking", and, as we were travelling in an open carriage, were obliged to take refuge under somebody's haystack.' Tally's brother, Chandos Wren Hoskyns recalled speaking twenty-one years earlier at the christening of 'the young squire'. With nightfall came a spectacular firework display, orchestrated by Henry Mortram, 'pyrotechnic artist by appointment to her Majesty's Court Theatricals, Windsor Castle'.[13] Another ball then followed from 7 p.m. until daybreak.

On Friday it was the turn of 1,000–1,400 tenants and labourers, 'strikingly Herculean types of the genus homo', to enjoy beef, mutton, poultry, vegetables, plum puddings and ale.[14] Afterwards, 300 children from the schools on the estate were entertained with plum cake and tea. The supervision of this part of the celebrations fell to Carey-Mary who were known to the children through their assistance at the schools. The Arkwright boys then organised sports before more fireworks were released. For those with the stamina, the whole three days were rounded off with a final ball in the house, led by Cox's band from Cheltenham.

Once the guests had departed, while John was recovering his strength, he must have reflected with satisfaction that the celebrations had united county society, landlord, tenant farmer and labourer at Hampton Court. He no doubt hoped particularly that the symbolism of the estate's unity was not lost on either his guests or his heir. Such occasions were designed to help cement and perpetuate the status quo.

With normality resumed, John could enjoy the rest of the summer holidays with his precious wife and dozen children. The £30,280 that he had spent altering Hampton Court in the 1830s and 1840s meant that it accommodated his large family and their visiting cousins and friends with ease.[15] John knew of no pleasure to equal that of sitting on his grey with his whole brood on horseback in the courtyard, starting for a gallop in the park and hearing the hooves clop on the wooden setts and re-echo under the entrance tower.

To the children, the gardens and estate offered boundless possibilities for amusement, with fishing in the Lugg, waterfalls on the Humber brook, cricket, archery and croquet on the lawns, and riding or sketching on Dinmore. The freedom that the youngsters enjoyed was punctuated by the call to meals of the bell on the drawing-room gable. The balance between freedom and a strict timetable fostered independence of spirit but promoted self-discipline and consideration for others, not least the staff who toiled to support the household. John's brother-in-law Sir James Wigram observed after his sons had stayed with the Arkwrights, that 'the mere *spectacle* of a family ordered as is yours, is more practically instructive than a whole volume of sermons'.[16]

All the children were avid gardeners. From their early years in the schoolroom they had given the cedars pet names (the favourite being Julius), chased butterflies around the Black Boy Arbour, and acquired the rudiments of cultivation from the long-suffering Head Gardener, Mr Gadd. During term-time, the girls sent their brothers garden news. In February 1850, Mary had added to Johnny and George's Eton hamper 'a little pkt of mignionette seeds which I hope you will sow in a box outside your window, & 8 nosegays to sweeten your rooms'.[17] The following year, there had been a plot afoot to 'drive Gadd & his potatoes from the territories they claim in the pink garden'.[18] As a result, Johnny developed a lifelong passion for the rose; Richard (Dick) and to some extent Henry contracted 'a mania for ferns',[19] so that a fernery was dug west of the kitchen gardens; George was dubbed the 'knight of the scarlet geraniums',[20] and Arthur enjoyed layering carnations. On wet days, they could pursue their horticultural loves in the conservatory that Joseph Paxton had designed for John in 1845.[21]

Before Johnny returned to Oxford and Dick to Trinity, Cambridge in the autumn of 1854, they visited their Derbyshire cousins at Willersley and at Sutton Scarsdale. Robert Arkwright's late wife, Fanny, had been a great favourite of the 'Bachelor' Duke of Devonshire.[22] It is little surprise therefore that Johnny reported: 'We picniced at Chatsworth on Thursday and were enchanted with the grounds and more especially the tropical houses for trees and shrubs . . . including gigantic cacti and the exuberant foliage of the prodigious what d'you call-it'.[23]

In these high spirits Johnny returned to Christ Church where he was 'the most popular man',[24] while at Hampton Court lessons were resumed in the schoolroom. The rhythm of the household, though, was thrown in November, when John opened a letter which revealed the fruits of the summer's festivities. The hand he knew well to be that of Berkeley Scudamore Stanhope, son of John's friend, Sir Edwyn Scudamore Stanhope of Holme Lacy, one of the most ancient houses in Herefordshire. Berkeley had shared county business with John and they had corresponded, for example, on school board meetings. However, Berkeley's letter to John of 16 November 1854 was on a subject entirely new:

> Through your & Mrs Arkwright's unvarying kindness in asking me from time to time to stay at Hampton Court . . . I have not failed to observe and admire

> the character & high principle of one, who brought up under the guidance of the kindest and best of parents, could scarcely fail to reflect at least in some degree, their many merits . . . Those excellent qualities & deep religious feeling such as a parent may well delight to see in a child, & which shine preeminently from your eldest daughter Caroline, have fully convinced me, that should you & Mrs Arkwright not consider me an unworthy aspirant, & I should hereafter be fortunate to gain her affections, I might indeed consider myself highly favoured . . . I determined on making you & Mrs Arkwright acquainted with my feelings before I had conveyed them to her, whom . . . it would be my pride & pleasure to win.[25]

If Berkeley's self-conscious unease made John smile and remember his own endeavours to win Tally, the letter's implications made him sit back in his chair, remove his pince-nez, and reflect. However much, as an older father, he wanted to perpetuate the pleasures that he had belatedly discovered in family life, he could not ignore the fact that the rest of the world considered it time that it drew to a close. John, though, was not ready to let Carey go. He discussed the matter with Tally before composing a reply of sensitive clarity:

> Mrs A & I wish to express our sense of the compliment paid to us and our family by one for whom we have always entertained the greatest regard. It is my wish & intention to be equally candid with yourself. And at once to state that Mrs A & myself have every reason to believe that she does not at present feel the least preference for anyone out of her own family & that if the proposal were at this time to be made to her come from what quarter it may, she would at once reject it . . . I know nothing as to how far you have considered the question of means should her decision (some time hence I selfishly hope) be in your favour.[26]

Berkeley was temporarily stalled until he had further advanced in his career in the Church. Although there would have been the utmost discretion outside the family, it seems that Berkeley's feelings were already common knowledge among them. The Valentine's Day postal delivery three months later caused consternation as Henry wrote to his father: 'I did not send Carey-Mary any "Valentines". Please to tell them that they cannot persuade me that they do not know who sent them. Hem!!!'[27]

The year 1855 was an important one for George who was due to forsake the protection of Harbin's vicarage and go up to Oxford. He had fancied that he might follow a career in the Army, but had been persuaded that the

Church was his vocation, a decision that arguably saved his life.[28] George might otherwise have been about to embark for the Crimea. John, though, was concerned that the reunion of George with the Etonians among whom he had been highly popular might undo the good that Harbin had wrought in his third son. Johnny pleaded the opposite case:

> An Eton man must meet with old friends in every college . . . I cannot help thinking that my being up especially in his first terms would be of advantage inasmuch as my experience and I must own it extravagance will put me in a position to prevent his falling into the same. Experientia docet. Now I know that the bills of the first terms residence are enormous, owing to ignorance. Furniture pictures and swell things for ones rooms run up frightful bills, before a man knows what he has done . . . my things will be transferred to his rooms and so save him all that . . . [I] can promise to be of far greater use to him in that way than I have ever been to myself – You have asked to know my money matters and so I have calculated that I have £129 in Smiths bank, 100 in the Oxford bank, 50 at Leominster, and owe 400.[29]

John derived rather more comfort from the knowledge that at Oxford George would be near his uncle, John Leigh Hoskyns, Tally's younger brother, who was vicar of Aston Tyrrold,[30] a fellow of Magdalen and canon of Christ Church. When George started at Oriel in 1855, Leigh promised to look him up. 'I do trust he will take to working hard,' Leigh wrote, adding, with characteristic simplicity of soul, 'he has chosen the happiest calling on earth.'[31]

George took heartily to Oxford life with rather less simplicity. He offered a timeless observation about study. 'Reading I find much harder work than I expected . . . it is one thing to sit over one's book, and another thing to derive any advantage from so doing.'[32] John, totting up his expenditure on George at the end of 1855, came to a total (despite Johnny's reassurances), including two bills of £150 for Harbin, of £820 17*s*. For a man who had lent over £40,000 to the Marquess of Normanby and over £35,000 to the Duke of Buckingham with stern penalties for default, John showed surprising incompetence over his children and their pocket money, turning to his brothers for advice.[33]

John was distracted from his concern about George by his nephew of the same name. In November 1855, George Arkwright of Sutton Scarsdale called John's attention to the political situation in Leominster. George had represented the Tories there since 1841 when John's brother-in-law James Wigram, the previous Tory MP, had been elected to the bench. In practice, it was John who opened any correspondence for George and harkened for any murmurings in the constituency. The political role expected of John as the largest landowner in the area was one not enjoyed by him, but endured. He had been asked repeatedly to stand himself, but had refused, being acutely sensitive to his status as a newcomer to the county and, in these post-Reform days, to accusations of buying his seat. He hoped that his responsibility might be fulfilled instead by supplying a suitable candidate.

John was a relatively liberal Tory, being on Sir Robert Peel's wing of the party.[34] He had, in contrast to his High Tory father-in-law, Sir Hungerford Hoskyns, supported the repeal of the Corn Laws, an exception for his landowning class that, since the Napoleonic Wars, had relied on protected corn prices, particularly wheat, for its living. John inclined, as he said himself, 'to the belief that the apprehension of the ruinous consequences [of removing protection for corn prices] is exaggerated and that ultimately "Free Trade" in corn will be most beneficial to us all'.[35] Almost a decade on, John's (and Peel's) position seemed to have been vindicated: wheat prices had been rising ever since 1851; there was renewed vigour in agricultural practice since the birth (at which Sir Hungerford had been present) of the Royal Agricultural Society of England in 1836 urging 'practice with science'; and since the late 1840s, advocates of High Farming had been encouraging farmers, with some success, to greater output.

John's dislike of politics dated from at least 1812 when he had helped his late brother Richard to canvass in Nottingham. To their father, John reported: 'My Lady Rancliffe canvesses in Person & Kisses the greasy chops of any person who will give her a vote. George Holcombe rides in the dicky of her barouche, and in that style they parade the streets with the mob. Whenever a vote appears coming into the town he is seized on by both parties, and unless very staunch, he is taken to a public house, made drunk and polled accordingly.'[36] He found distasteful the bile spilt over politics, causing unnecessary unpleasantness between men of opposing views, like his father-in-law Sir Hungerford Hoskyns and Sir Hungerford's son, Chandos, who was a committed Liberal.

He did not like, either, the implication that his tenants should have to follow his lead at elections out of fear of losing their farms. Before polling in the 1852 election of Members for the county of Herefordshire at which the third seat was being fought between a Liberal and a Tory, John refused to let Tory canvassers in Bodenham imply that he should like them to vote for the Tory candidate, asserting that he would 'preserve the strictest neutrality and should be sorry for the least degree to influence any of my neighbours'.[37] He furthermore refused to nominate one of the Tories on the hustings.[38] Equally, when the agent for the Liberal candidate George Cornewall Lewis (a future Chancellor of the Exchequer) asked John to give his tenants permission to vote for Lewis, asserting that 'The respect and regard which your Tenants and neighbourhood so justly entertain for you will induce them to act in entire accordance with your wishes',[39] John wrote back the same day to assure him 'that though I certainly am desirous to see Mr King and Mr Booker [the Tories] returned and intend to vote for them only, and have signified my intention of so doing, I do not intend to interfere as regards the other Candidates'.[40]

It would not be surprising then if an audible groan emanated from John's library in November 1855, when he read the latest letter from George Arkwright MP.

> I should like to have had a little more talk with you about Leominster. I very much hope that you will make up your mind to let John come in as soon as you think the most convenient time has arrived, & I think that he would not be so likely to get into bad company in the House as he might do elsewhere (though I have no great opinion of m^y of the MPs).[41]

George had raised this matter before, probably after the 1852 election. That July and August, in the immediate wake of voting, George had taken Johnny on a trip on the 'RYS Frisk' sailing from Portsmouth via Cowes to St Peter's, Guernsey. The weather had been as stormy as the contemporary election. During the days stuck in the port prior to their departure, George, older than Johnny by twenty-six years, had spun tales of his campaign and had infected Johnny with election fever. After devouring the newspaper reports, Johnny had written to his father, 'The accounts of the electioneering were very amusing as we came, but Leominster was not mentioned at length – of one unlucky candidate it says "although he fraternized with the tradesmen and smoked a short clay with the labourers it was no go".'[42] From Cowes, he had written about 'the yatch [*sic*] club . . . a very political institution I suppose from so many MPs having yatchs of their own'.[43]

In October 1853, John had got wind of some discontent with George's representation of Leominster and had brought the matter to George's notice. He suggested that George retire 'if such be your intention, for as to keeping your post till John is old enough, I have a decided objection to his being in parl^t till he shows himself disposed to attend to business of any kind'.[44]

By November 1855, then, John hoped that the idea had fallen into abeyance, and no doubt attempted to persuade George to drop the matter. However, fewer than three months later, the question of Johnny's parliamentary career was forcibly raised. George Arkwright died suddenly, at the age of 49, on 5 February 1856. John's immediate thoughts were for his brother Robert at Sutton, who having lost his fourth son in 1846 at the age of 28, and his wife in 1849, was now called to bear the sadness of losing George.[45] John could not, though, ignore the question of Johnny's candidacy. He at once telegraphed Tally's sister Catherine Hawkshaw, with whom Johnny was believed to be staying. Edward Hawkshaw wrote to John on 8 February that Johnny had left before the telegraph reached him, noting the strange coincidence that he and Johnny had talked of politics only the previous morning. 'One could have wished him a bit older before plunging into the whirlpool,' wrote Hawkshaw, '– but he will do well wherever he is – who could have looked for poor George Arkwright's death!'[46]

The interest created by Johnny's possible candidature was immense. In these post-Reform days in England (and post-revolutionary times in Europe) the succession of the 22-year-old son of the local landowner to the representation of the borough was keenly debated. Among his family, it seemed a good deal to ask of the young man. As Johnny packed a bag to return home, his friends at Oxford were agog with interest and imagined finding themselves in his position. That train journey to Ford was probably the longest that Johnny had endured in his three years at Christ Church. He could settle to neither the war reports from the Crimea nor to contemplation of the countryside that passed beyond the dissipating steam. He was not altogether comfortable with having to act so publicly and to justify his position to his peers. His dilemma was, he knew, being much discussed abroad, as must be his personal suitability for the role. He had been brought up with all the advantages that life could offer: an extensive estate that would one day be his, a close and supportive family, the best education and connections, a healthy body and mind combined with a keen sense of humour and enormous popularity. And now he had the chance of a place in the most influential club in the country. What a swell he would make at Oxford if he were to dive in and what a triumphant leave he would take of the House!

His thoughts must have rocked, with the camber of the track, between the fantasies of vanity and the reality of self-knowledge. Would he be able to fill his cousin's place? Youthful ebullience, ignorance and a sense of his father's standing in Leominster tempted Johnny to think that he might. What sport it would be to take up a seat alongside the leading men of the country in the spanking new House! What a swell he would be among his friends, whom he might invite to hear debates, and it would be flattering to have his opinions on the issues of the day sought over dinner. Presumably his father would set him up with somewhere in London. He would have to race up and down to keep up with the hunting diary and to look to his roses, but that would have the merit of keeping him in touch with his electors. His fiddle playing might suffer, but in London there would be no shortage of strings to make a quartet. What a prospect spread before him – 'Mr John Hungerford Arkwright MP'.

John, meanwhile, pacing his library, recognised in his anxiety the opportunity that he had sought to impress upon his heir his impending responsibilities. It was a chance that he must not squander, for all that he felt for Johnny in the difficulty of his position. The rheumatism in John's elbow and shoulder flared up as if to emphasise the urgency of seizing the chance while he had it. It was not only Johnny's immaturity that concerned John – he doubted the suitability of Johnny's character for the role of Member of Parliament. In the first place there was his early headmaster's assessment of Johnny as 'having a nervous habit producing confusion of ideas when pressed', being slow to absorb detail, and needing 'to acquire the habit of application'.[47] He had never been a profound thinker. Johnny had always been the sort of child who preferred racing round the estate on his pony to sitting indoors with a book. If he must be indoors, then he would play his fiddle or tease his younger brothers, but rarely would he sit still. This energy should stand him in good stead for the management of the estate that would one day be his, necessitating as it did active engagement with his agent and tenants. It was not, however, consistent with the patient, analytical contemplation of difficult items of legislation.

Therefore, when Edward Hawkshaw wrote to John again on 13 February that he was 'very keen to hear about John's commencing his Parliamentary Career',[48] and George reported from Oriel that 'everyone is enquiring for John in very anxious terms',[49] Johnny was having a most uncomfortable time. Locked in conference with his father, he was facing some searching questions: what did he expect of himself; what did he want from his future; how much did he wish to be in London and how much at home among his people? He also learned something of his father's estimation of him. John must have impressed upon his son that at Westminster he would find himself measured against the finest minds of his day, engaged in debates on policy of international import. Could he be sure that he was not struggling to pick fruit that was above his reach?[50] John had always instilled in him the need to 'win *the Race Intellectual* and defend conservatism since it is easier to find fault than to uphold & maintain'[51] but he must choose his field with care. Did Johnny really believe that he would stand out as a statesman, or might he not be better advised to make Herefordshire his arena and agriculture his sphere, where he might realistically hope to have some impact? Johnny knew little enough about running the estate as yet, but John could assure him that it was no good imagining that a capable agent could do the job in his stead.

Warming to his theme, John may have stated frankly to Johnny that he seemed hardly temperamentally fitted for hours of tedious debate on obstruse legislative questions. He had simply never demonstrated hitherto any real or nascent interest in the detail of policy and it was questionable whether he was possessed of the maturity to assume the responsibility. He would enjoy, yes, the tussle of canvassing, the tea-room gossip and mixing with his fellows, and he might follow events with interest as they unfolded at Westminster, but he could have all that at the Carlton Club or with his Eton and Oxford chums without undertaking Commons membership.

Having stated plainly his feelings, John left Johnny to decide. The young man, confronted suddenly with decisions he thought yet a way off, and having discovered abruptly from his father his opinion of him, had a good deal to turn over in his mind. He spent uneasy evenings and sleepless nights, rising early to pace through his beloved gardens and smoke, leaving his footprints in the frost. Was he simply going to follow the patrician road that rose up to meet him or listen to his father's voice of conscience?

TWO

The Season and its Harvest

In the face of all the expectation (and temptation) Johnny showed commendable self-knowledge and maturity when he declined to stand as MP for Leominster. He returned immediately to Oxford and endured the unenviable task of explaining himself to his peers. In Leominster, the decision once taken was quickly passed over. Other candidates were considered,[1] until on 11 February, George Arkwright's obituary was spotted in *The Times* by Gathorne Hardy, who at once 'hastened to town . . . and put my irons in the fire'.[2] Hardy won the candidature and at the election, exactly a fortnight after George Arkwright's death, he fought off the Liberal challenge from James Campbell to win by a majority of seventy-eight.[3]

The whole affair soon blew over. George wrote home to his father on 1 March that Cambridge had won the Boat Race by half a length because the Oxford crew had been third-rate – fifteen men had refused to pull because it would interfere with hunting. While in town for the race:

> I went to see the ruins of Covent Garden Opera House. It was the most piteous sight but still very *grand* . . . for there were all the iron pillars of the boxes & galleries left standing & the *subterraneous* arches (or rather *sub-scenic*) looked rather grand. The immense piles of bricks, which had been *red-heated* were still smoking, although 6 *days* had elapsed since the catastrophe. All the paint on the doors & windows of the opposite houses were raised in huge blisters & the glass in the windows *melted into folds*. They are afraid to let any carriages pass near lest the vibration should shake down some of the crumbling ruins.[4]

Johnny could appreciate his own cleansing through fire from a distance. From Oxford he wrote to his mother: 'The excitement I was suffering under this time last week has in a measure blown away – and I look back complacently on "free and independent electors" etc. etc. Many of my advisers (for I have very many now) say I ought to have gone in – "Oh just give me the chance you had" they say. Thank you, says I. Hardy I conclude is progressing favorably with his pro tem constituents.'[5] Johnny's brother Henry wrote to their father: 'I have been asked by many people why John did not stand but they all seemed to think him quite right not to "tie himself down as yet".'[6]

The plain speaking between John and his son had been timely. By the autumn of 1856, there had been a marked decline in John's strength and mobility. That October Henry hoped his father was recovering from the weakness that prevented him from riding, and in mid-November, George wished that his father was restored to health.[7] Henry and Edwyn's Harrow housemaster, Mr Middlemist, wrote in December that he hoped John could soon resume riding, 'which I know you so much enjoy'. In February 1857 George asked if his father was riding again, and in March, Henry hoped that his father was convalescing well.[8] John's recovery was not helped by an outbreak of scarlatina at Hampton Court from which Emily, in particular, suffered. In his illness it was noted of John that, despite being active hitherto, he bore increasing infirmity with calm resignation. He demonstrated a determination to savour existence, in particular the pleasure of having others about him. He was also unfailingly consistent, even when quite unwell, in attending chapel with the household in the mornings, however cold the day.

Despite indifferent health, in early 1857 John maintained his business activities. His Leominster solicitor Thomas Sale was instructed to buy land from Higford D. Burr for £4,631 17*s* and a cottage and land adjoining John's at Ivington, for £180. On 11 April, he purchased five allotments of land on the Grange in the middle of Leominster, totalling 2 rods and 25 perches. This plot was to become the final home of the half-timbered town hall which became redundant on the completion of a replacement and covered market in around 1855. The 1633–4 building by Charles I's carpenter, John Abel, obstructed the increasing flow of traffic at Leominster's main junction.[9] On 30 April 1855, the old hall was bought by Francis Davis, the town's (and the Arkwrights') druggist, for £95. This he probably did at John's instruction, since he sold it on, the same day, and for the same price, to John Arkwright.[10]

John's reasons for wanting to save the building are unclear, particularly since he had subscribed £5 towards the demolition of the black and white Butcher's Row in Hereford in May 1821.[11] The demolition in Hereford had been undertaken in the cause of health and modernisation, but it had cost the city some of its attractive vernacular architecture, a fact perhaps appreciated at the distance of thirty-five years. Leominster's town hall was dismantled in August 1855, and the Council, exasperated after heated debates about its future, invited John to do whatever he felt appropriate with the building. He amalgamated the plots that he bought at the Grange in April 1857 and there re-erected the market hall as a private dwelling, its ground-level arcade walled up.[12]

Alongside additions to the estate, there were changes in staff. John employed a new gamekeeper, Thomas Powell of Dinmore Hill, in October 1856, while February 1857 saw Henry Gadd, the head gardener and coachman, leave Hampton Court. John received a letter from Lord Middleton of Birdsall House, Malton in Yorkshire asking for confirmation that Gadd was sober, honest, steady, active and understanding 'in all his branches', and 'if with Mr Arkwright he has been accustomed to forcing Pines, Grapes, Flowers, Vegetables etc. and the care of wall fruit etc'.[13] Gadd was succeeded by Mr Langford.

James Tatlow, the butler at Hampton Court, delivered to John's library desk waves of correspondence of all kinds. Frequently included were requests for financial assistance from addresses as disparate as Holloway Prison and Chepstow Castle. John almost invariably opened his purse, although in some cases he sought confirmation of the claim before dispatching monies, for example when Margaret Hammond asked for £10 to assist her emigration to Texas. Consequently the posts brought notes of thanks, too, for his kindness. Vincent Corbet of Chepstow Castle described John as 'the best friend I have met through life', and Frances Boughton of Downton Castle in Shropshire thanked John – 'the friend I most value out of my own family' – for undertaking to be executor to her husband. Whether the cause was Christ's Hospital, Leominster Cricket Club, Bodenham Fishing Club or the Corporation of the Sons of the Clergy, he quietly contributed.[14]

Among the papers on his desk in early 1857 was a rental agreement with the Countess of Cottenham, for 15 Park Lane, London.[15] For six weeks, from 14 May until 25 June 1857, the Arkwrights took the house, with coach house and stabling, use of furniture, fixtures, china, glass and effects, for 350 guineas or £367 10*s*. The reason for this, besides the usual diversions of the summer, was to launch Carey-Mary in London society. For John, the season threatened his precious family circle, and it would not inspire in him the excitement of Tally and the girls. Tally must have used all her powers of persuasion to get John to acknowledge that it was high time that the girls be out more. They both knew that Berkeley was waiting, having secured the living of Bosbury near Ledbury.

The 1857 season would be invaluable too to the eldest boys now in London. For their second son, Dick, just beginning law in town, the season would bring useful introductions, besides helping him overcome a bout of unrequited love. Dick was nursing a smarting wound after his recent crushing disappointment with respect to the splendidly named Miss Isabella Elizabeth Catherine Twistleton Wykeham Fiennes. That April, Bel-Bel Fiennes had become engaged to another.

Bel-Bel's father, the 13th Baron Saye and Sele, was Archdeacon of Hereford and a family friend. The young lady herself had stayed with Carey-Mary at Hampton Court and through Tally's Hoskyns ancestors, Bel-Bel was a distant relation by marriage.[16] George commented to their father, 'I hope Richard is not past consolation for this sudden shock to his tender feelings. Tell him I can sympathize with him, and the best advice I can offer is to pretend that he never cared for her, and to make violent advances to some exceedingly old and disagreeable female – *out of spite*.'[17] The fortunate fiancé was Richard Webb of Donnington Hall, Herefordshire, who as an Etonian and Christ Church man was known to Johnny and George. George explained that Webb was 'called Spider Webb up here. I suppose it [Bel-Bel's decision to marry Webb] is on the principle that everything light and buoyant must have some ballast to keep it all right.'

The Park Lane house could not have been better located. Hyde Park was just over the road, and during a morning ride or stroll they might encounter numerous acquaintances. Carey must have been teased mercilessly by her brothers about going into the park through the nearby Stanhope Gate. To the north in Portland Place was the London home of John's brother-in-law and Tally's favourite verbal sparring partner, Sir James Wigram. They were within a short distance of the home of the late, incomparable Duke of Wellington at Apsley House, in front of which stood the ludicrous Wellington Monument. This arch, topped with a vast equestrian bronze, was known in jest as the 'Archduke'. It was so disproportionately large that, unfortunately for its subject (who had died in 1852), it cast Apsley House into shadow for most of the afternoon.[18]

Just up Piccadilly (next to Berkeley Street) was Devonshire House, well known to John's brother Robert, and Stratton Street, where Angela Burdett-Coutts, the Duke of Wellington's former favourite, lived.[19] Further up Piccadilly, near the Royal Academy, was that Arkwright landmark, the Burlington Hotel on Cork Street. It was here that John and his brothers always used to meet and collect hampers from Willersley when they were at school, and they had used it for get-togethers in town ever since. John's sons were now perpetuating the tradition.

For the Arkwright girls, more accustomed, as their uncle Joseph put it, to 'vegetating in the county', the excitement must have threatened to be overwhelming. If the round of balls, dances, dinners, concerts and picture exhibitions became too much, they could visit Henry and Edwyn at Harrow, and Arthur at Eton on 4 June. John, though, remained practical, like the eye at the centre of the storm around him. He organised repairs to his coach at the Coach Manufactory at Park Street, Grosvenor Square. It was returned to Hampton Court by train in August with a request please to forward his 'old chariot' at once.[20]

In July, after the lease was up, Johnny headed for Ireland to stay with Hoskyns relations, and the rest of the family returned to Hampton Court. Four weeks of concerts, balls, picnics, boating on the Lugg, sketching trips, horticultural shows, croquet and cricket ensued. On 29 and 30 July, the Arkwrights probably made the trip back to town for Henry's final cricket match against Eton at Lord's, when the dazzling slow round-arm bowler captained the Harrow side to a 10-wicket victory. Henry took 3 wickets for 25 runs, and in the second innings 5 for 27.[21] He was carried aloft by the team.

To crown the season's excitement, Berkeley summoned up the courage to ask Carey to marry him. He was accepted, and John and Tally gave their consent. On 4 August, Berkeley's father, Sir Edwyn Stanhope wrote to John:

> Berkeley has announced to us that he has been fortunate in winning the affections of your eldest daughter, and that he has obtained your's and Mrs Arkwright's consent to her union with him. I trust I need scarcely assure you of the heartfelt pleasure wh: this announcement has given us, feeling as we do how eminently Carey is qualified to make him happy, and how delighted I am at the prospect of having so sweet & good and amiable a daughter in law.

She could, Sir Edwyn admitted, have found a wealthier partner, but not a better. 'I know for the most part how unacceptable to Mammas and Papas a poor *younger son* is.'[22] He was, he added, glad to hear that John was in better health. Berkeley wrote on 4 August, from his vicarage at Bosbury, to confirm 'how cordially my good parent consented to my marriage with Cary . . . I feel that I have truly won a treasure.'[23] John could not but concur.

Despite John's private feelings, he could not be more content with Carey's choice. Tally's Hoskyns grandmother was a great-aunt to Sir Edwyn Scudamore Stanhope, so Berkeley and Carey's union was fitting. Berkeley's choice also indicated to John the extent to which his children were considered part of the county establishment. John's policy of keeping his head down in local affairs, his residence in the county, his patronage of local causes and his care not to abuse his position and wealth had won him popularity among his peers. His insecurity about his precise place in the county would not dog the next generation.

With the date for the wedding set for 27 January 1858, John and Tally went to Dover for a precious last holiday with the girls in the autumn, returning in time for a visit to Hampton Court by the Earl of Essex, from whose family John's father had purchased Hampton Court in 1810. From Dover, Johnny set off on a grand tour including Paris and Florence before the wedding, and Rome and Naples afterwards. Henry, meanwhile, had gone up to Cambridge where, from 61 Park Street, he wrote to his father. 'I feel rather strange here, as I suppose is universally the case with freshmen. I have a very nice next room neighbour – Norman the Captn of the Eton 11, so we fight over old battles.'[24]

The financial negotiations for Berkeley and Carey's marriage were entered into over the winter. Sir Edwyn went to Devon in late November, and wrote to John from the Ship Hotel, much amused that a barge from Bremen had run aground and spilled its cargo of rum into the water, 'making a harbour of *grog*!'[25] On his return, he, Berkeley and John tried to get their figures together. John wrote to Berkeley on 15 December to tell him, with typical Arkwright financial clarity, that Carey had interest on legacies of £8,000 from her grandfather Arkwright, £2,000 which would be added at Christmas, and £10,000 from her uncle Charles at his widow Mary's death, giving Carey about £620 per year.[26]

Berkeley wrote to John on 19 December that as vicar of Bosbury he received £400 per year, to which his father was adding £100 for a curate. On the death of the vicar of Holme Lacy, he hoped to take that living, which would mean an increase to £578 per year. On his parents' death he would receive £1,450, his share of monies settled on Lady Stanhope on her marriage, plus £7,000 which was to be charged on ample and freehold estates.[27] The finer details were checked by Thomas Sale with the Stanhopes' solicitor, R. Underwood of 8 Castle Street, Hereford.

In the new year of 1858, John suffered another bout of ill health, worrying everyone in the run-up to the wedding. However, John was able to write to Sir Hungerford on 22 January that he was really much better and that the wedding preparations were progressing. Johnny was just back from Florence and had been to a ball at Hereford the night before. George and Henry were home too, and the other boys, Edwyn, Arthur and Charlie were expected from school.[28]

The wedding day, Wednesday 27 January, dawned dry, giving hopes of a fine day. The reporter from the *Hereford Journal* arrived in time to watch a nervous Carey and her bridesmaids descend the stairs beneath a moss arch clustered with snowdrops supported by pillars of ferns. Johnny had organised his brothers to raise it the night before. 'The effect was singularly charming. The tiny flowers, fit emblems of modesty, seemed stooping to salute their maiden queen, or looked like strings of nature's pearls twined for the brow of purity herself.'[29]

Waiting for Carey by the door into the courtyard were her parents, John with a proud smile and Tally wearing 'a costly creamy-white and green striped figured silk dress, double skirts, with deep vandykes of green let in the skirt, richly fringed with material of the same colour'. Her bonnet 'was of white Terry velvet, with flowers and white feathers'. Johnny was also there, having seen Berkeley and his parents, Tally's family, and the eight bridesmaids off in a ribbon of carriages drawn by greys.[30] The four of them stepped into their carriage which turned around the courtyard and was waved off by the staff.

Their route down the drive and along the road was punctuated by arches of flowers, some with crowns and Union Jacks, some bearing inscriptions such as 'May help and happiness attend the happy union', and 'Long life to the happy pair'. As they rounded the turnpike corner and climbed the slope towards the church, they saw a throng of spectators, 'dressed in their holiday garb, and wearing bouquets and wedding favours'. A crimson carpet led up the path to the church door, where the Bishop of Hereford was waiting.

As Carey stepped out, her dress of rich glacé silk, trimmed with two deep flounces of Honiton lace, looped up with white satin ribbon, was seen for the first time. The jacket was of the same material, fringed with lace, and fastened at the bosom with gold buttons. White satin boots covered her feet; massive gold bracelets with diamonds set in turquoise graced her wrists; and the bouquet included orange blossom, azaleas, camelias, lilies of the valley, and snowdrops, 'grouped by one of the first French *artistes* in the metropolis'. A magnificent Honiton lace veil (fastened at the head with a brilliant diamond pin) fell gracefully to her feet.

The decoration of St Mary's had been supervised by Joseph Yates, Edward Colley's assistant at the estate office. Here again were evergreen pillars and snowdrops, but it was the scent of early violets and primroses that captivated the senses. The pews were full, and Hope's schoolchildren thronged the gallery. Carey entered the church on her father's arm to a whisper of excitement from the congregation. The Bishop of Hereford and Carey's uncle, Leigh Hoskyns, moved to the altar to conduct the ceremony.

With the vows exchanged, Mr and Mrs Scudamore Stanhope signed the register and the bells 'rang out as joyous a peal as sinew and goodwill could make them'. As Carey left the church, the children of Hope School presented her with an address of gratitude for her 'kind teaching and Christian example'. She and Berkeley were sent off to a loud shout and chiming bells. At the end of the drive to Hampton Court, the horses were unfastened and forty local men drew the newly-weds home, stirred on by the band of the Hereford Militia.

Inside the house, the party proceeded to the dining room for the wedding breakfast, overlooked by the Wright of Derby pictures of Sir Richard Arkwright, of John's parents, and of John and his siblings as children.[31] Here it was the food that drew the attention, including a boar's head, and a magnificent wedding cake topped with a chalice of flowers. Mr Merrett of Hereford had again been called in to assist Mrs Kitchen, the unlikely named cook at Hampton Court, who had undertaken much of the work, aided by the housekeeper, Mrs Mitchell. Between eighty and a hundred people enjoyed lunch and speeches by the Bishop, Berkeley, Lord Saye and Sele, Johnny (who toasted the Queen with 'pleasing allusions' to the marriage, two days earlier, of Princess Victoria to Prince Frederick William of Prussia) and Dick, who proposed the health of the bridesmaids.

Meanwhile, in another demonstration of estate unity, the laundry that John had built in 1854 had been converted into a dining room for John's tenants and labourers. Prime Hereford beef from John's herd fed 300–400 people. Before the meal, Berkeley said grace and Carey cut the first slice of beef, which was offered to Thomas Gatehouse who had been employed in the gardens for over fifty years. After the meal, Mr Colburn of Bodenham spoke of their regret at losing Carey.

'Of Mr Arkwright,' he continued:

> it was not too much to say that he had always shown himself a just and yet generous employer. Possessed of a magnificent estate, he did not, like too many of the aristocracy and landlords of the present day, go abroad to spend

> his money, forgetful of the adage that 'property has its duties as well as its right'; but, like a true 'old English gentleman', stayed at home, spent his money among them, and was always well pleased if he could by advice or assistance contribute to their comfort and happiness. [Loud applause.]

Colley then distributed up to 5*s* to each guest. For those not present, there was a share of 100 gallons of good ale. Besides this, the inhabitants of the parishes of Hope, Newton and Wharton collected enough cash to give a total of 1,300lb of beef to the local cottagers, each family receiving between 7lb and 13lb of meat.

After the breakfast, the wedding presents were on view in the Museum.[32] At 3 p.m., Berkeley and Carey left for their honeymoon. 'A splendid equipage and four greys decorated with wedding favours, drew up to the principal entrance of the Court', and bore them away, against a volley of 'artillery' from the tower. From Ford Bridge station, they took a train north to Gwysaney near Mold in Flintshire, the seat of Carey's cousin John Clowes.[33] As the train passed through Leominster station, the Priory bells rang out.

In the evening, a ball was given for the Hampton Court staff in the Coningsby Hall, at which, 'throwing off for a while the conventionalities of fashionable life, the family of Hampton Court and their visitors . . . led those around them to believe that they had their enjoyment at heart'. A huge fire illuminated 'the massively splendid marble chimney-piece and the happy-looking group of musicians on its pilasters', and 'the belted knight on his noble charger on the picture-lined walls'.[34] Supper was served at 1 a.m. and the revelry continued until nearly daybreak. The next day, Thursday, brought another ball, and on the Friday, 'a dramatic entertainment written for the occasion by Richard Arkwright', was performed by all six of his brothers, 'in which they displayed considerable histrionic powers'.

After the excitement, the decorations were taken down, the plants were returned to the hothouses and conservatory, and normality resumed. Johnny packed for Rome. Young Charlie wrote to his father from Little Berkhamsted in Hertfordshire that the school had been to the theatre in Drury Lane.[35] Three weeks after their departure, Berkeley and Carey returned to their new home at Bosbury, where Mrs Drake and her staff welcomed their new mistress.[36]

The report of the newly-weds' return appeared in the *Hereford Journal* on Wednesday 24 February 1858. By then, their joy was extinguished.

John had fallen ill once again, rapidly declined and Carey had hastened home. John was troubled at the end by the financial problems of his father-in-law. Sir Hungerford had large debts but he refused to turn to his own son Chandos and had instead confided in John. John used his dwindling strength to make Johnny promise that he would not become embroiled in Harewood's affairs under any circumstances. That much ascertained, he could finally be at peace. John Arkwright died a month to the day after Carey's wedding and the day before her twenty-seventh birthday. William Glading, carpenter and Master of the Estate Works, undertook the melancholy final duty for his employer of making his coffin from estate oak.

The following week the deaths column of the *Hereford Journal* bore the simple announcement:

> ARKWRIGHT. – Feb 27, at Hampton Court, in this county, John Arkwright, Esq, aged 72.[37]

John was buried at Hope Church on 5 March, with, at his request, the minimum of pomp consistent with his station. Black horses led a very different procession from the house shortly after 1 p.m. The *Journal* reported that:

> The hearse, drawn by four horses, accompanied by the pall bearers, mourners, private friends, tenantry, servants and tradesmen . . . was met at the entrance to the grounds by a number of highly respectable tradesmen and others from Leominster, who had expressed a wish to pay the last tribute of respect to one so justly beloved and esteemed, by accompanying his remains to the grave. At the same place the children (about 100 in number) attending the school at Hope, in which the deceased and his family have always taken so great an interest, joined the procession.
>
> Crowds of persons from the neighbourhood came to witness the funeral of a gentleman whose loss will be severely felt by all classes, particularly the poorer people, who have been bereft of a kind friend and benefactor.

The clergy heading the procession were followed by around fifty of the tenantry, led by Colley, all wearing hat-bands, scarves and gloves provided for them, and walking in pairs. Behind them came the pall-bearers including one of John's oldest friends, William Mitford, his neighbour Daniel Peploe of Garnstone, his Leominster friend Bonham Caldwall, and Sir Edwyn Scudamore Stanhope. They preceded the hearse, alongside which walked the underbearers, and behind whom came the mourners. These included all seven of John's sons and Berkeley, Sir Hungerford, Lord Auckland, Lord Saye and Sele, various Arkwright nephews, Chandos and Leigh Hoskyns, Richard Phelips and Edward Hawkshaw. They were followed by private friends, the servants, tradesmen and schoolchildren, all two by two. The whole service was conducted 'in the most impressive manner' and with 'the greatest order'. In the evening, a muffled peal of bells tolled from Leominster Priory.[38]

THREE

Master of the Estate

Johnny Arkwright would not be going to Rome. He urgently required instead a grand tour of his own acres and their management, territory as foreign to him as Florence had been a few weeks before. There was little time to be lost – the first rent day fell within three weeks of his father's death. As Johnny pushed against the heavy oak door cut into the gates and stepped over into the freshness of an early March morning, he was embarking on the longest journey of his life.

He began to walk past the stables. He would not usually have been able to resist a check on his hunter, but his sense of his own predicament, an unwillingness to see his father's redundant old grey horse, and the sight of the unforgiving hands of the Tompion clock in its turret drove him on.[1] He passed the bothies that lined the north wall of the kitchen gardens and noted the smoke of the hothouse fires curling into the morning air. The beating of waterwheels accompanied his approach to the estate works and home farm where he was to meet his fate.

Johnny had an experienced chaperone to guide him through the estate's labyrinthine affairs, one wise to the tricks that might be tried by more experienced men on the ingénu. Edward Colley had been the agent or steward of the Hampton Court estate since the late 1830s. With Colley's advice Johnny's father had increased the size of the estate from the 6,220 acres that Richard Arkwright had purchased in 1810 to its present extent of 10,257 acres.[2]

Colley had been employed by John Arkwright when John's father, Richard, was still alive. Richard had insisted that meticulous records be kept for every aspect of the estate, and John had learned the importance of careful bookkeeping through having to report to his father on Hampton Court, using information supplied by Colley. That punctiliousness now proved invaluable to Johnny. Colley had carried out a full survey of the estate on 12 September the previous year, with maps indicating holdings and defining boundaries.[3]

Colley's office was at the estate's home farm, known as Green Farm, or The Green, west of Hampton Court. As he walked through its door,

Johnny entered a different world, one of coloured terriers, measuring wheels, compasses and dividers, theodolites, samples of corn and oilcake, magnifying equipment, shelves of ledgers, racks of correspondence from Sale, farm particulars, cogs and broken parts from machines awaiting attention, calendars marked with auction and market dates, and copies of agricultural journals.

In this stimulating environment, Johnny's responsibilities were made clear. He was already no doubt aware that Herefordshire was, when evaluated by 'the number of persons engaged in agriculture in proportion to the entire population . . . the purest agricultural district in England'.[4] Within that county, he now headed one of the largest estates. Colley showed him that his land extended over twenty different parishes, from Leominster Borough in the north, to Hereford city 15 miles to the south. Seven and a half thousand of the acres focused on Hampton Court itself in the parishes of Hope, Wickton, Stoke Prior, Risbury, Bodenham and Pencombe. This land was divided between 43 tenants, farming between 40 and 391 acres apiece. Besides these there were smallholders and cottagers with an orchard or paddock who, combined, rented another 821 acres.[5] The biggest farm on the estate was The Green itself at 728 acres, which was farmed for the landlord by his bailiff.

Each of the tenants paid the annual rent in two instalments, due on Lady Day (25 March) and at Michaelmas (29 September). These rents plus the profits from timber sales and from farming The Green would constitute the majority of Johnny's income, there being no mineral deposits or other sources of income from the land. The rents currently amounted to around £10,500 per year. Unfortunately, profits at The Green were not healthy, but this was common on estates, where the landlord set an example to his tenants by fertilising the soil generously and investing in the latest machines.[6]

The highest rents on the estate were taken from Wharton Court and the Woodhouse. High rents, though, were no use if they dissuaded potential tenants from applying for empty farms that needed to be re-let as soon as possible. In 1865 Johnny wrote: 'I do not wish to let my farms at the highest possible value, but of course must take care of myself . . . I want tenants who will stay and treat farms as far as they think right as if they were on lease.'[7]

Rentals were actually paid over three days to Colley and Yates at the public houses belonging to the estate, such as the Oak at Hope-under-Dinmore, and England's Gate Inn, at Bodenham.[8] In return, any petitions for repairs or improvements to the farms could be lodged with the agent the same day. When the business was concluded, the landlord provided a supper at the inn.

Requests for repairs and improvements were constant. This was not exclusive to Herefordshire, but the variety of crops that the county's rich red open loam soil could support – cereals, roots, hops, apple and pear orchards, besides pasture for Hereford cattle and Radnor and Ryeland sheep – demanded an unusual diversity of buildings on each farm. The Hampton Court tenants required sheep cots, pig sties and cattle sheds as well as folds for handling stock, barns for grain storage and chaff and turnip cutting, oast houses for hop kilns, and cider milling sheds, in addition to the usual buildings for carts and wagons, and stabling horses. Besides the calls for improvements in the farmyard, there were the perpetual demands for improvements to the tenants' homes and to the farm labourers' cottages.

When Johnny asked approximately how much was spent on repairs, Colley could tell him that in 1854, for example, an outlay of £3,566 had been made, of which £120 was spent at Bowley Farm, £148 at the Woodhouse, £133 at Marlbrook, and £115 on Mr Lloyd's at Risbury. In the year before that, £3,204 had been spent.[9] The average for 1852–4 was £3,329, around one-third of the income from rentals in 1857, a fact that must have made Johnny rapidly reassess his annual income of £10,500.[10]

The change in estate ownership emphasised the value of a good agent. Crafty tenants might try to fool Johnny that his father had promised improvements to their farm, but Colley's rent-day notes could confirm or refute this. Even so, in December 1858, Johnny wrote (on mourning paper) to each tenant to request 'a list in writing of repairs improvements & buildings which you consider have been promised on your farm'. This was to be sent to Colley by 12 December 'after which time no claim for promises will be allowed!'[11]

Repairs and improvements were carried out at the estate works by craftsmen employed by Johnny. The works were located south-west of The Green, and included operations such as timber- and stone-cutting, brick-making and iron-working. Under William Glading toiled highly skilled masons, carpenters, a glazier, painters, blacksmiths and quarrymen. They carried out repairs to the Court itself besides manufacturing farm carts or repairing stone walls, and making the gates, hinges and gateposts for the estate (which, as was customary, bore Johnny's initials).

At the estate works, too, Richard Arkwright's influence was felt. No man in Britain was better placed to benefit from Sir Richard Arkwright's ingenuity with water power. Sir Richard had turned his Matlock spinning frames with the waters of the Derwent, and although he was not the first to use water power for textile production, he was extremely successful in doing so. After his example, Richard Arkwright repaired the weir on the River Lugg running past the works, and harnessed its power to drive the saw- and stone-mills. The works too required expenditure – between 1849 and 1854, John Arkwright had laid out £3,592 on the sawmills alone.[12]

The estate works and the estate office were at the core of the enterprise. Both interacted with all the properties on the estate, including the Court, and with all its departments. For example, the sawmills might supply timber to the gamekeeper for rearing pens, besides poles for the hopyards on several of the farms, and wood for a new glasshouse in the kitchen garden at Hampton Court. In each case, the foreman, whether the head keeper, a tenant, or the head gardener, kept a note of what had been received, while the head of the sawmill recorded what had been supplied by him. Every month, there was a great reckoning at the estate office, when poor Joseph Yates and his clerks had the unenviable task of trying to make the amounts tally. The estate office, therefore, was the clearing house of a small independent economy.

Johnny's role, he now learned, was to define the direction of that economy. During the final decade of his father's life, High Farming had become popular. This was a theory born of the demand from Britain's growing population for greater agricultural output, particularly of wheat for bread, and, as the standard of living rose, of meat. With the enclosure process completed by 1820, there were no further significant acres to bring into production. The repeal of the Corn Laws meant that foreign competition was a threat and British produce would have to be competitively priced. To increase supply and lower prices, in recent years efforts had been made to fertilise the soil to achieve greater yields per acre.

High Farming evangelists, including James Caird, Philip Pusey and John Joseph Mechi, depicted the increase of output as the only way forward for agriculture.[13] They advanced soil fertilisation and the overwintering of stock indoors, to bring beasts to maturity more quickly and enable the farmer to garner manure for spreading on the fields, so producing better feedstuffs for overwintering stock the following year. In this way, a beneficial, self-sustaining cycle would be established.

There was little mention of the costs of building cow and sheep sheds to overwinter stock, or of importing fertilisers. Landlords, though, were accustomed to starting cycles of improvement through their own financial outlay. High Farming therefore demanded of landowners an optimistic view of agriculture while offering a clear alternative for those who did not believe that a return to the protection of the Corn Laws was realistic.

John, by his own assessment 'somewhat of a Free Trader',[14] had taken the advice of the High Farming advocates. In 1849 he had purchased some of Lawes's superphosphate for spreading, and in difficult years began to provide fertilisers for struggling tenants in lieu of, and in some years in addition to, rent rebates.[15] Besides using fertilisers, John had also followed the movement by acquiring ploughs, a steam-driven threshing machine, and a Hussey steam reaping machine seen at the shows of the Royal Agricultural Society, the Bath and West of England Agricultural Society and Herefordshire's own Society in the 1840s.

The improvements seemed to have paid off when, in 1853, like bright sun after rain, agricultural prices had improved, the upturn being partly effected by the blockage of Russian grain supplies during the Crimean War. Meat prices also began to climb and continued to do so (along with most dairy prices) until, between 1850 and 1868, they had risen by 50 per cent.

By the end of his interview with Colley, the way forward for Johnny was clear: he should follow his father's High Farming lead although it would mean significant further expenditure on the estate. He would have to lead by example at The Green, and on the other farms that his father had had in hand – Hillhole and Henhouse.[16] John had spent generously on the house during his years at Hampton Court; Johnny would invest in the land that supported it.

Before Johnny could embark on his plans, he faced the melancholy reading of his father's will, drawn up with Sale on 2 December the previous year, and proven at Hereford on 1 April 1858.[17] In it, John established a trust or 'Estate of Inheritance' of Hampton Court, nominating as the trustees 'my friends the Rev. Berkeley Lionel Scudamore Stanhope Vicar of Bosbury . . . and Bonham Caldwall of Leominster'. This meant that neither the acres themselves, nor Hampton Court, nor the buildings, nor the implements passed to Johnny. Instead, he inherited only the rents and incomes from the estate for his lifetime. They passed thereafter to his son.

John instructed that £1,000 be paid to Tally within a month of his death. Thereafter, she was 'to have the personal use and occupation of my mansion house with the offices gardens and appurtenances belonging thereto at Hampton Court . . . for her residence until some person or persons being of the age of twenty five years shall be entitled to the possession of the same'. She would also draw a quarterly jointure from the estate, totalling £1,000 per annum.

Each of Johnny's brothers was to receive £15,000 on his twenty-first birthday, as well as a further £5,000 payable on Tally's death. Each daughter received £10,000 at 21. John had noted that Richard had bequeathed to each of his grandchildren £5,000. Since Emily, Alice and Charles had not been born in 1843, John gave each of them £5,000.[18]

Trusts of the kind established by John's will were quite common. However, Johnny must have wondered privately about his father's intentions, and some of his unease over the Leominster parliamentary candidacy must have stirred. John had ensured that although Johnny would have the income from the rents plus any profit that he made from farming The Green (which depended on agricultural prices), he was not free to dispose of any of the land without permission from Berkeley and Bonham. Might this have reflected his father's mistrust of him or suspicion that he might want to sell off the farms to fund an extravagant lifestyle?

He had no idea what to make of the fact that none of the stock or machinery had been left to him. Everyone assured him that it was an oversight on the part of Sale, but it cost him dear. The value of the stock including the Hereford herd, the deer in the park, and the machinery was assessed at £9,873 – more than a year's disposable income for Johnny – which at once became a debt from Johnny to the trustees. Dick and George, meanwhile, having attained 21, found more than one and a half times that sum credited to their account at the bank, and they had none of the worry of running the estate.

Johnny could not share these misgivings with Berkeley since, besides being a trustee, he was his brother-in-law. The other trustee, Bonham Caldwall, by Johnny's own account 'the gingerbread and barley-sugar man of my childhood' and 'the riding-master and teacher of all good and sound sports', was of his father's generation, and dated his first visit to Hampton Court to 1816.[19]

The one person who could truly appreciate Johnny's position was his uncle Chandos Wren Hoskyns. Like Johnny, Chandos was almost irrepressibly energetic. He had trained in law and was enjoying a successful career when he married Theodosia Wren, the last descendant of Sir Christopher Wren, inherited Wroxall, her father's Warwickshire estate, and took his name. Faced with a rapid apprenticeship in agriculture, Chandos not only maintained but improved his unpromising clay-soiled estate, while other, more experienced, Warwickshire farmers struggled.

For thirty years, Chandos, under the pseudonym Talpa – the mole (a renowned soil improver) – wrote up his experiences at Wroxall in a column for the *Agricultural Gazette* and subsequently compiled them into a volume entitled *Talpa: The Chronicles of A Clay Farm*. He blended with his subject immense charm and humour. He looked at farming with the eyes of the outsider and broadened participation in agricultural debate.

His first priority at Wroxall had been to drain his clay fields. He described with characteristic verve the reaction of his sceptical foreman to the theodolite used to calculate the fall of the land. 'If you ever saw a dog put his nose to a wasp's nest,' Chandos wrote, 'you may form some idea of the mistrustful curiosity and hesitating aversion with which he brought his face into close contact with his arch-enemy.'[20]

Chandos's great achievement was the promotion of guano to fertilise the soil. Between 1841 and 1845, annual imports of guano rose from 2,881 tons to 283,000 tons.[21] Through his column, he, as it were, took Peruvian penguin excrement out of the farmyard and into the drawing room. As far as his mother, Lady Hoskyns, was concerned, he had done so rather too literally when, after Theodosia's death in 1842, Chandos made his second marriage (in 1846) to Anna Fane Ricketts, the daughter of the British Ambassador to Peru. In Lady Hoskyns's opinion there hung inescapably about poor Anna the musk of 'the guano of the penguins of the Pacific'.[22]

More important to Johnny than Chandos's agricultural credentials in these early days was the empathy of this uncle who was blatantly disparaged by his father. Sir Hungerford Hoskyns was an old-fashioned father, whose voice was noted for carrying an unusual distance. Sir Hungerford's temper was not helped by his significant indebtedness by the 1850s owing to injudicious investments and ill-fortune. Furthermore, his son and heir, Chandos's older brother Hungerford, had suffered a breakdown, in part due to the overweening personality of his father. Young Hungerford would never recover sufficiently to run the estate and in 1842 was removed to the Brislington asylum near Bristol.[23]

Chandos therefore faced the future responsibility for the encumbered Harewood estate. Father and son, however, could not have been more different; Sir Hungerford was an eighteenth-century patrician aristocrat, stubbornly against change, High Tory in his politics and self-pitying in his predicament. Chandos (perhaps as a result) enjoyed nothing more than to shake the establishment and to challenge accepted norms. He was mild-mannered, affable and sensitive, a leading Free Trader and a Whig by party, ready always to make the best of a difficult situation. As Sir Hungerford's financial problems became apparent, John Arkwright had tried repeatedly to persuade Sir Hungerford to inform Chandos of the position, but the old baronet would have none of it.

In the end, John Arkwright and Sir Hungerford's other son-in-law Richard Phelips had to deny Sir Hungerford any help until Chandos be apprised of the situation. This worked, but Chandos was often reduced to frustrated tears by his father, with whom the advice of his agent at Harewood counted more than that of his own son. 'The agony,' wrote Chandos to Tally, 'will never be effaced from my remembrance, of what I went through last year . . . If there was more intelligence there would be more sympathy.'[24] The evidence of Sir Hungerford's low estimation of him nevertheless wrought its damage. Chandos wrote of himself to Tally 'a son, however unpopular is still a son'.[25] The strife brought Chandos little but unhappiness. To save Harewood for the family, he had to sell Wroxall in 1861.

While Chandos returned to Herefordshire in the teeth of his father's resentment, Tally recognised her brother's abilities and encouraged Chandos to help Johnny. The extent to which Chandos empathised with Johnny is clear from his letter of 24 May 1858. Of estate work he wrote, 'It gradually gets, I think, less onerous as the business gets to be one's pleasure. But oh! for the grace of the days that are fled! The Hills of Manhood look beauteous from afar but oh! the ragged sides they have as you begin to climb!'[26]

In recognition of his contribution to agricultural improvement, Chandos had, since 1854, sat on the Council of the Royal Agricultural Society of England (RASE). Through his influence, in 1862, Johnny was appointed to the RASE Council. The Council was at the forefront of the drive to make agriculture more scientific and productive through the exchange of ideas and displays of agricultural excellence at the Society's annual show. The organisation of the peripatetic show was the Council's principal task, but it also published figures on outbreaks of disease or pest, reported on trials of different fertilisers or compared regional practices.[27]

Chandos's views in many areas of agriculture were influential. He had been innovative with fertilisers, field drainage, and the removal of hedgerows.[28] He was an outspoken critic of traditional attitudes, including primogeniture and the type of entail through trust that John had just established for Hampton Court. As Chandos knew from Harewood, these shackled the hands of the man responsible, particularly if he needed to raise funds for capital investment. Chandos encouraged the industry to look at itself critically for the sake of improvement. He advocated the centralised collection of agricultural statistics, believing that it was only from the pooling of information that knowledge might emerge and progress be made. English farmers, in their ignorance of such information, he characterised as more backward than those in Scotland or Ireland where 'the experiment of collecting agricultural statistics has been attended with greater success'. Chandos's aim in collecting agricultural statistics was 'to exchange doubt for certainty, guesswork for fact, error for truth; and in so doing to hold up a mirror that can neither flatter nor distort'.[29]

The British farming community, however, was slow to change. At the 1862 International Exhibition, Chandos was asked for the total amount of the agricultural produce of England. 'To French, Germans, Austrians, Portuguese, Americans and Canadians alike, he was obliged to return the humiliating reply that we had no means of ascertaining what was the agricultural produce of the country; and so surprised were these gentlemen that they seemed to be really incredulous of the fact.'[30] Finally, in 1866, the annual Agricultural Census was introduced, recording the use of every acre of land in the country as well as the numbers of sheep, cattle, milking cows and pigs.

For his innovative approach and through *Talpa*, Chandos became a respected agricultural figure. His influence was most memorably acknowledged, nine months after John Arkwright's death, by Charles Dickens. Chandos was chairing a dinner at the Castle Hotel, Coventry, organised to present Dickens with a gold watch for his reading of *A Christmas Carol* in aid of the Coventry Institute. The great author proposed the following toast to the Chairman. 'In my ignorance of the subject, I am bound to say that it may be, for anything I know – indeed I am ready to admit that it is – exceedingly important that a Clay Farm should go for a number of years to waste; but I claim some knowledge of the management of a Clay Farmer, and I positively object to his ever lying fallow. In the hope that this very rich and teeming individual may speedily be ploughed up, and that we shall gather into our barns and storehouses the admirable crops of wisdom which must spring up wherever he is sown, I take leave to propose his health.'[31]

Sitting on the RASE Council alongside his esteemed uncle and reading the Society's *Journal*, Johnny was exposed to all the innovations of his industry. That exposure, blended with the zeal to improve and the fact that Chandos was now living at Harewood, emboldened Johnny to embark on major changes at Hampton Court. His eagerness was fed by the staging of the 1863 RASE show at Worcester, where Johnny first showed cattle from his Hereford herd. He won the £25 first prize for his bull, Sir Oliver II.[32]

Johnny began to practise High Farming in spite of less propitious indicators. In 1858, the golden age of the middle of the century had ended abruptly, at least for grain prices. The following year, the tenants at New House and Hill House asked for a rent reduction. Johnny convinced the New House tenant to stay at the same rent with an allowance of superphosphate. At Hill House, the rent fell from £280 to £260 for the year, with the addition of two tons of fertiliser, £200 expenditure on altering fences, and land drainage.[33] The same year in November, to recoup some of his losses, and presumably with the consent of Berkeley and Bonham, he tried to sell Redwood, the worst-paying farm on the estate, but the tenant offered only £6,200, less than their reserve.[34] Johnny followed his father in paternalism too, offering a widow who lost £106 worth of cattle through yew poisoning £50 of his own.

Johnny also spent on farm machinery. In 1860 he bought a wind pump from Southwark, and the following year a mower from Burgess & Keys of Blackfriars and a steam engine from Humphries of Pershore. In 1862 he bought two more mowing machines and in 1863, after taking advice from Chandos, he bought a hay machine and horse rake from Nicholson of Newark-on-Trent, and a bone mill from Crosskill of Beverly Iron Works.[35] During meetings with Johnny, Colley must have noted that the young squire's admirable (and unexpected) appetite for hard work seemed to be paying off, for he was becoming entirely familiar with land management and its principles.

The momentum of Johnny's expenditure grew with his confidence. Chandos's influence was clear in Johnny's most significant project, land drainage. Since the late 1830s and early 1840s, when it became possible to produce tiles and pipes on site using mobile equipment, drainage had become more widely undertaken. Indeed, it was to become the chief agricultural improvement of the nineteenth century. At first, Johnny, like his father, had made piecemeal improvements. Then, the government, keen to increase agricultural production and appease the disgruntled landowning and farming classes after the repeal of the Corn Laws, offered loans for estate improvements through new land drainage companies.[36]

In 1862, Johnny applied to the Lands Improvement Company for a loan.[37] It was approved. In June 1863 he borrowed £1,097 and in December £1,084.[38] He began drainage on Green Farm and circulated his tenants with his terms – 5 per cent of the outlay and all the hauling to be undertaken by the tenant. For building improvements, the tenants contributed 2 per cent. The following year, Johnny borrowed over £2,000 in two tranches. In 1865, he increased his borrowings dramatically, to over £5,100, most likely because the results of drainage and building repairs were seen by more cautious tenants who now began to take up his offer.

The 1865–6 drainage at Hampton Court was done by William Bowles of Shrewsbury.[39] The work involved digging trenches into which to lay pipes, 13yd apart and 4ft deep across the whole of any field, whether it needed it or not. Careful calculation had to be made to get the fall of the ground correct. Lower Wickton and The Ford were drained,[40] but the biggest project was at Wootton, where a total of 141 acres, 2 rods and 7 perches were drained at a cost of £988 7*s*.[41] The costs, at an average £7 2*s* 6*d* per acre, were on the high side of the national average of £4 to £8. Still, Johnny thought it worth it, for he continued to borrow, though never as much as he had done in 1865. In 1866, he borrowed over £3,000, £1,605 in 1867, £2,660 in 1868, and so on, until by the end of 1874, he had borrowed a colossal total of £27,451 6*s* 5*d* (over £1.1 million at today's rate), with a total in interest over the 25-year repayment period of £18,608 5*s* 3*d* (£755,670).[42]

Improvements going beyond wear and tear were made by Johnny in farm buildings over these early years to meet the needs of High Farming. From 1865 to 1866, he also laid new farm roads. With Colley he moved fences to amalgamate farms, and he experimented with new products. In 1864 he was testing manure and lime on ten squares that he had pegged out in the park. In June the same year he costed mowing part of the Great Meadow immediately east of the house by hand and by machine, concluding that, although he had bought three mowers in the last couple of years, it was cheaper by hand.[43]

After all this activity, Johnny checked himself in May 1864, probably to establish that he could afford the 1865 drainage loan. Johnny noted that he was a tenant for life, holding assets of his own to the value of £21,634. He owed the estate trustees (including the original sum for the stock and implements) a total of £17,000.[44] He was living beyond his means. His yearly income from estate rents had fallen to £9,956 15*s* 4*d*, and when that was combined with income from the residue of his father's estate (including shares in the Macclesfield Canal and railway companies) it amounted to £14,463 9*s* 4*d*. From this he deducted a sum for repairs (not including those on the house) of £2,463 9*s* 4*d*, making a net income per annum, of £12,000. This had to cover both annual obligations as well as private expenditure. The former included land tax, chief rents, charitable obligations attached to properties, and his mother's annuity of £4,000 per annum, and totalled £5,043 4*s* 8*d*.[45] His private expenditure over the same period showed an average of £7,481. He was therefore out of pocket by around £500 per year.[46]

Furthermore, Johnny was investing very heavily in the estate, with no guarantee of returns. However, like his peers, he believed it the primary duty of the landowner to risk capital to set in motion the virtuous cycle of demand for farms on the estate, high rents and plentiful employment for the labour force. He had heeded advice that he had read, such as that given by David Milne in his *Report of a Visit to the Farms*, of 1850, that 'those who have the most capital will, ceteris paribus, make the most profits'.[47] Chandos, too, had written in the *Farmer's Magazine* of 1856, 'it is true that capital cannot be applied profitably to agriculture beyond a certain limit . . . but . . . [that limit is] . . . a point so high, so far above the ordinary scale of farming, that for the present question it is as though that limit did not exist'.[48] Critics scoffed at this absence of economic rigour. Sir Robert Brisco warned the Wigton Club in 1864 that 'it is high farming though it may not be profitable farming'.[49] He, however, could no more than anyone else formulate the optimum level of investment per acre.

Johnny was not the only High-Farming optimist in Herefordshire. Over at Shobdon, Lord Bateman, Lord Lieutenant of Herefordshire, had asked Johnny's father in 1852 to be shown 'an inkling' of Hampton Court book-keeping.[50] Now he was following the example of the Prince Consort on the Norfolk, Shaw and Flemish Farms at Windsor by establishing a model farm with a new agent's residence and state-of-the-art farm buildings at his home farm, Uphampton.[51]

Lord Bateman's new buildings measured about 190ft × 150ft. The ground floor housed horses and cattle. Upstairs was grain and straw storage. The corn was brought to the building by tramway and immediately threshed by a nearby machine driven by a twelve-horsepower engine. The same engine powered an Archimedian screw that transported the threshed grain up to the granary. The straw, meanwhile, was carried upstairs by Tuxford's Patent Straw Climber, cut into litter and conveyed 70ft by creeper until it dropped through trap doors onto the pile beneath, to be forked into the cattle pens and horse stalls. The whole process used minimal manpower and was driven by just one engine, which also ran a pulper for crushing cattle cake, oatmeal and beans for the animals, turned the apple mill and powered the cider press.

Johnny did not go to such lengths at Hampton Court but was concerned not only with the quality but also the appearance of his land. He rebuilt stone walls and set about repairing hedgerows. In February 1860, two men from Warwickshire, Joseph Arch and John Ivens, came to Hampton Court for twelve days' hedging work.[52] They had been at Harewood with Chandos before coming to Hampton Court and their Warwickshire roots suggest that Chandos had employed them at Wroxall before that.

The 35-year-old Joseph Arch who arrived at the estate office was a small, square and powerful man. He had begun his working life at the age of 9, scaring birds in the Warwickshire fields for 4*d* a day. Later, he tried gravel-digging and wood cutting, but by the turn of the 1850s 11*s* a week was an insufficient wage to keep a wife and two children. He worked as a drainage contractor, but specialised in hedge-laying. By the late 1850s, he was highly skilled, winning prizes at shows, which brought Arch work all over the country hedging, draining, ploughing and mowing.[53]

Colley put Arch and Ivens to work over at Hill House in Bodenham and at Newton Court. Over the twelve days, the men laid 101½ perches of fencing, for 26¾ of which they were paid 1*s* 3*d* a perch and for 74¾ of which they were paid 1*s* a perch. At a work rate of nearly 8½ perches a day, each man was earning at least 4*s* per day. With a labourer's wage in Herefordshire being 10*s* or 11*s* per week, their work came at a premium. Johnny admitted that it was generous, but 'our own hedgers could not have done the same amount of work. This incident, more than anything else in my experience, has proved to me that wages must be gauged by individual capability, not by a fixed tariff.'[54]

The question of pay and conditions for labourers was beginning to stir. Why was it, the labourer wondered, that if the landowner had all this money to build model farms and scatter fertilisers, he, the labourer, was feeling none of the benefit? The tenant farmer might get increased outputs from his plot, but precious little of the wealth thereby created seemed to be trickling down to the workers. All they got from higher yields were harder days harvesting denser crops. The improvements in communications resulting from the circulation of trains, the penny post, and newspapers had brought the rural labourer closer to his urban equivalent. Their lots were more easily compared, and urban union activity was noted. However, the memories of Tolpuddle in the year of Johnny's birth, when seven men were deported after forming the Agricultural Labourers Union, kept them quiet.

The labourer was, thanks to industrial and economic growth, increasingly scarce and therefore in a stronger position. The increase of his power, however, was barely perceptible to the labourer, with his eyes down hoeing between rows of turnips. All he knew was that at key times of the year it was becoming harder to find hands. The phenomemon was first really noticeable nationally at harvest time in 1859. Between the 1851 and 1861 censuses, there was an overall fall of 2.8 per cent in the number of agricultural labourers in England and Wales. New industries such as sewage works, brewing and gas companies sapped labour from the countryside and took them to the towns and beyond, in the case of the American gold rush. The increasing mechanisation of agricultural work inclined some to leave. Others exchanged jobs on the land for employment on the railways, as stationmasters and signalmen, or as police constables.

The labour shortage had been observed earlier in Herefordshire. In 1845, when the Hereford to Monmouth railway had been under construction, it had been difficult to find hop pickers.[55] There was also competition from the mining and japanning industries of the Welsh valleys. During the mid-century depression, wages for some had dropped to as low as 6*s* per week, but had picked up again with the golden years after 1852. Even so, quarrymen or railwaymen could earn 2*s* or 3*s* a day, but labourers only about 1*s* 4*d*. During the Crimea, the recruitment of men for the Militia had coincided with an abundant harvest in June 1857, and the Green Farm mowers had rejected the 3*s* 10*d* per acre rate they were offered. Joseph Yates had the unpleasant task of informing Johnny's father that they would not work for under 4*s*. Herein, no doubt, lay the germination of the switch to mechanical mowing on the estate.

Poor wage rates meant difficulty in paying cottage rents. The agricultural labourers were employed and housed by Johnny's tenant farmers. While the labourer's employer owned his cottage and paid his wages, the worker's disposable income was effectively fixed by the tenant farmer. In aggravating the farmer by taking action to improve his lot, the labourer risked the roof over the heads of his wife and children. This had been mentioned by Mechi during his visit to Herefordshire in 1848.[56] Then, Mr T. Batson of Kynaston had claimed (to cries of 'Shame') that in some parts of the county, labourers' wages were as low as 5*s* a week, with half a dozen children to feed and a cottage rent of £10 to £14 per year to find. Batson's figures were queried by W. Bennett who insisted that the average yearly rent was between £2 and £5. Whatever the average, at the lowest end of the scale, there was considerable hardship.

In response to this issue, from Lady Day 1859, Johnny took back from the tenant farmers all his cottages and let them himself from the estate office. In 1863, he also began erecting cottages on the estate using prize-winning plans for a double labourers' cottage from the RASE of 1861.

Weekly wages rose gradually from their average level for the county of 8*s* 5*d* in 1850 to 9*s* 1*d* in 1860. By 1861, when Arch worked at Hampton Court, they were 9*s* 9*d*, rising to 10*s* 6*d* in 1867–9. Wages for task work, like that done by Arch, went up by 25 per cent or more. For those not tempted away, there was more work to do, since High Farming needed extra hands for winter foddering and littering, the lifting of root crops and hauling, and spreading of fertiliser.

Johnny had learned from hiring Arch and Ivens the importance of having the right man for a job. In these circumstances, the employer did not resent paying good money. Acting on this, in 1867, Johnny helped to create the Herefordshire Domestic and General Farm Servants' Registration Society, administering this early employment agency himself, his intention being to match employers' demands with workers' abilities. The Society soon had 260 employers and 323 farm servants on its books, but it was short-lived, many farm servants preferring the old hiring fairs on parishes' patronal festivals.[57]

Alongside this innovative and paternalistic work there went too a self-serving motivation. Johnny, like his illustrious great-grandfather who had established textile workers' dwellings at Cromford with schools, shops and churches, knew that a healthy, well-fed, educated and rested workforce produced the best profits for its employer. For the same reason, from 29 May 1868, Hampton Court estate workmen were given a half-holiday on Saturdays. Johnny also staunchly supported his mother in her work at Hope School, because, more than ever, as unskilled labourers broke expensive machinery, the need for a literate, educated workforce was felt. However, the profit motive rarely accounted entirely for the responsibility felt for the workforce. On numerous occasions, men well past their best years were retained, or tenants' widows given jobs as housekeepers and their offspring as domestic staff.

Of all the improvements that Johnny undertook in his first years in charge, that which gave him the most pleasure was the expansion of the pedigree herd of Hereford cattle established by his father. These burnished claret-red beasts, with their curly-haired white faces, crest and tail tuft, and placid temperament, were his pride and his joy – his 'ruby-moos'. An irksome day at The Green could always be alleviated by a peep into the stalls where the great creatures raised their wet noses at his approach. During his father's lifetime, it had been customary for oxen to work for five or six years before being fattened for market. By the 1860s, the race was on to bring cattle to maturity earlier, and the Hereford was unrivalled in his ability to fatten quickly even 'upon nettles'.[58] Furthermore, the Hereford carried the most flesh exactly where the prime joints were wanted, and the beef had the beautiful marbled appearance of lean flavoured by fat.[59]

For the cowman, the Herefords' virtue lay with the cow's immunity to disease and infection, her extremely low tendency to abort, and her splendidly rich milk, ensuring a strong start for her offspring. She also had a long breeding life, from 3 to 14 or 15 years old. While careful breeding in the eighteenth century had established the uniformity of the classic Hereford markings, such repeatability in the conformation of each beast was not so easily achieved. Every year, breeding cows were put to different bulls in the search for the best-quality offspring. Painstaking records were kept by breeders, so that successful lines could be inter-bred. The Hereford Herd Book, established in 1844, centralised the pedigrees' breeding records.

Johnny enjoyed crossing prize bulls with his finest cows and anticipating the calves' arrival. To encourage improvements in his tenants' stock, Johnny instituted an annual livestock show at Hampton Court in 1863 and the following year offered £1,000 in prize money. For Johnny, unlike his father, part of the pleasure in breeding Herefords was the public success of winning show prizes, and the knowledge of possessing the country's finest beasts. After success with Sir Oliver in the 1863 Royal Show, Johnny showed again in 1865 at Plymouth, but did not win until 1868 at Leicester, when his home-bred bull Sir Hungerford, and heifers Hampton Beauty and Hampton Oliver won their classes.[60]

These successes a decade after his father's death were especially rewarding. In response to the scrutiny following his inheritance, Johnny had rolled up his sleeves and worked hard. His forward-looking approach had kicked up a dust-storm of change on the estate. Colley's workload meant that in 1860 his son, Henry Colley, had joined his father as a clerk, and in 1867, additional rooms at The Green were requisitioned as estate offices. Ten years after the overwhelming responsibilities and private insecurities of 1858, Hampton Court looked in better order than anyone could remember. No wonder if the champagne flowed in the RASE Councillors' marquee. To Johnny, victory with the Herefords vindicated his sense of natural justice, that where investment was made it would be rewarded. He now understood that for the landowning man, his acres were indistinguishable from his person. His investment in them was therefore an investment in his own future and position.

FOUR

Mastering the Family

The Hills of Manhood incorporated for Johnny not only the virgin slope of estate responsibilities, but also some tricky uncharted terrain as head of the family. After John's death, Johnny's mother, brothers and sisters struggled with overwhelming insecurity and a sense that things would never be as safe or carefree again. All the old certainties seemed to have melted, a feeling doubtless reinforced by the publication, a year later, of Charles Darwin's *The Origin of Species by Means of Natural Selection* which undermined so many fundamental tenets. It was as if the features in a well-loved landscape had shifted slightly, altering the light and the perception of everything that was formerly familiar. Johnny accepted instinctively that, like the estate, the well-being of the family, its health and happiness, its comfort and the quality of its marriages, would reflect on him.

For Mary and his three younger sisters, Fanny, Emily and Alice (known as the Three Graces) and for little Charlie in particular, Johnny wanted to dispel any sense of diminished security, so that they might enjoy a carefree youth as he had. It was a matter of pride with him that 'dear old Hammy', as they called their home, should remain a haven, with either Mamma or himself always at its heart. Hampton Court would continue to open its great gates to shelter the wider family.

Despite his resolve, there was little that Johnny could do to dim the pain of 'first times since'. Arthur's fifteenth birthday fell three days after the funeral, on 8 March, and Charlie was 12 on 2 June. Tally herself was 50 on 26 May, when she went to visit her sister Caley and husband Rev. Richard Phelips at Cucklington. Johnny's first birthday since his father's death, his twenty-fifth, on 12 July, was spent in London. A family gathering of young took place at the Burlington Hotel where his mother's birthday wishes found him. 'My Dear John,' she wrote,

> if you could read my heart you would see it *very fond* full of love for you . . . You are early called to the 'battle of life' with more than usual cares

> & responsibilities, but the prayers & love & *gratitude* too of a Mother ever attend you.[1]

Tally's first trip to Willersley without John came in April 1859, 'a *sad* one, for former remembrances'.[2]

At the end of May, it was Johnny's turn to be away. Complaining of bad headaches, probably owing to the pressures of his responsibilities, he went to London to see Dr Burrowes. Tally tried to cheer him.

> We had gay doings on the occasion of my birthday yesterday, and in a *lottery* in the evening, *you* gained the first prize! . . . a painted tin hot water jug! Langford went to Leominster Flower Show, with a cargo of plants for which he gained *the 1st Prize* no others being exhibited . . . the Cloth of Gold [rose] is in such splendour![3]

While amusement was plentiful during the outdoor months, the shorter days presented a greater challenge. That first winter, while Chandos was being toasted by Dickens in Coventry, Fanny started a book of poems.[4] A favourite game was to write verses to a given title including two or three set words. Johnny was given 'How do you like Books?' to include 'Beetle' and 'Crusher'. He summoned up the following:

When Books stand round on every side
How can I say I hate them?
French, Hebrew, Syriac inside
I could not underrate them!

Should a living housemaid dare to dust
Or approach with an ostrich brusher;
May an antediluvian centipede,
Or a huge black beetle crush her!

The choice for Mary was revealing: 'Do you ever fish for compliments?' using the word 'terror'. Her response was the didactic:

I go out early in the morning
And I fish the live-long day
But I never get a compliment,
So my fishing does not pay!

The river may be full of them,
But they never take my bait,
I see them swimming all around
While drearily, I wait.

Perhaps they see my line too plain
In terror, take their flight,
And never come that way again
If I fish till ten at night.

So now, my friends, be warned by me,
For compliments don't fish
But wait until you see them lie
Before you in the dish.

Few guests were spared these agonies. Mr and Mrs Grane, the Hope vicar and his wife had to try, though she appears to have been less than enthusiastic, for Fanny was set: 'Why does not Mrs Grane write poetry?' using the telling word 'Paragon'. Chandos and his daughter Cathy, Berkeley, and a visitor, Mr White, all had to contribute. Despite their execrable rhymes and trite metres, the subjects set revealed contemporary talking points and family developments. 'Are you fond of comets?' 'Do you like wooden legs? – on the subject of the Free Wing to the Royal Hospital', 'Has Fanny any right to choke while Mrs Arkwright is reading?' 'What is cotton wool useful for?' 'What is the news of the day?' (using the word 'Baby' when Carey and Berkeley produced a son), 'Where is California?' and 'What's moral philosophy?' were all tackled.

Then, in April 1859, Fanny finished her poem, 'Each with his own sweet thoughts is busy;/as George is – when he thinks of Lizzie!' 'Lizzie' was the Hon. Elizabeth Kenyon, third daughter of Lord Kenyon of Gredington, Flintshire, and younger sister of the wife of William Townley Mitford, of Pitshill, one of the bearers at John's funeral.[5] By July 1859, they were engaged, and Lizzie was staying with the Arkwrights at Hampton Court while George was travelling in Norway. As poor Lizzie pined, Tally reported to Johnny that she 'does not add much to our animation, sweet as she is! A letter from George . . . does not allude to *coming home*, which, *entre nous* caused some sad tears and a very pale face ever since'.[6]

The errant George returned safely to his distressed damsel, and married her at Hanmer in January 1860. As with the *Hereford Journal* at Carey's wedding, the *Shrewsbury Chronicle* burst forth with a tide of prose, asserting that 'never was enthusiasm more manifest nor rejoicing more general'.[7] When the couple left, 'the old custom of throwing the slipper was not forgotten, for a complete shower of all sizes was hurled after them'. The following year, Johnny gave George the living of Pencombe. Their first child, Cecil John, arrived nine months after their marriage, but died in January 1861. In October 1861, a second boy was born, Bernard George, and by 1863, Lizzie was expecting their third child. The rector of Pencombe built a new home for his growing family as well as rebuilding the church. Tally laid the first stone in 1863.

Johnny showed no sign of following George's example and settling down – quite the reverse. Confronted with the considerable pressures of keeping home and estate together, Johnny was playing as hard as he worked. He was wildly popular. Legions of At Home invitations included those from Viscountess Palmerston, Dowager Lady Shelley, the Countess of Ashburnham, Lady Louisa Douglas Pennant, the Duchess of Montrose, Lady de Rothschild, Miss Burdett Coutts and the Duke of Devonshire.[8]

As a young man of £10,000 a year, Johnny was a good catch, as well he knew. Masking his private insecurities, Johnny could swagger with the best. He revealed a taste for fashion when he decided to cultivate (besides his rosebeds) a beard, soon to be adopted too by the Prince of Wales. For this manifestation of virile vanity, Johnny suffered chaffing from the family. Tally signed off two letters from Tenby in October 1860: 'Shall I ever see your chin again?' and 'we all write in full tide of loves and kisses to you and your beard'.[9]

Johnny was probably led on by his greatest friend of this period, Sir Velters Cornewall of Moccas Court near Hereford, who sported splendid handlebar moustaches and bushy Dundrearies. Sir Velters was a tall, thin man, with a rakish demeanour. Being fond of gambling, he was said to have wagered his estate and lost, but had been offered a reprieve if he could reach it on horseback before daybreak. Both men had been in the Herefordshire Militia since the 1850s. In 1858 Johnny and Sir Velters became joint Masters of the Herefordshire foxhounds after a run of difficult years for the pack, when the Master had changed every season.

The Herefordshire met three times a week, on Monday, Thursday and Saturday, and Johnny seldom missed a day. There was no feeling on earth to match the intoxicating physical contrasts of hunting: the obedience of the hounds at the meet and wild instinct in the chase; the social etiquette at the outset and abandonment to splashing along puddled tracks be-spattering shining boots and fine fabrics; the creak of leather and the jingling of curb-chains; the grinding of horse-tooth on bit and the crack of horseshoe on stone; the clarity of frosted air and fugginess of sweat; the thunder of the gallop and the ear-straining silences; the pain of low boughs whipping the face or of frozen feet jumping to earth and the delicious comfort of a hot bath and meal at the end of the day; and the horses' furnace-flared nostrils and heaving flanks of exertion compared with their be-rugged comfort as they swished through fresh straw in the stalls, when visited after dinner.

The opening meet was always at Hampton Court in early November, where around a hundred people sat down to a breakfast at 9.30 a.m.[10] Thereafter, hounds and followers met at private homes and public landmarks including Credenhill Park, Stoke Edith, Foxley, Moccas, Kentchurch, Holme Lacy, Garnons and the Trumpet crossroads. The followers were far from exclusively the county's grandees. The fox was a pest to the squire's home farm stock, the tenant's lambs and the cottager's chickens alike. In law, nobody but the landowner had the right to kill ground game, so it was Johnny's duty to kill the foxes and he was determined to enjoy it. It was also the delight of everyone else to join him as he did so. The hunt rode over land only with the permission of the farmer, be he yeoman or tenant, and all who could followed on foot, in fly or on horseback, relishing a day off work. In the supremely revolution-conscious country that Britain was after 1848, hunting was even credited with 'the bringing together the different ranks of society', in pursuit of the common enemy.[11]

Followers also came from neighbouring shires, and the provision of plentiful foxes, of a good pack and runs across well-tended country, could be greatly to the county's credit. For the Master, this meant a gruelling if pleasurable schedule, and Johnny needed to draw on a full stable of horses. He hunted Promise in October 1859,[12] and Grey, Kitten, Forester, Sunflower, Hiawatha, Brenda, Harlequin, Ratclyffe, Bayleaf, Comet, and Squirrel, besides George's Bay and Edwyn's.[13] His stable expenses rose from £887 in 1858 to £1,287 in 1859.[14]

Johnny kept a hunt diary, listing the location for the meet, covers drawn, his mount, the number of foxes killed and the duration of each chase. He reserved his more expansive descriptions for the pages headed 'Observations'. These illustrate the knowledge that Johnny acquired of virtually every fox, hound, field, track and gate in the county. In his haste to record the detail, his punctuation and grammar were let go. On 18 December 1858, ten days after Fanny began her poetry book, the meet was at Burley Gate and Johnny was on Forester.

> Found directly in Cowarne Wood. Tried Westhide and headed away towards Broxash and ring round Stoke Lacey for Hall Court. 35 minutes – hunted him on slowly for Canon Frome and lost
>
> 2nd fox at Balk Copse. away at good pace for Cowarne gorse and pointing for Broxash – good ring to Hall Court and killed him in Ashbed. Time 2 hours and a very good hunting run it was – Charter and Actress do a deal of harm each in its own way. C always ahead mute and Actress wide. Colonel Stretton – De Winton and other Monmouth men out with us.[15]

On 15 February 1859, they met at England's Gate Inn. Johnny was on Kitten.

> Darley coppice Longmans Hill blank. found in Henner Wood our old friend of Venn Wood (see Janry 3) He took us his old line but being headed by woodmen at Hackwood we got on the line of a flying fox and while Starlight and Nancy stuck to the right one by their skirting propensities the body of hounds hunted the flyer slowly over the Stone farm nearly to Bromyard and gave him up – No second fox to be found.[16]

Johnny bought some property and established the Hunt Kennels at Whitecross, Hereford. By 1863, the kennels housed 49½ couple.[17] Out of season, the breeding of hounds was almost as time consuming as the winter sport. By 1867, the Herefordshire were crossing their bitches with dogs from packs including the Duke of Beaufort's, the Belvoir, the Duke of Buccleuch's, the Quorn, the Duke of Grafton's and Johnny's uncle Joseph's pack, the Essex.[18] Many of the dams were similarly diversely sourced. The acquisition of dogs and horses gave Johnny and Sir Velters ample excuse for forays to town to spend an afternoon at Tattersall's by the Albert Gate to Hyde Park.

The thrice-weekly sales at Tattersall's were useful for meeting old friends and cementing acquaintances made fleetingly in the field.[19] Johnny often ran into his uncle Joseph or cousin Loftus Arkwright from Mark Hall. Just as he sought the advice of his uncle Chandos for the improvement of the estate, Johnny looked to his uncle Joseph regarding the Herefordshire Hunt. In 1857, Joseph had become Master of the Essex Foxhounds, and it was as Master rather than Vicar that he was remembered after his death in 1864. This was partly due to Anthony Trollope's characterisation of the hunting parson. Five seasons of Joseph's term as Master coincided with Trollope's residence at Waltham House, where the novelist enjoyed his most prolific period.[20]

'For myself,' wrote Trollope, 'I own that I like a hunting parson. I generally find him to be about the pleasantest man in the field, with the most to say for himself, whether the talk be of hunting, of politics, of literature, or of the country. He is never a hunting man unalloyed, unadulterated and unmixed – a class of hunting man which is perhaps of all classes the most tedious and heavy in hand.'[21] Trollope further asserted in his *Hunting Sketches* of 1865, that 'Among those who hunt there are two classes of hunting people who always like it, and these people are hunting parsons and hunting ladies. That it should be so is natural enough.'

It might have been natural enough, but Victorian society expected its clergy to overpower the natural urges. Trollope explored the hunting parson's dilemma through Mark Robarts in *Framley Parsonage*. Robarts falls into debt through his contacts made on the hunting field, illustrating Trollope's belief that 'I know no vice which hunting either produces or renders probable, except the vice of extravagance; and to that, if a man be that way given, every pursuit in life will equally lead him.'[22]

If extravagance and a love of hunting were mutually perpetuating qualities, then Joseph was a clergyman of truly Trollopean proclivities. He had indulged in hunting since Cambridge, when he had stabled no fewer than four horses (and excused himself to his father for his admitted extravagance).[23] Like many contemporary clergymen, Joseph delegated most of his work to a curate, and hunted as many days as the season allowed. He was far more often in the saddle than the pulpit and was able to indulge his passion in the superior hunting country of Leicestershire, too, for on his father's death, Normanton Turville had been added to Joseph's inheritance of Mark Hall.

Joseph's fourth son Loftus inherited both his father's love of the field and his Mastership. He went further by marrying Elizabeth Reynolds, a young lady as passionate about the chase as Loftus.[24] Ladies had ridden to hounds since at least the 1830s and their numbers were growing. Despite Surtees's disapproval, they could not be denied after the Empress of Austria dashed across the fields of Leicestershire and Northamptonshire in the 1870s. Trollope refuted allegations that the indulgence of hunting by ladies led to flirtation, to 'ways and thoughts which are of . . . the stable and strongly tinged with the rack and manger'. However, he admitted that 'all the pretty girls delight to be spoken to by the Master! He needs no introduction, but is free to sip all the sweets that come.'[25] The mere sight of a pair of hunting tops could make a young lady blush. Sir Velters and Johnny undoubtedly fancied themselves a couple of swells.

The Mastership did no harm to Johnny's self-confidence and it certainly contributed to the delectations of the Hunt Balls.

By the end of the 1860–1 season, Johnny was encouraged by the quality of hunting in Herefordshire. On 14 March 1861, the meet was at Hall Court. Johnny rode Hiawatha and Forester. He noted:

> 1st fox for Bromyard, turning left Broxash earths his farthest point back to Hall Court and killed him. Time 1.10. 2nd fox Cowarne ring through Felkton leaving Moreton woods on right over hill between Coomeshill & Broxash across Holly bush lane to Wootton – up dingle over Eydon Hill past Marston firs & killed him at Dayhouse farm (Herring). 1.17 – a very good run. The best day I ever saw in Herefordshire.[26]

The week after, however, came the fall that followed his pride. Johnny 'got a bad fall on Monday laid up'. This was not unique. He took such a crashing tumble in 1864 that Joseph Yates at the estate office ominously noted it in his journal.[27] With good reason, Tally grew increasingly uneasy with Johnny's hunting, and quite possibly with Sir Velters's influence. Lines of inheritance all over the realm ran the risk of snapping if young men would insist on hurtling over rails and ditches. In 1868, Loftus, as Master, fell and broke his back. He never rode again, but followed in a phaeton.[28]

Although it threatened ancestral lines, hunting also perpetuated them. One of the Monmouth men out with the Herefordshire in December 1858 may have been Samuel Courthope Bosanquet, to whom Mary became engaged in early summer 1862, while up in London for the International Exhibition. Courthope was a lawyer and heir to Dingestow estate in Monmouthshire. When the news broke, Johnny literally ran across town to tell Chandos and Anna at Berkeley Square. Three days later, he did the same again when Dick became engaged to Lady Mary Byng, second daughter of the 2nd Earl of Strafford from Wrotham Park in Hertfordshire.[29]

The brace of weddings made a hectic summer in 1862, a year that also saw Johnny become High Sheriff. Dick and Minnie were married on 22 July and Mary and Courthope at Hampton Court on 7 August. Johnny was determined that Mary would be provided for every bit as generously as had been Carey. Consequently, labourers and tenants were fed on beef and plum pudding, meat and bread were distributed to the parish poor, and children bolted buns and enjoyed donkey races in the park. Flowers and bridal arches decorated the house and the road to Hope church, the guests were fed on sumptuous food and fine wines and Mary was dressed in glacé silk with flowers and diamond stars in her hair. Of her dozen bridesmaids in white grenadine muslin dresses, little Augusta Arkwright from Bodenham stole the prize for the most charming.[30]

The wedding went off with great credit to Johnny, as Mary wrote to acknowledge the following day, while Courthope serenaded her on the flute. The calm of Harewood 'seems such a great contrast from our bustling life the few last days. We talk over the wedding, and think that nothing *could* have been better, kinder or more delightful than the arrangements were altogether, for which we have to thank you; as we do a *great* deal. How good and generous you were . . . your father-brotherly care of us all . . . has been most wonderful.'[31]

Tally echoed this sentiment a couple of years later, when she wrote, 'I often think with sorrow how much you must have fetter'd yourself with undue expenses in order to give us so happy a home for so many years!'[32] After Mary's wedding, Tally reported: 'Excellent accounts from Mary and Courthope somewhere about Mont Blanc and they saw such a sunset as is *rarely* to be seen!'[33]

By early November 1862, Tally and the three Graces were at 22 Waterloo Crescent, Dover, where the girls were riding and sketching, weather permitting. Dover was a strategic choice: Arthur was in barracks nearby at Shorncliffe; Henry's regimental band, the 84th, were performing on the front; honeymooners Dick and Minnie could pass through on their return from the Continent, and Mary and Courthope were to pop across from Paris before heading for the south of France again. The family's pleasure ended, though, with news of the death of Sir Hungerford's brother. Sir Hungerford himself had died on the last day of February, almost exactly three years after Lady Hoskyns.

Tally was hard hit, went down with 'a case of low fever' and was moved to the Brunswick Hotel, London, from where Fanny, as the eldest unmarried daughter, reported her progress to Johnny. On 12 December, she wrote: 'The two doctors came at 1 o'clock and now allow us to say "better" – the fever is diminishing, and of course mother feels her weakness very much now. She has today begun champagne every 2 hours, and it agrees very well . . . Poor mother wonders how ever she shall get strong again.'[34]

Fanny assumed the supervision of Emily and Alice and, after they returned to Hampton Court, for the household there. Through their responsibilities, she and Johnny became close, his paternalistic instinct complemented by her protective streak. For the first six months of 1863, they ran the enterprise together, Johnny combining hard work field-draining with preparations for the Worcester RASE show. In August, he went on his annual grouse-shooting trip, but for the first time, the invigorating Highland fresh air and the relaxation and 'musicking' with friends failed to work their restorative magic. He returned south in a mist of depression that would not lift.

After five years in charge, Johnny understood that his responsibilities were not just heavy but relentless. As the novelty of his position wore off, a view of his lifetime's work stretched ahead, the foreground features only hiding, he now knew, further difficulties beyond. The need to protect his family from reality, to get the estate running on exemplary lines, and to maintain his public duties required boundless optimism and energy, to say nothing of money. It could also be a solitary experience. His popularity as a capital chap and thoroughgoing roisterer meant that he could not confide in Sir Velters, and his uncle Chandos was now overburdened with Harewood's problems. Johnny's headaches returned, and he could not shake off the depression and introspection that they induced. He suggested to Fanny that they make a trip to Aix-la-Chapelle.

A few carefree weeks restored his perspective, and the waters at 'Aches' revived his vigour. He returned home convinced that there was no cure for the troubled mind like occupation, as if *labor vincit insomnia*. Perhaps he thought of the Arkwright family motto '*multa tuli fecique*' – 'much we wish and we achieve it'.[35] He burst once more on to the county stage in autumn 1863 by establishing the Herefordshire Philharmonic Society (HPS) to promote instrumental and vocal practice among amateur musicians in Herefordshire, through the performance of at least two concerts a year (usually November and March).[36] Membership subscriptions would cover the expense of concerts and provide a library of music for members. Johnny himself took on the roles of Secretary and Treasurer for the first year, and thereafter he remained Secretary, helped by Henry Colley at Hampton Court estate office.[37] He also led the 'band' as first violin, and this is probably why he bought a Stradivarius violin (for £200) the same year.[38]

Believing in excellence in all things, Johnny enlisted the 40-year-old Henry Leslie as conductor. Leslie had been a cellist and ended up with a knighthood as the most celebrated British choral conductor of his day.[39] Johnny also inveigled Sir Frederick Gore Ouseley, Precentor of Hereford Cathedral and Professor of Music at Oxford, to be the Society's President until his death in 1889.[40] Chandos, a fair cellist, became Vice-President.[41] Apart from Leslie and Ouseley, the HPS orchestra benefitted from professional musicians, some based in London, others locally. By 1872, the

HPS orchestra included the Elgar brothers of Worcester (Edward Elgar's father and uncle Henry) on violin and viola. Edward Elgar joined the HPS in 1883.

Johnny's enthusiasm attracted opening subscriptions of 126 non-performers, 92 vocal performers and 26 instrumentalists, making a total of 244. By 1865, this had risen to 315 and included legions of Arkwright relations and most of the county's leading families.[42] The first practice was held on Wednesday 14 October 1863 at the College Hall in Hereford. Rehearsal for 'the band', as it was termed, began at 1 p.m., and for voices at 3 p.m.[43] The first concert, at the Shire Hall, Hereford, in November 1863 combined music by Haydn, Mendelssohn, Mozart and Rossini with some of Leslie's own compositions.[44] By the practice of 22 December, the band had moved on to Beethoven's Symphony No. 1 in C, Auber's Overture to *Gustavus* and Ouseley's march *Polycarp*. The choir was rehearsing more madrigals, a glee and two part songs, which were performed at a concert in January 1864. For HPS members, the Society wove another thread into county life and whenever enough were together, after dinner, or during house parties, impromptu concerts ensued. Fanny was, in later years, to liken rehearsals to 'a monthly bird call, which gathers the flock again'.[45]

For Johnny, HPS rehearsals complicated a frenetic winter schedule. Besides hunting three days every week, with Master's duties and checks on the kennels in between, his days were spent shooting, at the Magistrates' court, in discussion with Colley and the architects about building and draining plans, corresponding with musicians, obtaining music scores, liaising with the rehearsal and performance venues, chasing overdue subscriptions and organising the printing of programmes. Between November's concert and December's practice in 1863, he was also in London for the agricultural show at Smithfield and an RASE meeting at Hanover Square, probably meeting Leslie at his 59 Conduit Street home to discuss music for the next concert, and running errands for his mother to acquire decorations for the Christmas tree. It was, though, the sort of hectic lifestyle on which Johnny thrived, and it kept the blue devils at bay.

While Johnny was roaring to and fro prior to Christmas 1863, Fanny was at Mary's home, Wonastow near Monmouth. Mary was enduring a difficult but precious pregnancy after a previous miscarriage. While there, Fanny was 'appointed Mary's housekeeper and having ordered dinner, I now proceed to fill the tea caddy . . . [Mary] cannot walk much yet. 10 minutes are quite as much as she can do out of doors.'[46] Fanny returned to Hampton Court for Christmas. In the new year of 1864, when Mary had moved from Wonastow to 12 Wellwood Park, Torquay, Emily, just 19, went to stay with her. On 29 January, Emily wrote to Johnny about the town, Mary's health, and a Church Missionary meeting of the previous day.[47] Almost immediately afterwards, Mary wrote to tell her mother that Emily was severely depressed. Mary was alarmed and Tally gave instructions for Emily to come home.

Back at Hampton Court, Emily improved. On 26 February, Tally wrote to Johnny: 'She has not cried much this morning . . . slept for ten hours last night, with only the *half* of her sleeping draught . . . She is very cheerful this morning and I hope we shall do well through the day . . . Emily is charmed with your letter.'[48] Tally's concern switched to Mary. 'I have made up my mind to go to Torquay for a few days and comfort Mary, who is making herself very unhappy about Emily.'[49] Unfortunately, after Tally and Alice's arrival in Torquay, Mary again miscarried. Tally wrote in despair: 'What must be said to her? After all of the nursing and *lying down* you have heard of regarding Mary . . . you must guess at the consummation w[h] has brought her a second disappointment.'[50] Mary and Courthope's dreams of a family were finally fulfilled the following year, when a daughter, Maud, arrived in May, and thereafter an heir, Samuel Ronald Courthope (Ronald) in 1868, and another son, Vivian, in 1872.

Fanny, having nursed her mother through low fever at the Brunswick, accompanied Johnny to Aix, and cared for Mary at Wonastow, was now left at Hampton Court with Emily. Her descriptions to Johnny of Emily's symptoms led him to confide in Fanny his own former state of mind. She replied on 27 February:

> Did you really get dreadful ideas into your head which you now know were quite your own fabrication, and still not be able to shake them off? Emmie knows she cannot think right but still cannot persuade herself that these melancholy thoughts are entirely imaginary. I suppose you were *just* able to refrain from saying melancholy things, but did you feel as if you should (if you had spoken) have said things you did not mean? . . . It is such a support to me to talk to you about it, and how true you are in saying that the bright promises of the Bible are for her.[51]

Emily's condition stabilised but it became clear that longer-term help was needed. Johnny consulted London's best physicians and looked for a house nearby. Fanny, Emily and a nurse called Greenhead moved into Lime Hill at Tunbridge Wells, around 20 March. The arrangement put Fanny in the extraordinary position of being head of her own household. When not worrying about Emily or receiving visits from medics or family, she exclaimed to Johnny, 'It is *great* fun keeping house here.'[52] She giggled at having been addressed as Mrs Arkwright and at having been 'sent a card with list of prices for the tuition of my daughters'.[53] 'So you must think of us as very comfortable in the dear little house you prepared for us.'[54]

Charlie, Dick and Minnie visited, and Johnny dispatched champagne to keep their spirits up. In mid-April, once Mary was gaining strength, Tally joined the girls at Lime Hill. Her mother's presence gave Fanny a rest but it was clear that she could not care for Emily indefinitely. Tally, after a few days playing croquet with Emily, set out for London to engage some help.

At the end of May, Miss Brown arrived at Lime Hill and even the protective Fanny reported to her mother, 'Miss B is extremely kind and asks all sorts of questions about the ways, and so nice in her manner with Emily.'[55] Fanny's devoted care of Emily led her siblings to fret that instead of being out in society, Fanny was becoming a sick nurse. Johnny invited her to Scotland with him, but she refused.

> Dear little Minnie said to me the other day 'we want to take you away from Mother and Emily'. But she does not know how cruel it would be to poor Mother this year to leave her. Emmie's illness has been such a shock to her that I am sure she ought not to lose her only strong daughter.[56]

Fanny was soon back at Tunbridge 'in the old house again', but Emily had grown bored of Lime Hill, and a move became inevitable. By the end of July, they were at Greenwood Lodge, Wargrave, Henley-on-Thames, and had engaged a Miss Stokes, a clergyman's daughter and governess of fifteen years' standing.

Physician Arthur Noverre, 'much beloved for his gentleness of character and the high professional standards',[57] continued to visit Emily, 'when he stopped her tonic and gave her soothing medicine'. Fanny informed Johnny that

> she has been much better. The brothers' visits now do her the greatest good, and I really do not see that she is so *down* when they go as she was before . . . She played and sang quite a long time with Uncle Leigh, of course stopping very often, when he encouraged her on . . . Arthur comes again tomorrow. Edwyn and Charlie next week.[58]

The engagement of Miss Stokes enabled Fanny to return home again. She spent a golden late summer around her twenty-fourth birthday on 22 September. 'Carie and I had a delightful ride yesterday. 4 hours we were out and we went round 4 hop yards to see all the hop-pickers . . . The country is scented with hop-drying.'[59] She also 'planted my dear Water Lilies in hampers with stones tied to the bottom near the Hampton Bridge where the yellow ones live'.[60]

Dick's wife Minnie was more successful in getting Edwyn out than she was with Fanny. Minnie's brother, Francis Byng, who had held the perpetual curacy of Holy Trinity, Twickenham, gave it to Edwyn. Edwyn, having graduated from Merton, spent the early summer travelling before settling to his new role. His trip to the Italian lakes had included a verbal tussle with a French train conductor who would not believe that Edwyn had lost his ticket and made him buy another.[61] Such larks were commonplace for his peers, but Edwyn suffered with a degree of deafness probably caused by a childhood illness. As a result, he occupied a particularly soft spot in his mother's affections. Tally had been horrified when Edwyn was bullied by his housemaster Mr Middlemist at Harrow, but Edwyn scorned self-pity.[62] He played the cello to a creditable standard, threw himself enthusiastically into theatricals, and displayed a natural aptitude for his clerical vocation in his concern for those less fortunate than himself. When Tally was set the poetry-writing task of 'Can you define a Heart?' using the word 'alarm', she wrote:

Oh tender-hearted Edwyn, prone to pity
Is it thy *heart* that shall inspire my ditty
Then should it tell of pure and tender feeling
Ne'er deaf to sound of want or woe appealing.

Yet should th'*alarm* sound at early morning,
Deaf wouldst thou be to all its noisy warning;
Then prosper in thy thoughts of mercy still
Nor let the world's cold blast thy bosom chill.
Mamma[63]

Far from being chilled by the 'world's cold blast', during Fanny's hectic summer of 1864, Edwyn was glowing with joy. He had fallen in love with Lady Muriel Campbell, daughter of the second Earl Cawdor, John Frederick Vaughan Campbell, of Stackpole Court in Pembrokeshire and

Golden Grove in Carmarthenshire.[64] Within weeks of Edwyn's return from Como, Tally wrote to Johnny that Edwyn had

> been accepted by Lady Muriel Campbell and everybody seems very much pleased. I hope you like it, as much as you can. She is a fortunate girl to have won such a heart as his. Tomorrow I am to go to luncheon at Minnie's to be introduced to some of the family. When shall I be introduced to *your* wife?[65]

Despite general approval of the match, Lady Muriel fell ill almost immediately. Perhaps she had misgivings about her choice and was sickened with worry. If she did, she kept it from Edwyn, for on 25 July, Tally wrote to Johnny that 'Edwyn talks of his marriage in December, but Muriel is not *at present* any better.'[66] Not until October did Alex Stables, agent at Cawdor, feel able to write to Lord Cawdor: 'We were very glad indeed to hear of the great improvement in Lady Muriel's health.'[67] The same month, Edwyn wrote to Johnny to ask for permission to bring some of the Campbells to Hampton Court. Soon after, however, Edwyn's engagement to Lady Muriel was broken and the wedding never took place.

It was a blow that hit Edwyn hard and he never married.[68] Johnny tried to intervene on behalf of his vulnerable brother. He wrote to Lord Cawdor suggesting that some trifling misunderstanding between Edwyn and Muriel had been misconstrued by Muriel as a result of her ill health. Cawdor did not thank him for implying that Muriel had been out of her right mind while unwell – a rebuttal that must have hit Johnny hard given Emily's condition.[69]

Mercifully for Edwyn, Francis Byng helped again. In 1865, Byng was appointed Chaplain at Hampton Court Palace, where he stayed until 1867. Edwyn was made Assistant Chaplain, an informal arrangement by which Edwyn deputised when Byng could not take services or attend to pastoral duties.[70] Edwyn's new prospects distracted him, but his experience made a salutary lesson for his unmarried brothers.

The phantom wedding date in December concluded a difficult year for Johnny – how appropriate that 1864 would be remembered for drought.[71] Emily's depression showed no sign of lifting and Johnny had weathered uncomfortable negotiations with Lord Cawdor on Edwyn's behalf. He now appreciated the difficulties facing the head of a family in attempting to steer it through society. Johnny's responsibilities and financial challenges made him see the companionship enjoyed by his married brothers in a new light.

FIVE

Foxley Hunting

At the 1866 election, Lord Derby formed a Conservative government. Since the Prime Minister sat in the Lords, the leadership of the Tories in the Commons fell to Benjamin Disraeli – 1866 was therefore the year in which the great bipolarism of the politics of the second half of the nineteenth century began. National leadership see-sawed between Disraeli and Gladstone until Disraeli's death in 1881. The axis on which the balance of these years often tipped was the fragile state of affairs across the St George's Channel in Ireland.

Johnny's younger brother Dick, who had now been at the bar for over six years, was elected for the Leominster constituency.[1] While Johnny was delighted to have such political influence so close to home, the old demons of insecurity stirred when he saw his first-class younger brother, who bore the great name of Richard Arkwright, come forward in the way that he had failed to do almost exactly ten years before.

Thankfully, Johnny was now distracted, for since the previous autumn's hunting and HPS rehearsals, his attentions had been drawn to Miss Charlotte Lucy Davenport. Lucy was the youngest daughter of John Arkwright's old friend, the late John Davenport of Foxley, Herefordshire.[2] The family acquaintance dated back to Derbyshire. The Davenports hailed from Westwood Hall in Staffordshire, and as Derbyshire county neighbours they had long been mixing in the same social circles.[3] In 1858, Lucy's eldest sister, Mary, had married Hon. and Rev. Arthur Bateman, brother of Lord Bateman of Shobdon Court.[4] Lucy's brother George was eleven months older than Johnny and had been up at Oriel (with George Arkwright), while Johnny was at Christ Church. Lucy's younger brother, Harry Davenport, was an exact contemporary of Johnny's at Christ Church.

At Christmas 1865, Johnny had paused for breath, and taken himself to the Arkwright home at Willersley. There he joined his old uncle Peter Arkwright and cousin Fred's party for the annual Derby Ball. It was a particularly happy New Year for the Davenport party, for George Davenport was to marry, in

February 1866, Miss Sophy Dashwood of Stanford Hall in Nottinghamshire. At the Assembly Rooms that year, the couples seemed to float on a sea of vast silk and satin crinolines as they danced to the latest Strauss waltzes. Amid dazzling gemstones and the scent of mulled wine, acute observers noticed a particular spark between Johnny and Miss Davenport.

On their return to Herefordshire they both attended rehearsals for the fifth HPS concert, scheduled for Friday 9 February. The programme included Henry Leslie's *Awake, Awake*:

> Awake! awake! while music's note
> Now bids thee sleep to shun,
> Light zephyrs of fragrance round thee float,
> For the young day has begun.[5]

Johnny was then invited to George and Sophy's wedding. Lucy, a bridesmaid, appeared to Johnny as vulnerable as an early rose as she watched her oldest brother marry. Since both Lucy's parents were dead, she would be living at Foxley with George and Sophy. Once they returned from honeymoon, Lucy, who had hitherto run Foxley, would have to defer to Sophy in all domestic matters. It would be a difficult transition and Johnny sympathised.

A few weeks later, in the early spring of 1866, they met again at Edwyn's house in Twickenham. Edwyn later recalled: 'I remember *looking* as you remind me, tho' I did not know that I beamed, at two people in a corner of the room at my tea party and arriving at a certain conclusion in my own mind about them.'[6] By now, the two concerned had reached definite conclusions about one another. On 10 April 1866, Johnny proposed to Lucy and was accepted. The euphoric Johnny must have ridden or driven home at a thunderous pace. After telegraphing George for his permission to marry Lucy, it was to his mother that Johnny wrote first. Then, he wrote to each brother in turn the briefest of notes.

> Hampton Court
> My Dear Henry,
> I am going to be married to Lucy Davenport best & dearest in England.
> Your ever most
> John[7]

For Tally, the news for which she had hoped for so long nevertheless brought sadness: she could not expect to remain at Hampton Court once it had a new mistress. Indeed she had been fortunate to remain there for fully eight years since Johnny had turned 25, when he might legally have asked her to move on. She replied to Johnny's note: 'What my poor pen can express tonight will ill convey to you the feelings with which your dear letter has been received! – That it astonished me I need hardly say (so safely had you kept your beloved secret).'[8]

As the news broke, letters of congratulation – all tenderly kept for posterity – began to arrive, expressing an overwhelming tide of joy at the announcement.[9] Among the first was one from the Arkwright cousins 'next door' at Bodenham Vicarage. The real flood began – indeed it seemed that everyone wrote – on 12 April. George, brother, schoolmate, fellow undergraduate and now near-neighbour wrote from Pencombe Rectory: 'I was at the top of a very high ladder hanging water-colours when your joyful note arrived. My feelings on reading it well nigh precipitated me down onto Lizzie . . . How we all love and look up to you as the ideal of what an eldest brother can be.' Edwyn remembered his tea party with joy, and Dick confessed he thought them well suited. Henry was playfully cool, writing from his barracks in Dublin: 'I congratulate you in all fraternity.'

The next day Carey wrote from Mary's at Wonastow. She recounted how 'Neither of us slept for joy. The first time joy has kept *me* awake since the night that Berkeley told me *he* was thinking of being married.' Mary pointed out that 13 April was their parents' wedding anniversary, and added her own thoughts. 'Should not dear Papa be happy now – and would he not welcome her warmly as his child.' Fanny passed on Emily's reaction: 'She says "Lucy" often and talks about a walk she had with her at Foxley of which she has a very happy remembrance.'

Arkwright relations from Derbyshire weighed in with a good show of letters, including one from Spondon Hall, Derby, which remembered the Christmas ball. 'Deaf people are proverbially quick sighted – & Frederic has said to me many times since the Dec^{ber} Derby Ball "is John going to marry Miss Davenport?"' Letters came, too, from Anna Arkwright at Mark Hall and from Godfrey at Sutton Scarsdale. From Park Row in Liverpool another cousin, Louisa Arkwright, asserted that 'You will find henceforward every pleasure doubled, every care (if you have any) halved and every thought enhanced by being partnered. Make the most of this great privilige by *confiding fully*, and you will find your confidence repaid a thousand fold.'

Brother Arthur's response came relatively late, on 22 April, when he wrote from Hyde Park Barracks, 'I was quite taken by surprise by your letter (I mean the contents of it). You were such a "*sly dog*"! . . . It's all over London already. You'll be no end of a *swell* when you come up.' A friend of Johnny's, L.H. Ward,[10] at Hyde Park Barracks with Arthur, also sent his congratulations, 'trusting that you will run as pleasantly in double harness as you have in single'. Sir Velters wrote from Moccas:

> We are all very glad to hear that you are going to marry Miss Davenport and think you could not have done better. We were all afraid that we might lose her out of the county and the course you have taken to keep her in it is first rate . . . I think you were quite right to choose a lady for a wife who was quite as much a favourite of the ladies as the gentlemen.

Velters's brother, George, echoed the sentiment, saying: 'I have always thought her *the* young lady of Herefordshire by very long odds.' Berkeley's father, Sir Edwin, reflected similarly, from his club in Pall Mall: 'Miss Lucy Davenport has always been a great favourite at Holme Lacey', and Henry Cotterell at Garnons wrote: 'You were very deep and mysterious on Monday, but I suspected *something* was coming.'

George Davenport, honeymooning in Marseille, telegraphed his consent and wrote on 19 April:

> I have telegraphed the 'Yes' and in so emphatic a manner that I fear the Leominster Official Receivers thereof will be somewhat astonished . . . I do indeed welcome you as a brother and my consent is given with the most perfect assurance that had my parents been living, they would have trusted you entirely with my sister's happiness.

Letters from Lucy's side reflected upon her many qualities. Henry Longley, son of the Archbishop of Canterbury, had married Lucy's sister, Diana, in 1861.[11] He wrote to Johnny from Lambeth Palace on 16 April:

> I have felt with her in the most severe trials and sorrows wh can happen to anyone and particularly to a girl; I don't speak merely of losses but of family and domestic troubles . . . I don't think any of us will ever forget the comfort and support wh her sympathy and kindness and good sense and perfect temper gave to everyone who was with her, though in each case she was perhaps the chief sufferer.

The approval of Johnny's choice was universal, and was best summed up by his mother who wrote from her childhood home, Harewood, where she was staying while Chandos and Anna were in Italy. 'There is only one opinion all over the world about your darling "Lucy" and to say that I shall dearly love her and take her to my heart as a real daughter and worthy of the *best* of sons is only simple truth.' Tally had visited the bride-to-be. 'I am glad I went to Foxley yesterday because the first meeting was a nervous affair . . . Poor dear Alice was much overcome.' The news reached Chandos and Anna in Italy, and Chandos's daughter Cathy reflected that

> Ever since the year of the Exhibition – 1862 – when you came to us in Berkeley Sq and told us of dear Mary's engagement and three days after were the bearer of similar tidings about Richard, we, who then thought that perhaps the week would not pass without your third appearance to bring the same news of yourself – have expected in vain and now the joyful intelligence has had to travel a 1000 miles.[12]

The date for the wedding was set for 12 June, a month to the day before Johnny's thirty-third birthday. They were to marry in the fifteen-year-old church of St Mary the Virgin at Yazor, at the foot of Foxley's drive.[13] A fortnight after their engagement, Lucy visited her future home, where she won over the household. Johnny, seeing Lucy in his own surroundings, seems suddenly to have understood that she would banish the solitude that he had hitherto felt in his role. The dam of self-containment once breached released from Johnny a tide of unstaunchable affection and a wave of confidences that obliterated past hurts. He wrote in rapture on 26 April:

> So much of my day dream years and years old has been within the last two days filled that I feel as if fancies must be ever hereafter facts . . . You have filled every heart here with joy to overflowing and your first visit to your nest under my present happy planet will never be forgotten.[14]

The public excitement at the impending marriage grew to extraordinary heights over the next six weeks. Tenantry and staff on both estates collected together funds for gifts, and planned celebrations both at Foxley and at Hampton Court. Schoolchildren were to be entertained and parish poor fed; public dinners had to be organised, speeches and testimonials written. Advertisements appeared in the local papers to inform the public of the plans for the day. Lucy wrote to Johnny on 6 June, having heard that private individuals at Hereford, Leominster and elsewhere wished to commission a window in Yazor church for her. 'I think Herefordshire has gone quite mad abt testimonials . . . George is quite gratified as it is a very inexpensive way for him to have stained glass windows put up in his Church, and he wishes he had a few more sisters to marry.'[15] The window was to be placed in the nave opposite that commemorating George and Sophy's marriage in February.[16]

The choice of subject for Lucy's window was topical. It depicted two men watching Ruth harvesting in the field, with the text 'Then said Boaz unto his servant whose damsel is this.' It recalled the passage from Ruth i.16–17: 'And Ruth said, Intreat me not to leave thee, or to return from following after thee: for whither thou goest, I will go: and where thou lodgest, I will lodge: thy people shall be my people, and thy God my God: Where thou diest, will I die, and there will I be buried: the Lord do so to me, and more also, if aught but death part thee and me.' The words were taken to be the pattern for a wife at this time although, in fact, they were spoken by Ruth to her mother-in-law. They had been used in 1864 in the same contextby Trollope in *The Small House at Allington* when Lily Dale vowed to Johnny Eames: '"If I cannot be to you at once like Ruth, and never cease from coming after you, my thoughts to you shall be like those of Ruth."'(It would be surprising if Johnny, as Chairman of the Executive Committee for Hereford's 1867 Three Choirs Festival, did not influence the inclusion of Otto Goldschmidt's oratorio *Ruth*, in which Goldschmidt's wife, Jenny Lind, 'the Swedish Nightingale' starred.[17]) Further text under the window read: 'Charlotte Lucy Davenport married June 1866 Blessed are the pure in heart.'

Great as the general excitement was, it paled by comparison with the intensity of Johnny and Lucy's love for one another. In their first letters, he was her 'own Darling', or 'Booby' and she was his 'own sweetest gazelle', or his 'own sweetest ruby'. The latter developed from Johnny's pet name for the Hereford cows, his 'ruby moos'. Thus, Lucy became his 'own Moo', though she was most commonly called his ''itti' 'ooman'.[18] While Johnny was irrepressible in his energetic excitement, Lucy was experiencing the symptoms of love's distraction. On 19 April she wrote to Johnny in a note enclosing violets.

> We started for a walk, but did not get very far, in fact we settled on the first cut down tree we met with, and sat in a row, and talked – or rather M[ary] and Di talked and I listened, or did not listen perhaps, for I believe I was thinking of some/thing/body else the whole time. The sky was very blue, and that reminded me of somebody's eyes.[19]

They did not have to be apart for long, for at the end of April they both went to London for a month, Lucy staying at 48 Dover Street, and Johnny at 49. Lucy was helped with her trousseau by her eldest sister Di, while Johnny celebrated the end of his bachelor days with his old friends. The honeymoon destination was also fixed. It was customary to go somewhere quiet before making a Continental tour. Carey and Berkeley had gone to the Cloweses in Flintshire after their wedding, and Mary and Courthope to Harewood. Lucy and Johnny settled on Wonastow at Monmouth, Mary and Courthope's home. Lucy wrote to Johnny:

> it seems to be the place of all others, the one gt advantage being able to drive there instead of going by rail and I do not think it can make much difference to us what kind of place it is, for we shall be together, and quite quite happy – and we know each other so well already, as you say, that we shall not be afraid of each other and we shall not be trying to think of something to say to each other all day long.[20]

Staying with Henry and Di Longley, Lucy saw their marriage in a new light as she considered her future relationship with Johnny. The choice of a subject for her Yazor window had led her to consider what the woman's role should be in marriage – a question presently under public debate. The previous autumn, the influential John Ruskin had delivered his lecture 'On Queens' Gardens' at Manchester and it had since been published with his 'On King's Treasuries' under the title of *Sesame and Lilies*.[21] Until now, it had been commonplace to differentiate between the roles of a married man and his wife by their spheres; the man was a public and political animal and his wife, private and domestic.

In 'On Queens' Gardens', Ruskin dismissed this 'idea that woman is only the shadow and attendant image of her lord, owing him a thoughtless and servile obedience . . . As if he could be helped effectively by a shadow, or worthily by a slave!' Instead, Ruskin promoted the idea of a complementary union in which neither sex was superior. He reflected on the chivalric ideal of courtly love, where the admiration of a woman inspired knights to valorous deeds. This model tended to be considered appropriate only for young lovers, but why should it not apply equally to marriage? That estate was, after all, 'only the seal which marks the vowed transition of temporary into untiring service, and of fitful into eternal love'.

In order to prepare a young girl for this role, her education, Ruskin asserted, should be afforded much greater attention. 'You bring up your girls as if they were meant for sideboard ornaments, and then complain of their frivolity.' A girl's education, he stated, 'should be nearly, in its course and material of study, the same as a boy's'. However, this was as far as Ruskin was prepared to go. He added that while a husband's command of knowledge should be foundational and progressive, 'a woman ought to know the same language, or science, only so far as may enable her to sympathise in her husband's pleasures, and in those of his best friends'.

The debate was given further impetus while Johnny and Lucy were in London. A paper was published by Emily Davies, the future co-founder of Girton College, Cambridge, called *The Higher Education of Women.* Miss Davies had the courage to push ahead where Ruskin had hesitated. This early member of the nascent women's movement, who had successfully lobbied for girls' inclusion in local examinations, pointed out that in the period before the Industrial Revolution every home had been a workshop where, besides undertaking the domestic responsibilities, women had worked.

Like Ruskin, Emily Davies denounced both the view that men and women's roles were entirely divorced and the notion that 'men are to be pleased, and women to please'. Such views were unhelpful in their implication that that which was manly was unwomanly and vice versa. Could courage be unwomanly or condemned when the case of Florence Nightingale in the Crimea was considered? 'Men have no monopoly of working, nor woman of weeping,' she stated boldly. She diverged from Ruskin's view, though, that women did not need a knowledge of the specifics of any subject. 'Women who act as the almoners of the rich and the advisers of the poor need for their difficult task something more than mere gushing benevolence.'[22]

While Emily Davies's views were too strident for women of Lucy Davenport's class, the courtly love ideal expounded by Ruskin was entirely in keeping with the Gothic Revival architecture of Hampton Court. Lucy returned to the question of her role four days before their wedding when she sent Johnny her copy of *Sesame and Lilies.* In the accompanying note she said: 'he quite expresses my idea of what a woman *might* be, and ought to *try* to be, but what unfortunately *very* few women succeed in being' – herself included.[23] What Johnny thought of most of Ruskin's work he did not say, but he believed in 'the superiority of the weaker sex'.[24]

While in London, Johnny was moved to write poetry to Lucy, perhaps inspired by Ruskin's references to Wordsworth's:

Three years she grew in sun and shower,
Then Nature said, 'A lovelier flower
On earth was never sown;
This child I to myself will take;
She shall be mine, and I will make
A lady of my own . . .

And vital feelings of delight
Shall rear her form to stately height, –
Her virgin bosom swell.
Such thoughts to Lucy I will give,
While she and I together live,
Here in this happy dell.[25]

Johnny keenly anticipated bringing his bride to Hampton Court. He wrote the day after his return: 'Our home is so beautiful in its breadth and sunniness that it is as perfect as landscape can be without one darling figure in the immediate foreground to light it up. Some day it will always be there and I shall be for one content.'[26] However, all was not unblemished joy, for he wrote on 26 May: 'I am badgered to death today – the Leominster people are going to water the town from the brook that brings me supply for house, gardens and irrigation – and just as I had a scheme for a fountain they want to steal my water!'[27]

Lucy wrote to Johnny the same day requesting a picture of him for her locket. He took her letter to morning service at Hope.

> I am afraid I read it several times when I ought to have been listening to the sermon but as he gave us 45 minutes without a check I consider everything above 20 minutes my own and did myself more good thinking of you than following maudlin verbage.[28]

On Monday evening, Johnny was to go over to Foxley to visit Lucy. He spent the afternoon in the walled garden gathering armfuls of flowers for her. He attached a note confessing that 'Although in an hour I hope to see you yet I cannot exercise sufficient self denial to stop writing . . . I have just packed your roses and kissed every flower.'[29] He stayed at Foxley until leaving for London on Thursday the same week. These were precious days together, offering a chance to grow yet closer, to express some of their fears for the future, and to reflect a little on the past. Though they were in the same house, they still wrote daily. Lucy recalled an incident early in their relationship: 'I told you this morning that I was surprised at your returning early from hunting that day at Harewood – and it was quite true, for I had not realised then how much you loved me.'[30]

They also recalled past losses, and grew closer through mutual sympathy. Lucy especially missed her parents at this emotional time. She wrote to Johnny on Thursday after he had left:

> I felt there was one who would *more* than make up for all I had lost in tenderness and love – and I was so happy and thankful and when you reminded me that they were really not far from us, the thought came back to me, one of my first thoughts when I knew you loved me, that *they* would also have loved you, and appreciated you, and that they were conscious of my happiness.[31]

There was sorrow, too, for Lucy at this time due to the serious ill health of her new sister-in-law, Charlotte. Johnny wrote to Lucy on 1 June: 'Moo, pretty, I never loved you more than I did in the conservatory on Wednesday night when I had the first joy of being allowed to kiss away a tear . . . I am very sorry to hear of Sophy's fears for her sister. It will make her young bride's days memorable for a dash of sorrowful experience.'[32]

Lucy was further troubled by losing Johnny's first ever note to her, and Johnny's loss of the photo of her that he carried in his watch. They discussed whether this could be a bad omen, but overcame their superstitions. Lucy was cheered by having George and Sophy at Foxley with her. She wrote to Johnny on 1 June: 'I wish you could have seen George and Sophy spooning last night – both sitting in one chair, in the Library, whispering and I imagine, tickling each other – Harry and I were quite ashamed of them.'[33]

The preparations continued and their letters were punctuated with more practical matters. Lucy decided to give her five bridesmaids, Fanny and Alice, Sarah Davenport, Henry Longley's sister, and Miss Coltman, a locket each, and she wondered how all her boxes were ever going to fit on the carriage to Wonastow.[34] Johnny was celebrating his forthcoming nuptials by the acquisition of two more farms, for which he borrowed £4,000 and £6,000 respectively. He also had to visit the Davenport family solicitor, Ward of Hereford, on 4 June with Lucy's brother George. Lucy's trustees in the settlement made on her marriage were her brother Harry Davenport, Henry Longley and Johnny's brother Arthur. Johnny could show from the

Lady Day rent roll for 1866 that the total acreage of Hampton Court was 10,617 acres, 3 rods and 28 perches. The nominal rental income for this acreage in 1866 was £15,000. In the event of Johnny's death, Lucy was to receive a jointure of £1,500 per annum from estate income. Lucy's father had left her £15,000 in her brother George's protection. She assigned whatever would be left of this after tax to the trustees of her settlement in favour of any daughters or younger sons she might have.[35]

Johnny and Lucy were to be married on Tuesday 12 June, and on the Saturday before, Johnny went over to Foxley, where the two families congregated. The groom's party included Tally and her sister Catherine and husband Edward Hawkshaw, George and Lizzie, Berkeley and Carey, Henry, Edwyn, Arthur and Charlie Arkwright, and the Bodenham Arkwrights. Amid the hubbub, bride and groom still found time to scribble notes. Lucy wondered, on Saturday evening: 'What can I *write* to you, when you are sitting close to me on the sofa!'[36] Johnny went home again on Sunday, after the whole party had been to church at Yazor, and returned on Monday morning. Doubtless the happy carriage was heavily laden with the very best produce from Hampton Court's gardens.

In Johnny's absence there was a great deal to do. It was Henry Arkwright who took charge of the preparations. With Johnny's marriage, Henry was to become the oldest of the unmarried boys, taking, as it were, his mother's arm on behalf of the family. Just as Johnny had seen to all the arrangements for Carey and Mary's weddings, Henry was determined that Johnny should have unclouded enjoyment of the day. Captain Arkwright took command of his younger brothers and Harry Davenport, and set to with the decorations of the church and the house.

On Johnny's return, on the eve of the wedding, Foxley was buzzing with anticipation. The scent of fresh flowers and polish was everywhere, teams of maids were hurrying along passages, distributing presents to the billiard room and trays of tea to the drawing room. After an evening of 'fiddling', Johnny found it hard to sleep. At 2 in the morning he could hear Lucy in her room. He pencilled a note to her:

> I will see no change in you darling tomorrow except that you will be in gorgeous array, which I shall fully revel in but dwell on no longer than to love as a beautiful thing. I shall then think of you as I have known you by your loving sympathy so long, and become your husband . . . may you never repent with one sigh the treasures you give me in yourself.[37]

The next morning, he threw open his windows and stepped onto the roof for a contemplative smoke. He whistled a tune that they both knew.

Once more I was watching her deep fring'd eyes,
Bent over the Tasso upon her knee,
And the fair face blushing with sweet surprise
At the passionate pleading that broke from me!
Oh Ruby! My darling the small white hand,
Which gather'd the harebell was never my own.[38]

Lucy replied to his note at 9.30 a.m., an hour and a half before the service:

> Do not suppose I do not hear you singing (or rather whistling) Ruby on the leads, but I cannot very well put my head out! . . . I am quite, quite happy, Booby, and thinking only of you and of our new life that is to begin today . . . Never has any little woman gone to Church with a more sincere and earnest desire and prayer to fulfil the vows she makes there than your wife will . . . I will try and keep my promise of looking into your eyes, my darling. Goodbye til then.[39]

Unfortunately, the day had dawned grey and stormy. An early train left Leominster, stopping at Ford Bridge, until it was filled with tenantry and well-wishers.[40] It wound its way to Moorhampton, the nearest stop for Yazor. Gaily dressed guests passed under an arch into the churchyard and up the carpeted path to the door. Inside, the nave had been decorated with flowers and inscriptions between the windows. Baskets of flowers hung from the roof over the aisle, and a continuous garland of greenery circled the church. At the focal point of the highly painted sanctuary was the altar, simply decorated with white roses. Lucy's window had not yet been inserted, but George and Sophy's was much admired.

Just after 11 a.m., word came that Lucy's carriage had arrived. Johnny and Sir Velters, his best man, walked down the aisle to greet her at the door, and then returned to the rail. Lucy entered the church on George's arm, followed by her five bridesmaids. She wore a white satin dress, trimmed with Brussels lace and orange blossom, and a full Brussels lace veil held in place with a wreath of orange blossom. The bridesmaids wore dresses of white tartalan, with blue silk scarves and white tulle bonnets also trimmed with blue. The *Hereford Times* noted that the congregation was literally on tiptoe at Lucy's arrival, but that she 'bore with composure the close scrutiny of the spectators as she passed up the aisle'. At the altar the party gathered before Arthur Bateman Hanbury, Lucy's brother-in-law, the rector of Shobdon, for their marriage.

Their vows exchanged (the groom's responses were given in 'a firm and clear voice'), the couple emerged onto a path strewn with flowers and rose petals, and gained their carriage. They were preceded in the drive to Foxley by the Hereford Militia Band, sporting new uniforms. During the day, the wedding presents were on display in the billiard room, the most prominent being a large silver replica of the Warwick vase, for which the tenantry and tradesmen had raised £200.[41] During the afternoon, it was removed and taken to the Royal Oak, Leominster, where a dinner was to be held for the Hampton Court tenantry to mark the occasion.

At half-past 2, Johnny and Lucy left for Harewood, via Hereford. Behind them, at Foxley, the revelry should have begun in the grounds at 3 o'clock, but the heavens opened, and it rained in torrents. Their route through Hereford had been decorated, particularly Broad Street and Eign Street. Mr Jennings, the saddler, an important supplier to Hampton Court, 'had his shop decorated with a flag and evergreens, with mottoes incident to the chase, and some heads of foxes'. By 2 o'clock Broad Street was thronged with well-wishers, and the cathedral and church bells pealed, but Johnny and Lucy did not arrive until half-past 3. The Green Dragon was gaily arrayed, as it was anticipated that the horses might be changed there, but the crowd was disappointed for they pressed on towards Harewood 'leaving the enthusiastic citizens in a state of sudden bewilderment'.

At Hampton Court, too, there were celebrations. At Bodenham, the bells were rung, and Rev. Henry Arkwright and his wife gave the schoolchildren tea. At Henhouse Farm, Mr and Mrs Morris held a supper and ball, finished off by a huge bonfire. In Leominster, the Priory bells pealed at intervals during the day, bunting was strung across the streets, and a dinner was held at the Royal Oak.

Everyone had their own memories of the day, and both the *Hereford Journal* and *Hereford Times* gave over columns to the festivities. The most touching account was given by Johnny himself, in a letter to Lucy:[42]

> My own sweetest Moo . . .
> A lifetime has opened on two loving souls apparently as suited to each other as can be imagined to lookers on. One is too full of self conceit and spoiled by having been what is called popular and the other too diffident from

a fancy that she has never succeeded in making some of her immediate relations happy. It will take a little time to weld into one golden medium these two excesses of useful vices or virtues for they are both.

I feel quite sure that there is nothing that they will not do for each other's good and that they will allow, even encourage each other to speak of any corner or edge which prevents a perfect fit and so unite two fond spirits into one eternal girdle of symmetry and love. Thorough confidence will trickle through all they do and they will have a defensive alliance against all the world and its bothers. Oh you unspeakably dear itti woman . . . I know only of one thing I fear – that time will go too fast for us. Bless you my beloved wife and make me more like yourself, every day.

Your devoted husband.

SIX

Sons and Mothers

Johnny and Lucy called at Harewood on their way to Wonastow, and it was to her old family home that Tally returned after their wedding. 'My Dearest John and Lucy,' she wrote to the honeymooners. 'My first few lines to my dear children! . . . You will believe my love for you both and all my thoughts and thankfulness for your happiness.'[1]

The absence of her parents and of Chandos, thoughts of Hungerford at Brislington asylum, the prospect of permanent estrangement from Harewood (which Chandos threatened)[2] and of alienation from Hampton Court contributed to Tally's melancholy. Every room unlocked memories of her own husband's visits there when she had been a girl, and of their courtship and marriage. Mercifully, her children had anticipated Tally's mood. It had been decided that after the wedding, Tally should tour the Continent with Henry, Fanny and Alice. Chandos was delighted. 'I feel sure that you will find it a new resource of life, & a fund of impressions & associations that no one should proceed to the end of life without including in their experience.' He hoped that she would get to 'Wengen-Alp . . . to watch the fall of the avalanches on Jungfrau one of which burst upon my bedroom window in the middle of the night, by its blast, last September'.[3]

Johnny and Lucy were due to return to Hampton Court on Thursday 28 June. Tally hoped they were 'making much of the remainder of your short honeymoon at Wonastow, for depend upon it you won't get much at Hampton Court. If you "shut the biggates" they will scale the tower and pop down into the Court.'[4] At Henry's command, elaborate floral arches decorated their route home, from Burghope Gate on the Hereford side of Dinmore Hill, over into the village of Hope-under-Dinmore, and then along the road to the Court and beyond as far as England's Gate. Particularly noted were those erected by the woodmen on the top of Dinmore Hill, and 'Speed the Plough' at the gate to Green Farm.[5]

A large crowd gathered on Thursday morning, but Lucy had fallen ill. By Saturday a rumour was racing through Hereford that 'Mrs Arkwright had sank gradually and was no more', but their return was merely postponed until Tuesday 3 July.[6] In the interim, Henry was telegraphed to go to London where he was informed of his appointment as ADC to the Duke of Abercorn, Lord Lieutenant of Ireland.[7] From town he left with his mother and sisters for the Continent, and therefore did not see the joy that his work gave to the returning couple.

Johnny and Lucy were preceded to the top of Dinmore by the Herefordshire Militia Band, cheered on by Mr Morton and the Bodenham schoolchildren. At Hope Gate a procession formed, including many Leominster tradesmen, while Hope church's bells rang. Right on cue, the sun burst through the hitherto cloudy skies, and a volley of cannon was set off from the Court. The *Hereford Times* journalist wrote memorably: 'The scene at this moment was something animating.'[8]

After their carriage had been drawn up the drive by the tenants and labourers, Johnny and Lucy alighted in the quadrangle beneath a central pole and floral garlands leading to all sides, pinned in place by mottoes such as 'love', 'hope' and 'peace'. While they were greeted by Johnny's brother George, sister Mary and her husband Courthope, Lucy's sister Mary Hanbury from Shobdon, and close friends, the crowd moved to the library steps on the south front of the house.

There, Johnny and Lucy appeared to rousing cheers. Jonathan Meredith, tenant of Wharton Court, and chairman of the organising committee, read an address, a copy of which was presented to Lucy. It alluded to Johnny's twenty-first birthday celebrations, and to the realisation since then of their hope that he would take after his father in kindness, forbearance and liberality. Another hope fulfilled was that Johnny might find a good and amiable wife: 'Right gladly and heartily we welcome you, fair lady . . . May you fulfil the responsibilities and realise the happiness of the wife of an honoured English country gentleman.'[9]

Johnny apologised for their delayed return and expressed their joy at the welcome they had received, which

> surpasses all our anticipations . . . I am not clever at expressing my thanks, especially when signs of sympathy and affection seem to reach a spot deeper than that from which words flow . . . you pay me a graceful and acceptable tribute in your appreciation of those points which I have learned most to value – the name of one who went before me – the scenes of my boyhood – my future home – and above all that I should accept gladly every celebration of to-day as addressed to the lady who is to be

its new occupant . . . As a landlord on a comparatively young estate, I acknowledge that I have a life-lesson before me, though I have for some years been making myself intimate with its details, and I hope to some purpose. I hope to lead an active life of advancement and friendship with my tenants, such as can be acquired only by a residence among them, not forgetting the labourer by whose toil Landlord and tenant live.[10]

Of Lucy, he said:

> Those who have known her longest . . . can testify that . . . 'the social duties of her position' are second to none, and that the welfare of the poor within reach is safe in her keeping. . . . A closer acquaintance between the tenantry of Foxley and Hampton Court cannot fail to help us on in sociable grooves, and on our return from Scotland we hope to give you an opportunity of asking them to see the insides of your houses and of ours, and though perhaps you will say that the less seen of some of my houses the better for my credit; yet I will remind you that Rome was not built in a day, and we are all young yet . . . may you never regret a jot of the demonstrations of to-day, or repent of having placed confidence in my wife and myself, should we live on without deserving it.[11]

Johnny and Lucy then withdrew, and by 6 p.m., 'the Court was restored to its wonted quietude'.[12] The following day, Courthope and Mary returned to Wonastow after watching Johnny and Lucy plant the acorn that they had gathered there near the Drybridge in the grounds at Hampton Court. On 5 July, Lucy took the first opportunity to thank Henry for their welcome. 'How very much we both admired all the decorations and appreciated your share of the work which was we hear very great.'[13]

On 3 September, Henry wrote home: 'We have ventured to try our luck higher up, as the weather is so warm and settled – as otherwise I should leave Switzerland without seeing a glacier.'[14] The Arkwrights, arriving after a dusty ride in a diligence, were thrilled by Mont Blanc.[15] To Henry's delight, their Grand Hotel Royal was situated midway between the fearsome Mer de Glace and the rugged Glacier des Bossons. The blinding brilliance that met his eyes and the clarity of the air that filled his lungs made him burst into renditions of his favourite anthem to aspiration, Longfellow's poem 'Excelsior'.[16] Having recovered from the responsibilities of Johnny's wedding and anticipating his promotion in Ireland, Henry felt supremely well and invigorated, at the peak of his 28 years. He was easily beguiled into an attempt at the ascent of Mont Blanc itself.

Mont Blanc had first been scaled by Jacques Balmat and Michel-Gabriel Paccard on 8 August 1786, eighty years before.[17] Ascents had become quite frequent of late, but it remained a significant undertaking. It would be folly to try the climb alone, or even to cross the Glacier des Bossons, so Henry found a guide and two porters. Accompanied by Fanny, and joined by a second guide and his client, they left Chamonix on 12 October, spending the night at the Grands Mulets cabin on the mountain. Departing at 6.30 a.m. the next morning, the 13th, Henry broke a bootlace, and Fanny lent him hers before waving them off.

While Fanny sketched, Henry's party zigzagged up through the Ancien Passage towards the summit. Suddenly, a crack was heard above them to the right, and within minutes, a terrifying avalanche swept the party away. Only the second guide, Sylvain Couttet and his client Nicholas Winhart survived. They recovered, lower down, the body of one of Henry's porters, before having to return to the cabin and break the news to Fanny. Realising from Couttet's face that something dreadful had happened, she knelt to pray before hearing his account. Fanny then joined Couttet and Winhart for the long walk back to the village, where she would have to break the news of Henry's death to her mother and Alice.[18]

At Hampton Court, the newly-weds had been settling in after their shooting trip to Scotland, when Alice's frightful telegraph reached them from the Leominster office, on 15 October:

> I tell you all our Grief at once. Henry was ascending Mont Blanc. An Avalanche came. All is over. I am telegraphing for Edwin to come at once. You tell the others.[19]

Having dispatched telegraphs to each of his siblings, Johnny took the saddest leave of his wife, and set off for London. Lucy, the death of whose own brother, John, in 1858, made her particularly empathetic, was left at Hampton Court.[20] The family instinctively gathered to sing Henry's favourite hymns in the chapel and to pray for him.

When Johnny reached Chamonix, Tally fell upon him in grief and relief. For two weeks, when the weather allowed, searches were made on Mont Blanc until only Henry's body remained unfound. In the sole surviving letter of Johnny's to Lucy during the useless days of waiting, he wrote numbly: 'I am very sad but think of you for comfort.'[21] By 7 November, hope of finding Henry's body was abandoned and the Chamonix party headed back. Lucy insisted that Tally come to Hampton Court rather than Harewood. Johnny resumed his responsibilities, going to London on RASE business and showing a heifer in Gloucester in December. He wrote to Lucy from there: 'May you ever be what you are now to me – the profoundest comfort and happiness that mortal ever possessed.'[22]

Christmas 1866 was one of the saddest at Hampton Court. Henry was absent yet omnipresent and the Christmas tree must have recalled the woods at Chamonix. Tally, leaving Johnny and Lucy to their first Christmas together, went to Byford Rectory near Garnons, where Berkeley had the living.[23] She wrote home on Christmas Eve, anticipating 'the holy day that brings back so many thoughts as well as looks forward . . . How many thoughts will be in every heart as to whether the dear one departed can still look down upon us.'[24]

In the new year, Johnny faced more practical matters arising from Henry's death, corresponding with William Herbert of Powis Castle, who wrote on behalf of Henry's regiment, now in Malta.[25] The officers paid for the installation of a memorial window in the east side of the north transept of Hereford Cathedral.[26] Henry's old Harrovian friend from the 1858 cricket XI, Captain William Clayton Clayton of the 9th Royal Lancers, oversaw the dedication of six of the marble columns in Harrow's new chapel to Henry's memory.[27] In time, a brass memorial was also erected in the Protestant church at Chamonix[28] and Tally ensured that a quarterly sum was paid to the three widows there.[29] However, nothing could be a more impressive token to Henry's memory than the great slumbering mountain itself. As a friend of Arthur's remarked in awe when he saw the pristine slopes, 'He has a magnificent monument.'[30]

Johnny was fortunate, as he struggled with the loss of his brother, that married life was a novelty. Nevertheless, when he was away in July 1867, he was caught off guard on finding black-edged mourning paper from the French trip in his bag. He wrote to Lucy: 'I take the only material I have in my bag and the depth of black reminds me that I mourn really as much and more than I did eight months ago.'[31]

Tally too had domestic distractions. In early 1867, she took Fanny and Alice to live at Llanforda Hall, Shropshire.[32] Lucy now began to run the household at Hampton Court herself, persuading the staff to bend to any changes she made, and checking for shortcomings in the linen cupboard. Management could be tricky and Lucy was as vulnerable to the artfulness of staff as Johnny had been to his tenants on his inheritance. The first years saw some clashes. In June 1869, Johnny was livid about the undisclosed behaviour of the Prossers. He wrote to Lucy: 'I don't believe I shall ever trust anybody again in my house or about the place – Sessions and Hewison, Anne too! seem all to be implicated, how far perhaps we shall never know.'[33] In June 1871 Lucy wrote from London to tell Johnny to expect the arrival of a new footman.[34]

When in London, Lucy stayed with Di and Henry Longley at 8 Lowndes Street. In 1868 she visited Heal's to look at sofas, chairs, valances and chintzes for the morning room. She ordered furniture and dispatched Johnny to check on its progress when he was in town. He reported in September 1869 that her chest of drawers was finished, and in March 1879, Lucy was sending him to Goode's after a crockery service.[35] In November the following year, Lucy was in London interviewing a housemaid ('no good') and choosing linen. In dismay, she wrote: 'I sat for an hour and ½ in a shop choosing Damask & Huckaback.'[36] It was her turn to take orders on 18 November 1870, when Johnny demanded 'a magnificent supply of things for our Xmas tree'.[37] She also leavened his blue days with gossip from the metropolis. In 1876 she spotted the Prince of Wales in Grosvenor Place. 'The Princess looked rather graver than usual, & I think was rather lumpy & no wonder – all the children were there, with sailor hats.'[38]

Technically Lucy, like every woman in Victorian England, was in a weak position in marriage. She had no enforceable entitlements (nor legal duties), her husband had an absolute right over her person and her property, she could not own any property, she had no rights of guardianship over any children that they might have, and she could not enter into any contracts independently of her husband.[39] Yet, as their pre-nuptial study of Ruskin's *Sesame and Lilies* revealed, Johnny and Lucy's was not the unequal partnership enshrined in law. Johnny certainly sought and respected Lucy's opinion on a broad range of issues. He brought the same forward-looking, perhaps surprisingly unconventional, attitude demonstrated on the estate to his marriage – one of many ways in which Johnny would not conform to the paterfamilias of popular Victorian myth.

Lucy, too, defies the image of the buttoned-up Victorian woman. Although Johnny might be expected to have taken to the sexual side of marriage with gusto, it appears that Lucy too revelled in the physical pleasures of the marriage bed. In their early days at Hampton Court, she resented Johnny's trips to London, and cold nights alone. She longed to feel the weight of his arm around her waist and his hand on her neck. Anticipating his return from Chamonix, she wrote: 'I never cease to think of you, all day long – you know *when more particularly*', and described herself as 'rather *hungry*, but will wait quite patiently for you'.[40]

Between them there was a clear delineation of responsibilities. Lucy had absolute dominion over the household, though she sought Johnny's approval on material matters like sacking the (notoriously foul-mouthed and licentious) laundrymaids wholesale and having the linen collected for laundering.[41] Otherwise, it was she who, in discussion with the housekeeper, devised menus, had beds changed, visitors' rooms aired, organised flowers, hired servants and paid the staff. She never interfered with estate business or the garden. Once, when Johnny requested his secateurs, Lucy confessed: 'I have been wracking my brains to think what a "secateur" is, a towel by chance? I hope you don't want it immediately for I can't imagine what to send . . .'[42] She did, though, support Johnny in his role, not least by managing his diary and reminding him of forthcoming engagements. When he had to run up and down to London, it was Lucy who consulted Bradshaw's timetable and told him which trains to take. On one occasion when Lucy was away, Johnny lamented: 'I am very tired of being without you & am all abroad with my engagements with nobody to remind me.'[43]

Johnny faultlessly acknowledged the joy that Lucy's love and companionship brought him. He never forgot her birthday, the anniversary of their engagement, which became known between them as 'mousetrap day', or their wedding anniversary. When Johnny's commitments meant that they were apart for any of these, the occasion was remembered in his daily letter. For example, on 12 April 1870, mousetrap day, he began his letter from London: 'Good morning my pretty, What did we do on this day four years ago?'[44]

Lucy, while conforming to the evolving role of the upper-class wife in the mid-Victorian marriage, learned quickly to manage her husband. She admired his irrepressible energy and came to gauge his mercurial moods. She was soon able to sense when sympathy was genuinely needed – usually concerning matters of the estate and family – as opposed to gentle teasing to restore high spirits. Johnny got little sympathy when he was ill through his own excesses. In November 1870 he had got lumbago and was miserable, being briefly too uncomfortable even to hunt. Lucy began her letter from Lowndes Street, 'My own dear Lumbago . . .'[45] and Johnny well knew that he should expect no more. He wrote to his wife from Garnstone near Weobley, just before Christmas 1872, where he was shooting with Daniel Peploe: 'Mrs P says that if she was you she would very soon put a stop to my hunting on cold damp days and getting rheumatism.'[46]

The novelties of domestic independence could not, though, veil the mundanities of estate work for long. Johnny's resignation of his seat on the

RASE Council in 1866 suggests a renewed focus on home, his wife and his estate. In anticipation of his responsibilities, Johnny totted up expenditure with Colley the same year, and found that cutbacks were essential.[47] Prior to their marriage, in devising Lucy's eventual jointure at 10 per cent of the rental income of the estate, he had estimated a rental income of £15,000 a year. On Lady Day 1866, the actual farm rents had totalled £10,437. Of these, Johnny had in hand (besides Green Farm and the Park) Henhouse, Lower Wickton, Hill Hole, Wootton, Stone Lodge and Marsh Court farms, and was jointly taking New House and Fishpools with Charlotte Grosvenor – rents he was paying out himself.[48] He had nearly 1,900 acres of the estate on his own hands. This was worth over £2,350 a year to him in ungarnered rent from tenants. His income from farm rents was therefore a maximum of £8,087.[49]

Repairs to the farms on the estate had been consuming around £5,000 annually.[50] Besides the farms, as Johnny had remarked after their wedding, the cottages were in need of expenditure. Between 1858 and 1871, £4,712 was spent on repairs to dwellings on the estate, 35 per cent of the income from them.[51] To ease the situation, Johnny persuaded the trustees to sell Redwood Farm to Edward Edwards on Lady Day 1868. The 185 acres raised £6,400. Later the same year, he disposed of Lower Buckland Farm to the Trustees of Captain and Mrs Heygate. The 202 acres went for £7,750. He went back to the trustees in 1871 and on Lady Day that year New Hampton Farm (142 acres) and the toll house were sold to tenant Richard Woodhouse for £4,223.[52]

These sales had little impact though while drainage of the estate was at its height. By the end of 1867, Johnny had borrowed a total of £14,052, and the repayments of principal and interest to the Lands Improvements Company (at subsidised interest rates) were now well in train.[53] Johnny's standard of living could not be sustained when confronted with such poor levels of profitability.[54] Although Colley might have seen this, the relation of income, profit and expenditure was not so clear to Johnny.

John Arkwright's will had sown confusion in Johnny's mind. It would appear that no form of trustee administration had been established to manage estate income. Rather, the trustees Berkeley and Bonham Caldwall played an advisory role, being available for consultation, and presiding over the disposal of any assets. In practice, the income on rent days was paid into Johnny's account and he met any estate expenses. Payments from investments for his siblings made under his father's will also came into his account and went to Tally in quarterly amounts of £950 to £970.[55]

He also covered capital improvements like drainage or cottage and farm building alterations, and lived on whatever was left, supplemented by whatever income he had from the profits of the land he was farming himself, and by whatever dividends might be paid on stocks that he held. It was thus never entirely clear in his own mind quite what the profit from the estate was and exactly how much he should be living off per annum. In this Johnny demonstrated a financial woolliness that his grandfather, Richard Arkwright, had disparaged in the aristocracy. More seriously, it left Johnny financially confused, and gave him a tendency to lurch from cash to crisis.

He did know, though, that hunting three days a week and keeping kennels was expensive. In 1865, the stable costs had constituted almost 10 per cent of his total expenditure on the house, gardens, stables and private expenses put together.[56] His mother, with the violence of Henry's death in mind, was also pressing him, in 1867, to give up the co-Mastership of the Herefordshire Hunt with Sir Velters.[57] This was a painful decision with its public acknowledgement of his poor financial position, and implication of shirking his duty and letting the county down. Appearances therefore had to be kept up on 5 June 1867, a year after his marriage, when Johnny was at the Whitecross Kennels for the sale of his hunters by local auctioneers, Russells. The lots included sixteen horses of Johnny's, for which he realised £615.[58]

He wrote to Lucy. 'It was sad to see my little horses sold to ruffians today and to have to say to enquiring friends that I did not expect to have to give up hounds all of a sudden and the like excuses for a general sale. But I believe it's all for the best – and I shall see more of my own dear 'ittle puff next winter.'[59] Johnny would regret cutting back on hunting just at this time. The 1867 season was the last for Sir Velters. Johnny's best man died at Moccas Court, 'after a long illness', on 14 October 1868, two years and a day after Henry.[60]

Sir Velters's death triggered a split of the hunt into the North and South Herefordshire, and Johnny assumed the Mastership of the North Herefordshire. By 21 April 1869, he was going to 'nip up to Tattersalls on Sat and back for I have heard of some likely horses', and he was buying hounds at Hereford.[61] Eventually, he built new kennels on the estate and took great delight in walking the hounds out of season.[62] By February 1872, he was, by his own admission, hunting like mad and by July the same year he wrote to Lucy: 'My two Rugby horses are come and the stable is getting on towards repletion.'[63] The same year the stable expenses reached a peak of £2,113, whereas in 1868, when he had temporarily given up, they had been down to £988.[64]

With hunting temporarily forsaken and his mother safely settled at Llanforda, Johnny and Lucy finally got away for their Continental honeymoon. Johnny's love for Lucy, far from being diminished by familiarity, was intensifying. At the Hotel Prince de Galles, Nice, on 4 January 1868, he wrote: 'I am very fond of the puffin's nest be it built under Dinmore Hill or on the South coast of France or in the mountains of the moon. The feathers that line it are so soft and enticing – too soft I sometimes think for one's general peace of mind and good behaviour in other mundane duties.'[65]

After a tour of Italy, as far south at least as Naples,[66] the couple returned home aglow with well-being. They reached Hampton Court in time to see Dick win another election in Leominster – a win for the Tories despite Gladstone's national victory for the Liberals.[67] However, the Second Reform Act and allied legislation since the previous November had deprived Leominster (and forty-four other boroughs) of one member, halving such constituencies' representation. In Hereford, the election was declared void and at the second vote in March 1869, Johnny's uncle Chandos, 'an ardent supporter of Mr Gladstone',[68] was returned.

If Lucy was disappointed to find that she was not pregnant after the honeymoon, she put it out of her mind by busying herself with another of her responsibilities, Hope-under-Dinmore School. This had been built in 1854 at Tally's insistence and at the sole expense of Johnny's father (£206 1*s* 11*d*).[69] Tally had taken responsibility for the establishment, liaising closely with the schoolmasters and mistresses, organising the timetable and visiting with her own daughters. To Lucy now fell the running of Hope School, while Johnny funded any capital improvements. Her first visit was recorded on 6 October 1866, a week before Henry's death.[70] Twelve months later, new teachers, Mr and Mrs James Sanders, arrived at Hope from Gloucester. Soon afterwards, Johnny paid £337 9*s* 9*d* for the addition to the school of earth closets,[71] heating apparatus, a new classroom, bell turret, paved walks, a stone fence and walls, and spouting cisterns and drains.[72] In 1871–3, additional bedrooms were added to Hope schoolmaster's house, at a cost to Johnny of £264 10*s* 11*d*.[73] In 1873, a village reading room and library was also established at Hope.

There were improvements, too, next door at Hope church. In 1865–6, John Arkwright's children had paid £402 10*s* for the addition of a north transept in his memory.[74] Hope Vicarage had been built by Johnny in

1860 with a water supply, coach house and pleasure gardens at a cost of £2,519 19*s* 6*d*. Its first inhabitants were Rev. and Mrs John Willis Grane. Mr Grane's incumbency (1858–73) saw innovation.[75] On 11 February 1866, the 'new selection of hymns' was first used, and on Christmas Day 1871, a harmonium, no doubt supplied by Johnny, accompanied the voices. Lucy occasionally played. In between times, in 1870, Johnny paid for sundry improvements at the church, including two seats for Arkwright servants at a cost of £13 6*s* 7*d*.

Although life appeared to roll on much as it ever had, the falling away of older members of the family reminded them that nothing remained the same for long. In 1864 Johnny's uncle Joseph had died at Mark Hall, and in 1866, both Peter Arkwright of Willersley (the last of John Arkwright's brothers) and Sir James Wigram (John Arkwright's brother-in-law) had died. Then, on 19 July 1869, a week after Johnny's thirty-sixth birthday, after some days in a coma, Tally died, aged 61.[76] Despite her irrepressible humour, Tally's widowhood had brought her considerable sorrow, partly over Harewood, but particularly with respect to her children. There had been the worries over Mary's pregnancies, Emily's mental state, Edwyn's broken engagement, and worst of all, the overwhelming grief at the loss of Henry, to whom she often referred, as Henry Longley recalled when he wrote in sympathy to Johnny. 'She spoke chiefly of the loss of your Brother Henry & of his singing 'Excelsior' as he parted with your sister.' Minnie's brother Francis Byng recalled fondly being 'brought up under her influence and example'. Chandos mourned the 'sister associated with all my happiest and saddest memories'.[77]

For Johnny there was comfort in re-reading Tally's letters recalling their shared love of the garden. 'I always feel when I look at your roses that I have something to tell you . . . Your General Jacquemins are beautiful now [1859] . . . What a deliciously sweet rose is Jules Margollin! [1863] . . . The roses here are so magnificent that it is a shame to leave them, & makes one almost cry to think you are not here to admire the fruit of your patient labours [1864].'[78] The most comfort, though, must have come from her gratitude that 'Whenever I have had your *presence* the sorrows of widowhood have been disguised to me.'[79] Tally was buried with John Arkwright at Hope-under-Dinmore church on 23 July 1869, Alice's twenty-first birthday.

Johnny and Lucy had now each lost both of their parents and one of their brothers, and their mutual support strengthened their relationship. In the summer of 1869, after his mother's death, and in the absence of children to increase their domestic circle, Johnny brought home a black and tan puppy named Greta. Snuffling about with her little tail waving in the air and her soft ears nearly to the floor, she became a focus for their devotion. In the middle of September, Lucy related to Johnny how Greta had just eaten a fish hook and menaced a mouse in the conservatory passage.[80] Johnny came to envy the house hound being adored all day by Lucy. Consequently, she started her letters 'My own House Dog', and 'Dearest of Black and tans'.[81] By November 1870, Greta had been joined by another puppy, Fritz.

Johnny, as head of the family, now had to take in Fanny and Alice, manage their finances and ensure that they were chaperoned at all times. All the 'corporate' decisions of the family fell to him too, though the feelings of his siblings had always to be considered. The public Johnny Arkwright, always sure to provoke laughter in a crowd, would cope with such additional responsibilities without turning a hair, but for the private man, the breadth and weight of his responsibilities could sometimes be crushing. His mother had always understood this, and now he was more grateful than ever to have Lucy as that most precious resource – the one person in whom he could confide and to whom he could safely reveal his insecurities. The new year of 1870 was one of those times when Johnny felt broken, not least because, under the terms of his father's will, on Tally's death he had to find no less than £25,000, around two and a half years' gross income, from the estate finances, £5,000 for each of his five surviving brothers. This would further deplete his income and leave him vulnerable to his tenants' ability to pay their rent. He wrote to Lucy from Hereford: 'I am in an awful state of depression which nothing but champagne can remove.'[82]

The legacy was particularly timely for Arthur Arkwright, who, in April 1870, married Agnes Mary Tufnell, of Witham in Essex.[83] Within ten months of their wedding, Arthur and Agnes had their first child, Wilfred.[84] The following year, they moved to The Mount, Oswestry, for the arrival of a second son, Harold.[85] Meanwhile, George and Lizzie had produced their sixth son, Richard, on 6 May 1870. On Lucy's side of the family, her sister Di had one son, John, and Mary two daughters and a son,[86] while her brother George and Sophy, who had married just before Lucy, had their first child, Charlotte Nest (always called Nest) in early 1871. Lucy travelled up to London on 18 February for the christening, at which, given the child's name, she was very likely godmother. She held every nephew and niece and recognised in the eyes of her sisters that ineffable, but in her own case apparently unattainable, joy. Lucy nevertheless managed to keep her spirits high. On the journey to Nest's christening, she was accompanied by HPS conductor, Henry Leslie, who, as she told Johnny, 'was most attentive to me, and so was the Guard (I think he thought I was eloping with Mr L!)'.[87]

Besides joy, children could also bring unimaginable grief, as the Arkwrights had cause to remember five months afterwards, in June 1871. Chandos and Anna's only son, Hungerford, then 18, drowned in the River Usk at Abergavenny. Lucy wrote immediately from London. 'I am *so shocked* to see the death of Hungerford in the paper.'[88] Hungerford had got out of his depth and his companion Arundel MacKenzie had not been strong enough to save him.[89]

Chandos and Anna's first son, Chandos Hungerford, had died in childbirth, and they buried Hungerford Chandos at Harewood on Friday 23 June. Johnny and Dick represented the Arkwrights at the melancholy service in the church where their parents had married.[90] Hungerford's death was a terrible blow to his father, and Chandos never really recovered. When he stood down as MP for Hereford in 1874, ostensibly in support of Gladstone, many held privately that he was a broken man.[91]

Hungerford's death was particularly cruel. Chandos, having done so much to keep Harewood together, would never now pass it to his heir. There was further injustice in the fact that, although it was Chandos who fought with his father, Chandos who parted with his beloved Wroxall to keep Harewood for the family, and Chandos who brought most honour to the Hoskyns name, his brother Hungerford, the 8th Baronet, in Brislington asylum, outlived Chandos by twelve months almost to the day, so that Chandos never even had the (unlooked-for) reward of the title. It passed to his brother Leigh and thence to Leigh's son, Chandos.[92]

Although Chandos railed against the principle of entail, the concept of continuity, of direct lines of inheritance reaching back into history and far into the distant future, was fundamental to the landed class. Johnny adopted the view without question. His ancestors' history might not stretch back all that far (Sir Richard had said only that he could 'plainly prove, on the best of all authorities, that Noah was the founder of our family, for he was undoubtedly the first Arkwright')[93] but Johnny assumed that his descendants and their association with Hampton Court and with Herefordshire would stretch into the future.

Yet as he stood with Dick in Harewood churchyard that June day, he must have reflected that there could be no guarantee that it would be so. By mid-1871, Minnie had been married to Dick for nine years, and

Lucy to Johnny for five, but neither had any children. For Lucy, who had married relatively late and was now 31,[94] the worry that she might never have a child must have begun to haunt her. Month after month she had faced the plain fact of her failure until months had become years. She had tried explaining her own inadequacy to herself, citing the upsets of Henry's death, the discomfort of travelling on honeymoon, and the grief of Tally's death, but had to acknowledge that these excuses were unfounded. She must have worried about the effects of her barrenness on Johnny's love for her, and to have begun to be angry with herself at her own inadequacy.

Every spring Hampton Court bore witness to the miracle that Nature wrought for God's creatures. The season brought fields of young and whoops of joy from Johnny at the birth of calves and foals. Lucy alone, or so it seemed in the fecundity of her surroundings, was overlooked by Him. At the fount of her femininity, where she yearned to feel a filial fist or foot, she knew only a growing knot of gnawing grief. Finally, by Christmas 1871, it seemed that she might possibly be pregnant. Knowing that it was early days, it was not until February 1872 that Lucy saw the family physician, Quain, in London.[95] Johnny apparently knew why she had gone. He began his letter of 16 February: 'Good morning, Fatty'.[96]

On 17 February, the day of Lucy's appointment, Johnny wrote coolly from Hampton Court of stocking the river with trout ova, and mocked his current 'fish mania'.[97] Lucy wrote that afternoon with ineffable excitement. 'I have seen Quain this morning and I scarcely believe yet that it is true, Johnny! It is almost too good to be true – I don't think you quite know how much I have thought about it all these years, or rather how I have tried *not* to think about it. And you have been so good, so *very* good, and never worried or showed very much that you really cared – and I know you have. If God gives us a little child I shall be too happy I think – but we must not think too much about it, as we may of course be disappointed.'[98]

By 20 February, Lucy could hardly wait to see Johnny. 'I have not been feeling *very* well the last few days, but Quain said I was not to mind that, and I am sure I do *not* if *it* is all right.'[99] Johnny, meanwhile, was experiencing that heightening of every sensation caused by the enormous joy that had suddenly burst upon his life. He wrote to Lucy on 19 February, 'After 60 hours rain without stopping the sun has just come out as if it never shone before, and the lawn is a mass of steam.'[100] Lucy stayed in London until the 22nd, interviewing housemaids (successfully this time), returning home that evening. Johnny's welcome is not recorded, but the extent to which he cherished his pregnant moo can be judged from a letter he wrote when in town seeking a house for her confinement, foreseen for July. He joked: 'I have taken the largest house in Belgrave Square for you, with the option of knocking a way into the adjoining houses on each side if there is not enough room for baby and nurse . . . There will be 40 policemen always on duty, and the traffic through that part of London will be stopped for 10 days.'[101]

During the latter stages of her pregnancy, Lucy and Johnny had convinced themselves that the baby was a girl (perhaps it was too much to hope for an heir first off). She wrote to Johnny on 17 May, while he was in town, 'The *tiny* . [Dot] is very troublesome today. I cannot manage her at all. She knows you are away, I think. *She* is rather a good girl today, on the whole, but did not at all like her little father leaving her so early this morning.'[102]

Lucy spent some of May and all of June in London, while Johnny to'd and fro'd to Hampton Court. The blissful days of expectancy could not obliterate entirely the realities of the estate. Johnny returned home on 6 July to attend the Hereford Rose Show, and was met by a terrible thunderstorm and a burnt-down barn. The next day, he 'was greeted this morning the first thing by five heifers on south Lawn with "foot and mouth" – so I cannot send any beasts to Cardiff', for the RASE Show.[103] But all was eclipsed by the great event that took place, finally, on 10 July, just two days before Johnny's own thirty-ninth birthday. Johnny was in Hereford at the Rose Show, when he was telegraphed.[104] Like lightning, he raced to the London train.

To everyone's surprise, Lucy was delivered, at 11 Lowndes Street, of a little boy, John Stanhope Arkwright, always known as Jack. By happy coincidence John had been the name of both Lucy and Johnny's fathers and of the older brother that Lucy had lost. Stanhope was chosen for Berkeley and Carey (Jack's godmother). Among the first letters to flood in was one from Mary who was to dispatch her own nurse, Mrs Morgan, to Lucy. George wrote appropriately from Pencombe: 'My great delight is to think how much more interest than ever you will take in all you do at Hampton Court.'[105]

From the estate there were letters from Colley and from Rev. Grane who told Johnny that:

> After a few solemn words of praise and prayer, at Mr Sanders' desire, I gave the children a holiday and, with many a shout, they started off in every direction, glad enough to bear such news. Then the Church

> bells took it up, and not long after the *cannon* did its best to roar – and now in every cottage there are hearts rejoicing with you and with Mrs Arkwright.[106]

At the Court, Mr Tulitt sent footman George to run up the flag on the tower, making everyone enquire what was up.

Friends wrote, among them the Chester-Master family of Cirencester, cousins of the late Sir Velters, and hunting companions. A.C. Master of Preston Vicarage supposed that 'you will look out for a pony for him immediately'. F.W. Chester-Master wrote from Stratton House, Cirencester: 'Don't lose your temper when your son helps you to dress for hunting and you find your best pair of tops floating in your bath!! I am beginning to get used to that sort of thing.'[107] But it was Johnny's uncle Edward Hawkshaw who best summed up the life-changing event. 'Hounds and Horses, Agricultural Prizes and Roseshows, Pheasants and Philharmonics all fade away before this little bud – the crowning rose of the whole wreath.'[108]

Johnny remained in London with Lucy until the end of July. From home, he told her his happiness was 'unbounded',[109] and Lucy replied on 29 July (although he was to return to her the next day) in blissful contentment. 'Dear, dear little Father . . . Dear Old Dog, I am still in a dream, and can't believe we have this blessed little thing all safe.'[110] He wrote again on 30 July instructing her to 'kiss the little changling for me on the top of his little nut. They call him the "blessed little Squire" about here.'[111]

The birth of the blessed little squire was cherished in part because it implied the protection of that equilibrium from which, for centuries, there had been little tendency to move. The tenants and tradesmen celebrated the implied perpetuation of their way of life – there would still be an Arkwright in residence at the big house to maintain their relationship to their mutual benefit; their sons would be doing business with Johnny's son. For landowners, it meant that one day they could discharge their duty to their forefathers by handing over the house and its acres to the next generation. To foster continuity, the heirs were brought up in virtually the same way as their fathers to a formula tested over generations. Thus Jack would be groomed by the nurse, governess, prep school, Eton and Oxford before returning to his estate to preside over his tenants and labourers, and take up county responsibilities. All that Johnny had risked to improve the quality of the estate would be redeemed by little Jack. That sense of natural justice that had inspired Johnny to take the risks that he had was now vindicated, and perhaps he would even have won his father's approval.

At Hampton Court, the excitement was reminiscent of that which had surrounded Johnny and Lucy's engagement six years earlier. On 5 August, Johnny reported that people had 'actually *advertized* for subscriptions to the celebration of the birth of the boy whom you have been rash enough to present to me'.[112] Lucy returned soon afterwards and Johnny barely let mother or son out of his sight for the rest of the year. It was a joyous Christmas. Di and Henry Longley stayed at Hampton Court, where the tree must have surpassed all previous attempts.

Johnny was a doting father, utterly infatuated with the lad. He wrote detailed letters of Jack's doings to his absent mother, letters which give the lie to the image of the distant patrician Victorian father. In February 1873, Johnny recounted how 'Jack has just rushed into the room to say that he has brought forth his first tooth – on the near side lower jaw and rattled his spoon against it.' Two days later: 'I have just taken him a rosy apple. He slobbered over it from his nose, his mouth, in fact from every pore, and crammed it of course into his mouth.'[113]

Johnny wasted no time in introducing Jack to the great ally of the patrician class, the horse. In May 1873, when Jack was 10 months old, Lucy was in town with Dick and Minnie at their new house, 8 Cadogan Place. She ordered a cot to be forwarded to Hampton Court, hoped to collect photographs of Jack and intended to visit Charlie at his new lodgings at 5 Saville Row. Johnny was loving having Black Jack to himself. He wrote to Lucy: 'I put Black on my knee on Comet and took him a long canter up the drive and back to his nurse who was in agonies. He crowed and screamed all the way with joy. He seems in rude joy and can stand a long time by himself playing on the sofa. He perpetually asks for Mammammam and won't believe that she is not dodging behind the screen.'[114]

SEVEN

Hodge Finds his Voice

The birth of an heir implied the perpetuation of the status quo between landlord, tenant and labourer, but changes were occurring in the countryside. The Second Reform Act (1867), in halving the number of MPs in Leominster and similar boroughs while creating new urban constituencies, had redistributed the weight of voices in Parliament, tilting the scales away from the countryside towards the growing cities.[1] The Act had also defined who should elect the new urban MPs. In the cities, most urban householders had been enfranchised by the Act, creating about half a million new voters at a stroke. In most large towns the numbers eligible to vote at least doubled. In Birmingham, the electoral roll trebled, in Leeds it rose fourfold, and in Blackburn more than fivefold.[2]

In rural boroughs like Leominster, the effects of the Act were less welcome. The power of those who had the vote was reduced, since they now returned half the number of representatives that they had before. The Act furthermore created a glaring discrepancy in the countryside. If a householder lived in a county division like the constituency of Herefordshire and not in a borough like Leominster or Hereford city, he still could not vote. This discrepancy created animosity between town and country. While Gladstone set sail on his mission to pacify Ireland, beginning with the disestablishment of the Church there, he trailed in his wake rural ill-feeling at home.

The enfranchisement of urban householders also irritated long-standing grievances among rural labourers. The young men beginning to move away from the countryside to the cities had prospects for improvement. If they could secure good work for reasonable pay, they stood a chance, in the future, of buying a house of their own and having a vote. Stuck in the countryside, the agricultural labourer, poorly paid and in his tied cottage, had no such prospects. He had little chance of saving money on his meagre wage and even if he could, there were precious few properties to buy – most had been swallowed up by the large estates. The self-respect of owning his own property, and its accompanying privilege of the vote, were unlikely ever to be his. Chandos acknowledged this in May 1871. Speaking at the dinner of the Central Chamber of Agriculture, he asserted that 'agriculture will thrive through ownership by all'.[3]

In moral terms, how could the ploughman or cowman be any less qualified to decide on the representation of his constituency than the factory worker was of his? Why should a man out in all weathers, his back turned to driving rain with little more than a grain sack tied round his shoulders to keep out the wind, and with no more to look forward to in his declining years than the rheumatism and arthritis that resulted, be deemed less of a man than the urban worker whom he toiled to feed? The rural worker was tiring of being represented in the press as 'Hodge', the ignorant clodhopper. The world seemed to think him less of a human being because he did not complain of his lot. Perhaps, as Darwin's new theories suggested, the survival of the fittest justified a hierarchy between the classes of man, but an accident of geography could not justify the discrepancy between the prospects of urban and rural working classes.

The difficulty for the agricultural labourer in making his case, by comparison with the factory man, was his geographic dispersal. The factory worker, as created by Sir Richard Arkwright, was, by definition, under the same roof (protected from the elements) as his fellows, and often billeted in the same street. For the agricultural labourer, the only way to meet his equivalent in any numbers was by journeying to the next village on foot. For one half of the year it was too dark to make the journey, and for the other half he was working up to fourteen hours from first light until nightfall. For him, there was little scope for the formation of any cohesive movement, such as the Trades Union Congress that had been founded in 1868. The last agricultural labourers that had tried to form a union, at Tolpuddle in Dorset, had been deported for their courage in 1833. The rural man was frustratingly dependent on his social superiors – those who owned his home and paid his wages – to put his case for him.

A couple of months before the death of Chandos's son, in March 1871, the discontent of local agricultural labourers had resulted in the formation of the North Herefordshire and South Shropshire Agricultural Labourers Improvement Society, in the north of Herefordshire, at Leintwardine.[4] The cause of the labourer had been taken up by the town's Methodist schoolteacher, Thomas Strange, who founded this Society which was 'destined to effect a real change in the condition of the labourer'.[5] He and others realised that the principal difficulty for the labourer was oversupply. Therefore, the union was founded not to promote strikes or action in the workplace, but instead to encourage labourers to migrate to other parts of the country, such as Yorkshire, Lancashire or Staffordshire, where men were fewer and wages were 16 to 17*s* a week, or to emigrate, particularly to the United States. Its motto was 'Emigration, Migration but not Strikes'. (Notably, the HPS programme that month included Bishop's song 'Let us seek the yellow shore'.[6]) Strange administered the Society as its Secretary, but he managed to secure for its President the Rev. David R. Murray, for forty-five years the Church of England clergyman for neighbouring Brampton Bryan.[7] As the President of the Society, Murray hosted meetings to provide labourers with practical information and assistance with moving away.

That a Church of England clergyman should take the part of labourers against the poor pay of their employers was particularly striking. The clergyman was usually appointed by the local landowner and if not his relation (as with George at Pencombe and Henry Arkwright at Bodenham) was sympathetic to his views.[8] As a result, the church in any village was generally allied with the 'big house'. As was later written: 'Hodge hates his landlord, and his employer but . . . above all he hates his parson . . . as the nominee of the squire, the friend of the landlord class, the supporter of "law and order" on the magisterial bench, and the autocratic manager of the school and other local institutions'.[9] To turn from the established church to the village chapel was often an act of defiance by villagers.

The identification of a man like Murray with the labourers' cause was seen by landowners as little short of an affront. Murray attracted criticism, but it was his vocation to help the poorest in society, to plead their case before those able to improve their lot, and he would not be turned from it. The formation of the union prompted a discussion on the labourer's situation in the columns of the *Hereford Times* during 1871. The debate reached a climax during the autumn months, when ploughing matches were held across the county and the labourer's cause was discussed during the dinners afterwards.

In 1870, a labourer at The Green at Hampton Court earned around 10*s* or 11*s* cash a week. His rent was between £3 and £5 a year. In addition, as was general practice in the county, he was provided with 2 quarts (4 pints) of cider per day in the fields while he worked.[10] Either or both of these increased at harvest. Besides this, a labourer's wife might be given the lease of small amounts of land after the harvest for gleaning wheat which she then sold. Additional perks such as the hauling of fuel from the coalyard to the labourer's cottage by the farmer's wagon and the provision of 5 to

7lb of beef at Christmas time were occasionally provided.[11] Bonuses, where applicable, were paid out from the office. Notes on the workmen dating from 1855 reveal that the 190 men then working on the estate for Johnny's father received a total of £32 between them. Those next to whom Colley had written – for example 'a very steady man' (William Bethell and William Lawrence), 'Very constant at work' (James Colley in the gardens), 'A tidy man' (Richard Davies), 'Has an invalid wife' (John Badham), or 'Caught cold gathering Ice' (Samuel Merrick) – got additional amounts. Correspondingly, the seven workers found 'Tipsy at the Icehouse' that year went without.[12]

Much of the newspaper debate centred on an accurate assessment of the financial value of such gestures to the cottager. 'Observer', writing on 11 November 1871, estimated that a wagoner's cash earnings of 13*s* a week could be augmented by these extras to the equivalent of 17*s* 8*d* a week, that a shepherd on an average 12*s* per week, with extras at lambing time and shearing could be raised to 15*s* 8*d* a week and that an older, 'third class' man with weekly wages of 9*s* a week could in fact be getting the equivalent of 11*s* 8*d* per week.[13]

In the correspondence columns the following week, 'Bo-Peep' responded that the realistic totals were far nearer 11*s* 4½*d* for a first-rate man. 'Hauling or leasing . . . cannot be considered a part of the wages; they are little acts of kindness done by man to his fellow-man'. Of the labourer's living costs, Bo-Peep estimated: 'House expenses per week:– Half bushel of flour, 4*s* 5*d*; rent and rates, 1*s* 9*d*; firing and candles, 1*s*; 1½lb. of cheese, 1*s*; tea, sugar, and soap, 2*s*; total, 10*s* 3*d*.'[14] When wages were 11*s* 4½*d*, of which 1*s* worth was paid in cider, this left just 'one penny halfpenny per week' to buy boots, clothes 'and other necessaries for the family'. Finally, the anonymous correspondent warned that discontented labourers would indeed follow the advice of the Leintwardine Society and emigrate. As a result, 'the day may not be far distant when the fields may be golden with waving corn, the orchard loaded with clustering fruit, the fields rich in pasture, the markets high in price, but labourers so few that the crops cannot be gathered, nor the demand in the market taken advantage of'.[15]

Correspondence reached the paper from Burlington Mississippi. J.D. Butler LLD pointed out the stark truth that 'if a labourer has a wife and four children, his wages yield him only 1*s*. 6*d*. a week to each member of his family, for all expenses whatever – food, clothing, furniture, books, papers, amusements, &c. But in speaking of the gaol in Hereford, you state the weekly cost of the food consumed by each prisoner to average 2*s*. 3¾*d*; . . . Is there nothing rotten in a state where these things can be?'[16]

The case was put with clarity in a rare letter from a labourer's wife from Woolhope, south Herefordshire, to the *Hereford Times* on 25 November.

> I myself have been a farm servant for nearly twenty years, and now a labourer's wife for nearly the same period and the mother of seven children, who have to be maintained out of 10*s* a week, and £5 a year rent to pay, and £2 for firing. The farmers never think of hauling your firing on this side of the county; as for leasing, the pigs are turned into the fields instead of women. So instead of £70 I get £19 to support my family in the year. The extra money got in the harvest gets lost in the winter, when the snow is on the ground. The farmers say 2*s* a week for drink, but when asked for money instead of cider they boldly offer 1*s*, and will give no more.

It had been suggested by the Society that each labourer should be provided with ground enough for grazing a dairy cow, but others had responded that the labourer's wife would have no idea how to manage the beast. The Woolhopeian wife refuted that, for 'they most of them had to do it before they were labourers' wives, for the farmers' wives now a days think more of the piano or singing for their sons and daughters than the dairy. That falls to the lot of the labourers' daughters, who often bring disgrace on the mothers through the wealthy farmers' sons.'[17]

The debate was beginning to stir inter-class animosity which threatened the interdependence of the landlord, tenant farmer and labourer. There was particular fear of revolutionary sentiments in the year after the declaration of the Third French Republic in Paris. Rural unrest coincided with criticism lately directed at Queen Victoria who had been seen too rarely in the decade since Prince Albert's death. In November 1871, Sir Charles Dilke, MP for Chelsea, baldly declared that the royal family cost too much and wasn't worth it.[18] The contemporary emergence of this dangerous mood lent farmers and landlords ammunition with which to attack the Leintwardine Society.

Strange and Murray were undeterred. In early November the Society held two lectures on emigration, one at the Congregation Chapel in Leintwardine, the other at the Oxford Arms Hotel, Brampton Bryan. Mr J.B. Good, the American Consul at Birmingham, addressed the second meeting on 'the beauties and realities, and great advantages belonging to the United States of America; and what a glorious opportunity is afforded to the working classes whereby they may escape from the oppression and poverty they too often meet with in this country [cheers].'[19]

Good illustrated his address with a large map. He contrasted England, 'now as fully peopled as it ought to be (a Voice: And more so)', with the too sparsely populated 'millions of acres in America calling out to English people to go over and populate them'. He assured his audience that they would meet with no animosity there. 'We do not mind how poor you are so long as you will toil.' He spoke of vast mineral beds of iron, copper, gold, silver, natural gas and wonderful oil wells.

Good acknowledged the reluctance of many to 'cross a bit of a pond called the ocean and leaving dear old England', yet, if they wanted a farm at home, they were one of at least twelve in line to have it. 'If they would only step across to America with one year's rent of an English farm they could buy a large farm there.' There were no game laws in America '[cheers, and a Voice: The curse of the country]', nor tax on the poor, but a varied climate and better wages. 'Labourers were earning from £40 to £50 a year and everything found, and lived on the same fare as the family. Some of the best blacksmiths and carpenters were earning £1 a day.' After a vote of thanks, Strange read several letters from those who had gone to America 'from their own neighbourhood. All . . . breathed a spirit of thankfulness for having been guided to go to America, and every one represented the writers as being in a state of prosperity contrasting strangely with the state of poverty they were in before going out and advising all labourers to follow their example.'[20]

Murray acknowledged his critics but justified his support for the labourers:

> The present prospects of the agriculturists in this locality appear to be undoubtedly of the brightest order. Grain of every kind commands an excellent price, and stock of all descriptions is excessively dear, and likely to continue so, and the present appearance of turnips, mangels, &c, give an assurance of a produce most abundant, weighty, and luxuriant. But when I look towards the poor labourer, who is the foundation of all agriculture, what a sadly different prospect presents itself.

A Mr Urwick of Downton responded that 'If the farmers don't have a pull sometimes, they can't go on', implying that in the good years, the farmers had to put some money aside for the years of drought or flood and could not pass on all the benefit to the labourers. He and Murray agreed to differ.

A month later, in early December (when iron and coal workers were 'agitating' in South Wales)[21] the ploughing match of the fledgling

Bodenham Labourers' Improvement Society took place – the last that year. Owing to a hard frost, no ploughing could be done, just fencing. The dinner was held at Johnny's England's Gate Inn and he presided, with George and Henry Arkwright as vicars of Pencombe and Bodenham, and Bonham Caldwall among those present. In opening the business part of the evening, Johnny proposed the loyal toast, remarking that he 'regretted very much that certain people had of late thought fit to censure the Queen for her non-appearance in public and for a relaxation in her duties'.[22] Since Dilke's censure, Bertie, Prince of Wales had been struck down with typhoid, exactly ten years after Prince Albert's fatal attack. Public sympathy had been stirred and support had swung back to the Queen. Johnny reported during his toast that 'that day's papers contained a much more favourable account of the state of the Prince's health . . . He believed that the Prince was . . . especially fond of agriculture.'

In responding to the toast to the clergy, Henry alluded to the present class-skirmish. 'As to himself and the rest of the clergy . . . he thought they could not be too much thrown together with their parishioners, now that many enemies to mankind were trying to set man against man and class against class.' George pointed out that all men worked, either with their head or their hands, and he strove to find the connections between the classes rather than the differences. He stressed the importance of education and of persuading children to attend the Church of England-run schools. 'Everything was now being looked over, and the Church . . . itself was passing through a careful scrutiny . . . There were clergy who had worked long . . . to forward education . . . They were quite willing to hand over . . . to the Government, and . . . the expenses, too'.

Johnny, in his speech, addressed the labourers' debate.

> In a part of this county there had been started a labourers' society. Now he did not mean to say that the labourers had not a perfect right to meet and talk over their affairs; on the contrary, he believed it was their duty to make themselves intimately acquainted with their position, prospects and hopes for the future of themselves and their children, but he hoped they would be able to distinguish between the voice of the agitating charmer and those who knew something about the matter [hear, hear]. He thought they ought to set the labourers right and teach them that they could not all be landed proprietors or fill stations they were not fitted for [hear, hear].

Regarding each labourer having a cow:

> he was sure that they would all be most happy to give a sufficient bit of land to a man providing he had accumulated enough money in the Savings Bank to pay for it [hear, hear] . . . He really did not see how a cow could be kept on less than four acres. The only way to solve the difficulty that he could see was to keep a union dairy where the labourers might buy milk. These had been tried, but they were found not to be successful. A feasible suggestion he thought was that farmers should provide something like a dairy where at least the labourers on his own farm might get milk if they wanted it [hear, hear]. He believed that by paying sufficient attention to the cottages of the labourers, giving them ample rooms for the members of the family to live, and for the different sexes to sleep; by visiting them when they were sick, by inducing them to become members of some friendly society, and to see that they were properly educated was, he believed, the proper way to promote the interest of the labourers [hear, hear]. He hoped they would never forget the labourers; for his part he should always try to remember them and do the best he could for them [applause].

Where the estate was not already ahead of its times, Johnny was true to his word, as far as it went. The Hampton Friendly Society had been founded as long ago as 1845 to create a fund to support ailing or disabled farm labourers and their families. By 1883 it had 125 members.[23] Johnny had furthermore initiated the Domestic and General Farm Servants' Registration Society in 1867,[24] and his expenditure on the provision of education was already clear.[25] Since 1866, Hampton Home had been providing retirement accommodation for six estate labourers thanks to an endowment from Tally. The majority of the cottages had a garden and fruit trees,[26] and Johnny personally demonstrated the pruning and grafting of fruit trees to his tenants.[27]

On 20 April 1874, in response to the present dissatisfaction, the Hampton Court Savings Bank was established to encourage thrift among the labourers. They could pay money in from their wages before they left Colley's office and walked home past the temptations of the inn. Each saver had to take out all his money whenever he accumulated the sum of £5. By 1889 there were seventy-four depositors in all.[28] Exactly twelve months after the bank was begun, a dairy had sprung up at Home Farm. As ever, Johnny was taking an active role. He wrote to Lucy: 'Your dairymaid is a real treasure. I never saw a cleverer little chap & so clean withal. We churned 46lbs of butter last Monday.'[29]

Despite such gestures, the labourer wanted nothing so much as a bigger wage packet. If he were paid enough, he could save a little every week and not have to depend on the goodwill of the landowner in his retirement. It was this that drove on the Leintwardine Society until it boasted an extraordinary 30,000 members from six counties.[30] Such support attracted people of influence. In mid-December 1871, the Society held another meeting at the Oxford Arms in Brampton Bryan, to which men walked 7 or 8 miles in the dark after a full day's work.

The chair was taken by George Dixon, radical MP for Birmingham, who described himself (vindicating Johnny's scepticism) as 'one ignorant of their situation, not having been brought up in an agricultural community'.[31] He invited the labourers to put their case. Testimony was given by Messrs Clee, Kinsey, Holland, Owens, Lewis, Birrell, Tramper, Watkins, Morris and Hughes (and others who, out of fear, did not wish to be named). They complained of almost static wages over thirty years while the cost of living had risen. They sought a minimum wage of 15*s* a week, a holding on their cottage of at least six months, and exemption from the Poor Law contribution of 1*s* a week.

Dixon questioned the witnesses before commending their sincerity, simplicity and earnestness. He had often wondered how a man on 10*s* got on, 'but taking you all round you are not such a bad-looking lot [laughter]. I think you would compare very favourably with . . . Birmingham working men who get double your wages . . . I don't hesitate . . . to say that you ought to be . . . discontented. You would not be men – you would not be worthy of the name of men – if you were not discontented with your position [cheers] . . . your discontent is a righteous discontent [cheers]'.

Dixon turned to emigration and, in an allusion to the Tolpuddle Martyrs, commented that 'you have not been long in finding out that if you could only be transported – of course I don't mean by Government [laughter] – to New Zealand, Australia, or the United States of America, you would be converted from poor men into comparatively rich men'. He urged them to 'seek to improve your position by legitimate means', and 'Trust to no one, for no one will help you unless you help yourselves.' The meeting concluded with a stirring speech by Mr Strange. 'We mean by every fair and honourable means to get on higher ground and breathe in a healthier atmosphere, so here we are . . . shoulder to shoulder – determined to battle with wrong and to help and succour the weak . . . What class has been neglected and constantly neglected, as the agricultural labourer?'

The *Hereford Times*' reports of this meeting stoked the newspaper debate. H. Dawson Reid deplored the attitude of the county's MPs. He suggested that Sir Joseph Bailey (Conservative) feared that the Society would end in the extension of trades unionism to agriculture. Michael Biddulph (Liberal) he dismissed as even more 'patronising' (though he did agree with the principle of each labourer having a cow), and 'Sir Herbert Croft [Conservative and a friend of Johnny's] has had but little to say on the subject of labourers' wrongs, remembering, perhaps, that the more a dirty pond is stirred the more it stinks.'[32] Regarding wage levels and additional favours, Dawson Reid concluded: 'The fact is the actual wages of farm labourers is just precisely the sum paid to each in cash.' He, like Dixon and Strange before him, urged the workmen to stand together. 'Unity is strength – band yourselves together then and work as it were with one hand and one heart for your common good.'[33]

The census figures for Hope and Bodenham of 1871 and 1881 suggest that encouragement to migrate or emigrate had some effect. In Hope the 1871 population of 634 had fallen by 1881 to 504. In Bodenham the figure fell from 1,110 to 879, but both of these may in some part be accounted for by the more general move of country-dwellers to the cities.[34] Where the North Herefordshire and South Shropshire Labourers' Improvement Society was unquestionably influential was in the national propagation of agricultural unionism, as Dixon had foreseen at the assembly in early December. 'I should not be very much surprised if other agricultural labourers in other parts of the country were to begin to imitate you.'[35] By the beginning of 1872, agricultural unionism was growing in north Warwicksire, Lincolnshire and Leicestershire.

On 7 February 1872, Joseph Arch, who had undertaken hedge-cutting for Johnny in 1860, was approached in his Barford cottage in Warwickshire to speak at a meeting of agricultural labourers. Arch knew of the Herefordshire meetings the previous year as they had been covered in the Warwickshire press. As a Methodist preacher, addressing a meeting held no fears for Arch, and he spoke to the gathering under a tree on Wellesbourne green. He was a rousing success. A union was at once formed, and being near Birmingham, quickly attracted the attention of men like George Dixon and Jesse Collings, another radical and a close associate of Joseph Chamberlain. A second meeting was held three months later, at Leamington, where the National Agricultural Labourers' Union was formed with Arch as its President.

The national union demanded higher wages, reduction of the working day and education for young farm workers. Arch also alluded to the franchise discrepancy between town and country. As an article in the *Examiner* of October 1872 noted: 'Last week's meeting at Aylesbury saw them [Arch's union] demand a share in Parliamentary representation "such a share, it was added, as is not now denied to the negro labourers of America".'[36]

Arch travelled the country, speaking to labourers' meetings. Within three months, the NALU had 50,000 members. After two years the figure peaked at 86,000.[37] Already, though, the NALU was dogged by petty jealousy of Arch's fame. Nevertheless, the realisation of Sir Joseph Bailey's premonition that the Leintwardine Society's agitation would lead to trades unionism in agriculture was a sobering blow for landowners and especially for their tenant farmers, who, as wages rose, would be squeezed between rising costs and rising rents. Throughout 1872, the Herefordshire meetings continued, Arch attending one of them. Seventeen days after the birth of little baby Jack Arkwright, John Benbow of Marlbrook Farm on the estate, had his hayricks burnt.[38]

The efforts of the labourers caused some landowners to examine their claims. Johnny had again shown himself to be ahead of his peers in having taken all the cottages in hand centrally in 1859, so that the labourers did not owe their rent to their employer the tenant farmer, but to the squire. In 1872 he raised wages on his farms at Hampton Court to 11*s* per week.[39] To ascertain labourers' conditions under his tenants, Johnny canvassed eighteen of them.[40] Their responses in some cases reflected ill on both parties.

George Wilding laboured for William Parker of Sidnall in Pencombe, a farm of 256 acres and 17 perches for which Parker paid Johnny £340 6*s* rent in 1873. Notes for Wilding record:

> Does not wish to live under Parker. Did not engage to work for him regularly – Parker did not want him – Got 9/- a week in money and enough cider – Got 12/- from Rev. G[eorge] A[rkwright]. Impossible to live under Parker – He is harder than other farmers. Came at 6 and worked till he would let me go – at seven or up to 11 at harvest – Parker has taken a farm at Ullingswick and now wants a regular man – Had some potatoe land last year from Parker but he charged 7*d* a score (20 yards) which is 1*d* more than anyody else asks. We got from ½ a bushel to 1 bushel, in a fair year – Parker binds the wife to work at 7*d* a day.

Edward Beavan lived at Maund Common and paid £3 for his cottage. He was a wagoner for Richard Oliver of Rowberry Farm (211 acres 25 perches for which Oliver paid £327 10*s* rent in 1873). '12/- a week and £1 extra for harvest month, left on the 19th Feby '72 without giving notice to the Landlord – Mr Oliver could not get him to the horses early enough in the mornings – he gave Mr Oliver a week's notice and left.'

In May 1872, Johnny was checking the rent and extent of garden of all labourers not employed by him.[41] By June the following year, Johnny was writing to his tenants to ask whether the provision of cottages on their farms was sufficient for their labourers, and reallocating them where appropriate.[42] He was also checking the age distribution of his own labourers. In 1873 there were 178 of them in all, of whom one was over 90 years of age, and one over 80, 15 were over 70, 21 were over 60, 38 were over 50 years old and 34 were under 18 years old. This left 68 labourers aged between 18 and 50.[43]

NALU pressure continued, and again in 1873, on 21 March, Johnny raised his workers' wages to 12*s* per week.[44] Perhaps because of the extra costs, by 1875 the 178 workmen employed by Johnny had fallen to 152.[45] Following his studies of 1872 and early 1873, and after discussion with a few of his tenants the previous week, Johnny called a meeting of his tenants at England's Gate Inn on Monday 24 March 1873. Johnny opened the meeting by asserting that:

> it was simply childish to ignore the fact that the question of the agricultural labourers' wages had forced itself into notice. It now remained for sensible people to meet it on broad and public principles, and by no means attempt to patch it up or tide it over by narrow and private expediencies [applause] . . . He came there to-day to learn as much as to instruct.[46]

Johnny sought to negate the acclaimed agitation of Arch, Murray and Strange:

> The leaders of the present movement were merely giving an impetus to a mass of old efforts continually and perseveringly made for some time past by all those interested in the improvement of the agricultural labourers. Schools and clubs had done their work and made men at last respect themselves more . . . As to the Unions themselves, they were not to be confounded: there were Unions and Unions. There was the Warwickshire Union which openly fostered strikes; with that he had no sympathy, and

> quite disapproved of the principles it advocated [applause]. Then there was the West of England Association, of which Mr. Strange was the presiding genius. Of this Association the law of supply and demand seemed to be the principle, migration and emigration the appliance. Strikes were entirely discountenanced, and he must say that he could never see why it should be any more disgrace or hardship to a labouring man to move from one county to another in search of more remunerative work than for a professional man to migrate or emigrate in the interests of his profession [cheers].

In discussing the meeting's first resolution, 'That this meeting acknowledges the right of labourers to form unions in their own interests, but not in any way that shall tend to increase the price of provisions for public consumption', Mr Brassington of Woodhouse Farm, who had himself migrated to Herefordshire from the north of England, 'quite acknowledged the right of the labourers to unite for their own interests, if, in so doing, they did not violate the interests of others, and become exorbitant in their demands'. The meeting felt that labourers had to appreciate that raising prices would damage their own prospects, so that really farmers and labourers had a common interest. Henry Arkwright from Bodenham said that 'he could testify to a good deal of ill-feeling amongst the labourers and their wives in this matter against the farmers, just as if their interests were antagonistic'. Nobody welcomed the external interference in the relationship that hitherto existed between tenant farmer and labourer.

In his second resolution, Johnny stated that wages should be paid in full in cash weekly but that employers should offer facilities for the purchase of cider otherwise than at a public house. Johnny said that 'the great thing was the punctual payment of wages in money, weekly, if possible, so that the labourer might not be obliged to run up bills with the village shopkeeper', who then made money out of the labourer's misfortune. George Arkwright said that he 'had been present at one labourers' meeting at Pencombe, at which a great grievance was made of, and indignation expressed, at their being obliged to take cider as part payment'. After some amusement at the notion of labourers ever refusing cider, Mr Brassington observed that in the north, no such drink was given, and he 'thought the custom of part payment in cider very bad'. Major Heywood concurred and thought that 'this labourers' question would never be satisfactorily settled in Herefordshire as long as cider was given in part payment of wages'.

Thirdly, Johnny proposed that more definite agreements should be drawn up between the employer and labourer, specifying in particular the length of notice to quit. Johnny, as a magistrate, was seeing plenty of instances in which the absence of a written agreement caused difficulty. This was unanimously passed. Next Johnny opined that no settlement of the labour question should be made without consideration of provision for the aged and infirm labourer. He felt that it was the government's duty to provide a secure National Provident Society for labourers to save. In the meantime, George urged the farmers 'to induce their men by every means to become members [of the Hampton Court Savings Bank] – even to paying their subscription for them'.

At the end of the meeting Johnny asked what made a good labourer, what hours he should work and what he should be paid. The meeting felt

> that 15*s* was not at all too much for a good man, and as to the hours of work, a strong protest was made against the limitation to 9½ hours in summer which the Warwickshire Union demanded. In winter, the men often did not make more than six hours; would they consent to a reduction of 4*d* an hour for all under 9½ in winter? Of course not. An average of 9½ hours all the year round would not be out of the way.

In summing up, Johnny stated his satisfaction that not a word had been said against the labourers' meetings.

> We have agreed . . . that a good man should have good wages, a good cottage, a garden, and potato ground; if possible, co-operative stores to supersede village shops with their 200 per cent. profit; and certainly a good Provident club, guaranteed by Government, to provide allowance in sickness and pension in old age . . . There are many points connected with agriculture which do not come under the simple laws of other industries. The farmers cannot raise the price of their productions to make up to them for the advanced price of labour, as the coal merchant and ironmaster can do [hear, hear]. No other industry is to the same extent subject to the weather.

EIGHT

Down Corn, Up Horn

Higher wage costs for labourers could be tolerated while farming was healthy. In 1875, both wage and rent levels at Hampton Court peaked. Johnny's employees still numbered 152, and wages, thanks mainly to the efforts of the NALU, had climbed to 14*s* a week on Home Farm – a rise of over 27 per cent in three years.[1] Johnny's total rental income in 1875 was £17,000. Nationally, rent prices had risen from around 20*s* in the early 1850s to nearly 30*s* per acre.[2] Careful management of profitability was demanded of the tenant farmers who were paying for both increases. To landlords like Johnny, it appeared that faith that high levels of investment would result in greater profitability had been vindicated.

However, the outlook was not one of unclouded optimism. At the end of 1873, a House of Lords Committee had concluded that investment in land improvement 'is not sufficiently lucrative to offer much attraction to capital'.[3] It further suggested that those who had borrowed to finance drainage might easily be out of pocket on that alone, without taking into account outlay on farm buildings and cottages. Nevertheless, in 1874–5, Johnny took out a further loan of £825 from the Lands Improvement Company. His last loan was taken out in 1878. The total capital borrowed since 1863 stood at £27,451 6*s* 5*d*, with an additional £18,608 5*s* 3*d* in interest due, a round figure of £46,000 in all (equivalent to approximately £2.06 million today).[4] The first loan would not be discharged until 24 June 1888 and the last not until 1899.

These were towering sums. Of other landowners in nearby counties, only the Earl of Powis borrowed comparable amounts – £21,847 between 1861 and 1879 and a further £28,308 between 1888 and 1899 – the latter including payments to build a laundry and lay on a water supply to Powis Castle.[5] The Earl of Dudley borrowed £12,683 to drain his Great Witley estate in Worcestershire, and the Duke of Beaufort £11,252 for drainage and farm buildings in Gloucestershire and Wiltshire over the 1861–79 period. In Herefordshire, only the guardians of the young Lord Rodney at Berrington came anywhere close to Johnny's levels, borrowing £21,583 against an estate of just 4,467 acres, let at £5,824 per annum.[6] The magnitude of the risk and the extent of his exposure were not lost on Johnny. In October 1874 he confided to Lucy: 'I wish I was going to school again and had no liabilities – they are almost more than I can stand, especially when I am alone.'[7] Six months later he wrote: 'I am counting the hours even the minutes till I clasp you to my waistcoat.'[8] Farming profitability in Johnny's highest repayment years between 1875 and 1888 was going to be crucial.

It was therefore troubling when wheat prices wobbled in 1874. After years of rising, the price fell by 10*s* a quarter and then stuck at around 45*s* until 1883.[9] The wheat price was still the main indicator of the climate of the agricultural sector, and it was a sensitive barometer. Between 1850 and 1875, wheat had fallen to below 40*s* per quarter only once, in 1851. At the other end of the scale, it had climbed to 74*s* in 1855 and to 64*s* in 1867.[10] The price slump of 1874 hit hardest the wheat-growing specialists of eastern England, including the Mark Hall estate of Johnny's cousin Loftus. The diversity of West Country farming made Hampton Court less vulnerable, but the trustees nevertheless divested themselves of Hampton Wafer Farm, selling 394 acres to the Dean and Chapter of Hereford for £14,000.[11]

The agricultural census revealed that in the Green Farm parish of Hope, wheat acreage had increased from 242 acres in 1866, to a peak of 330 acres in 1875. In a direct response to the 1874 fall in prices, the wheat acreage in 1876 had dropped back to 207 acres, while pasture land rose by 125 acres.[12] The change of tack at The Green from corn into horn also coincided with the arrival of a new farm bailiff. George Sessions left Green Farm for work at the hunt kennels and was replaced by Mr W. Drynam, the former farm bailiff of Stone Farm.[13] Besides blessing the flexibility of their land use, Johnny's tenants could also be thankful for the removal of Excise Duty on hops in 1862 that had led to a beer boom. This, combined with a rise in the popularity of light ales (which had a negative effect on cider consumption) and the introduction of creosote for treating hop poles (which reduced the frequency of their replacement), meant improved profitability from farming hops.[14]

Most of all, though, as the direct switch from wheat to pasture demonstrates, Herefordshire farmers blessed their great red cattle. The Hereford breed was reaching the height of its popularity and Johnny was a leading breeder. Between 1859 and 1898, he was to win over 300 prizes and in 1869, he commissioned silver goblets of his champions' heads that made a novel addition to table settings.[15] By 1870, Herefords were by no means restricted to their native county, having grazed fields across the country since at least 1790. One Mr Westcar of Creslow, near Aylesbury, had visited the Hereford cattle fair annually from 1779 to 1819 and had encouraged among others the Duke of Bedford, the Duke of Manchester and Lord Talbot to adopt the breed.[16] Since 1855 the late Prince Consort had bred Herefords on his model Flemish Farm at Windsor.[17] However dispersed their popularity though, the annual congregation for buyers of the breed remained the Great Fair at Hereford on the third Tuesday and Wednesday of October, when the beasts were no longer tethered in the streets, but in the city's new cattle market.

The 1870 shows were a lean time for Hampton Court Hereford successes. To remedy this, Johnny went on a buying spree at one of the greatest Hereford sales of the day. William Tudge of Adforton was a champion of the breed's development and had consistently won prizes at county and national shows.[18] His greatest bull calf was the incomparable Lord Wilton, whose offspring founded herds across the world. In 1876, Tudge had suffered a stroke, and the Adforton dispersal sale was held on 20 September 1877. 'Universal opinion was that a better herd of Hereford cattle never came under an auctioneer's hammer.'[19]

Johnny enjoyed a healthy rivalry with his old friend, Lord Coventry of Croome Court in Worcestershire, who had begun breeding Herefords in 1874. The two men bid against one another with the result that the highest price of the day, 155 guineas, was paid by Johnny for a cow called Rosebud, who had taken the first prize at the Royal Show at Birmingham the previous year and at Liverpool in 1877. The verdict of one viewer as he looked over the rails at Rosebud was 'Perfection!'[20] Johnny also bought Beatrice who had likewise won at the Royal in 1877, for 100 guineas, and the bull, Mareschal Neil (4760) for 175 guineas. Lord Coventry was scarcely less extravagant, paying 140 guineas to acquire Giantess 'the best cow in England of any breed', who had come third to Rosebud at the Liverpool Royal. He also acquired another eight animals. In all the sale raised £4,029 18*s*. By 1886, Golden Treasure, the product of Coventry's Giantess and Johnny's Marschal Niel, was winning prizes for Lord Coventry and was hailed as 'the premier Hereford show cow of her day'.[21]

Johnny's care of his herd paid dividends at the Bristol RASE Show of 1878. Here, his home-bred, 10-month-old bull Conjuror won his class and his heifers were similarly successful.[22] Twelve months later, Johnny had another first prize with his young heifer, Antoinette, and the other heifers were again successful. Finally, at the height of this run of success, in the 1880 show at Carlisle, he won a prize with all five Herefords that he took.[23]

However, in 1878, the work of the Hereford Herd Book was threatened with collapse.[24] Johnny convened a meeting on 5 March at which the Hereford Herd Book Society was established to continue maintaining records of the herd. Johnny was voted the Society's first President. His Vice-President was Lord Coventry. The two of them, along with Sir Joseph Bailey of Glanusk and Sir James Rankin, presided for twenty out of the first twenty-three years of the Society's existence.[25]

It was a good time for Johnny to be hitting high-profile success with the breed. The great grasslands of the mid and far west of America were opening up, and demand for the finest stock was high. Although the Shorthorn had hitherto been favoured, the Herefords soon became 'supreme as ranch cattle, roughing it in extremes of heat and cold'. They could also 'walk longer distances in search of water than any other cattle'.[26] The first Herefords had been introduced to North America as early as 1817, but from the 1870s the trickle became a strong flow.[27] Great men like T.L. Miller of Beecher, Illinois, encouraged by his foreman, a former Herefordshire farmer, were introduced to the breed and quickly appreciated its virtues. Miller began to spread the word through the *Breeder's Journal* that he founded and others subscribed to the cause, including Adams Earl of Lafayette, Indiana, H.C. Burleigh of Fairfield in Maine, and A.P. Freeman of Huntington, Massachusetts.[28] In July 1883, Johnny had two yearlings heading for Chicago, and the presence of American buyers was noted at Leominster Agricultural Show in early September the same year.[29]

There was similar demand in Canada, where the Hon. M.H. Cochrane of Hillhurst Farm, Quebec, was considered the founder of the breed. In 1883 and 1884, he imported beasts from great Herefordshire breeders like John Price of Court House, Aaron Rogers of The Rodd, Philip Turner of The Leen and Stephen Robinson of Lynhales. Between 1880 and 1883, 'fully one-half of all the cattle imported by the St Lawrence route were Herefords'.[30]

Other Hampton Court Herefords found their way to Jamaica and to Australia,[31] where demand grew from their first introduction to New South Wales prior to 1839. After Johnny's Conjuror was 'triumphant'[32] at the Bath and West of England Show at Exeter in June 1879, his breeder was in negotiations (via correspondence from the grouse moor) with Australian buyers who wanted to purchase three young cattle, including Conjuror. Johnny asked 1,000 guineas, but was turned down. Conjuror won his class at Carlisle the following year, the zenith of Johnny's fortunes (although he continued to win prizes for as long as he showed).

Thanks to both the diversity of Herefordshire's produce and the resurgence of Hereford cattle, Johnny rode out the 1870s with few rent reductions. In this, he was unusually fortunate. However, he did not escape financial worries altogether. At the end of April 1876, Hoskyns family matters came to Johnny's attention once more. His uncle Leigh of Aston Tyrrold alerted Johnny to considerable problems with the trust for Cathy, Chandos's daughter by his first marriage. She was supposed to have had £1,600 settled on her by her mother, a further £3,000 settled on her by her grandfather Sir Hungerford, and a settlement of £4,000 against Harewood.[33] Johnny's father had consented to be a trustee until his death, but somehow, despite John's deathbed warning, the financial shortfall now touched Johnny. Leigh explained to him: 'The Trust Fund does not appear to have been duly guarded by the Trustees', but it was money to which Cathy was entitled and it must therefore be found. Leigh felt 'almost stupified by what is going on – the axe at the root of the old tree shakes every branch & spray & makes it quiver'.[34]

Immediately, Johnny went to Cucklington, home of Chandos's sister, the widowed Caley Phelips. There, he was joined by Leigh and his wife, Emma. Johnny most needed Dick's legal advice, but he was visiting Edwyn and Alice in Algiers, and was not expected home until the middle of May. Leigh, Caley, Emma and Johnny began to unravel the complicated picture and it became evident that they would have to raise significant sums to pay Cathy. Ominously, Johnny asked Lucy to 'enquire about Bijou'.[35] From Cucklington, Johnny went back to Aston Tyrrold with Leigh, and on to Harewood to see Chandos, before returning home.

Lucy went up to London, leaving Johnny to meetings about Hereford Three Choirs Festival, and incessant worries about Harewood. On 11 May, he wrote to Lucy that 'the award was to be signed in London yesterday – and I am afraid that the wretched business is by no means over yet – there are some hideous disclosures that may have to come out. I wish Dick was here.'[36] He was trying to keep the full extent of the Harewood problems from his brothers and sisters, particularly from Mary, as it looked increasingly inevitable that Harewood, the house and estate, to which Mary was particularly attached, would have to be sold. The following day, Johnny wrote again to Lucy: 'Every hour makes me more uncomfortable about it – as I know a good deal that is not yet public but will be any day now . . . Can't you find a rich man who doesn't know what to do with his money to put it on Harewood & save it for the family?'[37] Despite his attempts at secrecy, Mary descended on him at Hampton Court fewer than three days later, as he wrote to Lucy: 'with the most hideous reproduc^{n} of the ugliest new fashioned toadstool hat I ever saw in my life'.[38]

Lucy was as supportive as she could be at a distance. Johnny was candid with her, writing on 15 May 1876:

> I have succeeded in selling £3,000 of some bad stock at par . . . a corresponding weight has come off my pericardium. I may survive the six months without declaring bankrupt, but a heavier weight still has accrued from my discovering that probably by having signed my name touching Wroxhall [*sic*] soon after my father's death, I have made myself Trustee for all this hideous mess. I have found the letters asking me to do so at the time. I stoutly refused, with my father's last words in my ears, but cannot find my answer.[39]

Although Johnny had raised some cash, it was not enough to meet Cathy's claim, and Harewood would probably have to be sold. Chandos's brother Leigh wrote at the end of May: 'I cannot endure the thought of its entire & irrevocable alienation.'[40] A fortnight later, he wrote to Johnny again:

> As the time approaches I feel more & more how grievous a thing it w^{d} be to let Harewood go without some effort to save it from the hammer . . . Mallory has written to me suggesting a caveat on my brother Hungerford's behalf as the legal representative! – but I have always understood that the prospect passed *absolutely* to Chandos in 1858. Do you see any possible method of saving it?[41]

For Johnny, the sale of Harewood was frustrating. The idealist in him would purchase the estate and keep it for the family, but he was beginning to have to let reality and not aristocratic *noblesse* determine his affairs. He felt too the censure of the generations that had gone before. He communicated some of these feelings to Leigh, who replied in mid-June:

> Nobody feels more than I do what a hard thing it is for you to bear, more so because it could easily have been otherwise, but I must confess that I see no possible method of our saving it . . . Looking at it from all sides, I see nothing unless a millionaire could be found who would from sentimental motives put his money on it & release it for its old owners.[42]

Chandos, having suffered insult and injury over the place, was less sentimental, and in declining health. The sale day approached and particulars were drawn up. The property included 1,200 acres, farms, inns, cottages, the chapel and the house itself, a 'Noble Mansion . . . centrally placed in the Park, which is boldly undulating and ornamented with Timber of great antiquity and magnificent growth'.[43] On 14 July 1876, the bidding began at £45,000, and climbed to £75,000, but it was not as much as Chandos wanted, so it was withdrawn. Johnny reported to Lucy from the Carlton Club on 20 July: 'Harewood was not sold. I believe no bid.'[44] By now, the strain was telling on Johnny's health and he went to Bryn Tirion at Towyn on the Welsh coast to recover from a bronchial infection. There was no correspondence from Scotland this year. Johnny was uncharacteristically in no mood for the jollities of the grouse season.

After the abortive sale, Chandos's health continued to decline. At his London house at 41 Eccleston Square, on 28 November 1876, Chandos Wren Hoskyns died. His health had been declining for at least two years and he had lost the power of speech for some time before his death.[45] Leigh suggested also that Chandos had suffered heavy losses on some investments just before he died.[46] His body was brought back by special mourning coach from Paddington to Harewood chapel for burial.

At the end of January 1877, Leigh wrote to Johnny with some disgust at Chandos's will, which left everything to his wife, Anna, but made no provision whatsoever for Cathy, the unwitting cause of the difficulties. Leigh suspected that Anna had persuaded Chandos to exclude her step-daughter from his will, and Leigh cut off relations altogether with his sister-in-law, leaving Johnny to see to Anna and the girls. To Johnny, Anna bewailed the fact that she had her hands tied and could do nothing to disentangle the affairs at Harewood, not even to make a gift of the pianoforte to Johnny, as she wished. 'I try to be brave, as you wrote me, but it gets worse day by day as we realise our terrible loss.'[47] Anna did not have to wait long before her affairs eased. The contents of Harewood came under the auctioneer's hammer over four days, beginning on 24 March 1877. The Netherton, Pencoyd and Llandinabo parts of the estate were bought by Mary's husband, Courthope Bosanquet. Johnny marked his purchases in the catalogue, including a six-chamber revolver in its case, with fittings, for £1 3*s*.[48]

Another consequence of Chandos's death was that on 7 March 1877, the Royal Agricultural Society recommended that in Chandos's place Johnny be re-elected to the council from which he had withdrawn in 1866. The election was undoubtedly an acknowledgement of the work that Johnny had done to promote agriculture and in particular Hereford cattle, as well as of his popularity among his peers. It was an honour to be asked to rejoin the council, and Johnny accepted. Chandos's passing was regretted by agriculturalists, and particularly by the *Agricultural Gazette* to which he had contributed for nearly thirty years. 'No one', it asserted, 'ever did more to illustrate the influence of English history and of English legislation on the condition of English agriculture; no other English writer ever did so much to illustrate the charm and extend the interest now generally felt in even the commonest details of landowning and of farming.'[49]

For Johnny, the practical effect of his election was a return to the regular meetings in London of the general council and meetings of the sub-committees. In February 1877 he was in town for just such a gathering, and on 2 June he spent 'a very agreeable day at Woburn with the Chemical Committee'.[50] In April 1879, the council was joined by the Prince of Wales, who would host the Royal Show at Windsor ten years later. For now, Johnny wrote to Lucy: 'HRH was at our Council this morning looking very fat.'[51]

While the demand for British cattle was at its height, the opposite was true of British wheat. From 1874 when prices had first fallen, the decline had slowed but showed no inclination to reverse. The effects of Sir Robert Peel's repeal of the Corn Laws in 1846 were finally being felt. Prices had held up since that time largely thanks to the Crimean War in the 1850s, the American Civil War in the 1860s and the Franco-Prussian War in the early 1870s, when significant quantities of imported corn had just not been available to the British market.[52] Now, while the American push west was proving beneficial for cattle, it was catastrophic for British wheat. Vast tracts of corn-growing land were becoming accessible as the railroad rolled west. Johnny's uncle Richard Phelips had predicted in 1850 'that Wheat can be in future years imported into this Country at 36*s* per Q^{r}', and what had then seemed improbable now showed every possibility of being realised. He had further wondered: 'Can you grow it at that price and pay any rent?'[53] Others were less quick to appreciate the threat. They claimed that yields in America were half what they were in Britain and that 'transport costs are a most effective duty on foreign imports'.[54] The development of the railway meant that to move wheat from Chicago to Liverpool cost 15*s* 11*d* per quarter in the late 1860s. By the early 1900s, this would drop to just 3*s* 11*d* and afford no protection for home production.[55] British wheat farmers were struggling to compete, not least because the transport by rail in Britain of imported wheat was free, while home producers had to pay for their wheat to be moved by train.[56] The cry in agriculture became 'Down Corn, Up Horn!'[57]

Since 1874, the fall in wheat prices had been a worry, but farmers had seen poor spells in the past, and had no reason to suspect that the situation was anything other than the sort of temporary downturn that they had ridden out dozens of times before. They had yet to realise that by the end of the 1870s, the United Kingdom was importing nearly half her wheat consumption.[58] For those who had switched to mixed farming, where grain was principally grown as a stock feed, the impact was lighter. In Herefordshire, where shortfalls of profits from wheat could be made up with beef, hops and to a small degree with fruit, the situation was not serious. Rather than being a general depression, the downturn merely brought to a close the acknowledged Golden Age of agriculture of the middle of the century.[59] Farmers and landowners were not particularly concerned, except where, like Johnny, unrelated factors like Harewood also bore down on finances. The situation for Johnny's cousin Loftus at Mark Hall, among the wheat fields of Essex, was far more serious.

However, the Harewood affair had made an impact and Johnny had to act to meet his repayments to the Lands Improvement Company. In April 1878, Johnny wrote to Lucy: 'I did a great deal in the cellar, the garden & the school. Jack is very well & happy. He carpenters, eats & roams to even my satisfaction.'[60] As a result of this foray into the Hampton Court cellars with the Butler George Butters, Messrs Christie, Manson & Woods of 8 King St, St James's Square held a sale of 230 dozens of 'old wines, the property of J.H. Arkwright, Esq' on 3 June 1878. The lots included 1862 East India sherry, 1854 vintage port, and clarets from Châteaux Lafite, Latour, Leoville and Margaux.[61] Purchasers included Johnny's family and friends, John Heathcoat Amory, Henry Longley and Lord Lonsdale, with whom Johnny was shooting at Fettercairn in Scotland in August the following year.[62] The total made from the sale was £1,148 15*s* 10*d*.[63]

The trouble was also perceptible nearer home the same month with regard to Hope church. On 28 April, a Church Restoration Committee was established, which included Johnny and Colley as churchwardens. The nave needed work. Instead of Hampton Court producing the necessary finance, as it had in the past, the committee planned a series of fund-raising bazaars. One of these was held at Hampton Court and made £302 16*s* 7*d*. Lucy made the best of the second sale at Humber on 21 August and was proud of herself for having sold ferns from noon until 6 p.m. On 20 December another bazaar was held at Leominster Town Hall and made £43 13*s* 10*d*.

The work at Hope was duly carried out for around £1,000 in 1879, and the church was reopened on 18 November, when the Bishop of Hereford preached.[64] Again, in June 1883, when monies were needed for the new hospital at Hereford (of the funds for which Johnny was a trustee[65]), Johnny held a concert in the drawing room at Hampton Court, conducting and performing on the violin, accompanied by Lucy.[66]

Although western livestock farmers had so far largely avoided the difficulties from the fall in wheat prices, there was no escaping the British weather. The highest flood on the Lugg since 1852 occurred on 4 January 1877, but this was exceeded in 1879, when a severe thunderstorm on 11 June produced the worst flood in Hope in living memory – making a very unlucky thirteenth wedding anniversary for Johnny and Lucy.[67] It rained for the whole of the summer and produced a sodden harvest. In neighbouring Shropshire, cereal yields were cut by half.[68] Profitability was hard hit, since the crop, such as it was, still had to be gathered, but was barely worth the labour cost of bringing it in. It was hoped, though, that as usual, the small amount of marketable corn gathered would fetch a high price and so cover the costs of seed and labour expended in the spring.

There were poor harvests due to inclement weather every year between 1875 and 1882 with the exception of 1876 and 1880.[69] The unwelcome surprise, though, was that prices refused to compensate. The natural disappointment of farmers with the persistently poor harvests clouded analysis, but in time, it dawned upon agriculturalists that there were more menacing forces at work. Prices were not increasing despite the shortages because imports were arriving. In 1870, Britain imported 30 million hundredweight of grain. By 1900 this would be 70 million hundredweight.[70] Once this was understood, the situation became more sinister. Instead of pushing up prices, the shortage of home-grown grain was increasing the demand from overseas. Grain began to pour in through the docks from America, Canada, India, Australia and Argentina. The imports showed a relentless tendency to increase. Between 1867 and 1871 and 1894 and 1898, the price of English wheat fell from an average of 56*s* a quarter to 27*s* 3*d* – down by more than half.[71]

There were other, equally disturbing, outcomes of the wet weather for Herefordshire's farmers. Sheep began to fall ill with liver rot and in places entire flocks were decimated. By 1879 the RASE was so concerned about the epidemic that it sought to uncover the extent of the problem nationwide. For Herefordshire, Johnny undertook to canvass sheep rearers.[72] 'With zealous labour he communicated with upwards of eighty stock-masters. He found that the disease [liver rot] was widespread amongst both sheep and cattle; that it has extended over farms which from time immemorial have been exempt from flukes: several of the valuable pedigree-flocks have been sufferers, and fatal cases have also occurred amongst several of the fashionably descended Hereford herds.' Hereford Market's auctioneers, Edwards and Weaver, stated that sheep that should have fetched between 50*s* and 63*s* per head if sound were instead selling for 7*s* 6*d* to 27*s* a head.[73]

For some, the effects of disease were catastrophic, but the incidence could be very localised. Henry Moore, farming Fields Place on the Garnstone estate, had lost or had to sell as diseased, every one of his ewes. On his other farm, Chadnor, adjoining, however, they had remained sound. Thomas Rogers, The Homme, next door to Moore, had also kept his flock sound. Mr Bull of Bear Farm, Weobley, however, was left, out of a flock of 92 sheep, with 20 ewes, after selling a dozen at skin price and losing the rest. Instead of having 100 lambs, he had only 13. John Ludge of Ivington Court was left with just 10 surviving sheep out of 125 that he had bought at Hereford from Mrs Evans of Swanstone. Thomas Green of Kinnersley had lost all of his sheep and many cattle from liver rot and had been forced to give up farming altogether.

Of Johnny's own flocks, he reported that rot was unknown until 1880, when sixteen cases occurred. Shropshire Down sheep seemed to suffer more than the Leicesters, and 2- and 3-year-olds more than lambs.

> No explanation can be given of the introduction of the disease; the running stream, river, and pools are not considered injurious to the sheep: no particular plants or weeds are observable in the meadows . . . Frost and severe weather generally lead up to the first symptoms . . . Dry food and salt are believed to be the most effectual remedies for preventing rot and arresting it in the early stages.[74]

The sixteen cases in 1880 had occurred up at Stone Farm and on the undulating Pencombe land which was dry and well drained. Other than a proliferation of blue 'carnation-grass' (thought injurious to the sheep) there was no discernible cause, such as an increase in snails. Liver rot had also been contracted by the deer in the park. Of the 160 with which the park was stocked, 50 contracted rot in 1879 and 20 in the first half of 1880. The keeper had also found many dead hares and rabbits with enlarged spotted livers, distended stomachs and intestines, but no flukes.

For tenant farmers, who had been bearing the costs of increased wages for labourers and the highest-ever rents, the sliding wheat prices, combined with the rot of stock, caused severe hardship. To add to this, by 1879 there were outbreaks of pleuro-pneumonia in cattle that persisted until at least 1882.[75] In addition, overseas competition for hop production increased markedly from 1878, although it took a while for output to respond. In Herefordshire, hop acreage had increased from 4,500 acres in 1850 to 5,738 acres in 1869.[76] By 1878 it stood at 6,000 acres, but this was its peak. Increased overseas competition, processing improvements in brewing, and rising productivity per acre of hops led to a fall in acreage.[77] Where the farmers were hard hit they could not continue to pay the NALU-increased wage levels. By the end of 1879, NALU membership had fallen from its 1875 peak of 86,000 to just 20,000, and wages too had fallen.[78]

In response to the crisis, in 1879 Disraeli established a Royal Commission into the conditions in Agriculture, a very public acknowledgement of the industry's problems. In May 1880, Johnny gave evidence to the Richmond Commission. Having managed to ride out the 1870s with few rent reductions, the picture Johnny drew of his Hereford estate was unrecognisable to grain producers further east.[79] Of the estate's 10,030 acres, 2,920 were arable, 5,950 pasture and 1,160 woodland. Only Green Farm was bigger than 500 acres (at 734 acres), 22 farms were 200 to 500 acres in extent, 12 of 100 to 200 acres, 2 of 50 to 100 acres, 4 of 20 to 50 acres and 36 were smallholdings of under 20 acres.

He could report no increases in tenancy changes of late, no bankruptcies and no distraints for rent for twenty years, although in some cases late payment had been allowed. Regarding difficulties resulting from the wet seasons, low prices and the increased costs of labour, Johnny confirmed that changes had been made. The rotation of crops had been much varied and 'many acres seeded down in consequence of the low price of produce, and the increased cost of labour'. Figures that he supplied showed that the average yield of wheat per acre had dropped from 18 to 12 quarters since 1878, meadow hay had dropped from 15 hundredweight (cwt) per acre to just 1, and hops had fallen from 6 cwt to 1 quarter, 'if that'.

Even as the Commission sat, the rain fell, increasing cases of liver rot in sheep, and pleuro-pneumonia in cattle. Farmers had very little healthy stock left to sell and the wheat situation showed no signs of improvement. Johnny's estate, despite the expensive drainage, could not escape the difficulties. His farmers, taking their beasts to Leominster or Hereford markets, realised low prices for their stock, rendering the ravine between income and high costs (including rents and labourers' wages) at best treacherous and at worst, unbridgeable.

As farmers' income fell, demands for rent allowances began to be heard. In 1879, few rent reductions had been made on the estate, although Samuel Smith farming Bury of Hope was allowed 20 per cent that year.[80] By November 1880, within six months of Johnny's evidence, his tenants were demanding reductions. In the past they might have been pacified by an increase of capital outlay. However, Johnny, post-Harewood and with the drainage loans to repay, was in no position to increase his expenditure. Too late, he could see the wisdom of having alternative sources of income, as landowners had at the beginning of the century. There was now, unfortunately, no one wanting to buy his land for railways at £200 to £300 per acre, and no prospect of minerals being discovered under the red soil.

Johnny's 1880 rent days drew a very different picture. William Proudman of Winsley, Edwin Jones of Hill House, John Davies of Lower Wickton, Robert Bemand of Risbury, Henry Lambert of Risbury Court, William Parker of Sidnall and John Pitt of Pencombe Court all demanded allowances of 20 per cent. Also, George Bemand of New House Farm, Pencombe, a scrupulously consistent payer of his £205 rent throughout the 1872–9 period, asked for and got a 20 per cent allowance on his rent in 1880, and in 1881, 15 per cent.[81] Some allowances persisted until 1883, although reduced to 15 or 10 per cent.

To keep his tenants, Johnny was obliged to drop the rents in November 1880, thus reducing his own ability to meet his financial commitments. It was policy at Hampton Court, as elsewhere, that the rents were paid by the tenants, but the rates on the land by the owner. While Johnny was granting reductions in rent, the government was making no concessions on rates, so he, like other landlords, was being squeezed in the middle. To compound the farmers' problems, in 1880 the first shipment of frozen mutton slipped quietly into Britain from Australia.[82] The pattern of overseas competition that had begun with grain now showed every likelihood of being repeated with livestock. As one observer noted: 'A few years ago it was our boast, that although the Indies, Australia and the almost illimitable virgin prairies of the new world could and would furnish us with breadstuffs, yet in the case of our live stock we had nothing to fear. Now all is changed.'[83] To add to the Tory landowners' misery, Gladstone returned to power in 1880 and the same year passed the Ground Game Act, permitting tenants to shoot hares and rabbits on their land, hitherto the much-begrudged preserve of the landowner.

Johnny had shared his rent-day blues with his wife. Lucy showed a surprising understanding of the issues. 'I am glad to hear you have settled the 7 Tenants, altho' I am very sorry you were obliged to give way about the rent – but anything is better I suppose than letting them go, & having the farms on your hands.'[84] The same story was being repeated all over the country. Indications of financial difficulty for landowners were multiplying, but they were rarely acknowledged. Ominous news of reining in passed between households. When Johnny stayed at Stanage, near Brampton Bryan, in early November 1880 for some 'musicking', he met Lucy's brother George. He revealed to Lucy that George 'has made up his mind to lease Foxley at least til March next year, & live at Stanford to help out Lewis Dashwood' (Sophy's brother).[85] Lucy, staying with Mary at Tanhurst in Dorking, was not impressed. 'We are all *very angry* with George D. . . . If he found that he could not afford to live at Foxley, there w^{d} be nothing to say, but as he has distinctly said he *can* afford it, one can only say that it is very wrong to live away from your own people & duties & to let yr children grow up away from home.'[86]

Johnny was not immune. After giving way to the tenants, something had to be sacrificed. At the end of the same month, he acknowledged to Lucy a humiliating truth. 'I do not see my way at all to doing the [hunt] ball this year.'[87]

NINE

Algiers to Aberystwyth

For Johnny, the Richmond Commission, the return of Gladstone to power, the passing of the Ground Game Act, and the reduction of tenants' rents at Hampton Court, made 1880 a trying year. Lucy, meanwhile, was becoming a tenant herself, of Alice's London house, 7 Lowndes Street, next to Di and Henry. Johnny was to visit 'the Algerians' – Edwyn, Alice and Fanny – for three months, from February 1881. In his absence, Lucy would live in London with the children. Since Jack's birth in 1872, Lucy had produced a daughter, Geraldine (Pinkie) on 23 November 1875 and a second girl, Evelyn (Wee) fifty-one weeks later. When Lucy had informed Johnny of her third pregnancy in May 1876, Johnny had 'a suspicion that we were once more three of us. I pray you do not disclose our disgrace – rabbits are nothing to it!'[1]

Johnny set off for Algiers, with an ailing knee, on 11 February 1881. He wrote to Lucy from the Hotel Bristol, Place Vendôme, reporting a rough crossing to Calais, before proceeding via Amiens to 'Parry'.[2] The wagon-lit took him, by 12 February, to the Grand Hotel Louvre and Paix, Marseille. Two days later, he was on one of the Messagières Maritimes Company's steamers, bound for Algiers.[3] He set sail in rough weather owing to a mistral from the north, but once he was off Majorca, he was speeded, wrote Johnny quoting Milton, by 'a south, mild wind of Araby the blest'.[4] Lucy wrote: '*I do wish I was with you.* I knew I should not like letting you go, but I tried not to think of it – & when it came to the point, it was almost more than I could stand – but *please* come back a great deal better . . . Pinkie divided her pudding at luncheon into 2 portions & said one was France & the other Algiers, & milk . . . for the *sea* & a little lump of pudding in the middle represented "Father's ship".' His girls enclosed a Valentine.[5]

The 36-hour journey gave Johnny time to reflect on his adventure. Edwyn, Fanny and Alice had been living abroad for about seven years. For Edwyn the change had been a new start, and the climate relieved Alice's poor health. Fanny had been freed to join them by the reluctant removal of Emily to Ticehurst asylum in Sussex in 1873. Ticehurst, established in 1792, was the very best in residential care.[6] The converted country house stood in over 40 acres of grounds with 2 miles of footpaths through plantations, orchards and gardens. It resembled a well-ordered estate, not unlike Hampton Court, with sheep and cattle grazing in the grounds, and gardeners at work.

Emily was officially certified insane by physicians Arthur Noverre, who described her as 'incapable of entering into conversation or answering any questions', and George Fielding Blandford, who testified that 'she could not answer any questions but laughed to herself in a vacant manner'.[7] Johnny gave the supposed cause as 'overwork in the school room'. Emily was assessed as suicidal and dangerous to others, but not subject to epilepsy.[8]

Emily's care was regularly checked for the Arkwrights by Sir William Gull, who had, in 1871, attended the Prince of Wales during his bout of typhoid.[9] Her siblings visited frequently. Samuel Newington's notes suggest that at first she was closely observed in the hope of discernible change.[10] As the months stretched into years, hope of a cure evaporated. Emily remained at Ticehurst for the rest of her life, a total of fifty-three years. Only three people admitted between the hospital's foundation in 1792 and 1917 remained at Ticehurst for longer.[11]

There had followed a bewildering confusion of physical and mental illness among Johnny's circle in the 1870s. Lucy took the waters in Germany in the summer of 1874; her sister Mimmie Bateman at Shobdon was ill with a fever in November; on 8 December Johnny's first cousin Frederic Arkwright of Willersley died 'of congestion of the lungs'; and George began to suffer violent fits.[12] By the beginning of February 1875, Di had fallen ill. In the chaos, Dick resigned as MP for Leominster.[13]

From Charlie, travelling in North Africa in May 1875 (while Johnny was enduring London, 'horrible – inches deep in muck & smells'),[14] came the most bizarre news. Lucy reported that his companion 'Lord Ranfurly is dead, fm wounds from an animal. A *bear* they say.'[15] Two years later, Charlie too began to suffer fits, and Lizzie was cabling Lucy with renewed 'cause for anxiety' about George.[16] Alice, too, was unwell. Johnny circulated bulletins as they came in. With impeccable timing, Fanny returned, causing Lucy to observe: 'How strange that she shd have come to London just in time to help in illness, as usual!'[17]

By early August, Charlie was still not better, and George was complaining of pressure on his brain.[18] Throughout September, George's health deteriorated and on 5 October 1877, at the age of 41, he died. After a post-mortem, he was buried at Hope on 11 October. The well-being of Lizzie and her seven children was added to Johnny's responsibilities.

It was as well for Johnny that Herefordshire's farming had been healthy in the 1870s, because domestically it had been an exhausting time, the sickness coinciding with the worries about Cathy Piggott's payments. 'I think of you so much & all the worry & trouble & *sorrow* & wish I cd do anything to help you,' Lucy wrote in 1877.[19] Events beyond his control had threatened to submerge Johnny completely and the weight of the family's calamities had crushed him. When, a few weeks later, Lucy wrote from London to tell Johnny of Jack that 'I did not like leaving him face downwards on the sofa in an agony of tears, poor old fellow', Johnny could sympathise with his son.[20]

In conversations with George, Charlie or Emily, Johnny had been unsure whether his siblings even recognised him, and with Harewood it was hard to discern what was truth and what fiction. Visits to Ticehurst were especially frustrating, since Emily 'took no notice of me till I had gone – & then burst out crying'.[21] Furthermore, Ticehurst's gardeners and nurses spoke more sense than those whom they served. It was a topsy-turvy time, so steeped in improbabilities and requirements of Johnny to believe 'as many as six impossible things before breakfast', that he might have thought that he had stepped *Through the Looking Glass* himself.

Algeria promised Johnny welcome relaxation and an escape from the rain. Edwyn, Fanny and Alice spent the British winter there, returning to England for the season, like the family's own swallows. Algeria, taken from the Turks by the French in 1830, had come increasingly into fashion, especially after France itself had stabilised during the 1850s under the anglophile Emperor Louis-Napoleon.[22] More Britons started to visit, and doctors began to recommend the southern Mediterranean climate for its curative properties, above even Montpellier, Pau, Nice, Rome or Gibraltar.[23]

Britons had visited in increasing numbers through the 1860s. Influential in raising Algeria's profile was Barbara Smith Bodichon, a talented artist, who exhibited paintings she made of her adopted country in London, just as Frederick Leighton was constructing his Arab mansion in Kensington (1864–6).[24] In Algeria, Bodichon raised the social tone and promoted Anglo-French relations through the stimulation of her salons.[25]

From 1864, between October and the end of April, Algeria buzzed with the cream of Prussian, Polish, Russian and English society. Hotels were constructed and a new promenade was designed by Sir Samuel Morton Peto, bringing something of Scarborough to the Mediterranean.

The opening of the Suez Canal in 1869 increased traffic through the Sea, and many English on their way to India stopped off in Algeria, though few ventured from the city. It was to Mustapha Supérieur, higher up than Algiers, with wonderful views and walks, yet sheltered from the wind, that Edwyn, Fanny and Alice Arkwright had moved in the early 1870s.[26]

After several years' residence, Johnny's siblings were well established at Telemy. They found the insular social round irksome and rejoiced whenever they managed to avoid one of the Governor-General's balls.[27] The garden was their joy.[28] Alice's letters to Johnny blossomed with news of what she had planted, what was flowering and which plants she had recently painted. In 1897, Edwyn reported that they had just been to Juihaneh in the mountains and Alice had added over forty new botanical treasures to her store.[29] Flower shows were staged in Algiers, which Edwyn latterly helped to run.[30] The fertility of the soil and climate meant that everything grew with extraordinary speed. In 1899, Edwyn wrote: 'You English would never believe the weight and length of creepers etc. that we have to cut back.'[31]

Edwyn 'gardened' on a larger scale at his farm at Saidia, a couple of miles west of Castiglione on the coast.[32] There, among nesting eagles, he reared cattle (including Herefords, the rings through whose noses aroused great interest), grew tobacco and (getting back to his roots) cotton, asparagus, and Muscatel and Alicante wine grapes.[33] He also built a farmhouse where he employed a dozen men year round and taught them the care of dairy cows and poultry.[34] Willie Arkwright was a regular visitor, encouraging Edwyn to take Jerseys from Sutton and start a dairy herd. But it was not all easy going. On Christmas Eve 1883, Edwyn had his goats stolen and few of the Herefords survived.[35]

The Arkwrights were pillars of the British Church in Algiers, consecrated by the Bishop of Gibraltar in 1871. Edwyn was never officially the incumbent of Holy Trinity, but played a significant role. He and Alice also employed their energies in later years in the establishment of a little cottage hospital that opened next to the Presbyterian church in 1897.[36] Two years later, the physician for the English community in Algiers, Dr Gardner, left his Villa Regina to Edwyn for him to take in Englishwomen in difficulties. By April 1899, most of Alice's time was spent caring for patients there, though she hoped soon to find a matron. At that time, the hospital was caring for six patients, with two poor ladies in residence and a third to arrive shortly.[37]

Johnny, in need of some nursing himself, finally arrived in Algiers on 15 February 1881. From the sea, the port had been described as resembling 'a swan about to spread her wings'.[38] Johnny sweated through the kaleidoscopic streets to arrive at the haven of the Villa Arkwright. The next day, he wrote to Lucy: 'Slept like a top & woke in a brilliant sun & a garden of daturai, oranges & cloth of gold roses.'[39] Not surprisingly, the garden occupied many of his letters, and he described 'daturas, geraniums, rosas, hibiscus, violets, plumbago, Bougainvillea, Tacoma, bigumias (all sorts), wisteria, cineraria, verbenas, arums, lilies, incas, jasminium, wises, fuschias etc. etc. in profuse blossom out of doors'.[40] He no doubt visited the Jardin d'Essai, with its collection of 'flora of all climates and countries'.[41] With the warmth to cure his knee, his own small Kew Gardens outside, and endless novelties to explore, Johnny could hardly have been happier.

The only drawback was the ridiculous social scene in Algiers. 'We all see each other every day and sometimes oftener. Shake hands all round twice each time.'[42] He wrote on 23 February: 'People call here by dozens for tea & gossip & sing & play & garden . . . We play trios every day by ourselves.' Tennis was proving tricky, for there were few courts and great demand.[43]

Escape from social duties was a delicious prospect. 'Some day we mean to go to Saidia Edwyn's farm for a few nights & a visit to an ostrich farm is also on the cards.'[44] Of Saidia, a four-hour journey from Algiers, he wrote in more detail in March. 'It is a most interesting place on the site of an old Roman Villa. I think I shall like it better than the society here.'[45] They visited in early April, when he wrote: 'We have laid bare the bottom of the [Roman] bath covered with tessilated pavement with no doubt much more to come when they follow up the conduit.' They also visited sulphur springs and took a donkey trip into a pine forest.[46]

In his letters, Johnny described the 'Country all cactus, olives & mulberry, red soil, white tufa rocks & sandy roads.'[47] Many of these sights Johnny captured in his sketch book.[48] 'The old Moorish houses fitted up comfortably are most engaging & I never saw a prettier affect than the illuminations of last night. Chinese Lanterns seemed exactly right hanging in the arches.'[49] On 19 March, he wrote: 'Tonight there is a religious fête I believe worth seeing but in a fearful locality. They cut & gash themselves, run knives & knitting needles through their limbs, swallow live scorpions, chew cactus till the blood pours from their mouths, kill & eat raw chickens & sheep etc. etc. Quite the thing to see I am told. 30 ladies there last night.'[50]

The contrast with London in February could not have been greater. 'It is so horrid,' Lucy wrote, 'a sort of semi fog, always, & very raw and damp.'[51] Arthur was visiting on 16 February, 'having a turn at Dentists & Doctors'. On 26 February, 'Charlie looked in yest[y] – I am to go on Monday to help to choose a chintz, & Jack & I are to have Tea, after his riding lesson.' Of politics, 'They say Parnell is "suffering from nervous exhaustion", & gradually collapsing altogether.' Their own girls, Pink and Wee were sweeping all before them in town, and Lady Cecily Hardy had asserted that 'she had never seen such eyelashes & eyes as Pinkie's'.[52]

Johnny posted wonderful illustrated accounts to his children.[53] Lucy told him on 23 March: 'Pinkie is wild with delight at yr letter, & Wee is so jealous that she has insisted on writing also, in hopes of producing one for herself! It was a real beauty, yr. letter to P, & I am preserving it most carefully, as it ought to be kept as a family treasure.'[54]

The greatest excitement of the trip was provided by Fanny. Johnny wrote:

> When first I came I thought her [Fanny] really ill, & asked about it – She hardly spoke & lived in dreamland. One day Capt James by invita^{n} came to lunch the day before leaving for England. When really gone she could stand it no longer & had to make 2 telegraphs to Paris to a mutual friend to send him back again. And he is expected tomorrow . . . We met him several times – but all the time she could not stand it when he was gone & so it has come square. I knew nothing about it – and was sworn to solemn silence . . . He is a gentlemanly man well informed as far as I know him, very pale & with very little white hair. I believe [he] has only two relations in the world a married sister in England wife of a clergyman, & a brother in Melbourne on a large scale. Adjutant of some volunteers – captain in the 38th. That is all anybody knows of him. It seems curious to me that in four years nobody has ever taken the trouble to ask anything about him. They don't know any more even now, or as to his means. Try & find out.[55]

Captain Hill-James returned to Fanny in Algiers. Johnny reported on 6 April: 'The happy man has squared Banny & she can no longer leave it open . . . The world here are intensely surprised . . . It really is a wonder how they can have done it so quietly . . . Have you thought of "Fanny James"?'[56] Of his dearest younger sister, a bride-to-be at 39, Johnny reported, 'B[anny] as you may imagine is a totally new creation – she plays not having touched P[iano]F[orte] for 3 years – sings – sang at our concert with glee – and is astonishing everybody.'[57]

Lucy's reaction came in a letter dated simply 'Monday'. 'I am so electrified about Banny's engagement. I can't get over it at all. He must be a clever man to have wrung a "yes" out of her . . . I hope you like him, &

that it is satisfactory in every way.'[58] Lucy was, though, 'very sorry to hear he is so delicate – it is rather sad to think of Banny having to begin a fresh course of sick nursing'.[59] The talk of marriage made her reflect on their own anniversaries. '2 months tomorrow since we parted!! Next Sunday (10th) is Mousetrap day – & June will be our Copper wedding. I think I love you more now than I did then, dear old man, & yet I should have thought that impossible at the time . . . Please arrange for Edwyn & Alice to marry somebody before you leave them.'[60]

The wedding raised many questions. As Johnny wrote: 'It is not decided without you – but all the people here are bent upon the wedding at Hampton Court, & it will have to be done I am convinced.'[61] Lucy was trying to respond to 'frantic letters from the family this morning asking me what *I* have heard abt Capt James etc. . . . everybody seems to have an uneasy feeling that he *may* not be good enough for her'.[62] Indeed, Johnny himself seems to have been ambivalent about Hill-James, although it would be surprising if anyone would have been good enough for his Banny.

> The match seems to give great pleasure in Algiers so I suppose it is all right. I believe his sister is a Mrs Clarke – a widow. He seems to be quite poor & only hopes to get an appointment in *Jersey* some day. However as you may imagine nothing would alter the fact that they mean to be married. I am going to have a business talk some time with him – & as we intend to come home together . . . I shall have plenty of opportunity.[63]

Fanny's news made Johnny's an exciting return. Poor Hill-James suffered badly with seasickness on the crowded boat, and Johnny became frustrated. By 5 May, Johnny was back in London and besieged with enquiries about Fanny. He then returned to Hampton Court, where the overwhelmed children probably gathered around his luggage like pirates round a treasure chest.

The Algerians themselves returned to England on 9 June, and introduced Willie Hill-James to the family. Mary wrote to Johnny: 'We like our future brother quite as much as you do, & I see depths of kindness & dependableness in him which reveal themselves more the more you know him. Lizzie seems comforted about his health by this visit to Firlands in which she has tried to find out all she can . . . All our 3 [children] are *amusingly* devoted to him.'[64]

Fanny and William Hill-James were married at Hope church on 21 July 1881. At the end of October, Fanny was packing for a trip to Australia to meet her new brother-in-law. Johnny's opinion of Willie as a hypochondriac abated little over the years. In November 1885, he was affronted that Fanny could not receive him because Willie was unwell. When he did gain access, he found 'Willie covered with a white cloth as if he was going to take a swarm of bees – just crawling across the room.'[65] As a result, the Hill-Jameses spent from late November until May every year from 1888 at the Hotel des Princes, Biarritz, enjoying sea views and 'la cuisine la plus renommée de la station'.[66]

After the wedding, Johnny was hit with ill health and took himself to 'Hampton House', Droitwich Spa, for a series of treatments at the salt baths.[67] In between water drinking and swimming, he made trips to Malvern Wells and to Croome, home of the Earl of Coventry, while Lucy stayed at home and attended prize-giving at Bodenham School. She wrote to Johnny at the end of August that the children were all well, 'but disappointed that Papa is still away'.[68]

Taking the hint, the following month Johnny was at home prior to Jack's departure for prep school at Walton Lodge, Clevedon, near Weston-super-Mare. Jack was bright, but in May 1880 had 'contrived to get fast in the Gunroom'. To get the inquisitive 7-year-old out, the entire door had to be taken down.[69] He was slightly delicate but a keen gardener, with his own patches of kitchen and flower garden. The reflected warmth of the walled gardens at Hampton Court baked in Jack a lifelong passion for horticulture.[70]

In autumn 1881, Jack exchanged his sisters' company for the rigours of the prep-school dormitory. Johnny fidgeted and longed for news from his boy, but Jack's letter-writing was no better than Johnny's had been at school. He fretted to Lucy in July 1882: 'Jack has not written to me. I shall cut him off with a shilling.'[71] Pink and Wee were devoted correspondents, the ruled pencil lines of their letters keeping their handwriting even.

Johnny's choice of Walton had been carefully made. Among the other boys at the school were Richard Chester-Master, eldest son of Johnny's old friend from Cirencester, who owned the nearby Knole estate near Bristol,[72] and Gerald Parker, son of Johnny's friend Cecil, who sat on the RASE Council with him and was agent to the Duke of Westminster.[73] Johnny further hoped that Clevedon's sea air would be health-giving, but despite his visits to take Jack out for a good feed, the boy was frequently brought home to recover 'from school's plague'.[74]

On 4 March 1885, Jack went to Eton to sit the entrance examination. He wrote to his father from E.C. Austen Leigh's house, that Aunt Di,

Uncle Henry, Miss Peel, Sir Michael Hicks-Beach (Chancellor of the Exchequer and fascinating to the politically aware Jack) and several children accompanied him.

> Uncle Henry introduced me to Sir Michael H-B & Aunt Di declared she saw me blush, but I really cannot believe it!! . . . Howard won the history prize; I made the fatal mistake of writing 2 pages instead of 6 lines on the origin of the American War & so had not much time for 3 other questions; we only had an hour, so I have to console myself by thinking that I lost by knowing too much!!![75]

Jack missed his garden at home and Lucy dispatched primroses, violets and Lily of the Valley. More importantly, she responded to cries like that of 5 November 1882. 'I have really been rather hungry these last few days!!! I hope you will take my *hint* as you are in London (a city of bakers, and pastry cooks, and American apple sellers).'[76] Lucy was in London for the birth of their last child. It had not been a painless pregnancy. In September, while Johnny was shooting at Flikity, Inverness, her back was so bad that she thought she would 'have to take to the wheel-chair'.[77]

Johnny, too, soon had back pain. Out hunting on 3 October, he took a heavy fall and crushed his chest and rib cage.[78] This gave great cause for concern, especially as Willie Arkwright of Sutton had nearly killed himself in a similar fall a few years earlier. Between interviewing butlers and sorting out Lowndes Street for the confinement, Johnny reported to Lucy:

> Barton has just been here. He says I must be bound up with many yards of flannel or a straight waistcoat & have teetotal rest . . . He says that we shall have to watch the rigours of the heart which as I have often told you, beats for you alone . . . My dear old gal, when we think how easily it might be that this time of probation might never have been given me we may well be thankful – so don't cry![79]

The worry about Johnny was eclipsed when another baby girl was safely delivered at 1 Lowndes Street on 25 November – all three girls had birthdays within ten days of one another. The new babe was named Olive Katharine Mary, Olive most likely for her black button eyes which took Johnny straight back to Algeria.[80] She made good progress and was considered 'strong & forward'.[81] Lucy and Olive returned home in mid-December; Johnny was delighted to have another baby. He had been as proudly observant of Pink's progress as he had been of Jack's, writing to Lucy in May 1876: 'Gill has just cut a tooth on the lower jaw and looks beautiful.'[82] Now that Pink and Wee were lost to the schoolroom, here was another babe to play with. In July 1888, while Lucy was away, she knew that Olive would be indulged. 'I am afraid I shall have very black looks from your spoilt child when I come but she must try & endure me!'[83]

When Olive was born in 1882, Pink had just turned 7, and Wee 6. Despite Lucy's reading of Ruskin, the girls would not be going to one of the new schools. Since a governess was already engaged for Jack, they would be tutored at home in the traditional way. At the back of Johnny's mind, too, was the trigger given as the cause of Emily's illness – 'overwork in the school room'.

Initially, for Jack, a governess known simply as Mademoiselle had been brought to Hampton Court. She went on to Arthur and Agnes's children at The Mount, Oswestry, and in July 1883, returned home to Boudry in Switzerland. Next, Miss Emmeline G. Simpson – always known with affection as Simmie – arrived at Hampton Court. She was a great favourite during her five influential years, and seems to have been treated with all the respect that Ruskin advocated for governesses. In 1888, when Simmie returned after the holidays, she was engaged to be married, which excited the girls, but meant that she left them, becoming Mrs Dwyer and emigrating to New York, to be succeeded by Miss Marshall.[84]

The structure of the girls' academic year emulated that of Jack's so that the children's holidays coincided. In July 1890, Evelyn told her father that they 'played cricket in the schoolroom passage this morning – Jack & Olive against Geraldine & I. We got 15. They got 13.'[85] Naturally enough, the return to lessons was never popular, as Lucy told Johnny in August 1885. 'Pink & Wee are rather depressed at the thought of "Simmy" today & regular lessons again.'[86] Olive, meanwhile, was being nursed, as had been the others, by Pascoe.

The school room at Hampton Court was recommissioned for Jack and the girls. Judging by Pinkie's observation to Jack of January 1887 that 'Father has bought a new bird for the schoolroom', it was a stimulating environment, packed with artefacts brought back by members of the family from distant parts of the world.[87] In 1887, Johnny reported to his wife that 'The kids are quite well and stick to their lessons like Britons.'[88]

While their parents were away during term, the girls remained at home and at lessons, but during their holidays they often visited relations either alone or with their parents. In August 1883, when Johnny was in Scotland, the children went to The Mount to Arthur and Agnes, and then to Byford, to Berkeley and Carey, with their mother.[89] In December that year, Lucy was at home, while Johnny was in Perth, and Pink and Wee were again at The Mount.[90] Often the tables were turned, and Hampton Court was overrun with some of their twenty-five first cousins. Over at Bodenham were eight girls and four boys from Henry Arkwright's two marriages, who though second cousins, were close to the family at Hampton Court.[91]

Jack's holidays were keenly anticipated. In April 1882, Lucy wrote to Johnny: 'The excitement about Jack's arrival is becoming intense! Pink & Wee are wild about it.'[92] He returned with tales of tricks, friends, masters and routines that were full of wonder for his little sisters. When left in charge, Johnny and Lucy went to great lengths to amuse their offspring. Children of the post-Alice generation were no longer considered small adults, but had a world of their own. Johnny was far more likely to read his children a fairy story of an evening than a chapter from the Bible, as his own father had done. Toys began to come on to the market that took the new status of children into account. Jack requested soldiers at Clevedon,[93] and Pink and Wee would have been caught up in the magic of fairyland which swept the country in 1882. Doubtless Alfred Bye, the head gardener at Hampton Court, teased the girls about fairies in the fernery. In 1884, the Hampton Court nursery was being decorated with 'Kate Greenaway paper' for Olive.[94]

The same year, the family went to Aberystwyth and stayed at 61 Marine Terrace, near the bandstand. Johnny joined them, and then Simmie, when lessons resumed. On 24 September, they visited nearby Borth, where the sandy beach was safer for swimming. Lucy told Johnny: 'It was a lovely day & the children enjoyed themselves, but it is a deadly looking place.'[95] Within the month, Jack was back at Clevedon, but by 1 December he was poorly and Johnny was again tearing down to see him.[96]

TEN

Sized up, Seized up and Silenced

Despite the warmth and protection of the family circle, Olive was born at a time when the climate for agriculture was cooling again. Landlordism was coming under state-legislated attack in Ireland. Successive Land Acts were passed by the Liberals in 1870, 1881 and 1891 to establish fair rents, and to encourage tenants to purchase their own farms with government-provided subsidies, in the hope of lessening the antagonism between landlord and tenant. Back in England, anti-landlordism, which had flared up in the 1840s under the leadership of Cobden and Bright, was renewed. In 1876, a government survey of landownership in Britain had been published for the first time, earning itself the nickname of 'New Domesday'.[1] It was reworked by John Bateman into an alphabetical list of every landowner who held over 3,000 acres, provided that the rental income from those acres was at least £3,000, and published under the title *The Acreocracy of England*.[2]

It revealed for the first time to public scrutiny the astonishing extent of ownership by some individuals, and of their 'unearned' income. Some of the national statistics were staggering: a quarter of the land in England and Wales was owned by 710 people; 75 per cent of the British Isles was in the hands of fewer than 5,000 people.[3] The research revealed Johnny to be in the top 363 people who owned 10,000 or more acres in England – of which exactly half were peers.[4] Many landowners felt exposed by the findings. Joseph Yates noted that 'In the "New Domesday Book", JHA Hampton Court Leominster has 10,559 acres and £14,972 rent.'[5]

This figure put Johnny at the top of the landowning league in Herefordshire. Beneath him, in order, came Andrew Rouse-Boughton-Knight of Downton, who had 10,348 acres in the county, Robert Harley of Brampton Bryan with 9,901 acres (both in the north of the county near the seat of the Labourers' Union at Leintwardine), Lord Bateman of Shobdon Court 7,200 acres, Rev. Sir George Cornewall of Moccas 6,946 acres, and Earl Somers of Eastnor Castle with 6,668 acres of Herefordshire. Only

Johnny's acres were entirely in Herefordshire, the rest having additional land elsewhere.[6] Although there were few immediate results of the findings, the landowners' feelings of being sized up were novel and unwelcome. Their unease was not helped, either, by the arrival of the men from the Ordnance Survey department in 1883, who wished to map out every hedge and bridge of the country. In April that year, Yates was showing the surveyors around Hope and Bodenham, pointing out the estate's boundaries.[7]

Any mood of defensiveness was not helped by a renewed slide in wheat prices in 1883 which followed a brief levelling out in 1881 and 1882. The wheat-growing east of England had been particularly hard hit from the very beginning of the depression. Where Herefordshire could ride out the 1870s on the backs of its cattle and sheep, Essex had courted the king of crops and suffered when the revolution came. Mark Hall had experienced a storming of its own. Loftus Joseph Arkwright inherited at the age of 23 in 1889 when his invalid father died. Born in 1866, he had grown up with the uncertainty of modern farming, and was resigned to reality. Despite the love of hunting that he had inherited from his father Loftus and his grandfather Rev. Joseph Arkwright, Loftus sold off the kennels to Mr C.E. Green, a shipping magnate who was Master at the time.

Rev. Joseph's three unmarried daughters had continued to live at Mark Hall, and Loftus had been brought up at nearby Parndon Hall on the estate. Now, Loftus moved the three elderly ladies out and let the big house to Jonah Caldwell, an American merchant with a sugar plantation in Cuba. He let Parndon Hall to William Bradshaw, a solicitor, and moved into the farmhouse where he kept just one servant living in. Something of the old status would be restored when Loftus became joint Master of the Essex in 1892, but, like his father, he had a bad hunting fall and restricted himself to shooting thereafter.[8]

Shipping was certainly proving profitable at this time. From the mid-1880s, the improving technology of refrigerated holds meant that besides meat, butter, eggs and cheese could be imported, particularly from Denmark, reducing prices by 10 per cent or more.[9] Worse still, prices for mutton and beef that had reached a peak in the early 1880s began to imitate the price fall of wheat of the 1870s as imports of frozen meats began to climb.[10] With painful irony, the export of cattle like the Herefords to the Americas, that had helped Herefordshire through the 1870s depression, enabled producers there to improve quality. Overseas beef began to be imported into Britain, with corresponding effects on the price of the home-grown product. Between 1883 and 1895, the price of store cattle fell by one-third, as imports of beef rose by 50 per cent.[11]

By now, landowners could see that increased imports, whether of corn, beef or dairy products, would drive down home prices and bankrupt farmers. Many looked back on Peel's Corn Law repeal of 1846, which had removed the tax on imported corn, as the source of the present troubles. The landowning class began to demand the imposition of tariffs on foreign imports to protect the prices of their tenants' goods. In 1881, the National Fair Trade League was established to press the cause. In France and Germany, where farming populations still composed two-fifths of the national total, tariffs were indeed introduced.[12] In England, though, where urban populations had exploded in size, the agricultural interest was reduced to only one-tenth of the population.[13] Nine-tenths were glad of the difference that low food prices made to their disposable income, particularly during industrial depression. As the foremost industrialised nation in western Europe, Britain depended upon cheap food to keep its workers happy, and upon free markets into which to sell its manufactured goods. These interests were now more important to political parties seeking power than the protection of the livelihoods of country dwellers.[14]

In resisting the demand to protect her farmers, the British government was almost unique within Europe. Every other European country but Denmark and the Netherlands introduced tariffs. Bismarck imposed them in Germany in 1879; in 1885 German duties on grain were trebled, and they were increased again two years after that. France, Italy and Belgium introduced duties in 1887, and Switzerland followed suit in 1891.[15] The British government's refusal to heed the calls from the countryside was a 'momentous gamble', and surprising not just for its rarity within western Europe.[16] Hitherto, the landed class had ruled Britain, its scions had represented the country at Westminster and its interests had shaped British policy for centuries. The deaf ear that the government now turned to its concerns was indicative of what for Johnny's class was a sinister shift in the balance of power.

Landowners were just not as important as they had been. A gradual process of legislative change had been eroding their power and status within society over recent years. The reduction in the number of rural seats in the House of Commons meant that they could be outnumbered in votes on agricultural issues; there were plans to remove the county's administrative management from magistrates (chosen by the Lord Lieutenant) and place it in the hands of new county councils – in other words to supersede the 'rural house of Lords' with an elected body; the Land Acts in Ireland set implied precedents for change in Britain that would favour tenants' interests over landlords' as the 1880 Ground Game Act had already done; there was a gradual erosion of the power of positions like Lord Lieutenant and High Sheriff. The chronological collision of these factors in the 1880s with the financial difficulties of landowners, as illustrated in parish life – for example at Hampton Court with subscriptions for the repairs to Hope church – rendered landowners unable any longer to control county life to the extent that they had done for centuries.

The 1883 spasm of agricultural crisis was felt more keenly than any yet at Hampton Court.[17] Daniel Brassington of The Woodhouse, who had been a conscientious rent payer throughout the 1870s, was added to the list of struggling tenants and was allowed 10 per cent of his rents in 1883 and 7½ per cent in 1884. Henry Medlicott of Bodenham Court too had 15 per cent throughout 1884 and 1885.[18] These percentages outstripped the 5 per cent for drainage or 2 per cent for building improvements that the tenants had been supposed to contribute towards the Lands Improvement debts. Johnny was paying all his tenants' share of the improvements and more. Yet by 1886, Johnny's income from rents had fallen to under £11,500.[19] Consequently, wages to all his labourers on the estate were reduced in 1886 by 1*s* a week for all those earning under 14*s* a week, and by 1*s* 6*d* for all those earning above 14*s* a week.[20] Meanwhile, the rain continued to fall (high rivers sweeping away Ludlow and Onibury railway bridges) and the prices that Johnny was making from the produce of his own in-hand farms continued to slide. The amounts due to the Lands Improvement Company, though, made no allowance for the downturn. It was a frightening, helpless feeling as a yawning gap opened between the amount to be paid and the income with which to pay. In October 1884, after the Michaelmas rent day, Johnny wrote to Lucy, on holiday with the children in Aberystwyth: 'I never was more anxious to see anybody than I am to clasp you to my heart.'[21]

It was becoming alarmingly evident that the situation was unsustainable. It was now clear that Johnny and his fellow improvers had overstretched their capital during the 1860s and 1870s. However, the improvers could not and would not accept that the investment had not been worth it. The feeling of farm-owners and improvers was expressed in the contemporary writings of Richard Jeffries.

> Even now . . . I feel convinced that my plan and my system will be a success. I can see that I committed one great mistake – I made all my improvements at once, laid out all my capital, and crippled myself. I should have . . . grown my improvements – one this year, one next. As

> it was, I denuded myself of capital. Had the times continued favourable it would not have mattered . . . But the times became adverse . . . In a year or two I am convinced we shall flourish again; . . . – a depression is certain to be followed by a rise. That has been the history of trade and agriculture for generations. Nothing will ever convince me that it was intended for English agriculturists to go on using wooden ploughs, to wear smock-frocks, and plod round and round in the same old track for ever. In no other way but by science, by steam, by machinery, by artificial manure, and in one word, by the exercise of intelligence, can we compete with the world. It is ridiculous to suppose we can do so by returning to the ignorance and prejudice of our ancestors. No: we must beat the world by superior intelligence and superior energy.[22]

This sense was combined with the patrician instinct of landowners that if a man behaved honourably by his land, his stock, his tenant farmers, his labourers, his neighbours and his county responsibilities, if he stood his ground though it seem to rock uncontrollably beneath his feet, and if he fixed his eye with stoic resolve on a point in the future beyond the present troubles, all would, in time, come right. It had done before and it must do again. To give in and sell up was unthinkable. It would represent a betrayal of his ancestors and of his descendants. Although, morally, sale was not an option, legally it had become so. The influence of campaigners like Chandos Wren Hoskyns resulted in the passing of the Settled Land Act in 1882, enabling landowners to break entail imposed upon their estates and sell part or all of them.[23] Few would do so, though, without an immense struggle with their conscience. They had to keep faith that all would come right. There were moments, though, when it was difficult to sustain the confidence innate in Johnny's breed.

Much of county society was unwilling to discuss its misfortunes openly, although the difficult times continued to make themselves evident in subtle ways. In 1882 it was Hereford's year to host the Three Choirs Festival, the charitable festival that often struggled to make money in Hereford. The cathedral's capacity was less than at Worcester and Gloucester, owing to the collapse of the west end in 1786 and its only partial reconstruction. Given the agricultural climate, 1882 was going to be difficult. Johnny had, since 1864, been Hereford's Chairman of the Executive Committee. The city's decorations in 1882 included Venetian barber-painted poles through High Town – a comment, no doubt, on the appalling weather of Hereford's previous festival in 1879. But in 1882 Venetian gaiety masked a financially disastrous festival. Big losses were made and half of the 300 stewards who were supposed to contribute £5 to a guarantee fund refused to pay their share.[24]

Despite the struggle with their conscience, some Herefordshire landowners attempted to sell outlying acres. Johnny's neighbour Lord Rodney at Berrington, and Sir Geers Cotterell at Garnons tried unsuccessfully to dispose of small parts of their estates.[25] Lord Bateman at Shobdon had begun to piece together mortgages to enable him to remain at the Court.[26] The situation at Foxley was also grave and the entire estate seems to have been a possible candidate for sale in July 1884. Such a matter would never have been mentioned overtly in a letter for fear of falling into the wrong hands, so Johnny wrote cryptically to Lucy in July 1884: 'I heard from Sophy about Foxley. I believe you know as much as she told me.'[27] On 19 July, Lucy wrote to Johnny at Droitwich that she had heard from Di that Baroness Burdett Coutts was after Foxley.[28] Rumours of a similar kind raced through society, but the truth of the situation was that there were few buyers at such a time. Land values were driven down – farms which in the mid-1870s would have reached £54 an acre were, by the mid-1890s, fetching just £19 per acre.[29] More generally, the capital value of land in Britain between 1878 and 1890 fell by between one-sixth and a half.[30]

The scene in Herefordshire was familiar all over the country. Society was reluctant to talk about it, but the generality of the situation began to become ominously clear as word spread of families encountering difficulties. By the end of 1883, the problems were hitting even the fount of the Arkwrights' wealth, Willersley. Fred Arkwright married Rebecca Alleyne on 7 November that year, and in mid-December, Lucy wrote to Johnny: 'Katie [Arkwright of Bodenham] told me Fred is reducing expenses at Willersley, & has doubts about being able to marry & keep up an establishment without Susie [his mother]'s share in the expenses – I was rather surprised as I thought he was really comfortably off.'[31] In these last-expressed feelings Lucy might have been speaking for wives all over the country. With horror, the élite discovered that even apparently unassailable landowners were being hard hit. The awful truth began to become clear with a terrifying inevitability similar to that with which Sylvain Couttet had heard 'a crack . . . above us a little to the right' on Mont Blanc in 1866.[32] The avalanche was coming.

As the value of landowners' capital, the acres that they owned, began to slide, the banks from whom they had borrowed to make improvements, or to invest in stock and equipment, became nervous. Bank managers began to reassess loans and to demand the reduction of their exposure to the risk of bankruptcy. In order for landowners to find the money to pay back the amounts demanded by the banks, the sale of private household possessions was usually resorted to before the sale of acres (particularly when the price for land was low). There was no point in reducing one's land holding if things were going to pick up in a few seasons' time. All over the country, the barely perceptible but unmistakeable sound of picture chains chinking against walls made itself heard as paintings were taken down and transported to London for sale. In 1875 and 1878, the Munros of Novar had seen their collection of Turners and old masters go under the hammer for £100,000. The Duke of Hamilton cleared Hamilton Palace of its contents in July 1882. Many of Blenheim's treasures were turned out by the Duke of Marlborough: first the gems in 1875, next the enamels and old master drawings in 1883, and in 1886 a spectacular collection of paintings including works by Van Dyck, Rembrandt, Rubens, Breughel, Holbein, Kneller and Lely.[33]

In the same spirit, Johnny Arkwright, having cleared out his wine cellar, was in London on 6 November 1885, trying to sell his precious best Stradivarius violin for 250 guineas,[34] to someone to whom he referred as 'Baking Powder'.[35] This glorious instrument, itself a work of art, had been exhibited at the Historic Musical Instruments exhibition in South Kensington in 1872 and again at the International Inventions Exhibition earlier in 1885 at the Royal Albert Hall.[36] With a flood of best-quality items coming on to the market, the realisable prices were not of the highest order. The instrument was finally sold to the Hon. Odeyne de Grey in April 1886. The 'agony of parting with the loved one' as Johnny expressed it, was further inflamed when he spoke, seven years later, to a 'fiddle maker' in London who 'knows my Strad sold to Miss de Grey & says it is now worth £500. She had a bargain.'[37]

Cutbacks were under way in the garden. Johnny consulted with head gardener Alfred Bye.[38] 'He says the second stove has a separate fire, so we *can* do away with that & let it be only a greenhouse. I shd like to do this – & I shd also like to try & sell our bedding out plants, & turf up the bed round the pond & in the grass & leading up to conservatory – & either sow the horse shoes with annuals, or keep enough bedding plants to plant those beds.'[39]

There were other indications of the troubles. In 1886, the committee overseeing the restoration of Leominster's priory by Sir George Gilbert Scott was chasing payment of pledges. Its secretary, Rev. Augustin Edouart, wrote to Johnny on 6 December 1886 to remind him that he still owed £100 out of a total of £1,000 offered by him in October 1885. Edouart added that the committee was having to chase £600 worth of outstanding donations.[40] Symbolically, in June 1886, one of the pinnacles on the tower of Hereford Cathedral was struck by lightning.[41] In January 1885, Edwyn wrote to Johnny that there had not been a soul out in Algiers over the winter and many of the hotels were facing ruin.[42]

Nearer to home, when funds were needed to carry out work to another of Johnny's responsibilities, the Coningsby Hospital in Hereford,[43] a bazaar was again held to raise money.[44] Most telling of all, 1885 saw the unwilling reduction of the Hereford herd at Hampton Court. Johnny needed cash, and there was a good deal of it grazing the meadows at Green Farm if 1884 prices were anything to go by. August that year had seen another remarkable sale. American demand had been at its height for the dispersal of the late Mr T.J. Carwardine's Stocktonbury herd. The prize bull, Lord Wilton, was knocked down for a staggering 3,800 guineas, but the sale was never completed. Other bulls, Lord Grosvenor and General Gordon, made 650 and 750 guineas respectively.[45] Unfortunately for Johnny, by the time that he sold in 1885, the prices paid for pedigree Herefords were the lowest that they had been for some time and crucially there was a lull in foreign trade. The average price paid per beast for the 135 sold was a disappointing £31 and the highest price of the day was only 110 guineas for the bull Hampton Wilton.[46] With his ill-timed sales of the Stradivarius and the Herefords, Johnny was beginning to appear as unfortunate in his financial dealings as his grandfather, Sir Hungerford, had been before him.

The reduction in the economic importance of the shires and their landowners was driven home by the Liberal government's Third Reform Act of 1884 and the Redistribution of Seats Act of the following year. The 1884 Act ironed out the inequality of the franchise between urban and rural constituencies as borough privileges were extended to the counties, but what it gave to the labourers, it took from the landowning interest. Under the 1885 Act, the old Herefordshire county seats at Parliament were reduced in number from three to two when the county was split into the North (Leominster) Division and the South (Ross) Division. Significantly, the old borough seat of Leominster was lost as it merged with the county. Hereford City's representation was halved as its two MPs were reduced to just one under the same legislation.

Where Herefordshire had, before 1832, sent up eight Members, the entire county's representation was reduced now to just three men.[47] The old gentleman's agreement of sending one man of each persuasion up to Westminster was no longer an option. The scarcity of seats made them more valuable, and the competition to win them more intense, more professional and more expensive. However, any bias towards the wealthy in being able to spend more to ensure victory had already been removed by the 1883 Corrupt Practices Act which had limited the amount that could be spent on elections.[48] To compound the dismay of Johnny's kind in the face of these changes, at the election that followed in November 1885, all three of Herefordshire's seats went to Liberals.[49]

It appeared initially that in the labourers' first general election, the Conservatives had not done too badly nationwide, until the county results came in and, as in Herefordshire, unexpectedly produced a rout for the party. Of the 377 seats in the counties, the Conservatives' traditional heartland, the Tories won only 119. The agricultural labourer had overwhelmingly turned from his aristocratic betters. In the north-west Norfolk constituency, National Agricultural Labourers' Union leader Joseph Arch was returned as the Member of Parliament, having beaten no less a candidate than Lord Bentinck at the poll. Arch was now effectively the Prince of Wales's MP, since Bertie's Sandringham home was in the constituency. Sponsored by Joseph Chamberlain and Jesse Collings, Arch went to take his parliamentary oath in January 1886.[50] His brown tweed suit, seen among the frock coats, illustrated eloquently the changing order. Johnny was in the extraordinary position of seeing his hedge-layer of twenty-five years before attain the position that Johnny himself had turned down as being a fruit too high for him, as a youth.

The 1885 election produced the first influx of non-landowners into Parliament.[51] The broad-acred class could no longer count on support in the lower House at Westminster – they now constituted under a third of the Members in the Commons for the first time in Parliament's history.[52] For struggling landowners trying to pressurise some government action on tariff protection for agricultural goods, it was a depressing picture. The order of the country over which Johnny and his kind had held sway for 900 years was changing, both nationally and locally, beyond recognition. It was now that the Quarter Sessions, by which the county patricians dispensed justice, administered road and bridge building, oversaw school boards, and provided gaols and asylums, was attacked. Magistrates were increasingly being recruited from the middle classes, and it was an uncomfortable anomaly that the enfranchised labourers should not also be able to elect those who governed them at local level.

The Liberal government ran short of parliamentary time in which to introduce the Bill to bring reform at county level. It therefore fell, ironically, to the Conservative government to introduce the measures in 1888. County Councils would henceforth be elected, but aldermen could also be co-opted on to the Council, so that in practice influential landowners continued to have a hand in the running of county affairs. Many, though, could see where this would lead. Lord Powis, in neighbouring Shropshire, was of the opinion that although at present the landowner still had a strong hand, in time it would be 'the farmer and shopkeeper or tradesman, who will gradually elbow out the gentry'.[53] The Earl was right. Joseph Chamberlain recognised 'a peaceful revolution in the administration of our counties . . . second in importance only to the extension of the franchise'.[54] As the budget and workload of the County Councils increased, it was the sub-committees and full-time employees who undertook the tasks of investigating matters in detail and accordingly influenced them. The professionalism of the councils had to grow alongside their accountability, and this rendered amateurism, however well intentioned, obsolete.

At almost every stage, the milestones that had delineated life in the country for centuries, had altered. Landlords could no longer act with autonomy within their estate. The tentacles of government bureaucracy had now reached into the heart of their domain. From censuses of population and agriculture, via legislation such as the Ground Game Act, through to the New Domesday of 1876 and the Ordnance Survey of Britain of 1883, their acres had been invaded, evaluated and publicly scrutinised, and their power, influence and status eroded. At precisely the same moment that these changes had been taking place, the source of their wealth, agriculture, had suffered a crippling depression at the moment when many had large debts. The result was that land was becoming uncoupled from wealth and power in Britain.

Furthermore, the size of the world had shrunk, thanks to developments in the telegraph, shipping, canal-building and railways. Where once individual landholdings and their owners had wielded great influence within the nation, the scale had now altogether shifted to one of the nation states on the world stage. Leaders of government and those with fortunes approaching that of the Exchequer, made in mining, shipping, newspapers, or the manufacture of soap or beer, were the new equivalents of the old landowners in the global nation. The momentum of the change was unstoppable; its pace was breathtaking, and it left those that it affected most, the landowners, bewildered, betrayed, frustrated and angry.

ELEVEN

Arkwrights Act

There was a spark of hope for Johnny in an Act that was passed by the Lords in 1885. The Ramsden Estate Act rescheduled the debts of an individual to prevent him from declaring bankrupt. Early in 1886, Johnny asked his solicitor, W.T. Sale (the son of his father's solicitor) to ascertain whether such an Act might shift the debts incurred for improvements to the estate from his own account to that of the Hampton Court Estate Trust. He also wanted to borrow £50,000 against the value of the estate, and to have the debt that he owed the estate trustees for the purchase of the estate's stock and equipment after his father's death, written off.[1]

To draft the bill, Sale needed to establish the total spent by Johnny on estate improvements since he inherited, the acreage in hand and let, and Johnny's income from rental. Also required were the details of Johnny's personal and estate debts. The information dated back nearly thirty years, and it was a monumental task. Johnny and Sale were fortunate that Edward Colley, although 71 years old, still presided at the estate office, seconded by the equally dedicated Joseph Yates. Thanks to their experience and knowledge of the estate and accounts, the information was available by autumn 1886. Sale drafted the document and it was passed to Lincoln's Inn Counsel, George B. Rashleigh, for his opinion.[2]

In the petition,[3] Sale stated the peculiar nature of Johnny's inheritance, and the immediate debt bequeathed to him. It was asserted that when Johnny inherited, several of the recently acquired portions of the estate were in poor repair, and Johnny had been obliged to honour promises of improvements made by his father. John Arkwright had imagined that £2,000 per annum would cover the costs of repairs to the estate properties. However, since 1858, rather than a total of £56,000, Johnny had expended £129,843 on the estate, of which £16,000 was still due to the Lands Improvement Company. This work had produced, stated the report, 'one of the best-managed estates in Herefordshire'. Furthermore, it was claimed, 'Mr Arkwright's position has been caused entirely by his earnest desire to do justice to his tenants & to his estate, & it is beyond question that the whole of the money has been spent judiciously and in the true interest of the property.'

Sale also detailed Johnny's position. On his father's death, Johnny had personally met 'heavy claims for succession duty'. Then, in 1866, he had bought a new property to add to the estate, which had required him to take out mortgages to the value of £6,000 and £4,000. He had met his mother's annuity of £4,000 per year, and on her death had found £30,000 for his brothers.[4] Johnny's principal income was from the estate's farm rentals, but with the current state of agriculture, it was likely that further rent reductions would have to be made. Also, he had five of the estate's farms in hand, a total of 1,300 acres, in addition to the 800-acre Home Farm.

In sum, Johnny's total liabilities, including £50,000 due to the Scottish Equitable Life Assurance Society for the mortgage of his life interest and policies, £16,487 due to the Lands Improvement Company, £15,000 on his overdraft account, £25,078 due to the trustees of the estate, £5,000 outstanding to tradesmen, £5,000 owed to his brother Arthur and £1,000 to his sister Fanny, and £3,000 interest arrears, amounted to £122,565, with annual interest on this of £7,247.

Johnny's cash flow was demonstrably unhealthy. Annual income included £11,426 in rental, and £2,100 interest on £62,841 worth of investments, making a total of £13,526. His outgoings were the interest payments on his loans at £7,247, plus £3,476 rental of the house and lands in hand, totalling £10,723. This left him a disposable income of £2,803 per year. By his own reckoning, in 1886, his private expenditure was £4,050.[5] It was noted that

> Mr Arkwright has no Town House, & in fact no luxuries which gentlemen in his position generally consider as necessaries. The establishment at Hampton Court is as small as possible, & there have not been more than 4 horses in the stables for years & it can truly be said that Mr Arkwright has exercised the greatest unselfishness & self-sacrifice for years past for the benefit of his successors in the estate. [Nevertheless] Mr Arkwright is most seriously embarrassed.

Rashleigh delivered his opinion on 8 December 1886.[6] He asked that the petitioners give a fuller account of the fall in rents and the difficulty of finding tenants since 1858. He reinforced the points made, and added: 'I am instructed in conference that Mr Arkwright is the owner of curious manuscripts, china & other valuable articles said to be worth such sum as

1. Hampton Court, Herefordshire, north front, *c.* 1880. The fifteenth-century house was substantially altered by John Arkwright in the 1830s–40s, changes he later regretted.

2. Johnny's twenty-first birthday celebrations, 2–4 August 1854, included archery, and lunches in the Leominster and Hereford Horticultural Societies' marquees.

3. Willersley Castle, Cromford, Derbyshire, the house that Sir Richard Arkwright had built in the 1780s–90s, and John Arkwright's home before settling in Herefordshire.

4. John Arkwright (1785–1858), Johnny's father, and grandson of Sir Richard Arkwright, the first of the family to move to Herefordshire in around 1814.

5. Johnny's elder sister Caroline married Berkeley Scudamore Stanhope on 27 January 1858, exactly a month before John's death.

6. Johnny in the bachelor days after his father's death – a young man of £10,000 a year, and highly popular.

7. Edward Colley, the agent of the Hampton Court estate from the 1830s until 1888.

8. Bonham Caldwall, a trustee of the estate, and to Johnny 'the gingerbread and barley-sugar man of my childhood'.

9. Johnny's uncle Chandos Wren Hoskyns, a leading agricultural writer and major influence on Johnny's improvements to the estate.

10. Johnny with his violin at Aix-la-Chapelle in 1863, before returning home to found the Herefordshire Philharmonic Society, which premiered some of Elgar's works.

11. Johnny and the Three Graces – Fanny (standing), Emily (right) and Alice – with Charlie, outside the conservatory designed by Sir Joseph Paxton.

12. Sarah Arkwright, 'Tally', Johnny's mother, who wrote to him: 'Whenever I have had your *presence* the sorrows of widowhood have been disguised to me.'

13. The Herefordshire Hunt's opening meet at Hampton Court in 1866 or 1867. Johnny on his grey, with Sir Velters Cornewall, his co-MFH and best man, to the left.

14. Johnny's third brother, Henry, a crack bowler, who captained the Harrow side to victory over Eton at Lord's in 1857. He was to die on Mont Blanc nine years later.

15. Lucy and puppy Greta, *c.* 1869. Johnny's envy of Lucy's devotion to Greta led her to begin her letters to him 'My own house dog . . .'.

16. Johnny's nearest brother in age, Richard, a lawyer and MP for Leominster, at his home, Winkfield Cottage, Berkshire.

Opposite: 17. Johnny and young Jack in the gardens at Hampton Court. Johnny, contrary to the Victorian stereotype, was a devoted father to all four of his children.

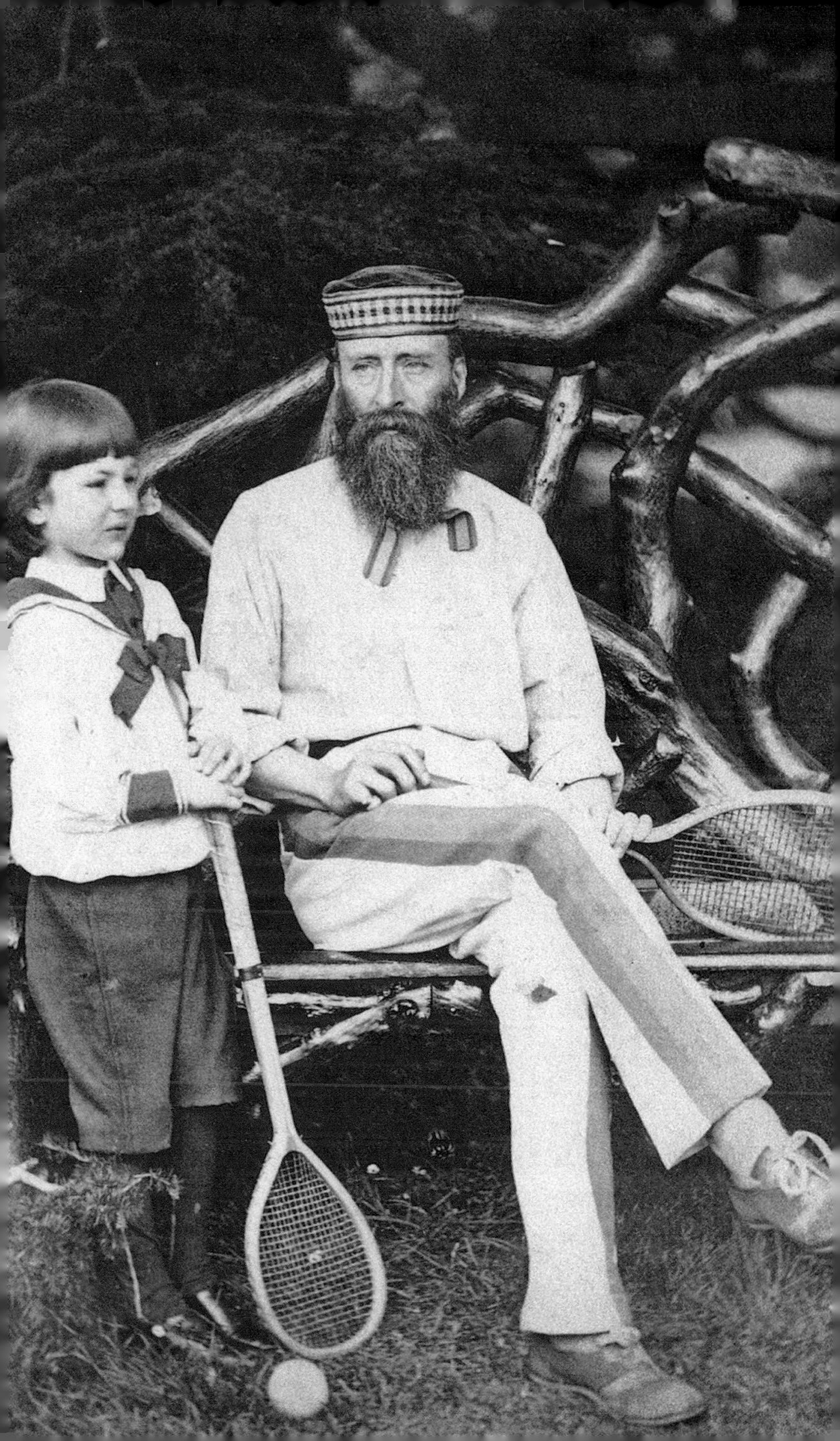

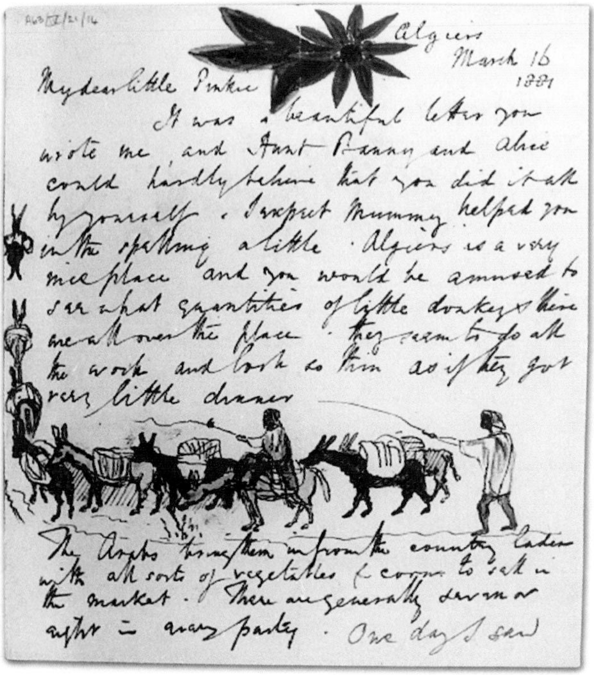

A63/III/21/14

Algiers
March 16
1881

My dear little Pinkie

It was a beautiful letter you wrote me, and Aunt Fanny and Alice could hardly believe that you did it all by yourself. I expect Mummy helped you in the spelling a little. Algiers is a very nice place and you would be amused to see what quantities of little donkeys there are all over the place. They seem to do all the work and look so thin as if they got very little dinner

The Arabs bring them in from the country laden with all sorts of vegetables & corn to sell in the market. There are generally seven or eight in every party. One day I saw

18. Johnny's splendidly illustrated letter to Geraldine (Pinkie) from Algeria in 1881. Edwyn and Alice lived there until their deaths in the early twentieth century.

19. Johnny (centre, holding Spring Jack) and Robert Eckley, his bailiff (right), with three prize-winning Hereford bulls – his 'ruby moos'.

The "Maidstone Fruit Trays."

"ARKWRIGHT" PATENT.

MADE IN ENGLAND.

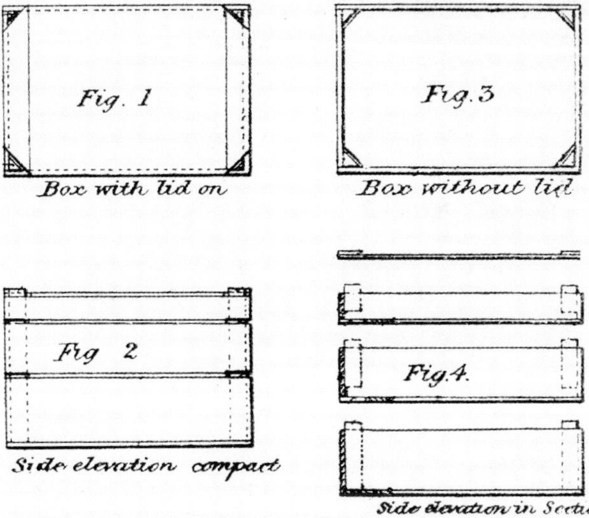

These Fruit Trays are designed to meet a very general demand for some sim; and safe receptacle for the delivery of fruit of a high class in first-rate conditio

They are made of varying depths for the careful packing and transit of F and Vegetables of all sizes.

Support is given to each by *inside* angle blocks, and it will be seen that a shock is equally received by all four angles.

Any number of trays may be fitted upon each other, forming one solid packa tightly corded round by hitches till the end of the cord receives its final hitch, a is sealed, if desired, by the sender.

It will prove invaluable to exhibitors of cut flowers or fruit, to families wh in London or on the moors, and to tradesmen for various specialités.

This invention, which is patented in Great Britain and abroad, claims the following advantages :—

1. No nailing is required.
2. No knots or waste of cordage.
3. The lid is reversible for "Return Empty."
4. They can be made of any size or materials as future experience may decide.
5. They are simple, light, strong, and cheap in the long run.
6. They are made in England.
7. They will be a good investment for those who live in towns and have no garden of their own to forward to friends in the country for "Return Full."

At present they are made in five depths, and half-size for the two shallowest trays.

PRICE 10/6 FOR FIVE TRAYS COMPLETE.

Separate Trays by the dozen at comparative prices.

MR. T. CLARE.

Hampton Court Works, LEOMINSTER, HEREFORDSHIRE.

20. An advertisement for the fruit trays which Johnny invented, and whose design is still familiar today.

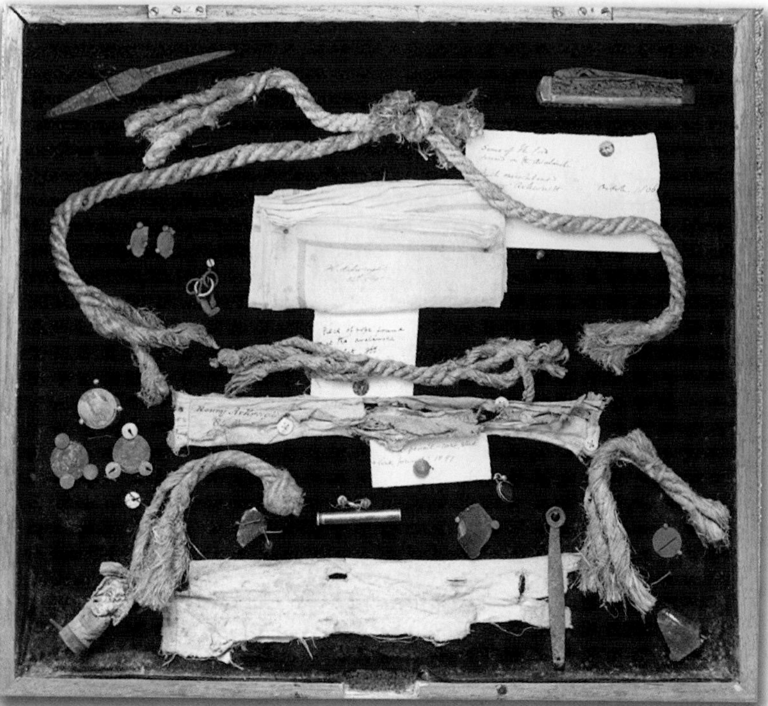

21. The case of treasures – articles found with Henry's body in the glacier on Mont Blanc in 1897, including the named collar and handkerchief by which he was identified.

22. Hampton Court, south front, around the turn of the twentieth century showing Paxton's original conservatory roof (far left) and the chapel (far right).

23. John Stanhope Arkwright, Jack (1872–1954), as Conservative/Unionist MP for Hereford City (1901–12) during the turbulent Edwardian years.

24. Richard Chester-Master (back right), ADC to Sir Alfred Milner at Government House, Cape Town, in the run-up to the Boer War.

Above: 25. Geraldine married Richard Chester-Master (13 August 1901) after he returned a hero from the Boer War. She went with him to Bulawayo shortly afterwards.

Left: 26. Johnny as Lord Lieutenant (1901–4). 'Herefordshire,' sneered the *Daily Express*, 'has to put up with a commoner as its Lord Lieutenant.'

Opposite, top: 27. Sutton Scarsdale, Derbyshire, *c.* 1902, the home of Johnny's cousin, William Arkwright, was another of the estates bought by Johnny's grandfather.

Opposite, below: 28. Sutton Scarsdale, *c.* 1998 after it had lost its roof, interior and garden statuary. Today, an English Heritage property, it overlooks the M1 between junctions 29 and 30.

29. Tally's home, Harewood, being blown up by the Royal Monmouth Royal Engineers as explosives practice on 22 March 1959.

30. Mark Hall, Essex, home of John's brother Rev. Joseph Arkwright, which has disappeared under Harlow new town.

£50,000. I think a valuation should be made of this property. Parliament may be induced to settle more on him because of the ready convertability of this capital to money.' Finally, Rashleigh insisted that the precedent of the Ramsden Estate Act be followed closely.

Sale implemented Rashleigh's recommendations. It was not going to be possible to keep the state of affairs private for much longer. Among the first to learn of Johnny's position would be Lucy's trustees. The jointure made to Lucy on marriage entitled her to £1,500 per year for life payable by the estate if Johnny predeceased her. If the Act went through, this claim would become secondary to that of Johnny's creditors. Lucy's trustees Harry Davenport, Henry Longley and Johnny's brother Arthur would have to approve the change in status.

On 1 March 1887, Lucy wrote a breezy letter to Johnny up in London. The day had begun with a fog so thick that 'We could not see the broad walk.'[7] Joseph Yates and Hemmings had come to Hampton Court to go through the silver plate kept at the bank. A 'Count Brazza' had arrived from Glanusk and would be put in the middle glasshouse or the conservatory until Johnny's return, and Jack had sprained his ankle at Fives. Almost as an aside, she added, 'Sale has sent me a copy of the petition to Parliament for the Act of P & asks my consent as a matter of form.'

Johnny replied the next day from the Carlton Club, 'We have a hideous fog & it is hard to breathe & smells of cheese & dead cats.'[8] The way that he continued demonstrated the extent to which the woman's position in society and within marriage was strengthening.

> I don't want you to look upon the 'Act' as a matter of form but to read it carefully with Arthur & Mimmie [Bateman-Hanbury at Shobdon]. Practically as affecting you it makes your settlement a second charge on the estate instead of the first as it now is for the purpose of borrowing the 50000 because people always choose a first charge as Trustees. With such a margin as we have it is really not inferior. This can be shown more easily to your Trustees than to strangers.

Johnny next wrote to Harry Davenport.

> I have calculated the cost, and find that it will pay me to go through with the proposed act *because* the alternative is an immediate collapse and a flight into unknown realms. If I get the Act I shall have an income just enough to keep up the place properly. I am told that there is no expense or responsibility

> for the Trustees beyond their consent to make Lucy's settlements a second instead of a first charge on the estate – and whereas the selling value of the estate would be about £420,000 and we want to borrow £50,000 on it there seems ample margin for any event.

He also told Harry that he had discussed the effects with Henry Longley.[9]

Arthur Arkwright communicated his assent to Harry Davenport. Harry and Henry Longley had had cause to speculate about Johnny's financial acumen in February 1878. Longley had written to Harry: 'I think the funds are all right now but it throws a suspicion on the soundness of JHA's mode of looking after his affairs to find that he is quite unconscious whether or not he has received the dividends on £15,000.'[10] It all smacked of Sir Hungerford's poor grasp of the finances at Harewood in the 1840s and 1850s.

The submission of the Act called for full details of all Johnny's siblings, their names, dates of birth, spouses and any children, in case there might be further demands on the estate. The dates and places of death of defunct trustees were also required and led to flurries of letter-writing. Johnny wrote to Lucy with shame and humiliation 'how astonished they will be who have not heard of my ways & means'.[11]

The earliest anticipated date for the presentation of the Bill to Parliament was mid-June 1887, and with the future of the estate depending on its outcome, the anxiety was intense. Either the worry made Johnny ill, or the humiliation made him unwilling to face friends in London, for in mid-June, Lucy went up to town alone. When the Bill was delayed, Johnny struggled with the impotence of waiting.

He wrote to Lucy under the shadow of the Act on 12 June:

> This is our wedding day and it is sad to be away from you. It is a much finer day than the original and except that age blunts one's senses sensibly I am happier than I ever was in your service than ever [*sic*].
>
> I am looking forward with anxiety which approaches the bounds of endurance for a finish to the little bill that some time or other I may know where I am & what I dare do for the future.[12]

He must have remembered writing to Lucy on the eve of their wedding: 'may you never repent with one sigh the treasures you give me in yourself'.[13]

The next day Lucy lunched with Lady Amory and dined with George and Lizzie's son Sidney. 'I am thinking so much of you & the "Bill" – it is such a worry for you my darling. I wish I cd tell you what I *feel* about it, but I think you know – bless you, you dear old thing.'[14] Again, on the 14th, she wrote:

> I am so puzzled to know what to do about coming home before this Bill business, or staying in or near London . . . I am waiting for a telegram from Dick who was to see Sale this morning to say if [*sic*] Sale considers that the Bill will really be about 27th . . . I am going to 8 Lowndes St for the Jubilee . . . I have just had a telegram from Dick to say we may be wanted the end of next week if not then the week after so I will decide not to go to Thoby [Priory, in Essex, now the home of Arthur and Agnes] this week but the Wedy in next week & there wait for the summons about the bill.[15]

The Jubilee of Queen Victoria's accession was one of several welcome distractions at this time. While in London, Lucy looked at rugs and kneelers for Hope church at Cox's in Southampton Street, and commissioned portraits of the children from artist Edward Tayler. She was delighted to see: 'On a little easel in the passage leading to the studio was a little picture of a child in a cap done from the photograph of Wee Wee.'[16] She also ordered balloons for the Jubilee celebrations from Whiteleys, who had sold out, like everywhere else. The big day for national celebrations dawned on 20 June, and it was also to be the occasion of the first large-scale distribution of honours. Lucy watched the procession from Henry Longley's Church Commissioner's offices in Whitehall, and wrote with a report to Johnny:

> Tuesday was a great success as you will have seen by the papers. I am very glad I saw it all, as it was well worth staying in London for & I did it so comfortably . . . Waiting in Henry's private room at the Office in cool & quiet, instead of in a stand or Club window like most people did, was a great luxury. I went out to see the illuminations on Monday & Tuesday nights . . . Did you see in the Times that Henry Longley is made 'CB'.[17]

Back at home, Johnny's celebrations had gone well, the three volleys of rockets set off at Hampton Court being seen 14 miles away.[18] With every rocket, Johnny must have offered up a prayer for Her Majesty's grant of the Act. In July, Johnny was able to report from the RASE Members' Reading Room at the Show Yard, Newcastle-upon-Tyne that Ivington Lass had come first at the Show.[19]

The Arkwright Estate Act finally came before Parliament on 23 August 1887. The facts were put plainly. First the terms of John Arkwright's will were stated, followed by information about each of John Arkwright's children. The necessity for improvements to the estate was explained, and the extent of Johnny's expenditure. 'The net income of the said John H. Arkwright has been reduced to a sum insufficient to enable him to continue to reside at Hampton Court aforesaid or to make proper provision for the said John Stanhope Arkwright.'[20]

The petition asked that the debt of £25,078 owed by Johnny to the trustees of the estate for the original stock and implements be released. It also asked that trust securities of £64,936 should be applied for, for the benefit of young Jack. A further policy of £15,000 should be vested in the trustees and 'kept on foot for the benefit of the inheritance'.

'Therefore Your Majesty's most dutiful and loyal subject the said John Hungerford Arkwright doth most humbly beseech Your Majesty that it may be enacted and be it enacted by the Queen's most Excellent Majesty by and with the advice and consent of the Lords Spiritual and Temporal and Commons in the present Parliament.' The Queen had evidently seen Hampton Court's distress flares, for Royal assent to the Arkwright Estate Act was granted with the words 'soit fait comme il est desiré'.

In granting the petition, the Act stipulated that Berkeley (who had just been made Archdeacon of Hereford Diocese), Bonham Caldwall and Johnny's brother Dick, the estate's trustees, should receive the rent, profits and annual produce of the Arkwright estate, oversee the discharge of outgoings connected with the estate's management, cover their own expenses in managing the estate, and pay and keep down interest on all charges and encumbrances affecting the inheritance. Until Jack was 21, an annual sum of up to £1,000 (or £500 if he died) was to be invested in shares or other securities, to maintain and educate Jack or any of Johnny's other children. From the age of 21, Jack was to receive £500 per annum quarterly for his lifetime, and up to £500 for any other of the children if necessary. After the above trusts and commitments had been paid out, the surplus of rents, profits and annual produce was to go to Johnny or to be used as he wished. In short, it established closer financial management of the estate than hitherto and separated the estate from Johnny's private accounts.[21]

Despite the relief, the conditions were a humiliation and Johnny would still have to cut back severely unless agriculture picked up. Economy was foreign to him, and frustrating, and the Jubilee did not see the only fireworks that summer. Alfred Bye was nearest to the house and caught the sharpest of his master's tongue. Johnny wrote to Lucy on 18 September:

> I told him that I must reduce work i.e. do less and do it better, & throw away his rotten worn out old ferns etc. etc. also that the apples & pears must be properly pinned. He broke out into a violent discourse of how I had for years been trying to drive him away – that I behaved as no man or gentleman would behave to a servant of 27 years! who had spent his life & spoiled his health in work. But he said that 'God Almighty' would take care of him when he was cast away by me.
>
> I stopped that briefly by telling him it was simply blasphemous to call on his gods on a matter of applepruning. Then I wrote saying that as he had expressed no sort of apology for this, I must sack him on Jan 1 1888. For this I got enclosed which is no apology especially as he did it once before & I let him off.[22]

Bye's apology said that for any

> Act or deed, in an unguarded moment, I have said to affect your position as a gentleman I humbly ask your pardon.
> I am, Sir, your obedient
> Servant A. Bye.[23]

The truce was a brief one, and by September 1889, Bye was asking for a reference.[24]

Dick's inclusion as a new trustee created tensions of a different kind. Dick was, out of habit and legal necessity, a man of precision, while Johnny was given to broad sweeps and the open-handed obligations of *noblesse*. Dick made sure that he knew exactly how the finances on the estate stood, which also meant that he knew precisely what Johnny was taking from it in income. This one-way relationship was not easy for Johnny to endure, reviving as it did lifelong insecurities about his brighter younger brother.

The humiliation of being overseen would have been less intolerable for Johnny had Dick not also taken to drinking heavily. Johnny found this lapse of behaviour incomprehensible, disgusting and unbecoming. Johnny wrote on 29 October: 'Dick comes here tonight. I could fill a volume but will write again tomorrow.' After his brother's arrival, Johnny wrote to Lucy: 'You see I did not go to Shobdon on Saturday, it would scarcely be fair to leave my guest *all* the time he is here.'[25]

Having laboured hard to see the Act through, Edward Colley resigned his position as agent of the Hampton Court estate on 31 March 1888.[26] He was succeeded by Joseph Yates. Yates's instructions from Johnny probably resembled the advertisement that Lord Harrowby had placed in 1886 when looking for a new agent: 'The strictest economy is necessary, and the agent is expected to diminish the large annual outgoings in connection with the estate.'[27] Colley's retirement was brief. He died on 22 November the following year, at the age of 74. Eight months before Colley's death, on 13 January 1889, Rev. Henry Arkwright from Bodenham had died. Four months after Colley's death, estate trustee Bonham Caldwall also died and was buried at Leominster Priory. An unsettling sense of shift was all-pervasive.

Johnny soon had occasion to reflect. In 1891, the estate celebrated the twenty-fifth anniversary of his marriage to Lucy, 'my little silver bride'.[28] Privately they were still a devoted couple and on occasion as passionate as ever in their correspondence. In 1889, Johnny had written to Lucy, while she was away: 'In a few hours I shall feel limp after many weeks of "stiffened splendour" it is your sweet company alone that I miss!'[29]

To mark the occasion publicly, Johnny and Lucy planted a silver fir in the gardens, and the tenants joined them and the girls in the music room for speeches and presentations, followed by tea in the Coningsby Hall,[30] at which 360 tenants, labourers, town- and tradespeople from Leominster gave the couple an appropriately silver Tazza vase, supplied by Leominster jeweller W. Ballard. The presentation was made by Mr T. Wood of Cold Oak, the oldest tenant. There were 175 signatories to a declaration read by Joseph Yates and presented to the couple by Robert Eckley of Green Farm.

The signatories testified to

> the great interest you take in the education of our children & your help in procuring for them a start in life. To many of us & to our sons have been afforded the means of learning a useful trade, without a costly premium & the restrictions which apprenticeship elsewhere brings with it. We remember, too, your desire to provide us with comfortable homes, with poultry, flowers, & fruit trees, &, to many of us, an allotment of land by which our wives & children are interested & usefully employed.

Next it was the turn of the 16 staff in the house and stables, 27 in the gardens and 20 in the buildings and repair workshop to present Johnny and Lucy with a silver chocolate jug. In reply, as the *Hereford Journal* reported, Johnny opened with the topical observation that 'his knees felt very weak, almost as weak as they were that morning, twenty-five years ago, when he was going to be married. He, nevertheless, felt he was bound to speak . . . after spending 25 years, with his beautiful & accomplished bride . . . learning the lessons of obedience to home rule'.[31]

Turning to the estate, he observed that since Jack's birth, he had sold four farms, Buckland, Hampton Wafer, Newhampton and Redhill, which were too distant to be looked after. Since 1820, he and his father had purchased 116 smallholdings, including 283 acres, cottage land and gardens. He had also undertaken a great deal of 'draining', for which, he explained with candour, he had borrowed from companies who lent for the purpose, but at the severe rate of 6¾ per cent. He had added 5 per cent to the rents, but that had long gone because of the bad times that they had experienced of late. He spoke of the severe depression of the last ten years, and of how landlords had been unable to live in country places, having to reduce 'their mode of life to an extent hitherto unknown'. He added, with the same frankness: 'I do not know why it should be a secret, I should not myself be here today had I not been able by a special Act of Parliament, to recoup myself to some extent for past expenditure on the estate.' Of the education of the children to which the tenants' declaration had referred, he expressed a firm belief in the three Rs, and thought that boys as well as girls should be taught sewing. In conclusion, Johnny affirmed his faith in the tripartite relationship of landlord, tenant and cottager, and in their interdependence.

New fears for Johnny's finances came when, that autumn, Jack made his way up to Christ Church, Oxford, to read English and European History in the first year, History honours in the second and Law for his finals. Jack was soon into the swing of political debate, beagling and publishing the *Christ Church Chronicle*. He was also acting. In 1893, he performed in a drawing-room comedy appropriately entitled *Debt*, in which one of the characters was the Hon. Tom Deepindebt.[32] Jack's father, exactly like his own and his grandfather before him, kept a close eye on his expenditure. In terms startlingly reminiscent of Johnny at his age, Jack defended his expenses at university. 'You may rest assured too that in whatever way I spend my money none of it will ever go like that of a good many people here, in betting, cards or anything of that sort.'[33]

With the Act passed and Jack settled at Oxford, the old Johnny resurfaced. On 8 March 1892, he wrote to Lucy: 'Tomorrow is the Shirehorse Show at Hereford, the HPS, Wye Board, Dioc[esan], Education all in the same hour.

I think I can do three of them.'[34] There was similarly renewed energy in Johnny's approach to estate business. He enjoyed astounding success with his Herefords in the 1890s. Every year between 1892 and 1898 (except 1894, when he was second) the RASE judged that the finest Hereford bull in all England was to be found in Johnny's Green Farm yard.[35]

Johnny's RASE work brought further pleasure. His old friend Hon. Cecil Parker (a son of the Earl of Macclesfield) was Director of the RASE Show from 1893 (when the show was held in Chester) until 1898. In April 1891, Johnny wrote home from London: 'Cecil P & I are hard at Committees today & tomorrow go dairying at Bayswater in the morning, Council midday.'[36] Two years later: he wrote, 'We have 3 days running of RASE but I have missed today.'[37] In June 1894, he was up at Cambridge for the show. He and Cecil attended a dinner with the Prince of Wales at Trinity College. He sent Lucy the menu with 'details of our orgy last night. I am hardly sober yet 2.30 p.m. Have just been to the Senate House to see all the degrees conferred. Princess Wales & 2 daughters were there & a very gay scene.'[38]

The Hampton Court dairy was also progressing. In 1889, Johnny entered some of his butter for the RASE Show. He wrote to Lucy on 22 June: 'Annie began churning at 2 a.m. I joined her at 5.15 – made an ice box partly at Droitwich on the Norwegian Kitchen principle finished by Mr Wood at home. Lined imperviously with felt – 3lb of fresh butter first, the salted 3lb next. It was quite beautiful, as hard as cheese, & broke up into curd to perfection.'[39] Agriculture even pervaded his trips to Scotland for the grouse. On 21 August 1889, he told Lucy that he was off to Ballindalloch Castle to see for himself the famous herd of Black Polled cattle there.[40]

Such devotion to agricultural duty earned Johnny some reward. He wrote to Lucy on 30 April 1898: 'I hear I am to be promoted tomorrow to Vice-President of the RASE for age not merit or intellect.'[41] He was in august company. The other vice-presidents were HRH Prince Christian KG of Schleswig-Holstein, H. Chandos-Pole-Gell, Rt Hon. Henry Chaplin MP, Johnny's old friend the Earl of Coventry, the Earl of Feversham, Sir Massey Lopes, Lord Moreton, Hon. Cecil Parker, the Earl of Ravensworth, Charles Whitehead and Sir Jacob Wilson.[42]

Nearer to home, the Herefordshire Philharmonic Society was similarly rewarding – Elgar was leading the band between 1891 and 1895.[43] On the twenty-fifth anniversary of the Society's foundation, Johnny was presented with a grand piano by the members. Henry Leslie was also honoured when he stepped down as conductor in 1889 and funds raised by the HPS established the Henry Leslie Prize for singing at the Royal College of Music.

Rehearsals for HPS concerts still resulted in riotous times with old friends. Johnny was staying with Leslie in July 1891 when Lucy wrote to check on a reference for Mrs Kitchen the former cook at Hampton Court. In high glee, Johnny replied: 'She was one of the suitable names on the list of servants we had at one period, Cook – Kitchen, Footman – Walker, Housemaid – Philpots, Gardeners – Greenhouse & Gatehouse & so on.'[44] Johnny wrote from Lily Hill at Bracknell during these years that he was 'rehearsing hard . . . Most of them went to a ball last night leaving Mary & Herbert, Ruth & myself. We dressed up a hideous ghost in the passage for their return home at 3.30, and sent a maid nearly wild meanwhile!'[45]

Johnny also embarked on some timely money-making schemes.[46] His first commercial venture was born of his love of horticulture. Out walking on Dinmore Hill, Evelyn had chanced upon a variety of the yellow native primrose. Johnny reproduced it under glass, and found that it came true and was a profuse flowerer, with blooms '2 inches across, being borne on long stalks'.[47] The primrose was shown at the Royal Horticultural Society's Show in 1891, 1894, 1896, 1897 and 1898, and won an award of merit from the Floral Committee in 1894. It was 'very much admired', and part of its success might have been owed to the contemporaneous flowering of the Primrose League in support of the Conservative/Unionist Party.

The Society's journal, the *Garden*, described a 'remarkable variety with its true primrose colour and enormous flowers of more than 2 inches across'.[48] Johnny told Lucy: 'I have written to Parr [gardener] to pack the best prim if it is still in top form & send it to Moon, artist to [William] Robinson Editor of the "Garden" who is going to give it a page life size. That will be a lift!'[49] Johnny's book of plant orders included one from Miss Jekyll of Godalming on 17 August 1897.[50] On 12 May 1898, while Johnny was at Llandrindod Wells,[51] he wrote to Lucy that 'Orders are rolling in. Kew Gardens have ordered plants & seeds & Veitch 6 plants & 100 seeds!'[52] The primrose was again on view at the RHS in April 1900, when Johnny reported: 'Prims . . . crowded with admirers all day.'[53]

The following year, he contacted patent lawyers Messrs Faithfull and Owen of 11 Victoria Street about acquiring patents for a gate latch designed by Henry Eckley, the bailiff at Green Farm, and for a fruit tray of his own invention. Hampton Court's gardens produced a magnificent selection of fruits and vegetables,[54] and the idea for the boxes arose from the poor condition in which the produce reached Johnny in Scotland or Llandrindod Wells. He recognised the need for a safe method of transporting soft fruit, vegetables, flowers, dairy produce or venison.

Johnny spent time at The Green with Clerk of Works Mr Clare, designing rectangular trays (still familiar today) of differing depths, which stacked by means of a triangular block in each corner. The shallowest of the trays was best for small red fruits like strawberries, or for flowers, and the deepest for vegetables. With a lid on the top tray, they were strapped together, making a compact tower. Taking a leaf from the book of his great-grandfather, the patents for whose water-powered spinning frame and carding machine had created the family's wealth, Johnny applied for a patent in 1899 and was successful.[55] He took the trays to the Royal Agricultural Show at Maidstone in June 1899, and they appeared in the official catalogue, priced at 10*s* 6*d* for a set of five trays, or 'at comparative prices' for separate trays by the dozen. He wrote home excitedly to Lucy: 'Just got an order for 100 strawberry trays . . . Everybody likes them & I have learnt a lot. A man came from Capetown wanting a small model but he did not get one as I think he wanted to make them for himself out there!'[56]

The climax of these relatively carefree times was Jack's twenty-first birthday, in July 1893, two days before Johnny's sixtieth. It was a valuable chance to reassemble the surviving siblings at the old family home. In May, when Johnny was staying at Sherfield near Basingstoke with the Lethbridges and Pink, the conversation turned to the party and presents. A portrait of Jack had been suggested by the tenantry as a gift. Jack wrote to his mother in June, 'A portrait of myself is the last thing I want, but one of you or Father would be an excellent idea.'[57] Jack requested a signet ring from his sisters, and Johnny and Lucy settled on a watch and chain from themselves. Jack, meanwhile, was turning his mind to his speech – 'No politics, I suppose.'[58]

As well as choosing caterers, Johnny and Lucy had to think of a gift for their guests. At Johnny's twenty-first, the tenantry had been presented with commemorative blue and white plates, cups and saucers. For Jack's birthday, 6-inch circular encaustic tiles, useful as teapot stands, reading 'John Stanhope Arkwright Aet 21 July 10 1893' were commissioned from William Henry Godwin's factory at Withington.[59] In addition, the men were each given a pipe bearing Jack's initials, and a pouch of tobacco.

Jack came home from Oxford to be greeted by an arch in flowers over the drive, wishing him 'Long Life and Happiness'. Flags fluttered on the top of the tower, and the ancient iron-studded doors said 'Welcome' in large letters.[60] The revelries were spread over Tuesday 11 and Wednesday 12 July, with family, friends and dignitaries on the first day, and tenantry, cottagers and workmen on the second, all enjoying lunch, a fête and tea. In the grounds to the south of the house was a variety of entertainments including a bandstand for the Hereford Militia Band, merry-go-rounds, swings, Punch and Judy, rifle saloon, fruit stall, coconut alley, 'a contrivance by which one threw at a mask for cigars', and a tent set up by photographers Jakeman and Carver. Manoeuvres by the Ludlow troop of yeomanry and sports were planned.

Of Johnny's siblings, only George and Henry (who were dead), Edwyn (in Algeria) and Emily (at Ticehurst) were absent. In all, 300 guests sat for lunch on the Tuesday. After the meal, they heard no fewer than ten speeches, of which Jack delivered two. In the first, he responded to the presentation of an illuminated address, which 'came from all classes, exhibiting a unity of welcome and of feeling at which he greatly rejoiced'. He particularly commented on the inclusion of signatures of the children at Hope School, as his father took such a lively interest in education.

Moving to the occasion in hand, he recalled reports at the time of his birth, referring to him being 'very fine and a very pretty and a very good-tempered little darling', and quipped that times had changed. He reflected on absent friends, including Bonham Caldwall, Rev. Henry Arkwright of Bodenham and nurse Pascoe who had cared for him and his sisters. He pledged himself to the justification of the honour done to him by the over 600 tenantry, tradespeople and townsfolk of Leominster in presenting him with the address, as well as the portrait of his father.

Johnny must have sat where his father had at his own twenty-first birthday and reflected on the changes since then, especially in the relationship between himself and those before him. At Hampton Court, the situation was utterly different from the order over which his father had presided nearly forty years before. Then, the rules of the game had been clear. John Arkwright had owned the land on the estate; Johnny did not – it was entailed for his descendants. The farms had been let to tenants who paid rent twice a year; these terms still stood, except that the tenants could not now afford to pay the rents. The tenants then had been left to farm the land in their own way within the constraints of the tenancy agreed between John and the tenants; now there was a high level of government intervention on behalf of tenants' rights, and landowners had to compensate tenants for improvements made at the end of a period of tenancy. Improvements to tenanted farms were made at the landlord's cost; this was still true, but landowners could no longer afford to pay for these improvements. The tenants had employed labourers at rates agreed between them; the labourer now had the backing of his union and wages had risen, squeezing the tenants' profits. The labourer had formerly known his place and been glad enough to occupy it; now, as Joseph Arch had shown, he could sit in Parliament. Even the labourers' children who formerly grew up to replace their parents, were now deserting the countryside for the towns.[61]

It is therefore not surprising that when Jack next spoke to propose the toast to the Town and Trade of Leominster, his words took a more political turn. He included with the town and trade, the tenantry, for, he observed, they all had to pull together if they were to see their grievances redressed. He proposed the formation of:

> a great agricultural party absolutely and entirely irrespective of any other party which was in the political arena [hear, hear]. They would have to talk to each other, so that the cottager should be able to go to his landlord and have access to him to lay any suggestion before him [applause]. Not until they had formed such an agricultural party, strong enough to enforce their righteous demands, would the golden days return to what was originally the greatest trade of this country – agriculture.

How far things had come! In 1854, when his own father had turned 21, the agricultural interest had been synonymous with politics, the interests of party politicians being overwhelmingly those of landowners.

There was unwelcome novelty, too, in Johnny's speech. He felt obliged to refer to:

> those who were opposed to gatherings of this kind, and said that the expense which was laid out might be better employed in the relief of agricultural distress or in other charitable ways. But he was not of that opinion himself [hear, hear]. Having made the promise twenty-one years ago when his boy was born that when he was able he should come and speak for himself he was determined he should do so [applause].

After the toast to the Ladies, the guests strolled around the grounds at Hampton Court, and the Hereford herd was displayed for their admiration. There was only one disappointment – it rained in torrents on both days – on their parade and on their cornfields.

TWELVE

Parasites and Mousetraps

The estate unity at Jack's twenty-first birthday was short-lived. The following year, problems hit farming with renewed vigour. The weather, as at Jack's party, was atrocious, both in 1893 and 1894, harvests in 1894 being very poor. The price of wheat per quarter finally bottomed at 22*s* 10*d* – just half its 1850s value, and the lowest for 150 years.[1] Not surprisingly, wheat acreage in Green Farm's parish of Hope-under-Dinmore had plummeted. In 1875 it covered 330 acres, but by 1895, only 35 acres of wheat were grown. In its place, acreage of barley, oats and hops had risen. Permanent pastureland had extended by 200–300 acres over the years up to 1890, but were back to around 1,400 acres by 1895.[2] Numbers of all stock had fallen considerably since 1875, in the case of sheep aged one year and over, by fully one-half from 1,444 to 665 in 1894, due in part to sickness. The numbers of cattle had also fallen, not surprisingly given the Herefords' sale in 1885. Nationally by 1894, 100,000 cattle were believed to have died from pleuro-pneumonia in twenty-five years.[3]

In the county as a whole, however, cattle figures had risen in a direct response to the poor performance of wheat and the resultant switch into stock. In 1869, there had been 71,362 cattle, including milk cattle, in Herefordshire. By 1909, this had risen to 103,627. Sheep figures, too, rose by 24,000. For Herefordshire as a whole, between 1869 and 1909, arable acreage fell from 192,000 acres to 129,500 acres. Of this, wheat had fallen from 60,887 acres to just 22,179, oats had risen from 12,032 to 23,670 acres, and hops fell from 5,738 to 4,997 acres. As a result of the wet weather that wrought havoc with root crops, turnip and swede acreage in the county fell over the same period from 27,000 to 15,443, and potatoes from 2,827 to 1,457. All of these trends were entirely consistent, over the same period, with changes in the comparable counties of Gloucestershire, Worcestershire, and Wiltshire, except for hops, which was barely applicable to Gloucestershire and Wiltshire, and which in Worcestershire increased in acreage.[4]

The change into stock, however, could not save beleaguered estates. With every improvement in shipping and railway technology, the opportunities for other nations to export meat into Britain increased. There was only one way for the price to go. Cattle of prime quality had been fetching around 6*s* per pound in London in the mid-1870s. By the mid-1890s, this had fallen to between 4*s* 3*d* and 4*s* 6*d* per pound, a decline of 25–30 per cent. Fat stock prices fell by more than store cattle prices. The former fell by 20–40 per cent and stores by 8–12 per cent between the mid-1970s and 1904 to 1908. To add to the misery, wool prices had also fallen sharply. Overall the picture in the mid-1890s was of prices that had fallen since the mid-1870s, in the case of wheat and wool by around half, and in the case of cattle and sheep by a quarter to a third.[5]

With the difficulties in agriculture, the NALU had become moribund by the late 1880s, but there were renewed attempts to motivate agricultural labourers after the successful Dock Strike of 1889.[6] Efforts centred on the eastern counties hardest hit by the downturn in farming, but north Herefordshire, with its pedigree of agricultural unionism was quick to respond. In early May 1892, in the run-up to a general election, a new Herefordshire Agricultural and General Workers Union was formed at a meeting in Kingsland (between Leominster and Leintwardine), having as its Secretary Rev. Arthur Auchmuty, the vicar of nearby Lucton.[7] Auchmuty was also a member of the General Committee of the English Land Restoration League (ELRL) whose aim was to break down 'the accursed system of landlordism and land monopoly', through 'revolution by due course of law'.[8] Joseph Arch had been returned again for north-west Norfolk and captured the mood by stating that 'land, land, land is what the labourer wants'.[9] In many counties, local workers' union organisers worked in conjunction with the ELRL against the interests of the big landowners, and in Herefordshire Auchmuty was no exception. He founded his new union in anticipation of a visit by ELRL campaigners to Herefordshire.

Johnny had given the land question thought back in 1886. He had written then that:

> since the year 1820, 113 strictly agricultural holdings have been added to the estate to the extent of 283 acres, all under eight acres, and kept as such – the greater part are called 'cottage and garden'. After careful inquiry I find that with scarcely any exception these tenements were sold because the mortgages on them made a sale to somebody compulsory or because the owners had found that they could not make two ends meet. In many cases the purchase money

> was converted into an annuity, the tenant being guaranteed the place for his life and that of his wife by my father . . . Allotments have been tried here 40 years ago and there is not one left today . . . I maintain that a man living in a purely agricultural district is better off with a rented cottage and as much garden ground as he can work himself, bearing a character which will ensure him a continuance of his holding, and a sound friendly society and old age pension at his back to call upon when downhill work begins, than he can possibly be as owner of his house, paying rates, and keeping his buildings in repair, for which he has no facilities . . . There are many landlords who would apportion and sell cottages with three acres attached (except to speculators), if it could be shown that there were a probability of continued success to the experiment.[10]

The ELRL sent speakers out in red gypsy caravans during the summer months from 1891 to agitate among the labourers and invite them to join the intended successor of the NALU, the Eastern Counties Labour Federation (ECLF). In 1891 the red vans had toured Suffolk, and in 1892, with the help of Rev. Auchmuty, van number four was sent into Herefordshire.[11] The visit coincided with the general election of July, when Gladstone was returned.[12] In all eighty-three meetings were held in the county in sixty-two locations. The red van usually parked at a prominent position in the town, and got children to distribute leaflets advertising the meeting for that evening at 7.30 or 8 p.m. The van displayed cartoons depicting wicked landlordism so that even the most illiterate passer-by could grasp its aims. At the meeting, after an hour's speech, a discussion was initiated, usually based on a local grievance. The proceedings would end with an invitation to farm labourers to join the ECLF.

The 1892 season in Herefordshire was productive for the ECLF. Thirty-five union branches were added to the nine that already existed in the county, and 553 new members were enrolled. The van was in Hampton Court's territory at Hope, Bodenham, Humber and Stoke Prior from 24 to 27 August. At Hope, the 'rather small attendance' was addressed by Mr Benjamin Riley of the ELRL. Riley stressed that the van represented no particular political affiliation. He noted the depopulation of Herefordshire, which he attributed to 'the present system of land tenure' under which

> the occupants had to work in order to produce rents for a few people who did not work. He had not a word to say against landlords personally . . . He believed that the people in Hope-under-Dinmore had a landlord whose character was estimable and admirable, and who evidently would do all in

> his power to make the lives of his tenants better and more comfortable. The objection of the Land Restoration League was not against land owners . . . but against the system which allowed them to own the land. A certain lady had a dislike to the fleas, not because they were innocent little animals, but because of their parasitical habits. That perfectly illustrated the objection of the League to the system which enabled a few people to live in luxury on the labour and hard toil of the majority.[13]

Here was vindication of the unease that landlords had felt at the exposure of the extent of their unearned income in the New Domesday survey twenty years before. Many, however, would have taken issue with the adjective 'unearned'. As the Duke of Bedford was to write in 1897 'I believe that most of us do work, [and] do run great risks.'[14]

The main rumpus involving the red van in Herefordshire surrounded the namesake of the author of Domesday, Lord Bateman. On 9 May, Henry Aucketill (Secretary of the ELRL) and Rev. Auchmuty had intended to address a meeting at Shobdon, in a room at the Bateman Arms. However, on arrival, the publican had informed them that:

> The secretary to the Lord Lieutenant . . . had been round and said it would be impossible for the room to be used . . . there being a certain clause in the lease which precluded him letting the room without the direct and divine permission of Lord Bateman [A Voice: 'Shame on Lord Bateman and his tenants'] . . . They then went out into the open to see if upon God's earth they could find some little space of ground on which to hold their meeting. This however was also denied them; for when in the road the Superintendent of the County Police . . . came up and . . . prevented the discussion of questions which affected the future happiness of themselves, their wives, and children [A Voice: 'That is like Lord Bateman']. Then they went to other places . . . but his Lordship's jackal had been round before them, and seen the various tenants, and told them they must not allow such a gathering to be held on their premises.[15]

As Auchmuty made clear in a letter to the newspaper, 'the unannounced and unexpected object lesson on "Life in our Villages", so frankly given at Shobdon, will . . . be far more effective in furthering the growth of the Herefordshire Workers' Union than the ablest and most convincing address that could have been delivered'.[16] Auchmuty had the last word. A meeting eventually took place at Shobdon on 11 July, when, the landlord and rector having absented themselves, Auchmuty spoke from the red van drawn up 'in an open space right in front of the lordly gates of Shobdon Court'. Its success was limited because 'so great was the terror inspired by the tyrannous privileges of the feudal lord, that it was found impossible to form a branch of the Union'.[17] The Herefordshire Union was still in existence in 1894, but it and others were already struggling with the effects of the downturn in agriculture resulting from the bad weather of 1893 and it had died out by 1900.[18] It had, nevertheless, damaged the landlords' cause.

By the mid-1890s, Herefordshire had been suffering the downturn in wheat and particularly in stock prices for over a decade. The renewed troubles of 1894 were compounded at Hampton Court by the retirement on 27 September of Joseph Yates after fifty-five years of service. Johnny gave this most faithful agent the rent of his home, Marlbrook, free for as long as he wanted it, and £50.[19] Yates ran his hand over the polished and bound ledgers one last time before he handed the business over to Harry Ashworth, the son of an old friend of Johnny's, on 1 October 1894. Ashworth was an Oxford man, and on closer than servant/master terms with Johnny. He came with a recommendation from Wilson Parr of Haigh Hall, Wigan, for whom he had worked for three years. Johnny offered Ashworth the low salary of £250 per year with Hill House rent free.

The markets for British produce showed little improvement around the turn of the century. By the mid-1890s, rents were in general back at the levels of the 1840s.[20] The effects of landowners' financial difficulties continued to make themselves felt. The Duke of Bedford had to remit 42.5 per cent of the rents on his Thorney estates in 1894.[21] In Essex, Loftus married Jonah Caldwell's daughter, Julia, in 1894, but by then the Caldwells had left Mark Hall, which was let to Newman Gilbey of the gin-making enterprise, whose family remained there for fifty years. Probably with Julia's money, Loftus was able to move back to Parndon Hall where a son, a third Loftus was born in 1895. Twin sons called John and Godfrey followed six years later, but Loftus and Julia were to divorce once the twins were 18.[22] In Gloucestershire, Johnny's old friend, Colonel Chester-Master was obliged to let The Abbey at Cirencester in 1894.[23] Further afield at Drayton Manor, the Peels, ironically, were unable to meet the cost of Dowager Lady Peel's jointure in 1899, and were obliged to break up and sell Sir Robert's great library.[24] No one was spared the humiliation.

Within two months of Ashworth starting, on 22 November 1894, further change was apparent. A meeting at Hope School considered the implications of the new Local Government Act. This wrested parish management from the hands of landowners and gave it instead to an elected local parish council – another change for which Joseph Arch had campaigned in order to eradicate 'many of the vile abuses at present existing' in the administration of charities and the Poor Law.[25] This manifestly hostile move, as landowners saw it, was combined with the government's introduction of death duties for the first time in its 1894 budget, at a rate of 8 per cent. It seemed that there was now no escape from the misery of decline, even in death. Worst of all, death duties meant that every acre of woodland and pasture would have to be gone over by a government representative whose duty it was to take the financial measure of every landowner. The indignity of the uninvited intrusion was, to many, intolerable.

Increasingly, the country's landowners gave up the struggle with appearances. Tenacity was fading in the face of mounting debts and dwindling income. In 1896, Lord Bateman was forced to part with the family's silver racing trophies, porcelain and pictures.[26] With every fall in the price of agricultural produce, the value of the land on which or in which that produce was raised fell too. Between the mid-1870s and the mid-1890s, the value of land sold in England and Wales fell from £54 per acre to £19.[27] As the Duke of Marlborough had commented as early as 1885: 'Were there any effective demand for the purchase of land, half the land of England would be in the market tomorrow.' As it was, land was no longer regarded as the best place to keep or grow capital. With gold and diamond mines being uncovered from America, through South Africa to Australia, and with industries like shipping and brewing producing new fortunes and new peers, there were plenty of alternative investments, like company stocks, or yachts, that would bring not just the wealth but the prestige of land in the past.[28]

Many landowners began to try to sell, but few could get the price they wanted. In the late 1880s and early 1890s those who were successful included the Duke of Newcastle and Lords Southampton, Ripon, Carlisle, Hardwicke and Tollemache. Unsuccessful sellers included Lords Wilton, Cholmondeley and Westmorland, besides more locally Lord Saye and Sele, and Lord Rodney.[29] Over the nearby border in Wales, prices held up better where pastoral farming predominated. Between 1894 and 1897, Lord Ancaster sold his Gwydir estate in the north. Nearer to home, between 1898 and 1901, the Duke of Beaufort parted with his Monmouthshire estate of 26,000 acres.[30] Along with the eight castles on the Beaufort estate, Tintern Abbey came under the hammer, being no longer 'sequestered from the commerce of life',[31] as it had been during the Picturesque days when Johnny's father had first come to Hampton Court.

By 1895, financial matters were again troubling Johnny. There was hollow amusement in the growing hypocrisy of keeping up appearances. In March 1892, Johnny wrote to Lucy from London after joining the Board of Christ's Hospital: 'You will see by the enclosed that I am a councillor of the new Board full fledged for I have made my affidavit tho' I am not quite sure that "I am possessed of £1000 after my just debts are paid" still Symonds said he thought I was!'[32] In 1889, when Lucy had accompanied Ronald Bosanquet to his presentation at the Queen's Levée, Johnny had written: 'Some day you will have to do it for Jack. But what a farce it is, when one is bankrupt or nearly so.'[33] Everywhere life as Johnny had known it was falling apart. It seemed even worse for men like his uncle Leigh Hoskyns, who after fifty years at Aston Tyrrold wrote to Johnny: 'Poor old Aston is going to the dogs, & farmers all missed, & nobody will buy the land. What is to be the end of it?'[34]

If Johnny were able to borrow against the value of the estate, things might be eased, but the entail forbade it. He began, therefore, to consider unravelling the legal ties that bound the estate to the future heirs instead of to Johnny himself. Sale at Leominster set about establishing the feasibility of the step, but it took a frustratingly long time. Johnny wrote to Lucy in late July 1895: 'I am firmly convinced that the lawyers are all making delay in order to charge for their time & run me up.'[35] A fortnight later he was even finding it difficult to enjoy the grouse shooting in Scotland. 'I don't feel as if I had any right to be here for I cannot keep my thoughts off the business at home & have no rest.[36] Tooth bad again today so I did not go on the hill.'[37] Matters were moving ahead finally by November, when Jack wrote to his father from 90 St Aldate's in Oxford: 'I shall be ready *whenever you like* to know further particulars about what you propose to do.'[38] Progress, however, was painfully slow.

There was hope when the 1895 election returned the Tory Lord Salisbury to power. Among landowners there was collective relief that what had felt like a landslide of unfavourable legislation would be stopped. The cabinet once more had the reassuringly familiar Tory, Anglican and landed silhouette and agricultural prices stabilised, albeit at their low level, in 1895 and 1896. Landowners were helped when Salisbury halved rates on agricultural land in 1896. However, the storm of Liberal (and urban Tory) protest with which the measure was met convinced Salisbury not to go further in the landed interest and not to lift the despised death duties.[39]

The year 1895 brought Johnny further joy when Jack won Oxford's Newdigate Prize for poetry with his epic poem on the subject of

Montezuma.[40] Jack had confided to his mother: 'I am not at all satisfied with it & am doubtful about sending it in. I think it is just above the average of a bad year.'[41] Nevertheless, 'Montezuma' won and was printed in June, slightly changed from the original.[42] Victory earned Jack the customary £21 in prize money and £5 for the copyright, his first earnings from poetry.

The excitement at Jack's triumph was immense, not least because the Newdigate roll of honour included Oscar Fingal O'Flahertie Wills Wilde, former student of Magdalen College.[43] Wilde had won the Newdigate with 'Ravenna' in 1878. One month before Jack's win, Wilde had enjoyed his greatest stage success to date with *The Importance of being Earnest* at the St James Theatre, London. By the time of the announcement of Jack's prize, Wilde had begun his sensational but professionally and socially suicidal libel proceedings against the Marquis of Queensberry, the father of Wilde's lover, Lord Alfred Douglas. Jack must have wondered quite what the literary future held for him. It might equally be wondered what Wilde would have quipped about the fact that one of Hampton Court's Hereford bull calves was named Montezuma in honour of Jack's success.[44] Gilbert and Sullivan, whose 1881 production *Patience* parodied Wildean ideas, would doubtless have relished the 'aesthetic transfiguration'.[45]

Having been presented at Court, Jack returned to Oxford and got his head down for more swatting. His sisters, meanwhile, were increasingly out in the world. Pink (Geraldine) was now 19 and Wee (Evelyn) 18. That June, 1895, both were called up by Jack to Christ Church for the Commem Week Ball. Johnny went to chaperone his girls, and Colonel Chester-Master, who in April, as Johnny reported to Lucy 'had a rattling fall with the Cirencester hounds but came up smiling – somebody told me they have never seen a man so plastered over with mud as he was', did the same for his daughters.[46] While Jack was toasted by them all for his Newdigate success, Johnny and the Colonel went over past times. Unnoticed by the men, Geraldine took her own heavy fall, head over heels in love with Colonel Chester-Master's eldest son, Richard. Dick, as he was known, being a couple of years older than Jack, had left Christ Church and joined the King's Royal Rifle Corps in 1893.

For Geraldine, Dick cut a glamorous figure being a man's man, loving his horses and hunting in particular. Although not robustly built, Dick's slim frame and elegant gait crackled with energy. Belying all the patrician bluff, though, were Dick's eyes. Their hint of vulnerability reinforced by the slightly protruding ears of a little boy, combined with his outward strength and self-assurance to make a heady draught for Geraldine. Before very long, Dick and Geraldine were entirely wrapped up in one another.

From Johnny's point of view, Dick could not have been more suitable. The Colonel had been at Harrow with Johnny's brothers, and young Chester-Master had been at Clevedon with Jack. The Masters were influential landowners in Gloucestershire and among his regiment Dick was known affectionately as 'the Squire'. In addition, he was related through his mother Georgina Rolls (sister of Lord Llangattock) to many of Johnny's Monmouthshire relations and acquaintances. Finally, through his father, Dick was related to Johnny's best man, the late Sir Velters Cornewall of Moccas.

Johnny and Lucy were soon aware of the attachment, and allowed Geraldine and the Master girls to exchange visits, a consolation for Geraldine when Dick was away soldiering. The following year, Lucy held a ball at Hampton Court on 21 May. She wrote to Johnny that 'G enjoyed her Home Ball last night – *He* is in Scotland so I did not see him.'[47]

Although they approved of Dick, Johnny and Lucy felt that at 19, Geraldine was too young to form a close attachment. They encouraged her to be in the society of many eligible gentlemen, organising trips to Ascot and other staples of the season. Geraldine, it was widely acknowledged, was a lovely looking young woman. Lucy's verdict on some new photographs: 'On the whole, *nice* I think but they none of them do Geraldine justice', might just as well have been passed on her daughter's suitors.[48]

Whatever Johnny and Lucy might intend for their daughter, it was Dick's role in international events on the other side of the world, in southern Africa, that was to determine Geraldine's future. At the end of 1895, the failed 'Jameson Raid' in the Transvaal further heated simmering tensions between the Boers and the British in the region. In the build-up to what would become the Boer War (1899–1902) Dick's regiment was called to Cape Town. He was to leave in April 1897.

It is not clear when Geraldine was made aware of this, but in February 1897 Lucy reported that 'G does not get on – so low & weak. Aycle is pouring in champagne. I think she must go away to the sea or somewhere for change – when she is well enough to move.'[49] They went to 40 Eversfield Place at St Leonards, where, a month later, Geraldine was 'almost unrecognisably better', perhaps because Dick wrote to her mother at the end of March, explaining that 'Miss Arkwright did me the honour of saying that she would like to add one of my photos to her collection and I am sending one.'[50]

After Geraldine returned home, Johnny gave permission for Lucy to invite Dick to stay at Hampton Court for a last visit. The young lovers must have spent bitter-sweet days hunting and walking over the Lugg and up on to Dinmore where the primroses were flowering. Seizing the opportunity before their enforced separation, Dick asked Geraldine to marry him. She accepted. On 12 April, the eve of Dick's return to Gloucestershire and two days after the anniversary of Johnny and Lucy's own 'mousetrap day', Johnny and Lucy were caught completely off guard by the young couple's announcement of their desire to marry. Johnny's situation was made no easier by having to leave at first light the next morning to go up to London.

He wrote to Lucy from the Carlton Club: 'I haven't got over G yet – don't know what to think. Suppose [Dick's] papa will write.'[51] Lucy in her turn wrote:

> I am thinking so much of that episode yesterday, & must tell you how kind I think you were about it. I did not know till Sunday evening that G *really* cared for him, but she was so sure of herself, that it took me by surprise – & I felt the whole thing could not be left in abeyance, for her sake – I am so sorry you should be worried about it, & as I said before, *if* she had not been able to make up her mind the whole thing might have been left to slide, & could have been brought up again or *not* when he came back from abroad – but as she seems to care for him so much, it cannot be left uncertain.[52]

Johnny assured Dick that in principle he had no objection to their engagement. However, in the circumstances of Dick's impending departure for an unknown duration, he advised that they might correspond but that Geraldine was to be left free of any official engagement until his return. He also suggested that Dick assess his ability to keep Geraldine on his current income.

On 14 April, Colonel Master did indeed write to Johnny from Knole Park. 'Whatever the two may mutually understand between themselves, I think you are very right in insisting on leaving Miss Arkwright perfectly free on his going to S Africa to join his regiment & also in desiring that they should wait for the present.'[53] Dick wrote to Johnny on 15 April after meeting the family lawyer in Cirencester:

> I came away with [the] conclusion that, in the present bad times, & from a heavily charged property, I cannot reasonably expect a sufficient allowance to marry on in the near future.

Meanwhile I shall return to duty with my regiment at Cape Town next week & shall not lose any opportunity of more remunerative employment should such arise.[54]

Johnny then replied candidly to his old friend,

There could not be a thought of any immediate decision for the 'modus vivendi' is not in view. She has no more than enough for her own pin money & I am penniless – without a chance of helping her – owing to the fact that I have nothing but a life interest in the acres which do not keep me solvent . . . In fact between ourselves I often think that I can no longer live here . . . I have seen very little of yr son – but what I know is all in his favour, & so we told him that he may write & so on, but that the future must decide any eventual pledge.[55]

There was convenient distraction almost at once for poor Geraldine. Towards the end of May, Lucy reported to Johnny that Fanny, who was back for the summer, had 'invited G for the jubilee, so the girls will be all right as I believe the Longleys will have Evelyn'. Jack would be all right too, as he had by now secured a pupillage with Hugh Fraser at Inner Temple. Appropriately enough, given that Sir Richard Arkwright's wealth had largely come from securing patents on his spinning and carding machines, Jack was practising patent and commercial law. For a man of lively and creative intellect, though, the rigours of 'the Turner Tyre case' left something to be desired. The same could be said for London, seen through the eyes of a gardener and a countryman, impervious to the superficial delights of society.[56] 'The weather is perfectly awful – thick leathery fog the colour of a rotten lemon combined with all the smells that dwellers in great cities are heirs to.'[57]

London was filled for the Diamond Jubilee celebrations and society gossip was rife, not least about Geraldine and Dick. Jack tried to suppress speculation. He wrote to his mother at the end of May:

Edith Woolaston Blake button holed me at the flower show & asked if I had any exciting news for her & when I said 'no' proceeded to beak gently to me in a loud voice all about it. I expressed astonishment & promised to make enquiries . . . I dined tonight with Ronald [Bosanquet] who discussed it as a matter of course but seemed to realize that the family alone were supposed to know. When his other guest arrived, a Barrister named Peacock, an old

Eton friend of mine, he (Peacock) said 'Is the Miss Arkwright who is going to marry Dick Master any relation of yours?' I said there were 3 Dick Masters to *my* knowledge & that Arkwright was a very common name in some parts of the country, that the weather had not been all that it should be, & upset the salt, & meanwhile Ronald changed the conversa^{n}.

But this is what I have to encounter hourly & almost minutely, & the strain is becoming great. I think G will really have to go in the Jubilee procession with a label on her, for the world seems to be agog about it. Mrs Wooley was literally trembling with excitement & evidently did not believe me . . . Now what do I do? Smile knowingly, deny the charge? express profound astonishment, or what? I shall avoid polite society till I have rec'd instructions.[58]

Another of Jack's letters reported: 'In court today I saw Betterton who suddenly said "I hear Dick Master is going to be married!" I gathered that he had got hold of the *other* Dick. I told him so. He finally said "Well I'm very glad our Dick isn't – as he's too good to waste!" He little knows the tale I could unfold.'[59] Of his own social life, Jack reported in July: 'The world is very male –!'[60]

THIRTEEN

Land Loss at Home, Victory Abroad

After Dick's departure for South Africa in the summer of 1897, Johnny took Geraldine to join Dick and Minnie, Fanny and Willie at Tor Castle, Fort William. The imposing house (said to have been the former seat of Banquo, murdered by Macbeth in Shakespeare's play) was located in a bend of the peaty River Lochy, and embodied much of the popular romance of Scotland.[1] Although Johnny's relationship with Dick remained sensitive, at Tor they could indulge their passion for fishing, a love shared from childhood. Quiet hours on the riverbank rolled back the years and the brothers no doubt speculated about Jack, who seemed to be emulating Dick's legal and political career.

Such were the pleasures shattered by the arrival of a telegram for Johnny on 25 August. He knew its contents the moment that he saw the French postmark. It read simply, 'Restes Henry Arkwright, péri Mont Blanc, 1866, retrouvés. Avisez. Payot, Maire.'[2] For thirty-one years, the unspoken 'When?' had hung in the air and now, as if distilled from the ether, the words had formed and dropped at last. Johnny's first duty was to break the news as gently as he could to Fanny, and to Dick.

Next, Johnny dispatched telegraphs, sending Jack ahead to Chamonix, with Arthur and Edwyn's servant Stanffer.[3] To the Mayor of Chamonix he replied: 'Mon fils et frere arriveront bientot. Reservez deux chambres.'[4] Almost before he can have been aware of it, Jack had crossed the Channel and was on the train from Calais to Cluses, his head reeling with instructions and questions.[5] His uncle Henry had been killed six years before he was born, and to him the whole affair was part of family legend. For Arthur, the telegraph had reopened very real wounds. Every circumstance of the weeks after Johnny's wedding remained raw. The long journey afforded him no respite from the swirling sounds, faces, places and smells that returned to him as if they had never entirely left.

For his journey, Johnny was joined by Fanny. The image of Henry bent over his broken shoelace in the minutes before he left the Grands Mulets cabin was again in front of her every time she closed her eyes. The nightmare of the long walk down the mountain, with only the prospect of breaking the news to Mamma and Alice, recurred as she and Johnny left Tor. Banquo's weary words whispered after them: 'A heavy summons lies like lead upon me, And yet I would not sleep.'[6] Alone at Hampton Court, Lucy mused that reclaiming Henry might be a fitting way finally to thank him for all he did over their wedding. No doubt she thought of Tally and her grief at the loss of a child, grief that Lucy could now understand so much better.

Arriving at Chamonix on 27 August, Jack, Arthur and Stanffer hastened to the Hotel Royal. In the ensuing days, they had to identify the body, find a clergyman to take the service, organise the funeral and choose a burial plot. All of this had to be accomplished in the teeth of a curious public. By many of the inhabitants of Chamonix, the Arkwright name was respected, owing to the financial support given by the family to the other bereaved since Henry's death, and all were considerate. It was the tourists with little to do but gossip and speculate that were the trial.

Chamonix became a fashionable alpine resort. Instead of the few thousand travellers who found their way to the Avre Valley in 1866, tens of thousands now came every year, particularly since the railway had reached Cluses.[7] The numerous tourists had little to do but exchange the gruesome news of the find. These included an Englishman who was walking on the glacier 9,000ft below where Henry had died, when he came upon the recovery.

> I . . . the only English person present while my countryman's remains were being brought from the glacier . . . was pressed forward into full view of them. Never have I experienced a moment so thrilling, so filled with painful interest . . . The right hand, which had once so firmly grasped the iron-plated pine pole that even after thirty-one years they were found close together, was marvellously life-like, the ice had even preserved in it the red tint of the blood.[8]
>
> There could be no doubt of identity. From the pocket of the gray waistcoat was drawn a white pocket handkerchief with a plain blue border. It was as strong and sound as if new; the marking-ink might have been used upon it that day so distinct were the works [*sic*]: H. Arkwright.

The words of the song that Henry had been singing as he left that morning now seemed eerily appropriate:

A traveller, by the faithful hound,
Half-buried in the snow was found,

Still grasping in his hand of ice
That banner with the strange device,
Excelsior![9]

Visiting the Protestant church, with its little stone spire thrusting defiantly into the air, in reflection of the Aiguilles de Chamonix that bristled on the skyline beyond, they paused at the memorial to Henry. Outside, at the rounded east end, they found a plot, next to Richard Nettleship, a Fellow of Balliol, Oxford, who had died on Mont Blanc 'of cold and fatigue' when Jack was at Oxford, almost exactly five years before.[10] Over the low stone boundary wall, cattle grazed the fields – a reminder of home.

It was after midnight when Jack wrote to his mother.

We have got the white handkerchief . . . stained through with blood . . . The body itself is still in the ice, having been put back there in a box immediately on discovery . . . Tomorrow morning . . . we propose to go up to the lowest point of the ice, where they had to leave him. Uncle Arthur seems very much upset . . . We are the objects of the greatest interest, & am afraid shall be greatly put to it before it is over. Today Payot brought the handkerchief to Uncle Arthur *in the street* with half the community looking round the corners.[11]

The Arkwrights were not alone in finding the circumstances difficult. For the families of the guide, Michel Simond, and porters François and Joseph Tournier who had died with Henry on the mountain, the discovery of the remains was painful. The surviving guide, Sylvain Couttet, was now an old man in Chamonix, mostly paralysed, but still recounting Fanny's bravery at the Grands Mulets. Arthur and Jack met the families and were touched by their support. The weekend's events were described by Jack on Sunday evening.

Darling Mother,
I am afraid much of this letter will not be cheerful reading . . . The discovery of Uncle Henry's remains was made as it were by chance. Pyott (?) [Payot – no direct relation of the Mayor] the guide, who lives by the glacier des Bossons, went with his son to a certain point in the glacier to plant a flag which was to indicate that it was safe to go to the spot. He had never been there before, & it is not really very clear why he went on this occasion. However, he did go & there he found the remains . . .

> Yesterday we went up, first to the place where he was found, & then on our way home we opened the box & saw the body . . . A man said to us in the train on the way 'I am afraid you will be very much shocked at what you are going to see' & he spoke the truth. Anything more awful than this state midway between real preservation and absolute dry bones it would be hard to imagine . . . That his identity is established is beyond any shadow of doubt; that he was killed instantaneously seems almost as certain. And now perhaps the most distressing part of yesterday – on our return to the neighbouring chalet we found a photographer who produced awful photographs taken by him on the day of the discovery . . . The photographs were seen by Stanffer in the shop windows this morning . . . The funeral will be at 3 o'clock on Tuesday . . . The papers here have been very truthful & in perfect taste & feeling about it all . . . None of this have [*sic*] ever been forgotten here, & the Simons [Simonds] know all the names of the family photographs which they produced yesterday though no names were upon them.[12]

Johnny and Fanny arrived on Tuesday 31 August, just as the procession was forming at the hotel to go to the church. Jack reported to his mother:

> The whole of Chamonix was there, & the scene was a most impressive one. Very many of the people were in black & the shutters were up in the shops which we passed, & the Union Jack was flying half mast high on this house. The Church was absolutely full; some idea of the number of people may be got from the fact that when we, preceded by some 50 guides, got to the Church, the end of the procession was well outside the Churchyard, & it this is some distance . . . The widows of the guides who were lost came just after the family.[13] The part taken by the Chamonix guides & their families, to say nothing of the town officials must have been very astonishing to visitors who did not know the whole story . . . I think Father was very much pleased; he said he thought it all very wonderful. He appears to be a good deal upset though glad now that it is over. I for my part am rather glad that he & Aunt Fanny were rushed at the last minute, as the trying part is now over almost before they knew they were in Chamonix. In opening a letter of condolence tonight he said that a letter of congratulations would have been more to the point.[14]

Lucy received Johnny's account on the black-edged Hampton Court mourning paper that he had taken with him to Chamonix.

It had rained nearly all the drive but just as we reached the valley the sun lit up the Bossons on the very spot & cleared off the clouds, as if it were on purpose . . . The Church was crowded to the last place. People have been remarkably kind to us all and the whole event has evidently made a profound impression. To me it has been a great relief more than a sorrow – tho' there are very ghastly details of the search.[15]

Of the feelings of the rest of the family, little survives. Fanny forwarded to Johnny an Alpine cow bell that she had bought in Chamonix.[16] From then on, some of the pedigree Herefords grazing near the house at Hampton Court always wore bells for a fortnight in October, as if the sound could keep Henry among them.[17] She wrote touchingly: 'I was so pleased and thankful to be with you. It is all like a dream. I have been with Arthur a few days since, as he was alone, and it is still in all his thoughts.'[18] The items found with the body were put into a glass case in the chapel at Hampton Court, alongside the marble bust of Henry.[19]

Chamonix was a turning point in Johnny's relationship with Jack. Jack had shown himself capable of bearing onerous responsibilities, sparing his father, uncles and aunts a painful burden. Johnny now looked for Jack to do the same at home, to assume an increasing role at Hampton Court as the estate's situation worsened. Daily Johnny's finances teetered on the edge of personal humiliation. One of the lowest moments came in March 1899, when Lucy wrote to apologise for 'the affair at the bank'. It seems that her account was overdrawn and a cheque may have been refused. Lucy explained that she had been paying for the girls' governess and the sums had mounted up. She was insisting that she sell some earrings, and felt very 'foolish and upset'.[20]

After Jack passed his Bar examinations in early summer 1898, Johnny tried to consult him on legal aspects of the estate's affairs. Jack, though, could see what his father was trying to do and resisted, straining their relationship. In February 1898, for example, Jack had written: 'At present all I can do is to make myself acquainted with the Law on the subject & consider hypothetical cases which may, or may not, resemble our own.'[21] Undeterred, Johnny tried to involve Jack by another route. The Leominster solicitor, Sale, requested of Jack an interview in July, to which Jack agreed, saying: 'I particularly wish to understand the position of affairs at the Bank.'[22] Correspondence between father and son quietened until 20 May 1899, when Jack wrote: 'I shall be very glad to discuss Estate finance with Ashworth & Sale. I think it high time the matter was put into the hands of a capable London solicitor.'[23] Jack advised that 'William Rowcliffe Esq,

1 Bedford Row' was 'of the highest standing'.[24] Rowcliffe assessed the situation at Hampton Court.

Jack was resisting distractions while trying to improve his political prospects. On 10 February 1899, the *Daily Telegraph* announced that he had been 'appointed private secretary to Sir Matthew White Ridley', Home Secretary in Lord Salisbury's cabinet.[25] Johnny reported to Lucy in March 1899: 'Visited Jack in the Office this morning. A great swell . . . he is looking very much stronger & better in face, & has plenty of fresh air – high ceilings & so on.'[26]

Johnny, always frustrated if not able to move things on by the sheer force of his personality, was further hit now by the demise of the Herefordshire Philharmonic Society to which he had given thirty years of his life. Evidence of the widespread extent of financial difficulties came in 1898 when members could (or would) not pay their subscriptions. In 1899, Johnny was unable to inject cash into this organisation to save it as he had done, for example, with the Hereford and West of England Rose Society in 1870.[27] As a result, the HPS folded and the twice-yearly concerts ceased, unpicking further the fabric of county society.

Meanwhile, the process of disentailing the estate was taking forever. John Daggs, the manager of Lloyds Bank in Corn Square, Leominster, became impatient for Johnny's overdraft to be reduced.[28] As the income that land generated had fallen, so too had its value, value against which many banks had lent. 'No security,' observed the *Economist* in June 1897, 'was ever relied upon with more implicit faith, and few have lately been found more sadly wanting, than English land.'[29] Once again, the prophetic Chandos Wren Hoskyns was proved right. As early as 1848, his mother had reported to Johnny's father that Chandos (then at Wroxall) was 'heartily sick of land – you need a fortune to run an estate and he thinks money in the stocks is the best kind of future'.[30]

The rising confidence and authority of the middle classes and the corresponding slide in status of the landowners was clearly demonstrated by Daggs's attitude towards Johnny. Wealth, status and power were closely interdependent, and deference towards landowners persisted while appearances were maintained. For Daggs, the transparency of Johnny's situation rendered deference defunct. Daggs was the son of William Daggs, who had organised Johnny's twenty-first birthday celebrations, and was therefore the grandson of one of Johnny's former tenants.[31] Under pressure from his superiors in Birmingham, Daggs began to insist not just that the loan be reduced. He demanded changes in estate management, and, from Johnny's point of view, had the effrontery to suggest that Johnny give up farming and let his land. On 13 October 1899, Sale was sacrificed to Daggs to stall the unpleasantness.[32] Four days later, Johnny's Green Farm bailiff, Robert Eckley, who had contributed to the success with the Herefords, died. Sale, evidently not enjoying the interviews with Daggs, wrote to Johnny that he hoped 'it might influence you in giving up farming'.[33]

While battle had commenced at home, war had broken out in South Africa on 11 October 1899. The Arkwrights were alive to what it might mean for Geraldine. Included in the British military build-up in South Africa had been two of Arthur Arkwright's sons, Cyril and Gerald. On 6 March 1899, Gerald died at Johannesburg. Alice wrote to Johnny from Algiers that she was 'thinking of the dreadful sorrow at Thoby'. Arthur's sadness compounded his lingering grief for his soldier brother Henry. Johnny and Lucy reflected, privately, on their wisdom at not letting Dick and Geraldine marry.

The shape of the Boer War (1899–1902) was dictated by attempts to relieve the towns of Kimberley and Mafeking in western Transvaal (besieged within a week of the outbreak of hostilities) and Ladysmith in the east, in British Natal. Two British columns set out to free them, the progress of each dictated by supplies, particularly of water which was scarce on the velt, making rivers and settlements' pumping stations key objectives. Arthur and Agnes's other son Cyril, a lieutenant in the 5th Lancers, was trapped at Ladysmith. They could only wait and pray.

Since early 1898, Dick had been Aide de Camp to Sir Alfred Milner, Governor of Cape Colony and High Commissioner for South Africa, at Government House in Cape Town.[34] Dick had therefore witnessed the build-up to war as one of six members of Milner's inner circle of staff.[35] At the outbreak of hostilities, Dick was released to become an officer in Rimington's Guides or Tigers.[36] Major Mike Rimington's men protected the western Army column from the ambush-style attack at which the Boers, with their superior knowledge of the landscape, were so adept.[37] Dick's own 'quick eye for country', honed out hunting, proved invaluable. The guides checked the territory, enemy positions and likely resistance, terrifying as they did so, vulnerable Boer women in farms on the velt.

Instead of the British celebrating victory by Christmas, as anticipated, they suffered three significant setbacks between 10 and 17 December 1899, 'Black Week'.[38] At home there was stunned disbelief.[39] Jack, meanwhile, had published another volume of poetry in July, and a 'Hymn for Use in Time of War' in November. The hymn was now eagerly taken up, expressing as it did, the public mood:

... Thou only art of Victory the Giver;
Our ears have heard the tales our Fathers told –
How they did cry, and how Thou didst deliver,
And led'st their armies in the time of old.

Johnny wrote to Lucy that 'his words are very good & he should copyright them as there may be lots of people who will want them for setting as they run so well for musicians'.[40]

Johnny's pleasure at the book's success was soon overshadowed. Johnny, Jack and Sale met at Rowcliffe's office in November 1899.[41] It was decided that Johnny and Jack should disentail the estate so that they could mortgage part of it to cover Johnny's debts. Ashworth was asked to calculate the total estate's debts and Sale to work out Johnny's liabilities, to ascertain the total amount that Johnny would need to borrow. Back in Leominster, Sale was again summoned to the bank to inform Daggs of progress. After their meeting, Daggs wrote to Sale to say that the plan proposed would take too long and he wanted Jack to guarantee Johnny's overdraft in the meantime.

Jack's New Year (and new century) therefore began with a letter from Sale asking him to offer security against his father's debts of £27,500 with his Law Life and Scottish Equitable Policies and their bonuses. Jack, no doubt appreciating the irony of his father's warnings to avoid debt at Oxford, dealt with the matter through his own solicitor, Rashleigh. Rashleigh confirmed in January 1900 that Jack would help but that 'In future Mr Arkwright should, it is mentioned in the interest of his family, take care that his estate and personal expenditure is kept within his income and that Mr JS Arkwright in fairness to himself and those who follow him ought not again to be asked for assistance.'[42] Johnny's situation was straining even his relationship with Jack.

Between January and Easter 1900, Sale and Ashworth calculated the total debts. However, Ashworth showed himself to be unreliable. First Sale rejected Ashworth's estimate of income on the estate as too optimistic. Ashworth modified the income downwards and resubmitted his figures. They still showed inaccuracies in the outgoings that both Sale and Daggs spotted. However, with time going on, Sale submitted them to Rowcliffe unaltered. By 6 April, Johnny, Jack, Rowcliffe, Sale and Ashworth had agreed on a mortgage. Johnny and Jack therefore spent Easter deciding which farms to offer as security.[43]

The mortgage involved consulting the trustees of all jointures and portions settled against the estate, just as for the Arkwright Estate Act in

1887. As the letters went back and forth, the bank overdraft continued to climb. Just after Easter, on 18 April, Daggs indicated that the bank's directors wanted further security. Jack agreed to facilitate the payment of the most pressing bills and returned to London. There, his solicitor Rashleigh said that he knew nothing of Jack's offer and Sale was summoned to London to work out the precise form that Jack's guarantee should take. Rashleigh made it clear that £10,000 might be used for only the most urgent items.[44]

By early July 1900, it emerged that Johnny and Jack needed a mortgage for £25,000. The bank's view of the crisis in land is illustrated by the fact that Daggs's directors demanded security against the £25,000 loan of £150,000 worth of land. With many of their agricultural customers going bust, the directors wisely foresaw that land prices would plummet and sought to cover themselves. Furthermore, with many acres now on the market and few buyers, the directors understood that the realisation of the land's value if offered for sale could require a long-term effort on their part. Sale recorded that Harry Ashworth, on hearing the sum, was 'aghast'.[45] Ashworth had the laborious task of tracing maps of the farms in question. Finally, on 9 July 1900, Sale was in a position to write to four mortgage brokers and ask for their terms on a £25,000 loan.

Scottish Equity offered £25,000 at 3¾ per cent against the security of the two available policies (Jack's) and the mortgage of Johnny's life estate. However, complications arose from the security of Lucy's jointure against the estate, and it looked as if Scottish Equity might pull out. Ashworth, Sale and Daggs scuttled about to keep Scottish Equity on board. They made a new proposal – the mortgage at 4 per cent in fee of property producing £6,462 per annum. Daggs declared it 'rather arduous', but as there was nothing else on offer, they must take it. Jack wanted to know which parts of the estate were being included in the £150,000 security. Rowcliffe insisted on a valuation of the relevant farms despite resistance from Johnny. Ashworth sat down in December 1900 to trace the boundaries, watercourses and woodlands of the properties. He was still at it five months later.[46]

Dick, meanwhile, was starting the twentieth century with the main column heading north towards Kimberley at Modder River Camp, where it had been halted by Boer General Piet Cronje at Magersfontein in Black Week. Some of the Tigers had gone on to relieve Kimberley with Major-General John French's cavalry, but Dick had had to miss the action. His moment was to come, though. Cronje, hearing about Kimberley, realised that he had British to the north and south of him, and began to retreat from Magersfontein. Dick spotted this and told Kitchener, only to be given the task of riding 40 miles overnight to instruct French to head south so that Cronje would be sandwiched. As a result of Dick's lonely but successful ride, Cronje was snared on 17 February 1900, and finally surrendered, with 4,069 troops at Paadeberg Drift on 27 February.[47] For his role, Dick was widely hailed as a hero. The British rolled on to Bloemfontein, the capital of Orange Free State, which Dick was the first officer to enter on 13 March.

The British occupation of Bloemfontein caused premature celebrations at home and a fatal pause there by General Roberts as 34,000 troops poured into the small city. The combination of overcrowding and unclean water resulted in an epidemic of enteric fever or dysentery that wiped out 16,000 British troops – only 22,000 were lost in the entire war. In these circumstances, Bloemfontein's water pumping station was targeted by the Boers, and Dick again played a key role, by ensuring the escape of Q Battery of the Royal Horse Artillery from the attack. For this Dick was mentioned by Roberts in his dispatch of 31 March.[48]

Pride for one branch of the Arkwright family was tempered by despair for another. Cyril Arkwright survived the siege of Ladysmith, which had finally been relieved on 28 February, but died eight days later. The news reached Arthur and Agnes only days after they had mourned the first anniversary of Gerald's death on 6 March. Lucy was in London at Alice's in July 1900, when Arthur called. She told Johnny: 'They have got Cyril's things at last – a letter found in his desk makes them feel so sad, written after he was supposed to have got over the worst of the fever – & saying he hoped to be home again & with them before many weeks were past! *Then* he took a chill & died in 10 days.'[49]

A rapid succession of favourable events, from the relief of Mafeking in May to the flight of President Paul Kruger to France in October, prompted widespread belief, in the last months of 1900, that the war was all but over. In fact it would continue until the end of May 1902. Milner was more cautious, fearing particularly an uprising of the Dutch in the Cape. To counter this, Dick assembled the Western Province Mounted Rifles to defend the northern districts of Cape Colony. He was made Officer in Chief of the Rifles in April 1901. Of Dick's efforts, Milner wrote to Lady Edward Cecil, 'Chester has got more than 500 mounted men in a fortnight. Good that. . . . But then Chester is Chester. I never in my life saw anybody work so hard.'[50]

Dick's standing was now very different from that when he had accepted Milner's ADCship. Besides the mentions in dispatches, he had risen to Captain and then Brevet Major and would be awarded the Queen's Medal with six clasps and the King's Medal with two clasps. Milner felt that Dick had outgrown the ADCship, and Dick had probably indicated to his boss that he would be prepared to return to South Africa if a suitable post could be found to which he might bring a wife.[51] Milner, considering the control of postwar South Africa, and understanding the importance of curtailing the power of Rhodes's Chartered Company, especially in the new Rhodesia immediately north of the Transvaal, needed men of unquestionable reliability to keep him informed of the Company's activities, men whose opinions and soundings he could trust implicitly – men like Dick Chester-Master.

On the strength of the good news reaching London from South Africa over the English summer of 1900, culminating with the annexation of Transvaal on 1 September, Lord Salisbury went for a dissolution of Parliament on 17 September. Rumours of an imminent election had been rife all year. In Hereford, as elsewhere, candidates had been jostling. Since 1893, Hereford City's parliamentary representative had been Conservative Charles W.R. Cooke of Hellens, Herefordshire.[52] Cooke now withdrew and Jack wondered whether to stand.

The sons of landowners were not going into politics as they had hitherto. The degree of professionalism now required of Members made them think twice. Jack, however, had handled more business at the Home Office than he might otherwise have done, because Ridley had been out of sorts after the death of his wife. The work had done nothing to blunt his appetite for political fare; indeed, he was eager to stand. He took family soundings and on 1 September Lucy informed Johnny: 'Jack wrote to you yest'y & told you he had made the plunge. Mr Ashworth was going in [to Hereford], so he sent a note to Beddoe.'[53] All month Jack campaigned in Hereford, although no Liberal candidate came forward. On 23 September, he was chuckling 'at a man he was canvassing saying he wished he was as sure of going to Heaven as *he* was of getting in!'.[54]

Nationally, the main election issue was the war. It was an ill-natured campaign, Lloyd George emerging into the spotlight for his pro-Boer stance and claims that Chamberlain's arms-manufacturing family was benefiting from the conflict. The Liberals, several of whose members had split from the party over Irish Home Rule and had formed the coalition with the Conservatives, couldn't shake off an image of disunity and disarray.

When Parliament reconvened in January 1901, with Salisbury still in Downing Street, Jack was finding his way around the House of Commons as the new Member of Parliament for Hereford City and PPS to Jesse Collings, the former radical agriculturalist MP and under-secretary at the Home Office. During his eleven years at Westminster (1901–12), Jack would see almost as many changes in Parliament as anyone in office for so short a time. The Tory leadership passed from the aristocratic Salisbury and Balfour to the Canadian-born Glasgow iron merchant, Bonar Law. Jack saw the top hat and frock coat superseded by the flat cap and tweed suit first worn by Joseph Arch. In 1901, the worst behaviour of Members was elbowing to get a view of the State Opening. In 1910 for the first time in its history, the House of Commons was adjourned by the Speaker as a 'disorderly assembly'. Finally, Jack saw the payment of Members introduced in 1911.[55]

Jack's first days in Parliament were overshadowed by the death of Queen Victoria on 24 January 1901, at Osbourne House. He got tickets for the funeral, and on 29 January was encouraging someone from home to come up for 'the most momentous state function that the world has yet seen'.[56] On Valentine's Day, Jack again wrote home describing the MPs' 'unseemly scramble' to the Lords' chamber for the opening of Parliament by the new King, Edward VII.[57]

> It was a very scandalous & surprising scene. Only a long football experience could have saved me.
>
> I saw the King & Queen on their thrones & I thought the Queen looked particularly well. HM's speech was audible everywhere & is considered a great success.[58]

The novelty of parliamentary attendance was short-lived. Eight days later, 'It is nearly 2 o'clock & I am weary. These days are interminably long. The H of C is the most unbusinesslike, timewasting, wearing place I could have imagined.'[59] Jack had been thrown into the seething Irish Home Rule debate. On 5 March he didn't get home until 1.30 a.m. The Irish had rioted and

> refused to clear the House for a division . . . Finally the police . . . entered & removed the recalcitrant legislators one by one till some 8 or 9 had been carried out, some kicking. The whole thing was as scandalous & disgusting as is possible to conceive. We might have been a tenth rate public being

> cleared after hours. I came here with a fairly open mind on Irish matters, but this sort of thing makes sympathy & concilia^{n} impossible, or at any rate very difficult.[60]

Between Parliament and the law, Jack was still writing poetry. 'Triumphans' had appeared in the *Daily Mail* after the Queen's death, and at the end of April 1901, as the Boer War ground on, he published a new volume, *The Last Muster*.[61] In the eponymous poem, the war dead reassure those who mourn that they have won eternal glory. There is, however, in the questioning of the fifth verse, a hint of that uncertainty which dogged the Boer War. Was it unimpeachably a war inspired by the noble cause of the defence of the downtrodden minority – the unenfranchised immigrant workers of the Transvaal? Or did the sparkle of gold and the fire of diamonds gleam in the greedy eye of the imperial power? Were the British in fact engaged, under another great Queen, in an act of modern-day piracy, singeing the bushy beard of the Boer? How unfortunate that 'mine' did not just mean a source of wealth, but also denoted its possession.

It is an uncertainty whose very existence Jack would have refuted, but, even unwittingly included, his words, 'Is there aught wherewith to upbraid us?' capture eloquently the suspicion.

> Speak! Was our course well run? Is there aught wherewith to upbraid us?
> Have we fled from the thunder of battle, or flinched at the lightning's track?
> Answer! What need of answer? By the God of Truth who hath made us,
> Thou knowest the Flag went forward, and never a foot went back!

Jack was excited to receive criticism from the most eminent poet of the day, 'Rudyard Kipling, who declares he read the book "with great interest", and specially liked the Hymn for use in Time of War'.[62]

The Last Muster had sold out by the beginning of August.[63] The late April publication date had assisted sales, for Milner had reached London, appropriately, on Empire Day, 24 May 1901. After four months of national mourning for Queen Victoria, Milner was met by corresponding rejoicing, a cabinet reception and a peerage. He then settled to business with Chamberlain. Milner was looking for a rapid end to hostilities in South Africa, to begin reconstruction and to get the mines working again to pay for the war. Beyond that, the establishment of government control in Rhodesia was key, and with a Resident Commissioner in place, Milner next wanted to reward Dick with promotion to Commandant-General of the police of southern Rhodesia, based in Bulawayo, from 1 October 1901.[64]

Milner had proposed the Rhodesian post to Dick before leaving Cape Town. Dick told Johnny, Lucy and Geraldine but not a word was to be breathed to anyone. Geraldine's excitement at Dick's imminent return contrasted with her parents' mixed feelings at the thought of their Pink being spirited away. Johnny was in Llandrindod Wells with Geraldine when Milner arrived in London. Lucy wrote to him: 'What a reception *Lord* Milner had – Jack got on to the platform at Waterloo with a ticket & saw it all. It is a pity Richard CM was not the aide de camp in attendance.'[65]

> I keep thinking of this appointment for Richard CM & of that little child being carried off from us to such a distant land. If only it had been nearer home! But I suppose one must not think of that as far as she is concerned I cannot blame her, I should have done the same in her case – if I had been engaged to you 4 years (instead of 2 months!) & the prospect of going with you to the North Pole or any outlandish place had offered, I would not have hesitated![66]

Geraldine responded to both of Dick's proposals with a clear 'Yes', and he and Geraldine, again acting very much according to their own minds, now announced their firm intention to marry after his return. Dick's father wrote to Johnny: 'The news is indeed "startling" about Geraldine & Dick – The latter seems to me to have jumped in about 6 months from a Lieut in his reg. to nearly Gen Com^dant!!! . . . Well of course I can only approve & think they both have been most patient & I am delighted you also consent.'[67] Finally, on 4 June, Lucy informed Johnny that 'A wire has just come for G from Chester Master. "All settled, but strictly private – am writing." . . . I hope there will be a cable soon from Richard to say he is starting [home].'[68]

Johnny visited the Chester-Masters in late June, to talk over Dick's return to Knole (which they were to attend), the wedding, and, doubtless, the dowry. He went to Knole from Cardiff, where the Royal Showground was being prepared ('I wonder how it can all be got ready by tomorrow. They must work all night').[69] He wrote to Lucy on the train:

> They all seem to prefer Hope Church for the ceremony but say that London & the Hereford Cathedral have both been discussed . . . his birthday is on the 28th . . . Am now in the Severn Tunnel & it is too dark to write. There is a damp smell like limpets & seaweed.[70]

While Johnny was at the Great Western Hotel in Cardiff, Lucy wrote from Di's where she was staying with Geraldine.[71]

> Last night we dined at the House with Jack & met Mr Walrond Lord Milner's private secretary! He talked freely ab^{t} RCM's appointment. . . . It is quite safe & settled by Milner & Chamberlain. Mr Walrond told us a lot about Bulawayo . . . It does not seem to be at all rough there except the washing which is a good deal battered about, but that we are accustomed to at Hereford![72]

Secrecy and the season were incompatible. With London agog at Lord Milner's return, Geraldine was an object of renewed interest. This intensified in June when *Country Life* featured Hampton Court.[73] Between writing announcements to the London and Hereford papers,[74] ordering the cake, and visiting Asprey's for the travel bag that Geraldine wanted for her wedding present, Lucy wrote:

> Several people have said 'I quite expect he will get some good appointment thro' Milner' & one has to look blank! G has often told her friends that she thought it probable that she w^{d} go out to SA when she married – so it all seems to come naturally – She is getting very tired of shopping.[75]

Dick's boat finally returned in early July, when an ecstatic Geraldine wrote to her father from 36 Seymour Street, at '6.30 p.m. . . . Dick has just arrived! & I have just given him his tea & Jack came in in the middle & tried to make him promise to go to see the Irish Members tonight!!!!!! He & his father are coming to dinner tomorrow.'[76] After four years, Geraldine was unwilling to let Dick out of her sight. She had to share him, though, not least with those awaiting his return at Knole, who were proud of their 'gallant officer'.

On Saturday 13 July, Dick returned to Bristol's Patchway station. Arches framed the route to Knole, and a procession formed of mounted tenants, men and women on decorated bicycles, Tockington Military Band playing 'See the conquering hero comes', and the cyclist corps of the Bristol Engineer Volunteers.[77] On Almondsbury Hill, Dick made a speech in which:

> Referring to the dates, April 1897, and July, 1901, on the arch, he said that the former re-called the mingled feelings of hope and sorrow with which he

> left England, the thought of friends and home and 'the girl I left behind me' would sometimes be uppermost.

In the following four weeks, the wedding announcement appeared in *The Times*, Jack and Dick met their solicitors on the House of Commons terrace to confirm Jack's trusteeship of Geraldine's jointure, and Dick went to Hampton Court to spend time with Geraldine.[78] Geraldine must have contrasted Dick on his last visit in 1897 with her husband-to-be, and been glad for a period of reacquaintance. Dick had been living at the boundaries of endurance, but now, at Hampton Court, he was utterly without responsibilities. Lucy hovered as discreetly as possible, trying to balance indulgence with indiscretion and understanding with the unseemly. She reported to Johnny that 'Dick & G did not come in from their ride till nearly 9 . . . I had to fetch them out of the garden at 10.30 p.m.'.[79]

Johnny had sent out 1,000 invitations to view the wedding presents (including luggage, saddlery, a camera and no fewer than nine silver toast racks) on Friday and Saturday, 9 and 10 August, for which a marquee and bandstand were erected. When Tuesday 13 August finally dawned, expectations of the day were high. As the *Hereford Times* reported, it was quite 'the wedding of the year so far as the West of England is concerned'.[80] Johnny went into his garden, as he had during the summer of his own marriage thirty-five years before, and harvested a bunch of Maréschal Niel roses for Lucy to carry against her white silk costume overlaid with black net. With the house quiet, the bride appeared, resplendent in white satin, trimmed with chiffon, and wearing her mother's Brussels lace veil. The household staff assembled in the quad to watch the coachman Frank Chilman drive Johnny and Geraldine to church.[81] There they were met by Johnny's uncle Rev. Sir John Leigh Hoskyns,[82] and by Berkeley, now Archdeacon of Hereford, who had married Carey forty-three years before at Hope. Johnny took his Pink on his arm, and, followed by six bridesmaids, they entered the church.

Outside, the large crowd noted that at her wrist, Geraldine wore the diamond and pearl bracelet given to her by the tenants, and at her breast the diamond brooch from Leominster friends and neighbours. Around her neck, she wore a diamond pendant from Fred and Becca of Willersley. Dick and Geraldine's carriage wound beneath floral arches on its way home to the wedding breakfast in the Coningsby Hall, whose centrepiece was a magnificent three-tier wedding cake weighing over a hundredweight.

Dick's best man was a fellow officer of the King's Royal Rifle Corps, Captain D.H. Scratchley DSO. His responsibilities included telegrams from Margaret, Duchess of Teck (sister-in-law of the future Queen Mary, whom Dick 'admired' and took out hunting frequently at the Cape[83]), Lord Milner from the *Saxon*, returning to South Africa, and Bend'Or, the Duke of Westminster.[84] At the end of the day, after the happy pair had escaped to Knole, three bonfires were lit and fireworks were ignited.

By the end of November, when Dick and Geraldine were expected to have arrived in Bulawayo, Johnny learned that Rowcliffe was finally in a position to proceed with the mortgage on Hampton Court, although the papers were before counsel until well into the following year. Less welcome, the Chester-Master solicitor Mr Ellert was starting to chase after the payment settled on Geraldine. Sale had to explain that 'with every desire to make things easy and pleasant' they could not really entertain his proposal, and made another suggestion.[85] Geraldine, blissfully unaware, sent her first letter home. 'Buluwayo [*sic*] is a sweet place. I adore it.'[86]

These demands, combined with the wedding bills, provoked another financial spasm for Johnny. By the middle of September, Daggs's directors at Leominster bank were demanding a fixed date for the repayment of Johnny's loan, but Sale could give no such undertaking, as the mortgage had still to be arranged.[87] The application of pressure did move matters on in one respect: Sir J.W. Ellis was appointed to value the estate.

Jack wrote with frustration to his mother of the 'want of a sense of propor^{n} in management [at Hampton Court]. Economising in pence and wasting pounds.'[88] He had confided to Lucy in June that he wished that

> Father would consult with Mr Cecil Parker, or someone of experience, in this matter of estate management. Seeing the interests involved, I don't feel as if I can acquiesce in my own useless posi^{n} much longer. It's all very well to say that I 'oughtn't to have to attend to these matters'. It would be a pleasure to me to do so, & in any case I feel I am responsible for every day that the present state of things continues, seeing, as I do, the extravagances & what they will lead to.
>
> I shall prepare a plain statement of what I think, but I shall not send it before seeing you.[89]

Everyone was soon distracted. In late November, Lord Bateman was suddenly taken ill in London, and died on the 30th, at the age of 75.[90] Three weeks of speculation about his successor as Lord Lieutenant ended when, on Christmas Eve, a black-edged letter from Downing Street, addressed to Johnny, arrived at Hampton Court.[91]

Dear Sir,
I have received His Majesty's command to propose to you that you should accept the office of Lord Lieutenant of the County of Hereford, now vacant by the lamented death of Lord Bateman. Hoping that you will see your way to complying with His Majesty's proposal I remain
Yours very faithfully,
Salisbury.

Under normal circumstances, this would have made for a very happy Christmas indeed. However, overwhelmed as he was by financial worries, alive to the hypocrisy 'when one is bankrupt or nearly so', and in weakening health, Johnny hesitated. Should the tempting fruits being offered to him be taken?[92] Most recent appointees had been young men, and at 68 years old Johnny wondered whether he was physically up to it.[93] Would he be required to answer piles of letters by every post, many of them soliciting donations to needy causes in the county, which he would simply be unable to honour? Would he be expected to chair endless meetings on subjects of which he was largely uninformed and quite possibly not interested, except insofar as they affected the county? In addition, he had never altogether overcome his aversion to public speaking. Besides all this, he suspected that much might be made of the fact that he had no title with which to dignify the position.

Johnny paced the gardens, retreated to the warmth of the remaining hothouse and smoked. He determined to seek advice, and consequently did not reply to the Prime Minister until 27 December:

My Lord . . .
His Gracious Majesty's proposal that I should undertake the duties of Lord Lieutenant of Herefordshire was so unexpected that I am still undecided whether I ought to enter upon so high and important an office, at my age, and when I am really obliged to retire as much as possible from county work. Tomorrow I hope to see friends in Hereford who may advise; and I ask meanwhile for your indulgence for a post or two.

At the foot of the letter, he added: 'I am very sensible of the high honour paid me.'[94]

FOURTEEN

Lord Looted

Immediately after Christmas 1901, Johnny sped into Hereford to find out what the Lord Lieutenancy would entail. It is unclear with whom he consulted, but on 28 December his old friend the Earl of Coventry wrote Johnny a warm letter of advice (notably using his christian name) from his seat at Croome, Worcestershire.[1]

> My dear John,
> I congratulate you very heartily, and I hope you will not hesitate to accept the post which has been offered you . . . You will have to succeed to a Ld Lt who, tho' no doubt he had all the wish, was unable, from circumstances which we deplore, to give large subscriptions: therefore they will not be expected – Then again yours is – I mean no disrespect – a comparatively quiet county, and you will not be pestered to call meetings on small subjects –
>
> I think you ought to attend a Levee in London once a year – and Quarter Sessions, as no doubt you do now, in your own county – you will not find the correspondence irksome; a few letters recommending names of gentlemen as magistrates – unless these are people who ought obviously to be justices, I generally consult the Chairman of the Board where they would sit – Then an order has recently come out that the number of Deputy Lieutenants is to be limited in future – often the number exceeds the limit, so I must hold my hand – I am sure your family and friends will feel that you ought not to refuse & I trust you will accept the post which is a very appropriate commencement of the new year for you, & with all good wishes, Believe me,
> Yrs very truly, Coventry.

Reassured, Johnny wrote again to Lord Salisbury on 30 December to say:

> that after reflection and a further knowledge of the duties involved I will undertake the position offered to me by His Gracious Majesty the King.

> I most heartily appreciate the honour which has been conferred upon me, and will use my best endeavours to maintain it.
>
> I take the opportunity of tendering the fullest assurance of my continued loyalty and devotion to His Majesty's person and allegiance to yourself in the cause now before the Country.

Johnny next wrote to his relations. Even he must have been surprised by the volume of letters that arrived. Lord Llangattock, Dick's uncle, wrote from The Hendre, Monmouth: 'The news . . . does not surprize me at all. We all determined here it could only be you if Justice was done. Who has ever done what you have done for Herefordshire? It is quite refreshing to see justice done for once.'[2]

Willie Hill-James wrote with the most accuracy: 'You have spent a life and a fortune in the interests of Herefordshire, as in a smaller degree did your Father before you, and the recognition of these services by your sovereign is as just as it is gratifying.'

Several people reflected on Johnny's near-scrape with the Membership for Leominster in the 1850s. The Rev. W.E. Edwards of Leominster wrote that 'Long ago your neighbours would have elected you to the highest position within their power but you preferred a quiet life – now at the King's command you cannot help coming forward.' Sale reported that 'Leominster people . . . seem to take it as a personal compliment to themselves'.[3]

At the House of Lords, the Letters Patent and Custos Rotulorum were prepared with Johnny's name, for which he was sent a bill for £100 14*s*. Besides this addition to Johnny's mortgage requirements, he had to pay for his dress uniform,[4] whose theatrical ensemble was dignified by the grey beard of Johnny's advanced years. The Court Journal described Johnny as 'an admirable example of that type of country gentleman on whom we specially pride ourselves as a nation'. Nevertheless, barbed comments about the appointment of a 'commoner' followed. In February 1902, the *Daily Express* noted that 'Lord Rodney [Johnny's former neighbour at Berrington Hall] is one of the very few noble landowners in Herefordshire, which has, in consequence, been dubbed the "peerless" county, and (like Cambridgeshire and most of the Welsh counties) has to put up with a commoner as its Lord Lieutenant.'[5] Whatever the national opinion on the subject, as Mary Heygate wrote to Lucy: 'At first, no one thought it would be possible a "Commoner" should be selected & how it's what everyone wished.'

Johnny, with characteristic frankness, alluded to his hesitation in accepting the position when he spoke publicly for the first time. 'He felt he was rather like an old hunter, that he would be the better for going out fewer days in the week.' Of the King's choice, Johnny felt that 'His Majesty . . . must have been thinking of the Whitefaces [Hereford cattle], of which King Edward had long been a fan.'[6] The high point of Johnny's three-year tenure of the Lord Lieutenancy would be the coronation of Edward VII in June 1902. Johnny spent the fortnight before the coronation in Llandrindod Wells where his swollen leg was massaged by a 'fat nurse'.[7] Lucy, meanwhile, was up in London, where she and Jack discussed the finances at Hampton Court. The 'Lord Lieut' was by now embarrassingly short of loot. It was now over two years since the decision to remortgage had been taken. Johnny's personal liabilities had continued to mount, so that, by February 1902, it had become clear that the proposed £25,000 was going to be inadequate. Sale had endured an uncomfortable meeting with Daggs on 11 February when he had been informed that Johnny's personal overdraft was now over £19,000.

> He wanted some definite information that he could put before his Directors at an interview he was having with them in Birmingham tomorrow & I could only repeat what I had said before but it became more & more evident that £25,000 w^{d} be insufficient for your necessities.[8]

Jack was particularly troubled by the expense of keeping the pedigree herd of Hereford cattle. To Jack it made no sense to tie up so much cash. He wrote to Lucy in May 1902: 'I quite agree about discussing things with you . . . I will send you a copy of the rough estimate of the difference in *£:s:d* between keeping a herd & running bullocks for market. I should be very glad always to explain to you my reasons for taking any particular view.'[9]

The Lord Lieutenant headed up to Fanny's town house for the coronation on 22 June 1902, having previously been to Harrods to order 'a one horse Brougham to carry 4 for the C^{n} week'.[10] The excitement in the capital had been heightened by the signing of the peace treaty at Vereeniging in South Africa on 31 May. As a result, Jack was 'overwhelmed with demands for Coronation & Peace Odes; but I have hardly any free time & shall not be able to do anything at all satisfactorily'.[11] Then came the shocking news that the King had undergone surgery for peritonitis. Jack wrote to his mother on 26 June: 'I don't at all like the last bulletin about the King. It was read with something like consterna^{n} tonight at the House, for it is known that the critical time is now.'[12] Edward VII was finally crowned in August.

With the passing of summer, reality resumed. By November 1902, having learned from Ashworth that the estate debts were standing at £3,930, and from Daggs that the bank overdraft was £20,691, Sale put it squarely to Johnny that a mortgage of £25,000 was 'manifestly insufficient'.[13] Sale, Johnny and Ashworth met at Hampton Court and decided that £3,000 more would be needed, but that they should ask for £5,000. They would go for the £25,000 first, and then apply for the further sum. For another three months, this was academic, for there was no appreciable progress in getting the plans of the estate to Rowcliffe. Sale and Ashworth caught the worst of Johnny's impatience during an interview at the end of January 1903. Sale recorded that Johnny 'had expressed yourself as most dissatisfied with the progress or non progress & you distinctly blamed us both not directly but indirectly'.[14]

Ashworth finally dispatched the traced plans at the end of February 1903, but they were back with him again by April for the addition of woods that he had omitted. In the event, the mortgage was split into two parts, one of £20,000, the other for £5,000. In early May 1903, Sale and a clerk went up to London to deposit the six boxes of documents and deeds with the Law Courts Branch. To their relief, they were successful. From the £25,000 mortgage, Johnny paid £22,146 to the bank to cover his overdraft, and £765 to Rowcliffe, with £50 interest, leaving £2,037 in a joint account with Jack.[15]

The relief of pressure on Johnny came just as he was celebrating the arrival of his first grandchild. Geraldine gave birth to a son in Bulawayo on 27 January 1903 (Carey and Berkeley's forty-fifth wedding anniversary). The child was given the Chester-Master family name of William. Once again, just as twelve months before, Hampton Court was inundated with letters of congratulation. As one of them put it: 'I saw it in this morning's "Times" that the King has got a new subject in Rhodesia.'[16] Jack accepted Dick's invitation to become Billy's godfather, as did Lord Milner, for whom the baby was given the second name Alfred.[17] Johnny and Lucy finally got to meet their grandson in September, when Geraldine returned home from Salisbury. She had moved there after Dick was promoted to High Commissioner of Rhodesia while retaining his role of Commandant-General of Police.

For Johnny there was at last the prospect, too, of an heir for Hampton Court. Jack had fallen in love that summer with Stephanie Robinson of Lynhales, Lyonshall, in Herefordshire. Her father, Stephen, was an old acquaintance of Johnny's as a breeder of Hereford cattle, and a past

President of the Hereford Herd Book Society. Stephanie herself was a thoroughly modern daughter of the landed gentry and a 'strong rider to hounds' in her youth.[18] Her education at home had been rounded off by two years at Cheltenham Ladies' College, the school then gaining ground under the inspired leadership of Dorothea Beale. This education made Stephanie rather a bluestocking. Schools like Cheltenham had been mocked by Gilbert and Sullivan: 'A woman's college! maddest folly going!/What can girls learn within its walls worth knowing?'[19] Geraldine's verdict after meeting Stephanie that September was 'quite delightful & suited to the part, & as beautiful as she was painted'.[20]

Jack did not feel quite so suited to his parliamentary part. After the spring session dealing with the Irish Land Purchase Bill (giving to Irish tenants financial incentives on generous terms so that they might become proprietors), now facing a diminished cabinet, and most of all overwhelmed with the desire to be in Herefordshire with Stephanie, the prospect of the return to London in September was unbearable. Jack contemplated giving up politics altogether. Geraldine warned: 'I shall be most disgusted if you give up the political world & brains, and go and vegetate at home.'[21]

Jack proposed to Stephanie and was accepted on 30 September. He wrote to his mother,

> The ring fitted most admirably. It was squeezed on & now I don't think it *can* come off! A good omen. She is very glad to think it comes from you . . . I am getting calmer, & the calmer I get the more certain I am that you will find her all that you could desire.[22]

Less happily, Evelyn had also fallen in love in 1903, with Thomas Percy Prosser Powell (TPPP). Although Tommy's father, the vicar of Dorstone in the Golden Valley of Herefordshire, was on the County Council with Johnny and Stephen Robinson, Johnny simply did not approve of Evelyn's choice, on the grounds of the Powell family's standing and, ironically, their lack of money.[23] Johnny would not consent to their marriage but Evelyn refused to let the affair drop. In his second daughter, Johnny had met his match. As a result of being too alike, the explosion of feeling between Johnny and Evelyn was powerful. Lucy wrote to Jack in August: 'E seldom speaks & is v grim.'[24] By Christmas, the two could hardly bear one another's company and Johnny and Lucy went to stay at Knowle Hotel, Sidmouth, Devon, for their health, taking Olive with them.

On their return in the new year, Johnny and his daughter were glad of Lucy's emollient effect as the TPPP affair ground on. Lucy's health, however, was not good, and, after being kept waiting outside the church at Hope one Sunday, she caught a chill. Her condition quickly worsened, and on 19 February 1904, Lucy Arkwright died, aged 64.[25] It was a cruel blow at a critical time. Jack lost his ally over estate affairs and now had to postpone his marriage indefinitely. Geraldine felt isolated by the distance. Evelyn lost a go-between with her father in the TPPP campaign. Olive had been her mother's close companion.

Overwhelmingly, though, Lucy's loss was suffered most keenly by Johnny. Throughout their married life, though mercurial in most matters, Johnny had been constant in his adoration of Lucy, and in his passion, affection and respect. She had been his essential counter-balance, measured, clear-sighted and calm while he rattled to and from London and Scotland to Hampton Court, forgetting his pipe, taking two left tennis shoes, falling off hunters and taking the wrong train. She had always known how to support him when required and chide him when appropriate. Whenever she had been away he had felt all at sea. Now that she was taken away, he sank. Lucy's death tore the heart and purpose from him.

Lucy's obituary noted that she had provided nurses for the poor, established clothing clubs and was secretary of the Herefordshire General Hospital penny scheme. 'No object of charity escaped her notice.'[26] The funeral took place on Tuesday 23 February, before Geraldine could get home. The family walked the private half-mile route from the house to St Mary's, cutting along the old main road, emerging by the school. At the church gates, the procession was joined by friends, household servants, tenants, workmen and forty schoolchildren. The service was conducted by the vicar, Rev. F.H. Tuke and by Carey and Berkeley's son, Rev. Lionel Stanhope. Mr Noakes, the schoolmaster, played the 'Dead March in Saul'. 'By Mr Arkwright's instructions the whole of the floral tributes were buried with the coffin.'[27] Johnny had no more need of flowers.

After the formalities, Johnny was inclined to retreat from the world. His financial situation was as bad as ever, and management of the estate was made difficult by his poor relationship with Ashworth. By Johnny's own admission the employment of a fellow rather than a servant was 'an utter failure'. Before Christmas, he had written to Jack: 'As we are today I hate being at home, for I cannot be on business terms with Ashworth.'[28] In his parlous financial situation and perhaps with Lucy's views in mind, Johnny caved in to pressure from Jack and agreed to the sale of his beloved

Hereford herd – the herd with which his name had been synonymous for nearly half a century.

The sale was announced in March, and a date set for October. Those who recognised Johnny's love of his Herefords, and his commitment to the breed acknowledged the blow. Sir John Cotterell wrote from Garnons: 'I am so sorry to see the dispersal of the Herefords announced.'[29] News of the sale reverberated around the county. Here was the man widely held as the epitome of the English squire, at the head of an exemplary estate, being forced, through financial difficulty, to sell one of the finest herds there was – the living symbol of the county and its prosperity. It was the end of an era, and many must have feared for the future.

There was no comfort for Johnny indoors. Evelyn, probably detecting the ebbing of fight from her father, was pursuing her relationship with Tommy, right under his deadened eye. Although Jack postponed his marriage to Stephanie indefinitely, Evelyn showed few such scruples. By 12 July 1904, Johnny's seventy-first birthday, Evelyn had wrung from Johnny his consent to her marriage to Tommy, though it was granted with poor grace. Olive reported to Jack that Johnny's

> one idea is to get Evelyn married as soon as possible. He says 'if I can be assured what she & Tommy will have to live on & can satisfy my mind it is enough & they will be all right I would rather it was done as soon as possible'. He says we shall know where we are, there will be one less person to consider, & she can be married quietly while we are still in mourning, & not wait till people will expect anything of us. All he wants now is to open up communication with the Powell family & find out how money matters are. He says of course he has been waiting for some 'Proposal' from Tommy but it has never come.[30]

Evelyn's wedding was foreseen for the following April. 'Father wrote me a letter last night from which I gather that everything is serene – as far as it goes. He said he preferred writing!' she told Jack.[31] A factor in Johnny's ill grace was that wherever he looked, his lonely misery contrasted with the happiness of his offspring. But there was not unbounded joy for all his children. On 1 August 1904, Geraldine was delivered of a second son, John Robert. To compound a miserable year, all was not well with the baby. He was little spoken of thereafter, although he lived to the age of 17. In 1913 Dick and Geraldine were to have a little girl, Lettice, who survived for just five days.

Through the summer of 1904 arrangements were made for the Herefords' dispersal. The sale was conducted at Green Farm, by Leominster auctioneers Alfred & Dearman Edwards.[32] Special trains stopped at Ford Bridge, luncheon began at noon, and the sale at 1 p.m. In all, 31 grand breeding cows and heifers, 16 2-year-old heifers, 17 yearling heifers, 13 calves and 8 bulls were sold, along with 10 of the tenants' beasts.

For the buyers, the sale represented an opportunity to acquire cattle from some of the finest prize-winning bloodlines.[33] The progeny of several of the lines, including the Livelies and Hampton Beauties were now in South America and the United States. Star of the sale was Whitfield (sire of two of the seven other bulls offered for sale that day), which Johnny had bought from Captain Clive of Whitfield three years before.

Johnny took himself off to Droitwich Spa, while at The Green, between 500 and 600 people lunched in the marquee. Johnny had asked that no speeches be made, but Sir John Cotterell toasted 'the health of the Squire'. Mr Edwards, brandishing the gavel, 'said he had to offer for sale the last of what had more than once been described as the oldest herd of Herefords in existence; and if it were not absolutely the oldest, it was not far from it'. Stephanie's father Stephen Robinson bought Beauty 16th for 27 guineas. Sir John Cotterell bought five cows for 167 guineas. The highest price of the day was 210 guineas paid by Mr Peter Coats of Sheepcote, Clifford, for Pearl 15th. The sale realised a total of £2,854 19*s* (around £166,131 today).[34]

With his wife no longer at home, his yard devoid of Herefords, his fiddle silent in its case, and autumn creeping across the gardens, there was a strong feeling about Johnny of a man dead to the joys of life, divesting himself of the trappings of his existence. On 24 October, Johnny added to this by resigning the Lord Lieutenancy. He received a generous letter of regret from Balfour at Downing Street. 'I cannot deny,' wrote the Prime Minister,

> the force of the reasons you urge for taking this step; and, feeling that they are of such a character that I should hardly be justified in pressing you to reconsider your decision, I must content myself with saying how very grieved I am to think that you will no longer be able to carry out the duties of an office which you are so well fitted to adorn.[35]

The position passed to Sir John Cotterell of Garnons, who was very much of the next generation, having been born in the year that Johnny and Lucy had married.[36]

This was not the end of the family's sadness of 1904. In November, Stephanie's sister, Lily Clegg, died at the birth of her fourth child.[37] Again, for Stephanie and Jack, death in the immediate family made marriage, for the moment, unthinkable. Evelyn's wedding, though, was still in prospect. Thankfully, the bride had a clutch of kindly aunts, who did their utmost to be excited for her. In particular, Minnie, Dick's wife, spent a week in March with Evelyn at the Hans Crescent Hotel in London.

On 25 April 1905, during Easter week, Evelyn and Tommy married at Hope church. Johnny and Evelyn walked up the path past Lucy's grave. The occasion was in marked contrast to Geraldine's wedding to Dick, but the newly-weds went away happy. Jack resumed his parliamentary duties in London and Olive stayed at home with her father. At the end of the month, Johnny went to a County Council meeting and sat on the Education Committee, apparently well, 'though stooping somewhat'.[38] On 21 May, he went to church, but fell ill on Monday. On Tuesday Olive, concerned by Hart-Smith's reports, wired for Jack and Evelyn to come home. Once Johnny had taken to bed, pleurisy set in, and he died peacefully at 10.15 a.m. on Thursday morning, 25 May 1905.[39] Remarkably, like his father before him, he died exactly one month after giving his daughter in marriage.

In death, Johnny Arkwright was remembered as a 'strong personality' and as one who 'felt the responsibilities as well as the privileges of an owner of landed property'. As a Master of Foxhounds, 'the memory of his conduct in the field, his liberality, his large-heartedness, his genuine kindness, and munificent hospitality, will never be effaced from the minds of sportsmen in Herefordshire'. His contributions to county education, charity, music, cricket, fishing, forestry and horticulture were all gratefully remembered, but it was for his promotion of the county's primary source of income, of agriculture, that he was posthumously most sincerely thanked.[40]

At the estate works, Mr Clare made Johnny's coffin, which was simply wheeled on its bier, like Lucy's before, over the fields to the church. It was followed on foot by Jack, Olive, Evelyn and Tommy. Among the mourners were Johnny's brothers Arthur and Dick, sisters Carey and Mary with Courthope, Fanny, George Davenport, Arthur and Mimmie Bateman-Hanbury, and Stephen Robinson. When they reached the main road, between 500 and 600 people joined them, including Colonel Chester-Master, Ashworth and Daggs. Berkeley and Tuke led the service, accompanied by other clergy from the estate. A mountain of wreaths surrounded the grave.[41]

Jack and his sisters returned to an uncharacteristically still Hampton Court. Johnny's death had taken the soul out of the place. For those around him, dependent on his way of life, the domestic staff, the agent, the tenants, the labourers, and shopkeepers, as long as Johnny's kind still existed, their way of life was secure. When they died or sold, life changed – for good. Insecurity now walked the corridors of Hampton Court. For all his shortcomings and mistaken judgements, Johnny had been larger than life, full of bluster and energy, making the house, gardens, home farm and estate run like a military exercise. In part, his problem was that, like his maternal grandfather, Sir Hungerford, he did not use the fruit of that order to his own benefit. He could make the estate office gather the information monthly, keep it in meticulous ledgers, and produce it on command, but he failed to take enough meaningful notice of the facts with which he was presented, allowing himself to be bound to too great an extent by form and tradition. He was a great leader, organiser and administrator, but no strategist. He felt that as long as the procedures were followed meticulously, everything would come right in the end. He believed that order had to come out on top, but could not comprehend the evidence of his own eyes, that the old order was changing for ever.

In many ways, this was symptomatic of Johnny's entire class. It was business as usual in estate offices, in London theatres, in the stands at Ascot, at Home Farm UK, and on the grouse moors of Scotland. But Johnny Arkwrights all over England were looking so hard at their account books, through their opera glasses and binoculars, over yard gates and down barrels, that when they paused to look up, the rest of the world had moved on. By going through the motions they had hoped to sustain their way of life. Johnny and his kind could not be blamed for their disbelief. The second half of the nineteenth century had raised a bloodless revolution, born of democracy, nurtured (ironically) by their own desire to modernise agriculture, fed by the farmer's oldest enemy, the weather, supported by market forces, and warmed by anti-landlordism. It only remained to reflect the revolution in the chambers of power at Westminster, and the time to do that was not far off.

FIFTEEN

Letting and Going

From Johnny, Jack inherited in 1905 the heavy responsibilities of the estate and its mortgages, along with the care of the tenants and labourers and their dependants. However, he was freer than Johnny had been in several respects; most importantly the estate once cleared of mortgages would be his outright to dispose of as he wished; he had been raised amid the uncertainty of agricultural depression, so that unthinkable questions had already had to be addressed, including the possible sale of Hampton Court; he had had closer involvement with the estate than Johnny had when he inherited; he had another career, the law (as well as Parliament and poetry); he did not have towering sums to pay to a large number of dependent siblings – only Olive remained unmarried; and he was more financially astute than his father (and it was less socially unacceptable to be so).

However, the demands of modern parliamentary Membership were the heaviest yet. Universal male suffrage had rendered obsolete set-piece speeches in town halls. Tours had to be made of factories, cricket clubs and working men's clubs, and speeches made at Primrose League meetings, in schools, at bazaars and in parish halls all over the constituency, even though there were few motor cars. As Lord Willoughby de Broke noted: 'the comfortable evenings at home had to give way, with distressing frequency, to the village meeting'.[1] When combined with the estate, the law, poetry and the family, it was a killing schedule.

Jack was immediately overburdened by the need to secure probate, pay death duties, pay portions to his sisters, and clear the mortgages.[2] Johnny had been unsure what was his to bequeath, when drawing up his will on 13 February 1894. In fact, his free estate amounted to £17,682 11*s* 6*d*, (approximately £1.025 million).[3] Jack paid £662 4*s* 3*d* death duty and had been granted probate by 19 July 1905 – within two months of his father's death.

Next there were the funds held by the estate's trustees, Berkeley Scudamore Stanhope and Courthope Bosanquet, on which duty was payable. They sold some of the £9,622 Great Western Railway 4 per cent debenture stocks that the fund held to pay this. Johnny's life insurance receipts were used to pay off the mortgages that Johnny had taken out, of £20,000, £5,000 and £6,500. This left the trustees with £1,926 11*s* 11*d* remaining from life insurance, as well as £2 11*s* 4*d* that they had in hand, and £40 worth of 3 per cent India stocks. Jack still had to find the money to pay the estate duty due on Hampton Court itself.[4] He sought advice from counsel and then arranged to pay the tax due on Hampton Court in eight yearly instalments beginning in 1905.

Meanwhile, Jack dealt with many personal requests from the family after Johnny's death. Jack's uncle Dick wrote to say that 'if there is anything which he wore in the way of jewellery I should be grateful to have it'.[5] Willie Hill-James asked for 'the case of the treasures found at Chamonix when we were all there'.[6] Many societies linked to Johnny wrote with suggestions for memorials to him. Herefordshire county leaders met in October to suggest a statue, painting or organ at the Shire Hall's music room, and Hope-under-Dinmore installed a new organ at St Mary's in his memory.[7]

Although overwhelmed, Jack exerted control over one area of his life. He settled with Stephanie that they should marry on 21 December 1905. Even this was complicated by the resignation of Balfour's government in November 1905, and the prospect of a general election on 14 January 1906. This time, Jack faced Liberal opposition for the Hereford seat from Colonel Edward Lucas-Scudamore.[8] The honeymoon was brief. The campaign against Scudamore was tough, but sympathy for the death of Johnny, Jack's aura of wedded bliss and the beauty of the new Mrs Arkwright helped to charm the electorate. Lucas-Scudamore polled 1,692 votes, and Jack 1,934. Jack was therefore returned with a majority of just 242. The newly-weds set themselves up with a flat in London at 56 St George's Square and rented Stephen Robinson's property, 'The Laurels', near Lynhales. On 13 January 1907, Stephanie was safely delivered of a little boy, John Richard Stephen Arkwright.[9]

Jack now sought a tenant for the house at Hampton Court. By 1 April 1908, Major and Mrs Evelyn Atherley, originally of Bishop's Waltham in Hampshire, were in residence. Letting wasn't an easy decision.[10] The notion of setting strangers loose among the sideboards and Chippendale was utterly foreign. As Lady Dorothy Nevill observed in 1907: 'The modern practice of letting one's country house would have appalled the landed proprietors of other days, when such a thing was undreamed of.'[11]

Although Jack held Hereford, the Tories were engulfed in January 1906 by a Liberal landslide victory. The surviving Tories found themselves in a minority of 157 against 513. Where previously, individual patrician candidates had lost to Lloyd George or Joseph Arch, this time they were defeated wholesale. It was as if the avalanche, high on the mountain that had previously claimed a few notables, had now crashed into the valley floor, making matchwood of the oldest and largest houses. Many landed families withdrew from politics for good. The extent to which established political figures were beaten was breathtaking. Balfour lost his seat, along with Henry Chaplin, the Tories' archetypal squire, who had sat on the RASE Council with Johnny and had held a seat in the house for thirty-nine years.[12] Change was sought all over Britain to reflect the ascendancy of the urban population which felt its fortunes swelling and desired a government that represented change.

In some of the more rural constituencies, the obliteration was not total,[13] but there were only 80 agriculturalists (reduced from 110) in the Commons after the election. In 1907–8 they briefly considered doing as Jack had advocated at his twenty-first birthday and forming their own party, but it was too late. By then they represented – even within the Tory Party – little more than a pressure group, and the idea was abandoned.[14] The Central Landowners' Association was, however, formed in 1906, theoretically to represent all agricultural interests, though in practice it became the patricians' mouthpiece.[15]

Nearly half of the Members were new when Jack returned to London for the 1906 session. Only 59 of the 377 Liberal MPs described themselves as gentlemen, while 40 per cent were businessmen.[16] There was a different feel about the place. Jack and his kind were now a minority, and not just in the political sense. At the age of only 33, Jack, as a landowning gentleman politician, belonged to a past generation and the previous century.

Ominously, the largely Tory, landowning, Anglican House of Lords now represented all that the Liberals and the electorate had just thrown over so categorically. There was a desire to reflect the new situation at Parliament, a desire that threatened the House of Lords' primacy.[17] Until now, their Lordships had had the right to veto any legislation sent up from the Commons. With the elected chamber representing views so different from their own, it was clear that any exercise of the Lords' veto would be seized upon as being counter to the will of the nation's electorate. Their Lordships were not cowed, however, and clashes with the Commons ensued. The Lords threw out the Liberals' Education Bill of 1906 and the Plural Voting Bill.[18] The Liberals' frustration at the blocking of their plans by an unelected and overwhelmingly Tory body boiled over in June 1907. Henry Campbell-Bannerman, the Liberal leader, moved a resolution to restrict by law 'the power of the other House to alter or reject Bills passed by this House'.[19] The fledgling Labour Party proposed that the upper house be abolished altogether.

Their Lordships' resistance created a close, revolutionary atmosphere laden with foreboding that crackled in the years between Johnny's death in 1905 and that of Edward VII in 1910. The most significant clash came over the 1909 budget, or Finance Bill. It was framed by the Liberal Chancellor, David Lloyd George. Ardently Baptist, Welsh, working class and Liberal, Lloyd George had ever been a loather of Jack's Anglican, landed, Tory class. Now, as a Chancellor framing his budget, he had the opportunity to exact revenge for all those he knew who had suffered injustice at the hands of the countryside's controlling interest. The means to fund the proposed Old Age Pensions, and the eight new Dreadnought battleships demanded by the Tories to counter the threat of German naval supremacy would be sweated from the fat of the land. The patricians had warned against becoming dependent on imported food.[20] They might already have paid for the shift to imports with the sale and export of their wine cellars, picture collections, musical instruments, furniture and even land, but now they would be required to pay to protect the free flow of the imports that had ruined them.

The 1909 budget included several measures specifically aimed at Jack's class.[21] Death duties went up by a third on estates of more than £5,000, unearned income was charged at a higher rate than earned income, and a Super Tax of 6*d* in the £ was charged on incomes of over £5,000. The real sting came with the introduction of four Land Taxes.[22] Although these taxes were later repealed due to the little revenue that they realised, they were seen as a direct attack by the Liberals on the ownership of property, particularly land.

The greatest success of Lloyd George's budget was in goading the House of Lords into direct confrontation with the Liberal government. In delivering the proposed changes in a 5-hour, at times incoherent speech on 29 April 1909, Lloyd George termed his measures a 'War Budget'. Though he publicly intended 'warfare against poverty and squalidness', he privately threw down the gauntlet to their Lordships.[23] The 1909 budget seemed to Jack's party a blueprint for socialism. It raised more revolt than revenue and caused the fiercest parliamentary battle since the Great Reform Act of 1832. The debate raged for fully 72 days and nights, and

550 divisions were called. Members were obliged to sleep, eat and work in the ill-equipped House, an exhausting situation exacerbated by the hottest summer in living memory.

The summer ground mercilessly on into autumn. Jack, as Secretary of the Tories' committee to oppose the Budget, was horribly overburdened with opposition to the Bill, demands from his constituents and worries about Hampton Court. The previous autumn, serious financial mismanagement had been revealed at Hampton Court estate office. Jack had sacked the cashier, Charles Duncan, but the agent, Harry Ashworth, had taken the matter personally. Jack declined Ashworth's offers to reimburse the shortfall but the affair resulted in Ashworth's mental breakdown and suicide. Rumours were rife, many concluding that it was Ashworth who had been in the wrong. Jack repudiated this utterly, stating that 'Mr Ashworth was an absolutely honourable man.'[24] While Jack sought a new agent, Harry Garstone, a clerk at the office, took up the reins. Jack passed the accounts, for clarification, to Herbert Ferguson Davie of Wilde & Ferguson Davie, at the appropriately precise address of 61½ Fore Street, London, but he had to try to keep a closer eye on estate matters as well.

On Jack, whose constitution had never been robust, 1909 imposed lethal demands. Stephanie became increasingly frustrated at how little she and baby John saw of Jack, and was genuinely alarmed at Jack's condition. On 2 October 1909, she wrote to Jack from The Laurels:

> I *do* want you to retire from Parliament, as I am quite certain you aren't strong enough for the work & I don't see why you should kill yourself to please anyone . . . All said & done I think you ought to consider me before your constituents & I can't bear to see you so thin & over-worked.[25]

Jack could not consider resignation, though, while Lloyd George remained on the offensive. As the Lords prepared to reject the Finance Bill that month, Lloyd George threatened them in a speech at Newcastle-upon-Tyne:

> Let them realise what they are doing. They are forcing a Revolution . . . Questions will be asked which are now whispered in humble voice . . . why 500 ordinary men, chosen accidentally from among the unemployed, should override the judgment . . . of millions of people who are engaged in the industry which makes the wealth of the country. It will be asked who . . . made ten thousand people owners of the soil, and the rest of us trespassers in the land of our birth?[26]

The Lords would not submit. On 30 November, they rejected the Finance Bill, and a general election was called for January 1910. The result nationally was the loss for the Liberals of their clear majority. They won only two seats more than the Conservative/Unionists (275–273), but with Labour (40) and the Irish Nationalists (82) on side, they could hope to push through their legislation, though at the cost of being prey once again to Irish demands. In Hereford, Jack was re-elected, beating lawyer E. Lewis Thomas. His majority more than trebled and now stood at 787.

Asquith returned to Downing Street and immediately framed the Parliament Bill: the House of Lords would be excluded altogether from interfering with the Finance Bill; any Bill would be able to pass into law without the consent of the Lords if it were presented in three succesive sessions of a single Parliament; and parliamentary life was to be reduced from seven to five years. On the evening these resolutions were passed, Asquith further warned that if the Peers rejected his Bill, he would advise the Crown on passing it directly into law, and if that was not done, his government would resign or recommend the dissolution of Parliament.

To the Lords, the threat of the loss of their right of veto was far more significant than the Finance Bill, which was now passed almost without notice. This was because the loss of their veto, as John Redmond, leader of the Irish Nationalists in the Commons acknowledged, was 'tantamount to the granting of Home Rule' to Ireland.[27] Nevertheless, the Parliament Bill emasculating the Lords was passed in 1910.

After losing the battles over the Budget and the Lords' veto, the surviving patrician and landed MPs, angry and frustrated, retreated and regrouped behind opposition to Home Rule for Ireland. This now became their last stand. The Tories under Disraeli had become the party of empire, and Ireland was geographically at the heart of empire. To let her go was more unthinkable than ever after men had so recently died in the Boer War fighting to colour the southern African colonies pink. However heated the passions aroused by the 1909 Budget, they would be as nothing compared to those that the Irish question inflamed.

The two sides were girding themselves for battle when, quite suddenly, on 6 May 1910, King Edward VII died. National feelings on the King's death in some measure resembled those at Hampton Court on Johnny's death five years earlier. Bertie's going was the final break with the certainties of the previous century and its Queen Empress. It was as if his reign had anchored the British liner to Victorian glory. Now, Britannia seemed to have slipped loose and she began to swirl around the vortex of class war in Britain, internecine war in Ireland and impending world war.

There were suggestions that the constitutional turmoil between the Commons and the Lords had hastened the King's demise, so over the course of the summer and autumn of 1910, a Constitutional Conference met twenty-one times in a futile effort to spare the new king, George V, the pressure of constitutional crisis. With the final breakdown of those talks on 10 November, war between the Houses broke out anew, over Irish Home Rule.

The angry landowners had capitulated over electoral reform, they had seen the agricultural interest bow before the needs of the cities, they would cede their constitutional right to veto legislation if they must, but they would not let Ireland go. Jack, true to type, was a supporter of the Protestants in northern Ireland. Among the Tories' leaders was Lord Willoughby de Broke who, at just three years older than Jack, had been moulded by an almost identical upbringing.[28] In July 1911 he stated that 'we have used every weapon save personal violence. I should not be averse to using even that.'[29] It was a conflagration that threatened to burn out of control, Catholic Irish nationalists and Ulster Protestants both arming themselves by means of (what became) illegal gun-running (especially in 1913), officers of the British Army in Ireland threatening disobedience (the Curragh 'mutiny' of March 1914), and the Tory leader declaring there to be 'no length of resistance to which Ulster can go in which I should not be prepared to support them'.[30] The spark of potential civil war was dimmed only when consumed by that greater conflagration, the First World War, in 1914.

A month after the breakdown of the Constitutional Conference, Jack was further taxed by grave domestic decisions. Stephanie's sister, Grace Evelyn was widowed on 8 December 1910. Grace's son, Lyndon decided to sell their home, Kinsham Court near Presteigne, and its estate in the north-western corner of Herefordshire. Jack now considered selling Hampton Court and moving to the more manageable Kinsham. Besides being a much smaller estate, the Georgian house would be cheaper to run and occupied a breathtaking position, the ground in front of the drawing-room window falling steeply away to a meadow in a hidden curve of the River Lugg. However, he had not yet cleared the remaining mortgages on Hampton Court, and he would have to purchase Kinsham before he could even begin to seek a buyer for Hampton Court. He did though have the funds from the September 1907 sales of all his Leominster property including the old Town Hall, Grange Court.[31] In total, nineteen lots had realised £10,735.[32]

The purchase of Kinsham now prompted Jack to make further sales. On 4 and 5 May 1911, he sold around 3,500 outlying acres of the Hampton Court estate by private treaty, and others by auction on 15 June through Messrs J.D. Wood & Co. The 106 lots realised £71,940 10*s*. Several of the tenants bought their farms, following the national trend at such sales.[33] These sales enabled Jack finally to pay out the mortgagees of Hampton Court in July 1911. Full ownership reverted to him and he was free to dispose of the house. Jack had the detachment to see that he had no future at Hampton Court – scaling down to Kinsham made financial sense.[34] It would be expensive to buy Kinsham before selling Hampton Court, but any debt would be entirely cleared by an eventual sale, and he would be left with a large lump sum to invest. Current opinion favoured investment in railway shares, mining, shipping, the Stock Exchange, breweries, newspapers, overseas bonds or foreign property. The new wealth élite was not in general landed, for reasons expressed by Wilde's Lady Bracknell. 'Between the duties expected of one during one's lifetime, and the duties exacted from one after one's death, land has ceased to be either a profit or a pleasure. It gives one position, and prevents one from keeping it up.'[35] The new super rich kept their dollars (for the really wealthy were now on the other side of the Atlantic) at the ready. As Balfour had put it the previous year: 'The bulk of the great fortunes are now in a highly liquid state . . . They do not consist of huge landed estates, vast parks and castles, and all the rest of it.'[36]

For all the enlightenment of his outlook, Jack was Johnny's son and it was unpalatable to scale down his land holding. He was, though, increasingly in the minority. Between 1809 and 1879 (a period that included the death of his own great-grandfather Richard Arkwright) 88 per cent of British millionaires had been landowners. Between 1880 and 1914, the proportion of British millionaires who owned land fell to 33 per cent.[37]

Jack had to come to terms, too, with the feelings that the decision stirred. As Lord Ailesbury said at this time: 'A man does not like to go down to posterity as the alienator of old family possessions.'[38] Furthermore, what was accepted in the privacy of Jack's study had to win the sanction of family sentiment. At the end of February 1911, Jack wrote to each of his father's surviving siblings to seek approval for the step that he was contemplating. On 7 March, Jack's youngest uncle, Charlie, replied. 'I am glad to hear from you, but I think you will be doing a very wise thing by selling'.[39] The next day came Arthur's reply.

> I cannot say that the contents surprised me. I am afraid that you have many anxieties & worries connected with the dear old home, and so had your father before you . . . It will be a wrench to say goodbye to Hampton Court, but you & Stephanie will be very happy in a smaller place, which you can look forward to as a future home for young John.

Jack's cousin Ronald Bosanquet who had forwarded Jack's letter to his mother, Mary, thought 'you are quite right, though I know how much it must have cost you to make the decision'.

From Algiers, Edwyn wrote for himself and Alice that

> what you write is common sense & a bowing to the inevitable – and however it may touch the tender chord to hear that the *decision* is made, one cannot shut one's eyes to the fact that for many years the *question* has been there . . . Possibly it is we old ones, who have the longest memories, who will have *only* sadness about it . . . you are doing the best thing, if not the pleasantest . . . You have Aunt Alice's & my own sincere sympathy and hearts good wishes in what must always be one of the big trials of your life.

Willie Hill-James and Fanny at the Hotel des Princes in Biarritz shared 'all your painful feelings', and thought Jack 'quite right in facing the matter now'. Berkeley, now living at The Grange, Much Wenlock, felt that 'H Court is a vast House . . . and I cannot but think you will be wise in selling it'.

Jack also consulted the Arkwrights at Willersley, where similar measures were being contemplated. Fred Arkwright replied from the Grand Hotel, Florence, that 'Seeing so much about the advisability of increasing the number of occupying owners of land in papers & speeches & thinking there is a good deal in it from a national or political point of view', he had offered his tenants the opportunity of buying their farms. 'The result is that 3 only have expressed a wish to purchase.'[40]

The benefits of creating 'occupying owners of land' had been promoted since the 1890s, particularly with regard to Ireland. It was believed that antagonism in the Irish question had its root in the landlord and tenant relationship. If that were eliminated, then the other polarisations along the lines of Protestant and Catholic, English and Irish would dissolve. Landowners in the south particularly hoped that the sale of land to their tenants would consolidate the Union. Instead it reinforced self-confidence and nationalism and left Unionist landowners in the south stranded.

In England, it was believed that the creation of more landowning farmers would counterbalance the growing threat of socialism. It was hoped, too, that ownership would reduce anti-landlord feeling and help to preserve surviving great estates. As Milner said: 'If the present social order is to endure, it is simply necessary, at whatever cost, to effect a great increase in the number of people who have a direct personal interest in the maintenance of private property.'[41] In neither case were complicated issues so simply resolved, but they do explain in part the desire of landlords to sell off farms to their tenants.

In April 1911, Jack sent out a second round of letters containing the particulars of the Kinsham Court estate. Berkeley's opinion was that 'It is beautifully place[d], with good fishing & motors now-a-days innihilate distance . . . The size of the estate is certainly very alluring.' Dick felt 'sure that you are doing what as far as human foresight can suggest, is right'. Jack's cousin, Sidney (George and Lizzie's son) revealed one of Jack's private preoccupations. 'Your son would have no reason at all to reproach you & it is not as if you had wasted your inheritance.'[42]

Alice wrote from Algiers that she was excited that he and Stephanie nearly had a new home, but was full of regret that she and Edwyn would never see it, as they no longer travelled back to England. 'I feel more & more how right you are to do it . . . We are *very* sorry for you & shall be glad for yr sake when it is over. We are so very sorry you are not well.'[43]

By 2 May 1911, Stephen Robinson was able to write to Jack from Lynhales, 'I must say that I am pleased that the transaction between you & Lyndon is nearly completed', not least because Stephanie was now expecting their second son, David, who was born on 15 September 1911.[44] Berkeley, too, was supportive, recommending auctioneers Frank Rutley & Co. who had disposed of his home, Holme Lacy, in 1910. Besides considering the family's views, Jack had to make provision for the staff at Hampton Court. He ensured that they all found jobs elsewhere if he could not accommodate them at Kinsham. Walter Heygate would become agent to Stephen Robinson at Lynhales, while Harry Garstone, who had proved himself in the wake of Ashworth's death, was promoted to agent at Kinsham. Reay and Childs would go with Jack and Stephanie, and William Bevan the gardener would move to Kinsham where his wife would become cook. With the motor car superseding the carriage, Frank Chilman was stood down. Jack made him landlord at the Railway Inn, Bodenham,[45] promising him that the moment one of the farms at Kinsham became available, his son John, who was keen to farm, would have the chance of it.[46]

The sale of Hampton Court now became public knowledge. The *Leominster News* of 10 May declared that the announcement was heard 'with considerable regret'. On 20 June, *The Times* reported that the outlying farms not taken to by tenants had been offered for sale at Leominster by John D. Wood & Co. of Mount Street, London.[47] Sales to tenants had realised £26,606 and auctions brought in a further £33,807.[48] The Hampton Court/Kinsham transaction was causing upheaval on the Kinsham estate, too. Lyndon sold off portions of the Kinsham estate, leaving the main house with around 2,500 acres,[49] which Jack now bought.

From 56 St George's Square, Jack wrote to each of his Hampton Court tenants personally:

> Dear Mr –
> You know that I am selling certain portions of the Hampton Court Estate. I am afraid that this has given rise to a belief that I & my family will come back to Hampton Court in the near future.
>
> That belief is, I am sorry to say, a mistaken one: Many years would have to elapse before we could return. For this & for other strong reasons I have decided reluctantly to try & find a purchaser for Hampton Court & to provide myself with a home elsewhere more in keeping with my circumstances.
>
> In taking this course I shall do what I can to see that the remainder of the estate is kept intact as far as possible, into whatever hands it passes, & that there shall be no more disturbance than I can help.
>
> I hope that the old personal friendships will long continue even though the relation of Landlord & Tenant come thus sadly to an end.
> Yours very truly,
> John S. Arkwright.[50]

Epilogue

On 13 July 1911, 101 years almost to the day after Hampton Court was conveyed to Jack's great-grandfather, Richard Arkwright, Jack paid off the mortgage on Hampton Court and it was his to sell.[1] Hampton Court joined the flood of houses on the market between 1909 and 1914. This slowed during the War (although the sales continued with surprising consistency) but picked up again afterwards. Between 1912 and 1920, between 6 and 8 million acres changed hands in England – around one-quarter of the country's land. In Wales and Scotland the figure amounted to nearly one-third of the land, and in Ireland the percentage was higher still. By mid-1910, 72,000 acres were on the market in thirty-six English counties.[2]

Hampton Court and its remaining 7,000 acres were sold by John D. Wood and Co. to Mrs Nancy Burrell of Carlisle in June 1912.[3] Mrs Burrell was 'an amazing "dyed in the wool" Northumbrian – very outspoken, highly eccentric – loved by children animals & the people who worked for her'.[4] She was the second daughter of Charles Perkins, heir to the Durham and Northumberland Coal Mines and Steel Works.[5] She was also an extremely keen and capable fisherwoman, and it may well have been the 6 miles of fishing on the Lugg that inclined her to purchase Hampton Court.

There was one further consequence of the sale. On 2 March 1912, *The Times* reported that Jack had 'applied for the Chiltern Hundreds on the grounds of ill-health and the necessity of undergoing an immediate operation'.[6] Publicly, the throat-tightening smogs of London and Jack's tobacco consumption had wrought havoc when the annual bout of influenza had struck. Privately, Jack's withdrawal from the House was almost certainly influenced by the sale of Hampton Court. In his mind, wealth, land, status and power were so inextricably interlinked that the loss of one must be compensated for by the sacrifice of another. The country house had ever been a powerhouse, symbolic of political supremacy whether that power was aspired to or had already been gained. When the house went, so did the position. To continue to occupy the seat that he had won under more fortunate circumstances seemed somehow dishonest.[7]

The loss of that power and position by the landed class in Britain has sometimes been attributed to death duties and the First World War. In fact, as the example of Johnny and Jack demonstrates, the process had started at least a generation earlier. Modern death duties were introduced in 1894. Initially they only applied at a maximum rate of 8 per cent on estates worth over £1 million. They rose to 15 per cent in 1909, to 40 per cent in 1919, to 50 per cent in 1930 and to 60 per cent in 1939.[8] When the late Duke of Devonshire inherited Chatsworth in 1950, he had to pay 80 per cent duty, a total of £4.8 million on a valuation of the estate at £6 million.[9] These increments contributed to the erasure of landed estates, but did not set the process in train. The First World War, cataclysmic as it was, was among the last of a passage of events that had begun to reduce the power, status and wealth of the landed class seventy years before.

The decline might be said to have begun with Ireland. After famine struck there in 1845, Sir Robert Peel repealed the Corn Laws.[10] The protection of landowners was simply unjustifiable in the face of the starving impoverished of 1845–6. Beyond helping the needy, Peel's removal of the tax on grain rendered agricultural interests secondary to those of the growing urban majority. Peel's decision broke the Tory Party and ultimately it broke the landowning class.

To appease landowners and to enable them to compensate for lost revenue by increasing the productivity of their acres, agricultural loan companies were established. These encouraged heavy investment in land to make it more productive. Agricultural improvements were made, in many cases, without due moderation – not least because no one could establish what the level of moderation should be.

Over-capitalisation was followed by bad weather, disease, increased production costs owing to unionism among agricultural labourers, and the explosive growth of imports. Together these factors created acute agricultural depression and serious financial losses at precisely the time when landowners' loans were due for repayment. The result was financial ruin which coincided with the undermining of the patricians' status by growing democracy and administrative professionalism.

Although electoral reform had begun in 1832, the measures then introduced did not have a great impact. The significance of the 1832 Act was rather that it represented the start of a process. Once introduced, reform would be hammered home with increasing force (in four blows in

1867, 1884, 1918 and 1928) until the log of patrician exclusivity was split open. The removal of the Lords' veto in 1911 was deeply symbolic. With Parliament lost, the patricians were lost.

The First World War hit hard a generation of the officer and patrician class, but the premature death of an heir could not alone end a way of life that had endured for centuries – it had, after all, survived the Wars of the Roses (1455–85). The aristocratic way of life had been waning long before 1914. Many families were only just maintaining their social position by the outbreak of war. The War represented, if not the cause of landed decline, the death rattle of the landed interest. For some landowning families, the War and death duties made a peculiarly cruel combination, where the landowner died at the country seat just before his heir was killed in Flanders. Jack witnessed this at first hand.

Dick's father, old Colonel Chester-Master, died on 14 November 1914 after one last fall from his horse.[11] Dick, who had returned from Rhodesia in 1908 to become Chief Constable of Gloucestershire Constabulary, sorted out the estate's finances, and rejoined the King's Royal Rifle Corps.[12] In March 1915, he was appointed second-in-command of the newly raised 13th Battalion, composed of 'Stockbrokers, Solicitors, Barristers, Country Gentlemen, Bank Clerks & so on'.[13] By August he was at Ploegsteert, north-west of Lille.

The stagnant conflict that was to set in during 1916 was not Dick's kind of war, but he again served with great credit to himself and the regiment, with mentions in dispatches, a DSO and bar, and frequent command of the entire brigade.[14] However, on 31 August 1917, four days after his forty-seventh birthday, during the Third Battle of Ypres, Dick was shot 'by a sniper from the right flank at short range', while trying to locate enemy dugouts.[15] Jack and Milner (who was now one of Lloyd George's five War Cabinet members and for whom Jack was working in London) were stunned. Geraldine, staying with Stephanie at Kinsham when she learned of Dick's death, wrote to Jack:

> I am so thankful I was here . . . Hosts of letters by every post come . . . Again I heard from Major Johns today & a full account of the funeral. If it had been in Winchester [Regimental HQ] it could not have been more imposing. Divisional Band, Battalion Buglers. 15 for Last Post. Lots of wreaths. And all in a Hospice garden with Mother Superior & Sisters to guard the grave in the future. GOC & Brigade Colonels all there . . . I was so glad to have Lord Milner's letter.[16]

On 7 September, Stephanie wrote to Jack. 'I gather from G that they will be *very* short of money with the double lot of death duties etc., & I'm sure any help with Billy's schooling will be a God-send.'[17] On 11 September, a memorial service for Dick was held at Cirencester.[18] Geraldine took support from reactions to his death, writing to Jack: 'The inhabitants of C'cester are walking about with their heads hanging down. The Police say the Force is ruined . . . Poor Ozzy Walrond is heart-broken.'[19] March 1918 saw more action in the Ypres area where Dick had died. The Germans took Mount Kemmel, putting the hospice at Locre into the front line for the first time. Geraldine was deprived of the comfort that the nuns would tend Dick's grave, and from the thought that Dick was well out of it, when Locre hospice was flattened by shellfire in April 1918. The cacophony and chaos might have woken the dead; the raining shells all but exhumed them. After the War, Dick's body was disinterred and he was reburied at Locre Hospice Cemetery nearby.[20]

Jack corresponded with Dick's brothers Andrew and Cyril about selling the farms at Knole to meet death duties on the estate. 'This blow has absolutely knocked the stuffing out of me,' Cyril wrote, '& I cannot realize the truth of it.'[21] The Chester-Masters, like many landed families, now found themselves with the insult of further death duties added to the injury of their loss. Their situation soon became untenable. On 17 January 1920, Geraldine's mother-in-law wrote that

> The irrevocable step is being taken! I have this day sent a line to Ronald Bosanquet to inform the trustees that I give up Knole on 25th March. I have done my best to keep the old home going for self & family but find having the gardeners to pay (wh I had not to do before dear Richard died), that even with the help of the PGs it makes the expense too great & I cannot pay my way, much less look to keeping the interior in order.[22]

Knole was let until 1931, when it was sold to a Bristol property speculator. Part of the house was taken as a school for the handicapped. Knole gradually fell into dereliction until it was finally demolished in 1970. Only the octagonal tower was retained, reduced and incorporated into an executive home.

On 7 April 1921, Geraldine and Dick's second son died and was buried next to his baby sister, Lettice, at Stratton. Geraldine and Billy withdrew to Roseleigh East in Cheltenham until 1927 when she moved to Quern's Lane House, Cirencester. The Abbey, the Chester-Masters' square mid-eighteenth-century house, built on the site of the twelfth-century St Mary's Abbey in the heart of Cirencester, was let until shortly after the Second World War. Thereafter it remained empty for over a decade while a tenant was sought. It was finally demolished in 1964. Flats for the elderly were subsequently built on the site, and Billy presented the former gardens to the town as a public park in 1965.[23]

Dick's death had come three weeks after Jack had achieved further recognition as a poet. In 1916 and 1917, while employed under Lord Derby, travelling around the country using his powerful oratory to help recruitment, Jack scribbled what would become 'The Supreme Sacrifice' on the back of envelopes, telegraph forms, and on War Office paper. The words were written to accompany a hymn tune he had heard, by Dr Charles Harris, the vicar of Colwall, near Malvern.[24] So profoundly felt was the resonance of his words that Jack's hymn was immediately adopted as the nation's favourite hymn of remembrance. It was sung on 5 August 1917 at Westminster Abbey at a service to mark the anniversary of the outbreak of war. It would also be sung at the burial of the Unknown Soldier, at the dedication of the burial flag of Ypres, and at the consecration of the Houses of Parliament War Memorial and of the Menin Gate Memorial. Jack's words were recited by the Premier of Canada over the transatlantic telephone at the unveiling of the Canadian War Memorial at Vimy Ridge.[25] The tune is still played annually at the Cenotaph in London on Remembrance Sunday.

The poem earned Jack the epithet of 'inspired interpreter of the nation's deep and inmost feelings'.[26] While the poems of Sassoon, Brooke and Owen expressed the experience of the men at the front, Jack's words seem to have touched a chord with those at home who lost men in the War. Time and again he received requests for the use of lines on headstones.

O Valiant Hearts, who to your glory came
Through dust of conflict and through battle flame;
Tranquil you lie, your knightly virtue proved,
Your memory hallowed in the Land you loved.[27]

Jack captured, too, in his expression of the extinguishment of knightly virtues, the sense of the end of an era and the extinction of a class. This intoned with the mood of change after the War. Between 1919 and 1930, death duties rose to 40 per cent. Art collections once again made their way to the auction rooms. London houses were sold. In 1919, Lord Salisbury sold the Cecils' Arlington Street home for £120,000, Lord Dartmouth disposed of his Mayfair mansion, and the Duke of Devonshire sold Devonshire House on Piccadilly, for £750,000.[28]

Country houses, too, began once more to come on to the market, including Stowe, former home of the Duke of Buckingham, in 1921–2.[29] However, the unprecedented number of properties available saturated the market so that between 1920 and 1939, 221 mansions in England, Wales and Scotland were destroyed (compared with 79 between 1870 and 1919), including the Peels' home at Drayton Manor.[30]

The other three surviving branches of the Arkwright family were obliged to follow Jack's suit and sell up. Fred and Becca's son Captain Richard Arkwright sold Willersley in 1927, four years after Fred's death, and moved to Worcestershire. The contents of Willersley were dispersed at a sale on 7 June that year, and included 'examples of Adam, Chippendale, Sheraton and Hepplewhite, suites, chairs, tables and a Sheraton Bookcase . . . pictures and drawings . . . [by] Joseph Wright of Derby, Houdecoeter, JMW Turner, David Cox', and others.[31] Willersley is today a conference centre for a religious foundation. It still overlooks the old Arkwright mill at Cromford, which constitutes an essential part of the Unesco World Heritage site on the Derwent in Derbyshire.

Willie Arkwright parted with Sutton Scarsdale in 1920, selling to an American but retaining the mineral rights. He moved to Devon, and on his death in 1925 made Jack's eldest son John his heir. Vandals got in to Sutton and it was decided to remove the lead from the roof before it was stolen. All detachable fittings were also stripped out, reducing Sutton to a shell, which was saved from total demolition when it was purchased by Sir Osbert Sitwell (one of whose ancestors had been married to John Arkwright's brother Charles, of Dunstall, Staffordshire) in 1955. Today, Sutton is owned by English Heritage, and its elegaic façade overlooks the M1 motorway, between junctions 29 and 30.

Part of Sutton suffered a bizarre fate, even for these years when houses were bulldozed or converted to schools. Three rooms were bought by William Randolph Hearst, the American newspaper magnate and collector. They were exported to California where they remained in crates for twenty years. They were then sold and went on contract to Hollywood where they became part of the film scenery for *Kitty*, made at Paramount Studios in 1945. Nothing could be more eloquently illustrative of the transition of values from silver spoon to silver screen than the nomination of this aristocratic cast-off for the Oscar for best film set at the Academy

Awards of 1946. The rooms were afterwards in part reconstructed at the Philadelphia Museum of Art where they can still be seen.[32]

It is the fate of the Essex Arkwrights that perhaps illustrates most eloquently the unstoppable process of democracy and urbanisation in Britain through the twentieth century. Mark Hall suffered two fires, in 1947 and in 1958. The remainder of the house was then demolished because of dry rot. Rev. Joseph's grandson Loftus lived out his reclusive final years at Parndon Hall. Of his three sons, the eldest disappeared in the 1920s and one of the twins died at sea in 1942. The remaining twin, Commander Godfrey Arkwright saw the family estates disappear under the new town of Harlow. Parndon Hall is today used for health service administration.[33] In September 1953, Loftus wrote magnanimously to the general manager of the New Town:

> As I sit at my desk tonight when all is quiet, writing . . . from my old home where my father and grandfather have lived before me and on the land which my family have owned for over 130 years, it is a very, very sad moment for me . . . but I admit the necessity for these satellites and accept the fact that it was 'just too bad' for us around Harlow that this area was chosen. I can only wish you every possible success with the progress of the new town.[34]

At Hampton Court the old order survived longer than elsewhere. Nancy Burrell turned the house into a hospital during the First World War.[35] Her husband died of pneumonia while on active service and she had to sell up in 1925. Viscountess Hereford then purchased the house. Lord Hereford remained there until 1972 when the contents, a few of which had been in the house for four centuries, were auctioned. Hampton Court has since changed hands six times and at the time of writing, is once again on the market.

Between 1945 and 1955, 400 country houses were demolished in Britain, reaching a peak of one every five days in 1955.[36] Many of the other houses in Herefordshire with which the Arkwrights were connected suffered this fate.[37] Lucy's home Foxley was demolished in 1948 and Harewood in 1952.[38] Lord Bateman's Shobdon Court estate was sold in 1933, and the house mostly demolished.[39] The Peploes' Garnstone Castle, built by John Nash in around 1807 was demolished in 1959.[40] Berkeley's home, Holme Lacy, is today a hotel, and its estate an agricultural college. The Cotterells' Garnons home was much reduced in 1959, but remains the family seat.

Sir Velters Cornewall's Moccas Court remains the home of Dick Chester-Master's descendants who have opened the house for fine country house accommodation.

Further afield, the Bosanquet houses, Dingestow and Wonastow in Monmouthshire survive, and Minnie Byng's home, Wrotham Park in Hertfordshire, is still owned by her family.[41] Today it doubles as a conference centre but is best known for its role as *Gosford Park* in the 2001 film. Lizzie Kenyon's home, Gredington in Flintshire, was partly demolished in 1947 and finally disappeared in 1982.[42] Thoby Priory in Essex was sold on 5 September 1905, after Arthur's wife Agnes inherited Hatfield Place, Witham from her father.[43] Thoby, of twelfth-century origins, was later pulled down. Agnes sold Hatfield in October 1917, after Arthur, haunted by the deaths of Henry and his sons, and depressed by the War and arthritis, committed suicide by cutting his wrists and throat on 4 May 1916.[44] The house remains a private home.

Johnny's experiences at Hampton Court and those of his cousins elsewhere were therefore typical of their generation, but there was one fundamental irony that added piquancy to their struggle. The landed class lost its position because of the growth of urban centres, whose enfranchised inhabitants came to outnumber those in the countryside, and whose contribution to the economy and industry far outstripped that of agriculture. These cities grew because of the system of manufacturing that Sir Richard Arkwright had invented, and the movement of the population to centres of employment. The question must therefore be asked: would the Arkwrights have been better off if they had remained with manufacturing and had not tried to assimilate themselves with the landed class?[45]

Perhaps the Arkwrights would have been better off staying with cotton manufacturing in the short term, but as a report of the Tariff Reform League of 1905 showed, the trade had been in decline for some time. The family had moved almost completely out of cotton by the time of the younger Richard Arkwright's death in 1843, a shift motivated by wildly fluctuating and severely declining profits. On Richard's death, his wealth was held not in cotton manufacturing but in government stocks, landed estates and mortgages. Johnny's uncle Peter inherited the spinning concerns from Richard Arkwright, but in 1844, the year after Richard's death, the original Cromford mill slowed to a halt. The water in the Cromford sough had become insufficient to power the mill because of lead mines upstream.[46] It was the beginning of the end for the old mill and for the association of the Arkwright family with cotton spinning.

The Arkwrights were wise to withdraw when they did. The four stages of the cotton industry's lifecycle have been characterised as growth (1780–1840), maturity (1840–72), deceleration (1873–1913) and recession (post First World War).[47] The Arkwright fortune had been made by capitalising on the exponential growth of the earliest years of innovation. Although the 1850s was a decade of great prosperity for cotton manufacture, it generated over-expansion that was followed by the Cotton Famine of 1862–4 when poor harvests and the blockades of the southern American ports by the northern states during the American Civil War strangled supplies of raw cotton. There was little chance of recovery before the Great Depression of 1874 hit Britain as a whole.

In parallel with the crises in agriculture, the cotton industry saw three spasms of depression between 1874 and 1896. After that, although the Edwardian years saw a brief period of hope, the industry, like everything else, was hard hit by the First World War, after which competition in the Far East picked up. The British cotton industry would never recover its former position of primacy. In exporting its finished goods to India and the Far East, British cotton was a 'suicidal industry', creating foreign markets and educating foreign competitors with whom home manufacturers would not be able to compete.[48] In this, the cotton industry resembled the British export trade in Hereford cattle, whose progeny returned to these isles to undercut its own production.

This is not the only way in which the two industries with which the Arkwrights were involved were alike. Firstly, each of the industries was supplying one of the three fundamental requirements of man.[49] Secondly, British cotton spinners were praised for creating an international cycle of trade, importing their raw material chiefly from America, processing it here and exporting the finished goods (as well as some of the imported raw cotton) to foreign markets. British farmers, following the innovations of High Farming, were 'just like any cotton lord', importing fertilisers and feeds which were 'processed' by their livestock, the young of which were then exported.[50] Thirdly, as the century wore on, cotton, like land, 'lost all its power of attraction as an investment for capital'.[51] Finally, in 1874, for the first time in the history of the cotton industry, Britain's imports of cotton were exceeded in value by imports of grain and flour. In 1898 they were surpassed by imports of meat.[52]

However, these industries' interests were more often antagonistic. Besides the immense contribution to urban growth made by textile production, in 1845 the import duty on raw cotton was abolished, arguably a precedent for the repeal of the Corn Laws the following year. Both of these acts of repeal illustrate the supersession of agriculture by cotton and by industry in general, in Britain.

Had some of the industries that were to grow in the nineteenth century to become highly lucrative investment opportunities, like shipping, brewing, newspapers, soap manufacture or mining, been available to Richard Arkwright at the beginning of the nineteenth century, he might well have put his money there instead of in land. The Arkwrights invested heavily, for example, in railway and canal shares when the opportunity arose. Where they could be faulted was in not switching their money out of land and into some of these ventures in the middle of the century. Acres, however, are not as liquid an asset as shares for all sorts of reasons – financial, practical and sentimental – as the new rich at the end of the century acknowledged by not putting their money into land in the first place.[53] Furthermore, to keep up with the wealth élite on the new global scale, the Arkwrights would have had to cross the Atlantic, like some of the labourers of the Leintwardine Union – a move not socially acceptable to their class.[54] By the beginning of the twentieth century the fortunes of even the wealthiest British were dwarfed by the richest Americans by approximately twenty times.[55]

Many of the difficulties faced by Johnny that seem specific to his situation were more general than they might at first appear. Arguably the greatest damage done to his fortune was its irreparable depletion by division between Johnny's eleven siblings. Under the terms of his father's will, £90,000 was paid out to Johnny's brothers and £50,000 to his sisters, a total sum that far exceeded the £46,000 that Johnny borrowed, and which ultimately brought him down.[56] However, large extended families were typical among the landed class at this time, and traps like the shortfall in the Harewood trust for his cousin Cathy Pigott were common hazards as a result.

Johnny was also, no doubt, by modern standards, extravagant in his private life, but when measured against his contemporaries, he is typical or even frugal in his refusal to keep a London home, staying instead at the Carlton Club or with Henry and Di Longley in Lowndes Street. There was extraordinary pressure during the Victorian period to maintain appearances at all costs, and those costs could be ruinous. Furthermore Johnny had been brought up among the very finest of everything that the family's erstwhile fortune could buy. This may be a lame excuse for drowning his every sorrow in champagne, but the refusal of men like Johnny Arkwright to settle for less has bequeathed to the nation houses and their contents of exquisite craftsmanship and quality – such as that of Johnny's friend Sir John Heathcoat Amory at Knightshayes, Devon – that can now be appreciated by everyone as part of the National Trust's portfolio of properties.[57] The expense of keeping a house of this kind could not easily be avoided, but Johnny did reduce staff numbers indoors from nineteen to thirteen between 1861 and 1901.[58]

Johnny's relative financial illiteracy might seem at first sight unusual, particularly given the value of the asset with which he was entrusted for life.[59] He was not entirely clear, for thirty years after his father's death, of the difference between the estate's expenditure and his own. Johnny's loose grasp of his situation would have made his Arkwright grandfather turn in his grave. However, it was not socially acceptable to be able to account for every penny and to do so smacked of trade. One was expected to have people to undertake the penny counting on one's behalf. It did not help that in Johnny's case the solicitor, Sale, in establishing the trust in his father's will (proved on April Fool's Day), failed to ensure that Johnny's father bequeathed to him the stock and implements on the farms in hand. To inherit a £10,000 debt was not a good start.

Johnny Arkwright was also typical of his generation in that he spent the family's fortune trying to do right by the Hampton Court estate and his descendants, its future owners. He believed unequivocally in excellence, whether training the Hope church choir or assessing the state of national agriculture for the RASE. Like his peers, he invested in his land, though perhaps to an unusual degree, but in this he was influenced by the zeal of his uncle Chandos, an acknowledged and admired pioneer of agricultural innovation. There was no one at the time who could indicate what a prudent level of investment might be. He was perhaps exceptional in being 'more paternalistic than most landlords, wanting his estate to "look good" rather than to be farmed at a great profit', and even today the Arkwrights are remembered in the county as exceptionally good landlords.[60] But Johnny was working on the theory that significant investment in the 1860s would reap rewards possibly for him but certainly for his heirs. He and his peers were making sacrifices for their descendants – sacrifices of which, sadly, they were not to feel the benefit. As has been written, 'a failing of the government drainage scheme was that its promise to landowners was based largely on the increased rents which tenants "ought" to pay and the increased livestock they "ought" to keep once the improvement had taken place'.[61] That unprecedented depression would follow the improvements could not be foreseen.

With hindsight, it is plain to see that Johnny Arkwright and his kind were living through revolutionary times. They could not see, though, that things would never be the same again. The landed aristocracy had ruled Britain since the Norman Conquest. Wealth, status and power had been an indissoluble trinity focused on land, in the same way that the 'big house', church and inn girdled every village green. That it should ever be otherwise required an immense leap of imagination that was at best unpalatable and at worst unconscionable. However, the crisis in agriculture produced the failure of wealth at precisely the moment when the irreversible eradication of political power was taking place alongside the erosion of status resulting from increasing professionalism in local and national life. The privileges of leisure had always been balanced by the responsibilities of local and national leadership. Once the responsibilities of leadership were claimed by elected or employed representatives, the privileges of position were unjustifiable.

The landed class had its foundations in the soil of the counties, but the cities produced by the Industrial Revolution to which Sir Richard Arkwright had contributed so significantly, ultimately overturned the pre-eminent position of agriculture in British society. Sir Richard Arkwright's contribution to the Industrial Revolution was made in the 1780s; the avalanche of changes that reversed the relative positions of country and city hit home in Britain in the 1880s, exactly a century later. The relegation of agriculture was almost impossible to grasp when food remained a most essential requirement of city-dwellers – the most fundamental factory fuel.

The history of the English country house cannot be divorced from the history of the estate by which it was surrounded. In recent times, it has been suggested that the fortunes of the country house are turning. Part of paragraph 3.21 of the 1997 Planning Policy Guideline (PPG7) permitted the construction of such properties again, provided they be of outstanding architectural merit and set within outstanding landscaping. However, by early 2004, of fifty applications made, only fourteen had been granted, and the Labour government had signalled its intention to withdraw the part of 3.21 referring to country houses. Those houses built will almost certainly be for residence without the responsibility of farming tenants; in other words they will be houses in the country but not country houses.

The outlook for agriculture is less optimistic. The issues surrounding food production and land usage remain unresolved a century after Johnny Arkwright's death. Producers face competition from cheap foreign imports not necessarily produced to the same standards imposed at home. Consumers spend ever less of their disposable income on food. Meanwhile, the rural economy is struggling to recover from depression caused by crises such as BSE and foot and mouth disease.

A century ago, in 1902, the writer H. Rider Haggard toured England asking those connected with the land (including Jack at Hampton Court) about the issues confronting Britain's farmers as they attempted to recover from agricultural depression. His observations remain surprisingly appropriate a century on, in an era of countryside stewardship and set-aside schemes.

> The impression left upon my mind by my extensive wanderings is that English agriculture seems to be fighting against the mills of God. Many circumstances combine to threaten it with ruin, although as yet it is not actually ruined . . . Of these the chief is unchecked foreign competition . . . The possession of land is becoming, or has already become, a luxury for rich men, to whom it is a costly toy, or a means of indulging a taste for sport. Than this no state of affairs can be more unwholesome or unnatural; the land should support men, not men the land . . . I am sure that one of the worst fates which can befall England is that her land should become either a plaything or a waste.[62]

Notes

The following abbreviations are used for items that occur repeatedly in these notes:

JA for John Arkwright (Johnny's father)
JHA for John Hungerford Arkwright (Johnny)
JSA for John Stanhope Arkwright (Jack)
CLA for Charlotte Lucy Arkwright (Lucy)
CWH for Chandos Wren Hoskyns

HRO for Hereford Record Office, where the main Arkwright Collection is located.

Kindly note that there are two versions of E.L. Jones, 'The Evolution of High Farming 1815–1865 with special reference to Herefordshire' (D.Phil. thesis, Oxford, 1962), one held at Oxford University, and the other, a late draft of the chapters pertaining to Herefordshire, at HRO. Unless otherwise stated page numbers refer to the Oxford draft.

Introduction, pp. 1–12

1. Herefordshire Record Office (HRO) A63/IV/56/2 JHA to CLA, 6 January 1870.
2. I have calculated the modern-day monetary equivalents used throughout this book by multiplying the sums by figures from the Bank of England's 'Equivalent contemporary values of the pound: A Historical series 1270–2004', which is compiled using figures from the Retail Prices Index and the Office of National Statistics.
3. The 1841 census revealed that of a total population of 113,878 in the county, 16,213 people were 'actively engaged in agricultural pursuits', over 14 per cent. T. Rowlandson, 'Farming of Herefordshire', *Journal of the Royal Agricultural Society of England*, Series 1, Vol. XIV (1853), p. 433. Johnny's position as the largest landowner in Herefordshire and as the 363rd largest landowner in the country is taken from J. Bateman, *The Great Landowners of Great Britain and Ireland*, 4th edn, 1883 Victorian Library Edition (Leicester, Leicester University Press, 1971).
4. *New York Herald*, 1 May 1843, quoted in R.S. Fitton, *The Arkwrights, Spinners of Fortune* (Manchester, Manchester University Press, 1989), p. 295.
5. G. Worsley, *England's Lost Houses* (London, Aurum Press, 2003), p. 23.
6. F.M.L. Thompson, *English Landed Society in the Nineteenth Century* (London, Routledge & Kegan Paul, 1963); F.M.L. Thompson, 'The Second Agricultural Revolution, 1815–1880', *Economic History Review*, Series 2, Vol. XXI (1968).

7. D. Cannadine, *The Decline and Fall of the British Aristocracy* (New Haven, Yale University Press, 1990).
8. HRO A63/IV/60/4, JHA to JSA, 25 January 1886.
9. The purchase price for Hampton Court was set, as Robert Fitton states, at £230,000, but Lord Essex removed some of the contents and solicitors were brought in by Richard Arkwright to settle the difference, see Fitton, *The Arkwrights*, p. 232. The final figure is confirmed in the surviving conveyance of the estate to Richard Arkwright of 7 July 1810, located at HRO A63/IV/305/11B. E.L. Jones, 'Industrial Capital and Landed Investment: the Arkwrights in Herefordshire, 1809–43', in E.L. Jones and G.E. Mingay (eds), *Land, Labour and Population in the Industrial Revolution: Essays presented to J.D. Chambers* (London, Arnold, 1967), p. 67. Jones was working on the figure of approximately £229,000 as the purchase price. As Jones makes clear: 'available figures on capital formation in British industry at the beginning of the nineteenth century are very approximate, but at least they indicate the orders of magnitude'.
10. It has been written that 'To Arkwright and Watt, England is far more indebted for her triumphs than to Nelson and Wellington', E. Baines, *History of the Cotton Manufacture in Great Britain* (London, Fisher, 1835), pp. 503–4.
11. Fitton, *The Arkwrights*, p. 187.
12. *Ibid.*, p. 296.
13. W. Rubinstein and P. Beresford, 'Richest of the Rich', *Sunday Times*, 26 March 2000, p. 32. Rubinstein and Beresford took the percentage share of NNI (an economic indicator akin to GDP) and multiplied the figure by the estimated gross domestic product for Britain at the end of 1999. The calculation, rounded to the nearest £100 million, gave them each individual's modern equivalent. From an estimate of Richard's wealth of only £1.2 million they thus came up with a modern-day figure for his wealth of £2.2 billion.
14. Normanton Turville cost £33,000; Mark Hall £100,000; Sutton Scarsdale £216,000; Dunstall £42,000. Fitton, *The Arkwrights*, pp. 230 and 234–5.
15. Fitton, *The Arkwrights*, p. 267.
16. Jones, 'Industrial Capital and Landed Investment', pp. 63–4 and E.L. Jones, 'The Evolution of High Farming 1815–1865 with special reference to Herefordshire' (Oxford, D.Phil. thesis, 1962), pp. 46–426.
17. Essex County Record Office D/Dar C3/26, Letter No. 95, M. Robinson, wife of the vicar of Bodenham, to Rev. Joseph Arkwright, 17 April 1829.
18. While employed at Hampton Court, Hanbury Tracy was appointed chairman of the committee overseeing the rebuilding of the Houses of Parliament, which had burnt down in 1834.
19. In August 2005, Toddington was bought by the artist Damien Hirst.
20. For a record of the work done and of the sensitive relationship between architect and client, see M.J. McCarthy, 'The work of Hanbury Tracy, Lord Sudeley, at Hampton Court, Herefordshire', *Transactions of the Woolhope Naturalists' Field Club* 38 (1964), pp. 71–5.
21. C. Beale, 'A Forgotten Greenhouse by Joseph Paxton: The Conservatory at Hampton Court, Herefordshire', *Garden History*, Vol. 30, No. 1 (Spring 2002), pp. 74–83.
22. HRO A63/III/72/1, Joseph Yates's Notes on the Hampton Court Estate. S. Jenkins, *England's Thousand Best Houses* (London, Allen Lane, 2003), p. 316.
23. Fitton, *The Arkwrights*, p. 293.

24. HRO A63/ II/304/1–35, JA's will, under the terms of which each of the boys except JHA received £15,000 at the age of 21 years, and each of the girls £10,000 at 21 years. Each of the boys was to receive a further £5,000 payable on Tally's death.
25. Jones, 'Industrial Capital and Landed Investment', p. 60.
26. Cannadine, *Decline and Fall*, p. 13.
27. HRO A63/IV/10/10, Dr Richard Okes to JA, 7 December 1847.
28. HRO A63/IV/56/1, JHA to Lucy Davenport, 27 May 1866.
29. HRO A63/IV/56/3, JHA to Lucy Arkwright, 17 May 1876.
30. H.C.G. Moule, *Memories of a Vicarage* (London, Religious Tract Society, 1913). The author was the youngest son of Rev. Henry Moule, Johnny's tutor at Fordington Vicarage, Dorchester, from 1843 to 1848.
31. *Financial Times*, 29 November 2003, p. W13.
32. Another outcome of the 1974 exhibition (and not unconnected) was the foundation of SAVE Britain's Heritage by Marcus Binney and other energetic campaigners, which has helped ensure the survival of several houses. Jenkins, *England's Thousand Best Houses*, p. xxii.
33. Figures supplied by the National Trust, Historic Houses Association and Visit Britain, December 2003.
34. Jenkins, *England's Thousand Best Houses*, p. xxii.
35. N. Coward, 'The Stately Homes of England', from N. Coward, *Operette* (London, Chappell, 1938).
36. Jenkins, *England's Thousand Best Houses*, p. 309.
37. The then owner of Hampton Court, Thomas, Lord Coningsby (1656–1729) was a Privy Councillor to King William III, whose preferred residence was Hampton Court Palace, part of which he substantially remodelled. Coningsby undertook work contemporaneously to the house and gardens at Hampton Court, Herefordshire. C. Beale, *Hampton Court, Herefordshire* (2000), published privately as the guide book when the gardens opened to the public.
38. Cannadine, *Decline and Fall*, pp. 10–11.
39. A. Trollope, *Can You Forgive Her?* (London, Wordsworth Editions, 1996), p. 1.
40. A. Trollope, *The Last Chronicle of Barset*, written in 1867 (Oxford, OUP, 1989), p. 623.
41. O. Wilde, *The Works of Oscar Wilde* (London, Spring Books, 1963), *The Importance of Being Earnest*, Act I, p. 151.
42. In 1850, Herefordshire was the only county apart from Cornwall not to have a railway, a significant drawback when, as was acknowledged by C. Stevenson in 1853, 'a railway is almost as essential to the agricultural prosperity of a district as thorough-draining itself'. C. Stevenson, 'Farming in East Lothian', *Journal of the Royal Agricultural Society of England*, Series 1, Vol. XIV (1853), pp. 274–324, quoted in Jones, 'Evolution of High Farming', pp. 173–4.
43. Figures from the Office of National Statistics population estimate for June 2001. It is important to note that the ONS does not include in the number of persons employed in agriculture those farming land who are salaried managers. This is the figure for regular workers in the industry, not seasonal. The 9,603 agricultural workers compare with 12,376 in manufacturing and 49,611 in service industries in Herefordshire.
44. Strawberry cultivation is not as new as might be thought (although the methods undoubtedly are). H. Rider Haggard noted in 1902 that Herefordshire had always been well known for its fruit, but that strawberries had lately been added to its industries and was adding to profits per acre. H. Rider Haggard, *Rural England* (London, Longmans, 1902), Vol. I, pp. 287–8.

45. T. Rowlandson, 'Farming of Herefordshire', *Journal of the Royal Agricultural Society of England*, Series 1, Vol. XIV (1853), p. 436.

Chapter One: The Heir to the Throne, pp. 13–26

1. The *Hereford Journal*, 12 July 1854 (no page numbers given), sets out the arrangements for the day in some detail, and the issue of the following week gave a very full account of the dinner. The narrative given here is re-created with careful attention to these first-hand reports.
2. By 1867, Daggs was a councillor for Leominster Corporation, Treasurer of the Local Board, manager of the Worcester City and County Banking Company Limited in Corn Square, Secretary and Treasurer of the Agricultural Association and a former Mayor of the town (Littlebury's Directory for Herefordshire, 1867). The census of 1871 reveals that in 1854, he would have been around 37 years of age.
3. *Hereford Journal* advertisement for celebrations of 12 July 1854.
4. Private collection, JHA to JA, 1 June 1854.
5. Essex County Record Office C1/188, John Arkwright to Rev. Joseph Arkwright, 4 November 1826, 'Our new road to Ledbury & Cheltenham is now open, the bridge by Hampton Court is finished all but the parapets.'
6. *Hereford Journal*, 19 July 1854, last page.
7. HRO A63/IV/9/14, John Arkwright, the education of his sons. George Arkwright to JA, 13 July 1854.
8. *Hereford Journal*, 9 August 1854, last page.
9. Mr Holt must have been known to John through the catering he did for Royal Agricultural Society dinners at Lewes and Lincoln. HRO A63/IV/9/1, quotation Radley's Hotel to JA.
10. HRO A63/IV/9/1, J.H. Brown to JA, 10 January 1855, the date that the picture was completed.
11. William Bateman-Hanbury, second Baron Bateman (1826–1901) had become Lord Lieutenant and Custos Rotulorum of Herefordshire in 1852. On 13 May 1854 he had married Agnes Burrell, daughter of General Sir Edward Kerrison, Bart of Brome Hall, Eye, Suffolk. They had six daughters and five sons. He was a lifelong supporter of Protectionism, who described free trade as 'an Utopian crusade . . . a Quixotic theory', I. Pfuell, *A History of Shobdon* (published privately, 1994), pp. 86–7.
12. The menu included roasted capons, boiled chickens, roast duck, venison, game pies, cold lamb, hams, tongues, lobster salads, shellfish, aspics, ornamental salads, potatoes and other vegetables, fruited jellies, fruit tarts, creams, cheesecakes, pastries, savoury cakes, chantilly baskets, dessert pines, hothouse grapes, cherries, strawberries, gooseberries, compotes, dried fruits, cakes, ices and punch. HRO A63/IV/9/1, preparations for JHA's twenty-first birthday.
13. Mortram traded from 15 Waterloo Road (near the obelisk).
14. *Hereford Journal*, 9 August 1854, last page.
15. HRO A63/III/72/1, Joseph Yates's Notes on the Hampton Court Estate.
16. HRO A63/IV/9/23/9, John Arkwright personal papers, Sir James Wigram to JA, 5 September 1852.
17. HRO A63/IV/21/5, Mary Arkwright to JHA, 27 February 1850.
18. *Ibid.*, 30 January 1851.
19. HRO A63/IV/9/15, Henry Arkwright to JA, 3 July 1856.

20. HRO A63/IV/21/1, Sarah Arkwright to JHA, 20 July 1850.
21. HRO A63/III/42/11, A63/IV/9/26 and C. Beale, 'A Forgotten Greenhouse by Joseph Paxton: The Conservatory at Hampton Court, Herefordshire', *Garden History*, Vol. 30, No. 1 (Spring 2002), pp. 74–83.
22. In 1849, the Duke confided to his journal that he was 'struck down today by news of Mrs. Arkwright's death . . . Of all the strong attachments I have had in my life mine to her has been the purest the truest the most salutary. O how I loved her!' J. Lees-Milne, *The Bachelor Duke* (London, John Murray, 1998), p. 182.
23. Private collection, JHA to Sarah Arkwright, 16 October 1854.
24. Johnny's friend Barker from Christ Church, speaking at the celebrations had said, 'they all had great affection and love for their young friend at Oxford, and he might say that he was the most popular man there', *Hereford Journal*, 9 August 1854, last page.
25. HRO A63/IV/9/7, Berkeley Scudamore Stanhope to JA, 16 November 1854.
26. HRO A63/IV/9/7, copy of JA's reply to Berkeley Scudamore Stanhope's of 16 November 1854.
27. HRO A63/IV/9/15, Henry Arkwright to JA, 25 February 1855.
28. HRO A63/IV/10/11, Rev. Charles Woolley to JA, 14 March 1853 and 15 April 1853.
29. Private collection, JHA to JA, 3 December 1854.
30. John Leigh Hoskyns was vicar of Aston Tyrrold for sixty-six years in total and is buried in the churchyard there.
31. HRO A63/IV/9/5, John Arkwright personal papers, John Leigh Hoskyns to JA, 26 October 1855.
32. HRO A63/IV/9/14, George Arkwright to JA, 21 February 1857.
33. HRO A63/III/42/13. In May 1844, Peter had lent nearly £127,000 to the Duke of Newcastle, Joseph £81,000 to Lord Chesterfield, Robert £71,000 to Lord Waterpark and Charles £71,913 to five different borrowers. From John, Lord Normanby wanted to borrow £12,000 in March 1852 and by December was behind with his interest repayments.
34. The second son of Sir Robert Peel, Frederick Peel had represented the Leominster constituency for the Liberals alongside George Arkwright from 1849 to 1852. During this time he was Under Secretary of State for War.
35. Journal, 17 January 1846, quoted by E.L. Jones in 'The Evolution of High Farming 1815–1865 with Special Reference to Herefordshire' (Oxford, D.Phil. thesis, 1962).
36. R.S. Fitton, *The Arkwrights, Spinners of Fortune* (Manchester, Manchester University Press, 1989), p. 267. John's natural inclination to shrink from making his views public had to be overcome when, in 1832, he had been High Sheriff for Herefordshire and had been obliged to chair a heated debate on electoral reform in Hereford's town hall. He had been against electoral reform.
37. HRO A63/IV/9/28, F.W. Davies to JA, 2 April 1852, and JA to F.W. Davies, 3 April 1852.
38. *Ibid.* John was asked to nominate James King of Staunton Park. J. King to JA, 25 June 1852.
39. *Ibid.*, F.L. Bodenham to JA, 21 June 1852.
40. *Ibid.*, JA to F.L. Bodenham, 21 June 1852.
41. HRO A63/IV/9/14, George Arkwright MP to JA, 22 November 1855. This is incorrectly filed among the letters from JA's son George to his father.
42. Private collection, JHA to JA, 9 July 1852.
43. Private collection, JHA to JA, August 1852 (exact date not given).
44. HRO A63/IV/9/6, correspondence with nephews and nieces. JA to George Arkwright MP, 8 October 1853.

45. Robert was to lose his second son William the following year, aged 47. Of Robert's four sons, only Godfrey now survived, and he held Sutton for life (until 1866), when William's son, also William (just a month old at the time of his father's death) inherited at the age of 9 years.
46. HRO A63/IV/9/4, Rev. E.B. Hawkshaw to JA, 8 February 1856.
47. HRO A63/IV/10/4, John Arkwright, the education of his sons. Rev. Henry Moule of Fordington Vicarage, Dorset, to JA, 17 December 1844, 26 January 1846 and 10 December 1846.
48. HRO A63/IV/9/4, John Arkwright personal papers, Rev. E.B. Hawkshaw to JA, 13 February 1856.
49. HRO A63/IV/9/14, John Arkwright personal papers, George Arkwright to JA, February 1856.
50. A. Trollope, *Can You Forgive Her?* (London, Wordsworth Editions, 1996), p. 323.
51. Jones, 'The Evolution of High Farming', pp. 426–7.

Chapter Two: The Season and its Harvest, pp. 27–37

1. The alternative candidates considered included Sir T. Gladstone and the future Lord Wilton.
2. A.E.G. Hardy (ed.), *Gathorne Hardy: A Memoir* (London, Longmans, 1910), Vol. I, p. 98, diary entry for 22 February 1856. He had stood unsuccessfully for Bradford in 1847.
3. Hardy went on to represent Oxford University from 1865 to 1878 and to have a distinguished parliamentary career, including service as Secretary of State for the Home Department, for War and for India. He was Lord President of the Council and Chancellor of the Duchy of Lancaster. He was created Viscount Cranbrook in 1878 and Earl of Cranbrook in 1892.
4. HRO A63/IV/9/14, George Arkwright to JA, 1 March 1856.
5. Private collection, JHA to Sarah Arkwright, 16 February 1856.
6. HRO A63/IV/9/15, Henry Arkwright to JA, 24 February 1856.
7. *Ibid.*, 26 October 1856 and HRO A63/IV/9/14, George Arkwright to JA, 10 November 1856.
8. HRO A63/IV/9/15, Henry Arkwright to JA, 1 March 1857 and HRO A63/IV/9/14, George Arkwright to JA, 21 February 1857.
9. Abel had the title bestowed on him for services rendered during the siege of Hereford during the Civil War. E. Turton, *Leominster* (Stroud, Chalford, 1996), p. 26.
10. HRO A63/IV/9/26, letters about the removal of Leominster's town hall, and A63/III/62/3, papers concerning the old town hall. I am grateful to Eric Turton, former Curator of Leominster Museum, for his help with John and Davis's roles.
11. This lovely row of Herefordshire's vernacular architecture is preserved in what is perhaps one of the best known of David Cox's works. He painted Butcher's Row, Hereford, in 1815.
12. As a house, the town hall was let to local solicitor, Henry Moore. The former town hall still stands on the Grange today. Hereford was less fortunate. Its half-timbered town hall, also by Abel, was taken down and lost to the city in 1861.
13. HRO A63/IV/9/28, John Arkwright personal papers, Lord Middleton to JA, 24 February 1857.
14. HRO A63/IV/9/26–28, John Arkwright, various miscellaneous.
15. HRO A63/III/42/26, rental agreement for Park Lane house.

16. Bel-Bel's mother had died in the year that she was born, and her father had married next the Hon. Caroline Leigh, third daughter of Chandos, first Lord Leigh of Stoneleigh. Tally's great-great-grandmother was a daughter of the 8th Lord Chandos, hence her brother's names of Chandos and Leigh. These are the same Leighs from whom the novelist Jane Austen's mother, Cassandra Leigh, liked to emphasise her descent. I am grateful to Sheila Weston for her generosity in sharing her painstaking research of the Hoskyns' genealogy.
17. HRO A63/IV/9/14, George Arkwright to JA, dated only April 1857.
18. The bronze, by Matthew Cotes Wyatt, weighed 40 tons. It was mounted on Decimus Burton's triumphal arch for a trial period of a fortnight, and stayed for thirty years, until the redirection of the roads around Hyde Park corner. The arch was then turned to its present alignment and the quadriga was added. The Archduke went to the British Army camp at Aldershot. The present equestrian statue of the Duke by Sir Edgar Boehm was set up in 1888. E. Longford, *Wellington: Pillar of State* (London, Weidenfeld & Nicholson, 1972), p. 370.
19. Among the surviving invitation cards in the collection at HRO is one from Miss Burdett-Coutts to Johnny, HRO A63/IV/22/7.
20. HRO A63/IV/9/28, John Arkwright personal papers, 5 and 8 August 1857.
21. Henry played for Harrow in the matches against Eton in 1855 and 1857 (both Harrow victories). He was a victim of the Eton headmaster's refusal to grant permission for his team to play at Lord's in 1856. Henry had at first bowled fast underhand, but in 1853 he changed to slow round-arm, 'which because he delivered the ball rather high and swung it, caused bewilderment amongst batsmen'. Charlie was to follow his brother and play for Harrow in 1864 (the year that overarm bowling was introduced by the MCC and that boundary ropes were recognised) in the presence of the Prince and Princess of Wales, and in 1865 (both victories for Harrow). R. Titchener-Barrett, *Eton v Harrow at Lord's since 1805* (London, Quiller Press, 1996), p. 15. Henry was, it has been claimed, 'the best amateur slow bowler in England'. F.S. Ashley-Cooper, *Eton and Harrow at the Wicket* (London, St James, 1922), p. 46.
22. HRO A63/IV/9/7, Sir Edwyn Stanhope to JA, 4 August 1857.
23. *Ibid.*, Berkeley Scudamore Stanhope to JA, 4 August 1857.
24. HRO A63/IV/9/15, Henry Arkwright to JA, 14 October 1857.
25. HRO A63/IV/9/7, Sir Edwyn Stanhope to JA, 27 November 1857.
26. *Ibid.*, JA to Berkeley Scudamore Stanhope, 15 December 1857.
27. *Ibid.*, Berkeley Scudamore Stanhope to JA, 19 December 1857.
28. HRO A63/IV/9/10, JA to Sir Hungerford Hoskyns, 22 January 1858.
29. *Hereford Journal*, Wednesday 3 February 1858, p. 6 – all details are taken from this account.
30. Apart from Carey's sisters, Mary, Fanny, Emily and Alice, the bridesmaids were the Hon. Maria Eden (daughter of Lord Auckland, the Bishop of Bath & Wells, an Arkwright relation through John's cousin John Hurt), Miss Cockburn, Anna Arkwright (Joseph's daughter) and Catherine Wren Hoskyns (Chandos's daughter by his first marriage).
31. HRO A63/IV/9/23/2. John had purchased these pictures from the sale at Burton upon Trent, Staffordshire, that took place on 25 June 1851, following the death of his brother Charles in late 1850. It appears that they were a second set of the family portraits, commissioned from Joseph Wright for Willersley Castle, that was made to hang at Stoke Hall, Curbar, John's childhood home. When Robert and Fanny moved from

Stoke to Sutton Scarsdale in 1837, it appears that the walls at Sutton, with their ornate plasterwork, could not accommodate the portraits, so Charles took them and hung them at Dunstall. For the portrait of Sir Richard, John paid £50. The pictures went as far as Worcester by train around 26 April 1852, from where John had them sent on.

32. They included a service of plate, a piano, vases, reading desks, writing and dressing cases, 'a costly ivory lady's companion', jewellery and ornaments, books, work in Berlin wool, Brussels lace, rich velvets and gold. A fine salver was given jointly by James Green the head keeper, Edward Colley the agent, William Glading the Master of the Works, Joseph Yates and Butler James Tatlow. *Hereford Journal*, 3 February 1858, p. 6.
33. Mrs Clowes, Caroline Elizabeth, was Peter Arkwright of Willersley's daughter (and sister of Rev. Henry Arkwright of Bodenham). The Willersley Arkwrights and the Clowes were inter-married twice over. John Clowes's sister, Isabel, had married Peter's son James in 1855. John and Caroline Clowes were to purchase Burton Court in Herefordshire in 1865.
34. This 'belted knight' was Godfrey Kneller's representation of Henry IV, the founder of Hampton Court, in armour and on horseback approaching Coventry for his famous duel with the Duke of Norfolk in 1397. It was commissioned from the artist by Thomas, Lord Coningsby, and was in Kneller's studio at the time of the artist's death in 1723. The marble chimney was also commissioned by Lord Coningsby and, although not surviving exactly as described here, still bears the Coningsby arms today.
35. HRO A63/IV/9/17, Charles Arkwright to JA, 6 February 1858.
36. For a full account of their return to Bosbury, see *Hereford Journal*, 24 February 1868, p. 6. Berkeley was vicar of Bosbury from 1856 to 1866.
37. *Hereford Times*, 3 March 1858, p. 5.
38. *Hereford Journal*, 10 March 1858, p. 3.

Chapter Three: Master of the Estate, pp. 38–53

1. The Tompion Turret Clock was removed from Hampton Court in 1972/3. It appears to have been installed on the stables there in about 1840 (or perhaps 1843 after Richard Arkwright's death, when John came into the money to afford such a clock), although it was probably put to work elsewhere in the 1720s. The clock was sold in 2003 for £50,000. I am most grateful to Michael Page for drawing my attention to this remarkable item, and to an article by J.E. Locke, 'A Thomas Tompion Turret Clock', *Antiquarian Horology*, Vol. 8, No. 2 (March 1973), pp. 172–4.
2. HRO C69, 'Acreage of Hampton Court Estate 1857', signed 12 September 1857 by Edward Colley.
3. HRO C69/219, valuation stock and crops, 29 September 1857.
4. This assessment was given by T. Rowlandson, *Journal of the Royal Agricultural Society of England*, Series 1, Vol. XIV (1853), p. 433, 'Farming of Herefordshire'. The figures used were those of the 1841 census, 'the returns for 1851 not having yet been published'.
5. These figures are taken from the 1866 rental list in HRO C69/229. In 1873 there were 388 tenants in all, paying a total of £14,825 16*s* 2*d*. HRO C69/312. In 1875 there were fifty-three tenants of 3 to 50 acres, HRO C69/312.
6. E.L. Jones, 'The Evolution of High Farming 1815–1865 with Special Reference to Herefordshire' (Oxford, D.Phil. thesis, 1962), p. 76.
7. *Ibid.*, p. 434.
8. HRO C69/312, 36 tenants paid the first day, 193 the second day and 154 the final day.

9. In 1853, repairs included £148 at Bodenham Court Farm, £573 at Rowberry, £216 at Marlbrook, £166 at Upper House, Risbury, £155 at Stone Lodge and £198 on the Priory Cottages.
10. Figures from HRO C69/236, Outlay for Repairs and Alterations, Improvements or Additions on the Estate.
11. HRO A63/III/50/5, repairs on the estate, 1851–68 etc.
12. HRO E41/290–295, O/L 360, Buildings and Repairs 1820–72.
13. Mechi spoke to the Herefordshire Agricultural Society in 1848. *Hereford Journal*, 16 February 1848, Special Supplement, 'Candlemas Meeting of the Herefordshire Agricultural Society'.
14. Jones, 'The Evolution of High Farming', p. 420, *passim*, says that JA wrote this to his son. Also, HRO A63/IV/9/9, Richard Phelips to JA, 1 March 1850, 'I do not quite agree with you in thinking Free Trade in Corn "un fait accompli".' Jones also notes (pp. 426–7) that in his Journal (which I have not been able to locate) JA's entry for 17 January 1846 reads: 'to Hereford to meeting in favor of the present protection to Agriculture though myself inclining to the belief that the apprehension of the ruinous consequences is exaggerated and that ultimately "Free Trade" in corn will be most beneficial to us all'.
15. HRO E41/11, O/L339, Hampton Court Rent Audits 1839–91, amounts received, arrears, allowances etc.
16. The figures from the previous September showed that Henhouse and Hillhole were stocked to the following extent: 55 Hereford cattle, 11 milking cows, 23 feeding cows, 21 3-year-old heifers and 131 oxen, making a total of 241 cattle. In addition there were 526 ewes of various values, 147 wethers, 15 rams, 372 ewe and wether lambs, and 9 ram lambs, making a total of 1,069 sheep, along with 39 mixed pigs. The 27 working horses included Smiler, Surly, Flower, Boxer, Folly, Bouncer, Bunting and Diamond, besides nine colts and hacks, including Black Bessy and the bailiff's mare. On Henhouse land John had been cultivating wheat, oats, beans, swedes, hay, apples and pears, while at Hillhole, wheat, barley, oats, turnips, hay, hops, apples and pears were grown. The total value of the stock and crops on these farms had been set at £5,124 2*s*. HRO C69/219–225. Green Farm valuation, HRO A63/IV/13/9.
17. HRO A63/II/304/1–35, JA's will.
18. John's other beneficiaries included Tally's sisters, Caroline Phelips and Catherine Hawkshaw, who each received £1,000, as did Rev. Leigh Hoskyns, Tally's brother. John then remembered his staff, including Eliza Jemima Ward, 'Governess to my children', who received £200, Edward Colley, who also received £200, the gamekeeper James Green, William Glading, Joseph Yates, and John's butler James Tatlow, who each received £100. Every servant at Hampton Court received one year's wages. All of the legacies were to be paid within six months of his death. In a codicil, John bequeathed £200 each to Berkeley and Bonham Caldwall. Since Carey had been given, on her marriage to Berkeley, £10,000 of 3 per cent consolidated bank annuities, John revoked his £10,000 to her. John's executors were his nephew Rev. Henry Arkwright of Bodenham and his brother-in-law Rev. Leigh Hoskyns. HRO A63/II/304/1–35.
19. Bonham Caldwall (1790–1889) was twice Mayor of Leominster and a magistrate for Leominster Division. He was also acting commissioner of taxes (1867) and President of Leominster Horticultural Society. He lived at 25 Broad Street and 116 Bridge Street, Leominster, *Littlebury's directory*. He is buried near the west door of Leominster Priory.
20. C.W. Hoskyns, *Talpa: The Chronicles of A Clay Farm* (London, Brimley Johnson, 1903), p. 22.

21. Jones, 'The Evolution of High Farming'. Lord Ernle cited similar figures, dating the first import to 1835. By 1841 only 1,700 tons were imported, but six years later, this had risen to 220,000 tons. R. Prothero, Lord Ernle, *English Farming Past and Present*, 6th edn (London, Heinemann, 1961), p. 371. F.M.L. Thompson gives figures of net imports of 119,940 tons in 1843–6, rising to 231,610 in 1854–8, then falling back to 209,460 in 1868–71 and to 18,780 in 1887–91. 'The Second Agricultural Revolution, 1815–1880', *Economic History Review*, Series 2, Vol. XXI (1968), Table 2.
22. 'She has not *half* the style & *consequence* that poor Dolce had.' Lady Hoskyns to JA, dated only 20 August, HRO A63/IV/9/12.
23. This was opened in 1804 by Dr Edward Fox (1761–1835) who retired in 1829 and was succeeded in the management of Brislington by his sons Drs Francis and Charles Fox. I am grateful for the assistance of Mrs Diane Pearce during my visit to Brislington. Information on Brislington at Somerset Record Office, Taunton at Refs T/PH/fx 2 s/2722 and T/PH/fx 3 s/2722.
24. HRO A63/IV/9/10, CWH to Sarah Arkwright, 2 May 1859.
25. *Ibid.*, dated only April 1857.
26. HRO A63/IV/21/15/4, CWH to JHA, 24 May 1858.
27. When Johnny joined the RASE Council, Chandos was already on the sub-committee for the *Journal*, and on the Chemical and Implement Committees. *Journal of the Royal Agricultural Society of England*, Series 1, Vol. XXIII (1862).
28. Fertilisers increased the productivity of the soil and field drainage increased the number of productive acres on a farm by bringing waterlogged soil into productivity. The removal of hedgerows was deemed necessary to increase acreage, remove shelter for vermin, and reduce the number of weeds in the days before weedkillers were available.
29. C.W. Hoskyns, 'Agricultural Statistics', *Journal of the Royal Agricultural Society of England*, Series 1, Vol. XXVI (1855), pp. 554–606.
30. C.W. Hoskyns's comments on the subject of agricultural education, 'The Report of the Weekly Council Meeting of the RASE, 23rd April 1864', *Journal of the Royal Agricultural Society of England*, Series 1, Vol. XXV (1864), p. 547.
31. Hoskyns, *Talpa*, introduction by J.S. Arkwright.
32. Sir Oliver II was 4 years old and bred by T. Rea of Westonbury, Leominster. *Journal of the Royal Agricultural Society of England*, Series 1, Vol. XXIV (1863).
33. HRO E41/30–33 O/L339, Rent Audits 1839–91, amounts received, arrears, allowances etc.
34. Jones, 'The Evolution of High Farming', HRO AJ68, Chapter XIV, p. 27.
35. *Ibid.*, p. 30.
36. These loan companies had existed to facilitate drainage since the 1840s, but only from the Improvement of Land Act of 1864 was money lent for the improvement of farm buildings. The passing of the Public Money Drainage Act of 1846 was not undertaken solely in response to the repeal of the Corn Laws. Momentum for financial assistance of this kind to improve farmland had been building for some years prior to this. D. Spring, *The English Landed Estate in the Nineteenth Century: Its Administration* (Maryland, John Hopkins Press, 1963).
37. The Lands Improvement Company had been founded in 1853. It was permitted to undertake improvement work, but in practice, it only ever lent money. By 1873, its loans amounted to £3,004,392. By 1880 they were £4,192,241, an amount exceeding that granted under the Public Money Acts of 1848 and 1850 which permitted up to £2 million of loans. Spring, *English Landed Estate*, p. 157.

38. HRO C69/244, Hampton Court Estate Drainage, Buildings &c 1863–74, amounts received from the 'Lands Improvement Company' to be repaid in twenty-five years with interest. See Chapter 8, note 4.
39. An advertisement for Bowles as drainer, contractor and engineer survives at HRO C69/285–311.
40. At Lower Wickton 113 acres were drained for £860 14*s*, and at The Ford, 84 acres for £683 3*s*, HRO C69/243, expenditure on buildings, repairs and drainage, 1857–64.
41. A statute acre is an area of 4,840sq yd. A rod or perch as a measure of length was 16½ft (5½yd) long, and derived from the length of the rod used by ploughmen to keep their oxen moving. A square perch is 30¼sq yd, 1/160 of an acre.
42. In all, between 1846 and 1881, the Enclosure Commissioners, or as they became known, Land Commissioners, oversaw loans totalling £13,597,620. Of this £8.2 million had been spent on drainage, almost £3.4 million on farm buildings and £823,190 on cottages. Spring, *English Landed Estate*, p. 176.
43. Jones, 'The Evolution of High Farming', HRO AJ68, Chapter XIV, p. 30.
44. *Ibid.*, p. 31.
45. There is some confusion about the amount of Tally's jointure – perhaps this is symptomatic of Johnny's state of mind. The document (HRO A63/II/305–307) that was drawn up on her marriage to John in 1830 allowed for £1,000 per year to be paid in four quarterly instalments, a sum consistent with about 10 per cent of the estate's rental income, as allowed for Lucy's jointure on her marriage to Johnny in 1866. His own notes of 1866 (HRO C69/282b) and Sale's submission for the Arkwright Estate Act of 1887 (HRO A63/II/304) showed that Johnny had been paying his mother £4,000 per annum (labelled 'annuity' in the 1866 notes). Tally's bank statements confirm that she was indeed receiving just under £1,000 per *quarter* from Johnny.
46. HRO C69/282a and b.
47. Jones, 'The Evolution of High Farming', p. 11.
48. C.W. Hoskyns, *Farmer's Magazine* (1856), p. 352, quoted in Jones, 'The Evolution of High Farming', p. 11.
49. Jones, 'The Evolution of High Farming', p. 13.
50. HRO A63/IV/9/8, Lord Bateman to JA, 27 October 1852.
51. As at Hampton Court, the home farm of 614 acres was mixed, with 268 acres of arable and the rest given over to meadow, pasture and orchards. About 600 sheep grazed the farm and there were about 100 store cattle. I. Pfuell, *A History of Shobdon* (published privately, 1994), p. 96.
52. From Hope, Arch and Ivens returned to Stratford-upon-Avon by train, the estate paying their 16*s* 2*d* fares. P. Horn, 'Joseph Arch in Herefordshire in 1860', *Transactions of the Woolhope Naturalists' Field Club*, Vol. XL (1970–2), p. 155, *passim.*
53. P. Horn, *Joseph Arch* (Kineton, Roundwood Press, 1971), pp. 1–12.
54. F. Clifford, 'The Labour Bill in Farming', *Journal of the Royal Agricultural Society of England*, Series 2, Vol. XI (1875), pp. 108–9.
55. Jones, 'The Evolution of High Farming', HRO AJ68, Chapter XV, p. 3.
56. *Hereford Journal*, 16 February 1848, Special Supplement, 'Candlemas Meeting of the Herefordshire Agricultural Society'.
57. A. Salt, 'The Agricultural Labourer in Herefordshire', *Transactions of the Woolhope Naturalists' Field Club*, Vol. XXXII (1947), pp. 95–102.
58. The improvement of pastureland contributed to the new speed with which beasts could be fattened. As Lord Ernle pointed out, the farmer 'sold his stock to the butcher

twice within the same time which was formerly needed to prepare them once, and that less perfectly'. Prothero, *English Farming Past and Present*, p. 371. Lord Berwick of Cronkhill referred to his bull, Tom Thumb, as 'one which will get fat upon nettles'. H.H. Dixon, 'History of the Rise and Progress of Hereford Cattle', prize essay, *Journal of the Royal Agricultural Society of England*, Series 2, Vol. IV (1868), p. 281.

59. This description of the breed is taken from W. Britten, 'Hereford Cattle', *Journal of the Royal Agricultural Society of England*, Series 1, Vol. LXXIV (1913), pp. 54–60, and from Dixon, 'History of the Rise and Progress of Hereford Cattle'.
60. In 1868, in the class for a Hereford bull 2 to 3 years old, Johnny won with his uncharacteristically cantankerous bull Sir Hungerford, bred by him. There were two other prizes for Johnny at Leicester. He won first with the in-calf Hampton Beauty, again bred by him, and was victorious with yearling heifer Hampton Oliver. He also got reserve and highly commended in the same class for another heifer. His bull Sir Hungerford was again victorious the following year at Manchester. Show catalogues of the RASE, 1842–1905.

Chapter Four: Mastering the Family, pp. 54–68

1. HRO A63/IV/21/1, Sarah Arkwright to JHA, 10 July 1858.
2. *Ibid.*, 6 April 1859.
3. *Ibid.*, 27 May 1859.
4. Private collection.
5. Mitford was MP for Midhurst in Sussex.
6. HRO A63/IV/21/1, Sarah Arkwright to JHA, 7 (no month) 1859.
7. *Shrewsbury Chronicle*, 13 January 1860, in Shropshire Record Office, Watton's Newscuttings, Vol. 10, p. 149.
8. HRO A63/IV/22/7. There are rarely year dates on these invitations, so they probably cover his entire adult life, and not just this period.
9. HRO A63/IV/21/1, Sarah Arkwright to JHA, 18 October 1861 and 7 November 1861.
10. Documents about Herefordshire Hunt are at HRO A63/IV/39.
11. John Cook quoted in E.W. Bovill, *The England of Nimrod and Surtees 1815–1854* (Oxford, OUP, 1959), p. 121. It has also been noted that 'Whatever their difference in status, a patrician and his tenant were both equal before a challenging fence, where skill and courage counted, and shared as equals the same memories at the end of a long day in the saddle', see D. Cannadine, 'The Theory and Practice of the English Leisure Classes', *Historical Journal*, 21, 2 (1978), p. 466.
12. Promise was formerly Hungerford Hoskyns's mount.
13. HRO A63/IV/39/45–50, JHA's hunting diaries.
14. HRO A63/III/77, JHA's expenses 1858–1905.
15. HRO A63/IV/39/45–50, JHA's hunting diaries.
16. *Ibid.*
17. Huntsman at the time was Thomas Carres, and the whips were Richard Hall and William Cross, *Field*, 31 October 1863.
18. HRO A63/IV/39/2, North Herefordshire Hunt.
19. Bovill, *The England of Nimrod and Surtees*, p. 86.
20. Anthony Trollope, who used the hunting parson as a character in his novels, lived from 1859 to 1860 at Waltham Cross near Mark Hall, and hunted with the Essex, of which Joseph had been Master since 1857. After a period at Leighton Buzzard,

Trollope returned to the Essex hounds in 1874 and in his last three seasons (he died in 1882) he hunted with the Essex three days a week. Lionel Edwards, in his introduction to Trollope's *Hunting Sketches* (London, Benn, 1952) suggests that Rev. Jack Russell in the West Country or Rev. E. Timson in the New Forest might have been models for the hunting parson, but remarkably omits Joseph altogether. For Trollope and hunting, see J. Hennessy, *Anthony Trollope* (London, Cape, 1971).

21. Trollope, *Hunting Sketches*, pp. 105–14.
22. *Ibid.*
23. R.S. Fitton, *The Arkwrights, Spinners of Fortune* (Manchester, Manchester University Press, 1989), p. 270.
24. H. Lake, *The Arkwrights and Harlow* (published privately, 1995), p. 49.
25. Trollope, *Hunting Sketches*, pp. 122–7.
26. HRO A63/IV/39/45–50, JHA's hunting diaries.
27. HRO A63/III/72/1, Joseph Yates's Notes on the Hampton Court Estate, 8 December 1864.
28. Whipper-in of the Essex, James Cockagne remembered that 'No matter what weather he came through the stables and kennels every day and expected each man in his place, washed and brushed up, with his boots well blacked and woe betide anyone discovered otherwise!' Lake, *The Arkwrights and Harlow*, p. 48.
29. HRO A63/IV/22/1, Catherine Hoskyns to JHA, 21 April 1866.
30. *Hereford Journal*, 9 August 1862, p. 4, 'Marriage Festivities at Hampton Court'.
31. HRO A63/IV/21/5, Mary Bosanquet to JHA, 8 August 1862.
32. HRO A63/IV/21/1, Sarah Arkwright to JHA, dated only 1 June, but, from the context, probably 1865.
33. *Ibid.*, 12 September 1862.
34. HRO A63/IV/21/6, Fanny Arkwright to JHA, 12 December 1862.
35. Fitton, *The Arkwrights*, p. 185.
36. HRO A63/IV/30–37 for all papers connected with the HPS.
37. Membership lists for the HPS are at HRO A63/IV/30/1–5.
38. Johnny had spent £178 10*s* of his inheritance on 17 July 1858 (probably his birthday present to himself that year) on a Giuseppe Guarneri del Gesù violin (made in about 1730–3). This he had purchased from Henry Gamble Blagrove (1811–72), a leading virtuoso of the day who was teacher to the Arkwright family. In 1892 he further purchased for 7 guineas a silver-mounted bow by Dominique Peccatte from Bela Szepessy of Wardour Street, London. David Murdoch, 'The Arkwright Guarneri del Gesu' (typed account, private collection). The 1732 Stradivari instrument was bought for £200 from or through the famous cellist Signor Piatti in 1863. Today the Guarneri is played by Kazuki Sawa, one of the leading violinists in Japan. Hugh Dodgson has recently established that Johnny's Stradivarius is today the property of Dr Joseph Manig-Sylvan, Professor of Music at New Mexico State University, USA. It is on loan to a young American violinist and will eventually be bequeathed to the Whital Collection at the Library of Congress 'with the binding stipulation that it be made available to aspiring artists "to be played and not idle in a glass case".'
39. Groves's Musical Directory.
40. Ouseley (who had written his first opera at the age of 8) had been precentor since 1855. He had an overwhelming vocation to raise the standard of church music and to that end founded St Michael's College in Tenbury Wells, Herefordshire, *Dictionary of National Biography*.

41. Chandos clearly shared Johnny's enthusiasm for music. He wrote to Johnny: 'Beethoven is like Shakespeare – the thousandth repetition brings out something not realised before.' HRO A63/IV/21/15/4, CWH to JHA, 10 December 1858.
42. HPS members included the Bosanquets, Hoskyns, Hawkshaws, Stanhopes and Clowes of Burton Court – besides the Batemans of Shobdon, Cotterells of Garnons, Clives of Whitfield Court, Bulmers of Aylestone Hill, Cornewalls of Moccas, Lady Foley of Stoke Edith, (Bishop) Hampdens of Hereford, King Kings of Staunton Park, Phillips of Bryngwyn, and Saye and Seles of Hereford. The 1868–9 HPS season saw the Baskervilles of Clyro Court near Hay-on-Wye join, as well as Miss De Winton of Graftonbury, the Heywoods of Ocle Court, Peploes of Garnstone, Rankins of Bryngwyn, and Rogers of Stanage Park. Finally, by 1872–3, the ranks were swelled by the Baileys of Glanusk Park near Crickhowell, Crofts of Lugwardine Court, Dunnes of Bircher Hall, Leominster, Kevill-Davies of Croft Castle, and Venables of Clyro (employers of the celebrated diarist Francis Kilvert).
43. HPS music was typically a blend of eighteenth- and nineteenth-century pieces, and included Haydn's Symphony *Letter Q*, the 'War March of the Priests' from *Athalie* by Mendelssohn, the Overture to *Idomeneo* by Mozart, and the Overture to *The Barber of Seville* by Rossini. The choir rehearsed three madrigals, 'Stay Corydon', 'Light of my Soul' and 'In Going to my Lonely Bed', and four part songs, of which two, 'Oh Hills, Oh Vales' and 'Morning Prayer' were by Mendelssohn, and two were contemporary, 'Ave Maria' by Henry Smart and Henry Leslie's 'Song of the Flax Spinner'. HRO A63/IV/34/6, HPS Vol. I, 1863–81.
44. The concert in December 1871 was deemed to have been of a good standard, but went on for 3 hours until 5 p.m. *Hereford Times*, 9 December 1871.
45. HRO A63/IV/21/6, Fanny Arkwright to JHA, undated, but from the context, probably before her marriage in 1881.
46. *Ibid.*, Fanny Arkwright to JHA, 17 December 1863.
47. HRO A63/IV/21/8, Emily Arkwright to JHA, 29 January 1864.
48. HRO A63/IV/21/1, Sarah Arkwright to JHA, 26 February 1864.
49. *Ibid.*, undated.
50. *Ibid.*, dated only March 1864, but approximately 20 March.
51. HRO A63/IV/21/6, Fanny Arkwright to JHA, 27 February 1864.
52. *Ibid.*, dated only March 1864.
53. *Ibid.*, 22 March 1864.
54. *Ibid.*
55. HRO A63/IV/21/6, Fanny Arkwright to Sarah Arkwright, undated (and filed with Fanny's letters to JHA).
56. *Ibid.*, Fanny Arkwright to JHA, 6 June 1864.
57. Noverre's details from *Medical Directory* (1885).
58. HRO A63/IV/21/6, Fanny Arkwright to JHA, 25 July 1864.
59. *Ibid.*, dated 14 September only, but almost certainly 1864.
60. The head gardener was now Alfred Bye. There were inevitably references to jobs being done 'by the Bye', for example 'the plants are all well, thank you . . . he had them done by the Bye', HRO A63/IV/21/6, Fanny Arkwright to JHA, dated only 14 September.
61. Fanny quoted Edwyn's letter in her own to JHA. *Ibid.*, 8 November 1862.
62. HRO A63/IV/10 1–28, letters to JA about the education of his sons, and letters from Edwyn to JA at HRO A63/IV/9/16, particularly those of late January 1857.
63. Poetry written by the family, private collection.

64. The Earl was also Thane of Cawdor, and owned Cawdor Castle in Scotland, but it was little used at this time. The younger generation of Arkwrights and Campbells were well acquainted. Photographs taken of the two families survive in an Arkwright family album (HRO BH78/2, photographs taken at Haynes Park, Bedford). Edwyn and Muriel's was a promising match. Lady Muriel's brothers were Eton and Oxford educated, her father had since 1841 been Conservative MP for Pembrokeshire, was a keen and innovative agriculturalist and a significant landowner. Her mother, formerly Sarah Mary Compton-Cavendish, had been a maid of honour to Queen Victoria.
65. HRO A63/IV/21/1, Sarah Arkwright to JHA, dated only July 1864. The agent for the Campbells at Cawdor wrote with his congratulations on 10 July 1864. Carmarthenshire Records Office Campbell/Cawdor Collection Box 141.
66. *Ibid.*, 25 July 1864.
67. Carmarthenshire Records Office Campbell/Cawdor Collection Box 141, Alex Stables to Lord Cawdor, 4 October 1864.
68. Lady Muriel married, 20 April 1876, Courtenay-Edmund Boyle CB, Assistant Secretary to the Board of Trade, a grandson of the 7th Earl of Cork and nephew of the 8th Earl. She died 30 September 1934. They had no children.
69. HRO A63/IV/22/9, correspondence between JHA and Lord Cawdor.
70. I am grateful to Canon M. Moore of the Chapel Royal, Hampton Court Palace, for checking their records for me and for explaining the probable role that Edwyn played there.
71. The drought was chronic in Herefordshire in 1864. Springs and brooks never known to have failed were dry, pasture was badly burnt, and by late August a bucket of water was selling for 6*d*.

Chapter Five: Foxley Hunting, pp. 69–82

1. The Reform Act, when it came, would deprive Leominster of one of its two seats, but in the election that followed in 1868, Dick polled nearly three times the vote of his Liberal opponent. W. Williams, *Herefordshire Members 1213–1896* (Brecon, published privately, 1896).
2. It was John Davenport who had recommended Charles Hanbury Tracy to John Arkwright as architect for the alterations at Hampton Court. He had bought Foxley, one of the homes of the Picturesque Movement of Landscape, from Sir Robert Price (son of Sir Uvedale Price, the co-founder of the Picturesque) in 1855. The Prices had ruined themselves financially with the building of the new Yazor church, begun in 1843, and now redundant. C. Flood, *St Mary the Virgin*, Yazor (London, Redundant Churches Fund, 1989).
3. Lucy's father, John Davenport, was a son of the founder of the Staffordshire pottery company that carried the family name. Lucy's grandfather, also John, had acquired factories at Longport in 1793 and he retired in 1830. The business was carried on by his sons in turn, Henry (until he died in 1835) and then William. By 1851 William had extended the business to become the largest china and earthenware manufacturers and exporters in the UK. HRO B/47 and E5 Foxley collections.
4. Mary married the Hon. and Rev. A.A.B. Hanbury-Bateman on 2 February 1858. They had three daughters and one son and lived at Shobdon Rectory. HRO AM12/181.
5. R. Ryan, 'Awake, Awake' (London, Novello, 1869). Music H. Leslie.
6. HRO A63/IV/22/1, Edwyn Arkwright to JHA, 12 April 1866.
7. HRO A63/IV/21/14, JHA to Henry Arkwright, 10 April 1866.
8. HRO A63/IV/22/1, Sarah Arkwright to JHA, dated only 'Weds eve'.

9. These letters are filed together at HRO A63/IV/22/1 and are therefore not all footnoted separately.
10. Ward was possibly also a relation of the Davenports. Mary Bateman-Hanbury, Lucy's sister, had the middle name Ward.
11. Henry Longley (1833–99) was the son of Charles Thomas Longley (1794–1868), Archbishop of Canterbury, who chaired the first Lambeth Conference in September 1867. The Archbishop was also Charles L. Dodgson's (Lewis Carroll's) most photographed male subject.
12. Further letters were received from Lizzie's family the Kenyons, the Wigrams in Portland Street and Place, W.S.W. Sitwell of Onibury, Aunt Sophie Philips at Gwernvale, Minnie's family the Byngs, Johnny's Hoskyns uncles, his father's old friend Bonham Caldwall, A. Chester-Master at Preston Vicarage, Cirencester, the Clowes at Burton Court and from the Batemans at Shobdon.
13. The architect of St Mary's was George Moore, who unfortunately died during construction. The rector, Rev. R.L. Freer oversaw the completion and was responsible for the remarkable decorated interior. *Visit Churches in Herefordshire* (London, Redundant Churches Fund, 1992). Unusually, the church is oriented north–south.
14. HRO A63/IV/56/1, JHA to Lucy Davenport, 26 April 1866.
15. HRO A63/IV/20/1, Lucy Davenport to JHA, 6 June 1866.
16. St Mary the Virgin, Yazor, is now redundant, but the windows remain. Lucy's window was designed by Heaton, Butler and Bayne, 'gold medallists at the Exhibition, London', *Hereford Journal*, 9 June 1866. It and that for George and Sophy ('And Isaac took Rebekah and she became his wife') were later judged by Pevsner 'uncommonly good'.
17. Lind's performance in *Ruth* was not well received, but of her singing in the *Messiah* the same year, it was written: 'The rendering of the sublimest of airs, "I know that my Redeemer liveth" by Madame Goldschmidt . . . was a marvel of artistic skill and profound expression.' A. Boden, *Three Choirs: A History of the Festival* (Stroud, Sutton, 1992), p. 83.
18. HRO A63/IV/20/1, Lucy Davenport to JHA, and A63/IV/56/1, JHA to Lucy, April and May 1866.
19. HRO A63/IV/20/1, Lucy Davenport to JHA, 19 April 1866.
20. *Ibid.*, 24 May 1866.
21. I am very grateful to Ruskin scholar, the late Lyle Eveille, for her assistance in identifying this work. Quotations given here are from J. Ruskin, *Sesame and Lilies* (London, George Allen, 1905), pp. 110–80.
22. The publication of Miss Davies's work (it had been read at the Social Science Congress in 1864) came at the time when the Schools Inquiry Commission (1864–8) headed by Lord Lyttelton (of Hagley in neighbouring Worcestershire) was ongoing and causing outrage by its suggestions that endowments to schools should be of benefit not just to boys but to girls as well. E. Davies, *The Higher Education of Women 1866* (London, Hambledon Press, 1988). By now two public schools for girls had struggled into existence: North London Collegiate School for Ladies, founded in 1850 by Miss Frances Buss, and Cheltenham Ladies' College (1854) of which Dorothea Beale was now principal. Nine women, including Miss Davies, Miss Buss and Miss Beale, finally gave evidence to Lyttelton's Commission. S. Fletcher, *Victorian Girls: Lord Lyttelton's Daughters* (London, Hambledon Press, 1997), p. 112.
23. HRO A63/IV/20/1, Lucy Davenport to JHA, 8 June 1866.
24. HRO A63/IV/56/1, JHA to Lucy Davenport, 7 June 1866.

25. Ruskin, *Sesame and Lilies*, pp. 140–1.
26. HRO A63/IV/56/1, JHA to Lucy Davenport, 25 May 1866.
27. *Ibid.*, 26 May 1866. This incident recalls the demise of Sir Richard Arkwright's first mill at Cromford. Its doom was signalled when the brook that powered it was rendered too feeble to turn the spinning machines by the drawing off of water by others further upstream. R.S. Fitton, *The Arkwrights, Spinners of Fortune* (Manchester, Manchester University Press, 1989), p. 228.
28. HRO A63/IV/56/1, JHA to Lucy Davenport, 27 May 1866.
29. *Ibid.*, 28 May 1866.
30. HRO A63/IV/20/1, Lucy Davenport to JHA, 30 May 1866.
31. *Ibid.*, 31 May 1866.
32. HRO A63/IV/56/1, JHA to Lucy Davenport, 1 June 1866.
33. HRO A63/IV/20/1, Lucy Davenport to JHA, 1 June 1866.
34. *Ibid.*, 2 June 1866.
35. HRO A63/II/304/1–35, extract from the marriage settlement of JHA with C.L. Davenport dated 11 June 1866.
36. HRO A63/IV/20/1, Lucy Davenport to JHA, 9 June 1866.
37. HRO A63/IV/56/1, JHA to Lucy Davenport, dated '2 a.m. Mon night'.
38. J.J. Lonsdale, 'Ruby', composed by Virginia Gabriel, for voice and piano.
39. HRO A63/IV/20/1, Lucy Arkwright (CLA) to JHA, 12 June 1866.
40. *Hereford Journal*, 16 June 1866, p. 3. Account of the union of J.H. Arkwright with Charlotte Lucy Davenport. Details used here are taken from this account.
41. This had been made by Hunt and Roskell of New Bond Street, stood 2ft high and weighed 248oz. It was engraved with an inscription in memory of the occasion, and with the Arkwright coat of arms.
42. HRO A63/IV/56/1, JHA to CLA, 10 June 1866.

Chapter Six: Sons and Mothers, p. 83–99

1. HRO A63/IV/21/1, Sarah Arkwright to JHA, 14 June 1866.
2. HRO A63/IV/21/15/4A, CWH to Sarah Arkwright, 30 June 1866. Tally had been discussing with her brother his return to Harewood after his travels into Italy. 'That however cannot be. Irrespective of repairs (necessary & ornamental) it has always exceeded my means, hoping each year (in vain) that it w^{d} grow cheaper, & reckoning on an income which the estate has never realized & never will.'
3. *Ibid.*, 17 July 1866.
4. HRO A63/IV/21/1, Sarah Arkwright to JHA, 27 June 1866.
5. A full report of 'The Welcome Home of Mr and Mrs J.H. Arkwright' was given in the *Hereford Times* of 7 July 1866, p. 3.
6. *Ibid.*
7. Henry was, by the start of 1866, billeted in Dublin. He had been captain of the Harrow cricket team, and got his blue at Cambridge before abandoning the university for the Army. Abercorn was, like Henry, an old Harrovian (and a governor of the school) and in August 1866 he was receiving requests for a donation towards the purchase of a new cricket ground at Harrow, for which £6,000 was needed. Abercorn's passions for Harrow and cricket could partly account for his choice of young Captain Arkwright as his aide-de-camp in Dublin. PRO Northern Ireland T2541, papers of Lord Abercorn.

8. *Hereford Times*, 7 July 1866, p. 3.
9. *Ibid.*
10. *Ibid.*
11. *Ibid.*
12. *Ibid.*
13. HRO A63/IV/20/1, CLA to Henry Arkwright, 5 July 1866.
14. HRO AM12/80, Henry Arkwright to JHA, 3 September 1866.
15. For an account of Chamonix at this period, see F. Loux, A. Ducroz and A. Pocachard, *Chamonix Autrefois; le Mont-Blanc et sa vallée* (Montmélian, Fontaine de Siloe, 1988).
16. H. Longfellow's 'Excelsior' was set to music and became a popular parlour song.
17. An Englishman, Edward Whymper, had become a great celebrity in 1865 for being the first to scale the Matterhorn, at the eighth attempt, but at the cost of the lives of four of his party, who fell to their deaths from a precipice. 'Rather than dampen the British enthusiasm for climbing, the Matterhorn incident – like all mountaineering tragedies, it seems – only served to enflame it', M. Jenkins, *White Death* (London, Fourth Estate, 2000), p. 131.
18. For a full account of the incident, *Harrovian* magazine, 20 November 1897, p. 102, and A. Le Blonde, *True Tales of Mountain Adventure* (London, Fisher Unwin, 1906), pp. 98–105, in which Sylvain Couttet, who had been 25 years old at the time of the avalanche, gave his account. I am very grateful to the author Gillian Linscott for her help in directing me to Le Blonde's account.
19. HRO AM12/84, telegraph from Alice to JHA, 15 October 1866.
20. John Coltman Davenport had served with the 1st Regiment of Dragoons in the Crimea, and in 1856 was awarded the Crimea medal with Sebastopol Clasp. He died on 27 July 1858. His health had been damaged on service and he never fully recovered. I am grateful to Major D.J.C. Davenport for confirming this for me.
21. HRO A63/IV/56/1, JHA to CLA, dated only 'October 1866'.
22. *Ibid.*, dated only 'December 1866'.
23. Berkeley Stanhope had been vicar of Bosbury from 1856 to 1866, when he accepted the living of Byford, Herefordshire.
24. HRO A63/IV/21/1, Sarah Arkwright to JHA, Christmas Eve 1866.
25. HRO AM12/83, letter from W. Herbert to Sarah Arkwright, 7 January 1867.
26. The window, by Wailes of Newcastle (who worked also at York and Ely cathedrals and whose work was frequently used by A.W.N. Pugin), survives, although the dedicatory brasses have recently been removed from the wall beneath the window. Part of the inscription reads: 'This window was erected by his Brother Officers serving and who had served with him in affectionate Remembrance of the many qualities which endeared him to them all.' The central light portrays St Michael, the patron saint of soldiers, slaying a dragon. The glass of the upper lights depicts symbols from the Arkwright arms, including the cotton boll.
27. Three of the pillars are close to the headmaster's seat and three opposite. *Harrovian* magazine, 20 November 1897, p. 102. Clayton was himself to meet an untimely death while playing polo at Delhi on Christmas Day 1876.
28. HRO AM12/89, notes of Sheila Powell.
29. HRO AM12/81, letter from Guide-Chef to JHA, 31 October 1866.
30. *Daily News*, 27 August 1897, cutting at HRO AM12/88. Also quoted in *Hereford Times*, 4 September 1897, p. 8.

31. HRO A64/IV/56/1, JHA to CLA, 4 July 1867.
32. HRO A63/IV/14/18–27, Sarah Arkwright's accounts for Llanforda show her ordering china, toilet sets, cake plates, egg cups, tart dishes, candlesticks, and claret glasses from Mr Jeffrey in Oswestry.
33. HRO A63/IV/56/1, JHA to CLA, 8 June 1869.
34. HRO A63/IV/20/2, CLA to JHA, 22 June 1871.
35. HRO A63/IV/56/1, JHA to CLA, 15 September 1869, and HRO A63/IV/20/2, CLA to JHA, 18 March 1879.
36. HRO A63/IV/20/2, CLA to JHA, 15 November 1870.
37. HRO A63/IV/56/2, JHA to CLA, 18 November 1870.
38. HRO A63/IV/20/2, CLA to JHA, 12 May 1876.
39. J. Harris, *Private Lives Public Spirit* (Oxford, OUP, 1993), pp. 73–6.
40. HRO A63/IV/20/1, CLA to JHA, 19 and 25 October 1866.
41. HRO A63/IV/20/3, CLA to JHA, 23 September 1887. 'The Laundrymaids are *very wild* just what I thought, so I shall feel no hesitation in letting them go.'
42. HRO A63/IV/20/4, CLA to JHA, 1 August 1890.
43. HRO A63/IV/56/14, JHA to CLA, 26 July 1879, when she was taking the waters in Wildbad.
44. HRO A63/IV/56/2, JHA to CLA, 12 April 1870.
45. HRO A63/IV/20/2, CLA to JHA, 14 November 1870.
46. HRO A63/IV/56/2, JHA to CLA, 17 December 1872.
47. HRO C69/282b, statement of income of JHA, 1 May 1866.
48. HRO C69/229, Hampton Court estate acreage and rental of principal farms.
49. *Ibid.*, Johnny had to pay rent to the Hampton Court estate trust established by his father's will, for any farms that he had in hand.
50. HRO C69/241–3, expenditure on buildings, repairs and drainings on Hampton Court estate 1857–64.
51. *Ibid.*, 1857–74.
52. HRO E41/1–4, register of property bought to add to the estate and of property sold. In 1866, Redwood's tenant had been Richard Jones, and that of Lower Buckland, Charles Steward.
53. HRO C69/244, table of borrowings made from the Lands Improvement Company, 1863–74.
54. HRO C69/282a and 282b, estimate of JHA's property 1864, and statement of his income 1866.
55. HRO A63/II/304, Arkwright family general and miscellaneous – the Hampton Court Estate Act. These payments are also shown in Sarah Arkwright's bank credits, HRO A63/IV/14/1–5, Smith Payne Smith account showing credits from JHA in March, June, September and December annually.
56. HRO A63/III/77, expenditure on the house, garden, stables, 1858–1905. Stable expenses had been £1,390 out of a total of £13,567 spent on the house, gardens, stables and private items.
57. HRO AM12/145, Sheila Powell's notes.
58. HRO A63/IV/39/2, White Cross Kennels sale, 5 June 1867.
59. HRO A63/IV/56/1, JHA to CLA, 5 June 1867. That September Johnny sold another five horses, including Lizzie, a 15.2 hands Irish brood mare, 'property of the late Capt H. Arkwright', making another £103 19*s*. HRO A63/IV/39/2, White Cross Kennels sale, 11 September 1867.

60. *Hereford Times*, 17 October 1868, p. 5, and 24 October 1868, p. 5, for the funeral which was 'of a most private nature'. There were only thirteen men present, eight tenant bearers and the estate's tenantry in pairs before the coffin. Johnny was not among those present.
61. HRO A63/IV/56/1, JHA to CLA, 21 April 1869.
62. The former kennels are still visible today at Saffron's Cross, on the A419 near Bodenham.
63. HRO A63/IV/56/2, JHA to CLA, 19 February 1872, and 30 July (no year), but logically fits here as there are references to baby Jack.
64. HRO A63/III/77, expenditure on the house, garden, stables 1858–1905.
65. HRO A63/IV/56/1, JHA to CLA, 4 January 1868.
66. For Johnny this completed the tour that he had been taking when his father died.
67. Dick beat his Liberal opponent, Dr Thomas Spinks QC by 432 votes to 147. W. Williams, *Herefordshire Members 1213–1896* (Brecon, published privately, 1896).
68. *Hereford Times*, Saturday 9 December 1876, p. 6. Account of the funeral and obituary of Chandos Wren Hoskyns.
69. Hope School remained open until the autumn of 2004, when, due to falling numbers, Tally's school finally closed. *Hereford Times*, 23 December 2004, pp. 8–9. I am grateful to the final headmistress, Gail Richard, for letting me see round the school.
70. HRO A63/III/72/1, notes about the estate made by Joseph Yates, the agent.
71. *Ibid.* The earth closet may well have been constructed according to the model of Johnny's own former schoolmaster, the remarkable Rev. Henry Moule of Fordington, Dorchester. Moule was the father of Horace Moule (Johnny's classmate), the great friend and mentor of the writer Thomas Hardy, whose parents were among Moule's parishoners. Moule patented his earth closet and experimented with using the waste as a soil improver, recording remarkable results in productivity.
72. In 1870–1, Johnny paid another £296 13*s* 11*d* for more earth closets, a wood and coal house, and an arch with baize curtain. HRO A63/III/72/1, notes about the estate made by Joseph Yates, the agent.
73. *Ibid.*
74. All figures for this paragraph taken from HRO A63/III/72/1.
75. Rev. Grane resigned following the death of his wife. See HRO A63/III/72/1.
76. *Ibid.*
77. HRO A63/IV/22/3, letters of condolence to JHA on the death of his mother: Henry Longley to JHA, 21 July 1869; Francis Byng to JHA, 24 July 1869; and Chandos Wren Hoskyns to JHA, 20 July 1869.
78. HRO A63/IV/21/1, Sarah Arkwright to JHA, 15 July 1859, 22 September 1863, and 21 June (no year given, but from mentions of Emily's movements, most likely 1864).
79. *Ibid.*, 7 June (no year given, but from other details, most likely 1866).
80. HRO A63/IV/20/1, CLA to JHA, 13 September 1869.
81. *Ibid.*, 25 January 1870 and 12 April 1870.
82. HRO A63/IV/56/2, JHA to CLA, 6 January 1870.
83. Agnes was the only daughter and heir of William Tufnell of Hatfield Place, Witham.
84. Wilfred was born on 7 February 1871.
85. Harold was born on 10 November 1872.
86. Henry and Di Longley's son, John Augustine, was born in 1866. Mary Bateman-Hanbury had Edith, born 1860, Constance, born 1863, and Arthur, born 1867. She would go on to have two further daughters, Mary, born 1874, and Winifred, born 1879. HRO AM/12, Sheila Powell's notes.

87. HRO A63/IV/20/2, CLA to JHA, 18 February 1871.
88. *Ibid.*, 20 June 1871.
89. Hungerford was being tutored by Rev. W. Faithfull, of Llanwenarth Rectory School. Pwll Cam, where the tragedy occurred, was a favourite place for bathing. Hungerford could not swim, but was walking in a shallow part of the river when he complained of weakness in his legs. His companion, Arundel MacKenzie, told him to get out, but Hungerford ignored him. *Hereford Times*, 24 June 1871, p. 5, 'Accidental Drowning of Mr H. Wren-Hoskyns'.
90. Chandos had made significant alterations to Harewood chapel in 1863–4. *Hereford Times*, 9 December 1876, p. 6, 'Report of the Funeral of Chandos Wren-Hoskyns'.
91. *Ibid.*
92. Chandos's brother Hungerford, 8th Baronet, died on 21 November 1877. *Burke's Peerage* (1888).
93. R.S. Fitton, *The Arkwrights, Spinners of Fortune* (Manchester, Manchester University Press, 1989), p. 2.
94. Lucy Davenport was born on 13 December 1839, *Hereford Times*, 27 February 1904, p. 10.
95. Sir Richard Quain (1816–98) was a consulting physician at the Brompton Hospital with a practice at 65 Harley Street. He was a prominent fellow of the Royal College of Physicians and its Vice-President in 1890. He was President of the General Medical Council from 1891 until his death. He was best remembered as the editor of the *Dictionary of Medicine*, published in 1882. He was appointed Physician Extraordinary to the Queen in 1890 and granted a baronetcy the following year. He was appreciated by his patients for 'sound commonsense' and 'good humoured geniality'. His friends included Millais (who painted him in 1896), Landseer and Charles Dickens. *Medical Directory* (1885).
96. HRO A63/IV/56/2, JHA to CLA, 16 February 1872.
97. *Ibid.*, 17 February 1872.
98. *Ibid.*
99. HRO A63/IV/20/2, CLA to JHA, 22 February 1872.
100. HRO A63/IV/56/2, JHA to CLA, 19 February 1872.
101. *Ibid.*, 3 March 1872.
102. HRO A63/IV/20/2, CLA to JHA, 17 May 1872.
103. HRO A63/IV/56/2, JHA to CLA, 7 July 1872. At this period, foot and mouth was not the notifiable disease that it is today. The condition had become endemic after free trade in livestock began, which also brought free trade in diseases. It was first noticed in Britain in September 1839. It made the animals sick for six weeks or so, and the blistered mouths and sore feet prevented them from thriving, hitting livestock farmers economically. It was therefore undesirable to spread it, hence the precautions for the RASE Show, but it did not herald the widescale slaughter that it does today. I. Pattison, *The British Veterinary Profession 1791–1948* (London, Allan, 1983), p. 21. I am grateful to Susan Cunningham for her help with this.
104. This is made clear by the letter (HRO A63/IV/22/2) from Caroline Master of the Abbey, Cirencester, to JHA, 14 July 1872.
105. HRO A63/IV/22/2, letters to JHA on birth of a son. Rev. George Arkwright to JHA, 11 July 1872.
106. *Ibid.* John W. Grane to JHA, 11 July 1872.
107. *Ibid.* A.C. Master and F.W.C. Master to JHA, 13 July 1872.
108. *Ibid.* E.B. Hawkshaw to JHA, 30 July 1872.

109. HRO A63/IV/56/2, JHA to CLA, 28 July 1872.
110. HRO A63/IV/20/2, CLA to JHA, 29 July 1872.
111. HRO A63/IV/56/2, JHA to CLA, 30 July 1872.
112. *Ibid.*, 5 August 1872.
113. *Ibid.*, 15 and 17 February 1873.
114. *Ibid.*, 15 May 1873.

Chapter Seven: Hodge Finds his Voice, pp. 100–113

1. The Act created 938,000 new voters who were added to an existing electorate in England and Wales of 1,057,000. The ballot was not introduced until 1872, so there was still room for influence to make itself felt. L. Woodward, *The Age of Reform 1815–1870* (London, Book Club Associates, 1979), pp. 187–8.
2. N. McCord, *British History 1815–1906* (Oxford, OUP, 1995), p. 259.
3. *Hereford Times*, 29 April 1871 and 13 May 1871, p. 6.
4. For a full account of the proceedings of the inaugural meeting, see *Hereford Times*, 18 March 1871, p. 3. E. Selley, *Village Trade Unions in Two Centuries* (London, George Allen & Unwin, 1919), pp. 36–7. The tenants of the Leintwardine area had been meeting in the town, too, to debate their relationship with their landlords, just a few weeks earlier. *Hereford Times*, Saturday 18 February 1871.
5. W. Hasbach, *A History of the English Agricultural Labourer* (London, King & Son, 1908), p. 277.
6. *Hereford Times*, 18 March 1871. This edition contained the meeting of the Leintwardine union and the programme details for the HPS's second concert of the eighth season.
7. Littlebury's Directory, 1867. Murray had been the vicar since 1826. The main landowners locally were Robert Harley of Brampton Bryan and Rev. John Rogers of Stantage Park.
8. To enable him to nominate the vicar he wished on the Hampton Court estate, Johnny had bought the privilege of granting the Hope living from the Bishop of Hereford for £1,300 in 1858. Three months later, Rev. John Grane had been installed. Murray's living was in the gift of Robert Harley of Brampton Bryan. The Harleys were descended from the statesman Robert Harley (1661–1724), 1st Earl of Oxford, Chief Minister to Queen Anne and collector of books and manuscripts.
9. *Hereford Times*, 16 July 1892, p. 16. A letter refuting the hatred of the labourer for the parson.
10. HRO C69/312, JHA's research into pay and conditions on the estate. In 1853 Thomas Rowlandson had noted that 'the ordinary allowance [or cider] to labourers being at the rate of 2 to 3 quarts daily, to mowers 5 or 6 quarts, reapers and harvest-men as much as they can drink – the latter classes are said to average 12 quarts daily'. T. Rowlandson, 'Farming of Herefordshire', *Journal of the Royal Agricultural Society of England*, Series 1, Vol. XIV (1853), p. 445.
11. HRO C69/312, Notes on Workmen. In 1876 a total of 947lb of beef was given to the workforce.
12. The seven were Thomas Adams, William and George Billings, George Davies, William Penson, Henry Reynolds the wagoner and Thomas Williams of Hope. HRO C69/312, Notes on Workmen, 1855.
13. *Hereford Times*, 11 November 1871, p. 10.

14. A bushel had been the standard imperial measure by volume of corn since 5th Geo IV, of 2218.19 cubic inches. Bushels were made from wood and stamped by the competent weights and measures authority. Corn was shovelled into it and levelled off with a 'strike' or stick. Cereal prices were usually quoted in quarters. A quarter was equivalent to 8 bushels, or around 540lb. C.A. Jewell, *Victorian Farming* (Winchester, Shurlock, 1975), p. 50, and P.J. Perry, *British Farming in the Great Depression 1870–1914* (Newton Abbot, David & Charles, 1974), p. 148.
15. *Hereford Times*, 18 November 1871, p. 9.
16. *Ibid*., 18 November 1871, p. 9.
17. *Ibid*., 25 November 1871, p. 8.
18. C. Lee, *This Sceptred Isle 55BC–1901* (London, BBC Books, 1997), p. 576.
19. *Hereford Times*, 4 November 1871, p. 6.
20. Bodies like the Leintwardine Union were successful in their mission. Emigration from the UK of adult male agricultural labourers peaked in the 1870s in 1878 at 6,097, fell away for a few years and then climbed again from 1882 (5,138) to a staggering 22,451 in 1888, by which time the USA predominated as the destination for these emigrants. P. Horn, 'Agricultural Trade Unionism & Emigration 1872–81', *Historical Journal*, XV, I (1972), pp. 87–100, Appendix A.
21. *Hereford Times*, 2 December 1871.
22. *Ibid*., 9 December 1871, p. 3. The account of the dinner and speeches is taken from this source.
23. Johnny chaired the Hampton Friendly Society, and Bonham Caldwall was the Vice-Chairman. *Leominster News*, 18 May 1883 (no page numbers printed). In 1879, Thomas Wargen, a member of the Society died at Hope at the age of 55. He had been confined to his bed for twenty years and had received a total of £298 6*s* from the Society. From its inception, Joseph Yates, Colley's colleague at the office had been the Society's treasurer, a responsibility that he was to hold for fifty-one years in all. HRO A63/III/72/1, Joseph Yates's Notes on the Hampton Court Estate.
24. For details of this early employment agency, see Chapter Three.
25. Johnny's father had given almost one-third of the public subscription of £640 which enabled the building of Upper Hill School on the estate in 1853. For the interest that she had shown in the education of local children, Tally was asked to lay the foundation stone of the Leominster National School in July 1857. The Arkwrights' expenditure on Hope School has already been summarised in Chapter Six.
26. The cottagers were to acknowledge the landlord's provision of gardens and fruit trees at Johnny and Lucy's silver wedding in 1891. *Hereford Journal*, 27 June 1891, p. 5.
27. *Hereford Times*, 27 May 1905, p. 6.
28. HRO A63/III/72/1, Joseph Yates's Notes on the Hampton Court Estate.
29. HRO A63/IV/56/13, JHA to CLA, 19 May 1875. Johnny did not patronise his staff. On 3 February 1875, he wrote to Lucy that he had played his fiddle all evening the day before with Darwall, one of the clerks in the estate office. Randle Darwall left the office in 1881. HRO A63/IV/56/3, JHA to CLA, 3 February 1875.
30. Hasbach, *A History of the English Agricultural Labourer*, p. 277. N. Mansfield, in *English Farmworkers and Local Patriotism, 1900–1930* (Aldershot, Ashgate, 2001), p. 53, makes it clear that Strange did not claim such a high membership himself, but that it was claimed by Arch and repeated by others.
31. *Hereford Times*, 16 December 1871, p. 10.
32. Sir Herbert Croft was not at this time resident at Croft Castle, but at Lugwardine Court.

33. *Hereford Times*, 30 December 1871, p. 9.
34. HRO A63/III/72/1, Joseph Yates's Notes on the Hampton Court Estate.
35. *Hereford Times*, 16 December 1871, p. 10.
36. J. Charles Cox and Henry F. Cox, *The Rise of the Farm Labourer. A Series of Articles Reprinted from the* Examiner *1872–3 Illustrative of Certain Political Aspects of the Agricultural Labour Movement* (London, E. Dallow, 1874), p. 10, 'The County Franchise', 12 October 1872.
37. P. Horn, *Joseph Arch* (Kineton, Roundwood Press, 1971), p. 70.
38. HRO A63/III/72/1, Joseph Yates's Notes on the Hampton Court Estate – 'Marlbrook'. The cause of this action is not recorded.
39. HRO C69/312, Notes on Workmen.
40. *Ibid.*
41. *Ibid.*
42. *Ibid.*
43. *Ibid.* Figures for 1873 and 1874. Some indication of the distribution of jobs within the labour force can be extrapolated from the 1865 figures available from the same source. Forty-four of the labourers were then employed on farm work, 34 in the woodland, 10 were masons, 18 carpenters, 1 a glazier, 4 blacksmiths, 22 labourers, 15 quarrymen, 13 garden men, 4 stable men, 9 gamekeepers and 6 were superannuated and earning between 3*s* and 12*s* a week.
44. HRO A63/III/72/1, Joseph Yates's Notes on the Hampton Court Estate.
45. HRO C69/312, Notes on Workmen.
46. *Hereford Times*, 29 March 1873, p. 11.

Chapter Eight: Down Corn, Up Horn, 114–127

1. G.M. Robinson, 'Agricultural Depression, 1870–1900', *Transactions of the Woolhope Naturalists' Field Club*, XLII (1976–8), pp. 259–78 (see tables) and HRO C69/312.
2. P.J. Perry, *British Farming in the Great Depression 1870–1914* (Newton Abbot, David & Charles, 1974), pp. 18–20.
3. Parliamentary Papers, 1873, IX Select Committee on Improvement of Land Report, pp. iii–iv.
4. HRO C69/244, amounts received from the Lands Improvement Company 1863–74. The total of £27,451 between 1863 and 1874 inclusive does not tally exactly with the Lands Improvement Company loans records at National Archive MAF 66/11–36, which record £27,116 borrowed from 1863 to 1879 inclusive.
5. The extent of the Powis estate against which the loan was made totalled 8,100 acres in 1866. The drainage work was undertaken on the Shropshire farms. PRO MAF 66/29–31.
6. Colonel John Lucas Scudamore of Kentchurch Court borrowed £12,871 for draining, embanking and watercourses, while Charles de la Barre Bodenham of Rotherwas estate in Hereford borrowed just £2,110 over the same period. PRO MAF 66/22–MAF 66/36, Lands Improvement Company Loans.
7. HRO A63/IV/56/2, JHA to CLA, 19 October 1874.
8. *Ibid.*, 17 May 1875.
9. Perry, *British Farming in the Great Depression*, p. 36.
10. *Ibid.*, pp. 18–20.
11. HRO E41/1–4, register of property bought to add to the estate and of property sold.

12. PRO MAF 68. Herefordshire is county No. 17; Hope-under-Dinmore parish No. 177. NB Between 1869 and 1891, the censuses did not apply to holdings under 0.25 acres.
13. HRO A63/III/72/1, Joseph Yates's Notes on the Hampton Court.
14. E.L. Jones, 'The Evolution of High Farming 1815–65 with Special Reference to Herefordshire' (Oxford, D.Phil. thesis, 1962). Herefordshire's hop acreage had increased from 4,500 in 1850 to 6,000 in 1878. Herefordshire and Worcestershire's output in the 1860s had been 10 per cent of the national total, but the quality of the hops in this region was greater than the majority of hops grown in the south-east.
15. HRO A63/IV/56/1, JHA to CLA, 14 September 1869. 'The silver bulls head cups are made and look very well.'
16. T. Rowlandson, 'Farming of Herefordshire', *Journal of the Royal Agricultural Society of England*, Series 1, Vol. XIV (1853), p. 450.
17. H.H. Dixon, 'History of the Rise and Progress of Hereford Cattle', prize essay, *Journal of the Royal Agricultural Society of England*, Series 2, Vol. IV (1865–89), p. 282. Up to 1867, Prince Albert's herd had won twenty-nine prizes, many of them firsts.
18. Tudge had formerly farmed the Great House, Llangunllo in Radnorshire. J. Macdonald and J. Sinclair, *History of Hereford Cattle* (London, Vinton, 1909; reprinted 1968 for the Hereford Herd Book Society), p. 154.
19. *Ibid.*, p. 159.
20. *Ibid.*
21. *Ibid.*, p. 160.
22. Gaylass IV won and Abigail came third in their same class. RASE Show Catalogue 1878, Bristol.
23. Conjuror again won first, a new bull calf, Broadward, was second in the 6–12-month-old class, Gaylass IV was second in the up to 3-year-old heifer in milk/calf class, Antoinette won Reserve and Highly Commended in the yearling heifer class, and Pearl 3rd won the 6–12-month-old heifer class. RASE Show Catalogue 1880, Carlisle.
24. Records of combinations of bloodlines used to improve the breed had first been kept by Mr T.C. Eyton of Wellington in Shropshire from 1845 to 1853. Eyton's work was then taken up by Mr W. Styles Powell of Hereford for four years to in 1857, Mr Thomas Duckham of Baysham Court, Ross, took over the publication of the Herd Book. For twenty years, Duckham maintained the detail of breeders and their beasts until he retired in 1878. MacDonald & Sinclair, *History of Hereford Cattle*, pp. 141–3.
25. Rankin was a future MP for Leominster and the north of the county.
26. W. Britten, 'Hereford Cattle', *Journal of the Royal Agricultural Society of England*, Series 1, Vol. LXXIV (1913), p. 57.
27. MacDonald & Sinclair, *History of Hereford Cattle*, p. 295.
28. *Ibid.*, 'The Breed's Extension: United States and Canada', pp. 295–355.
29. *Leominster News*, 6 July 1883 and 7 September 1883. One of the bulls that found his way into the Miller herd was Sir Richard II (4984), bred by Johnny in 1869 and bought the following year by John Merriman of Cockeyville, near Baltimore in Maryland. After crossing the Atlantic and spending six years with Merriman, Sir Richard moved on to Maine. Two years later, having left more progeny in Maine, he was sold to Mr Miller in Illinois for $500. After helping increase the Beecher and Lafayette herds, to whose owners he was hired, Sir Richard was purchased in autumn 1882 by Mr C.M. Culbertson, founder of the American Hereford Cattle Breeders' Association in 1881. By now, Sir Richard's offspring were reaching great prices. The same year, three of his heifers, together with another heifer and a bull, were offered for $5,000 the lot. Culbertson himself

bought two yearling heifers by Sir Richard for $800 each. His sons, too, were winning prizes. J.S. Haines of Kansas won awards for his bull Fortune who had been sired by 'Old Dick' as the bull was now affectionately known, and F.W. Smith of Missouri won prizes with Dictator, a grandson of Sir Richard II. When, finally, the old bull was slaughtered, he weighed just over 2,000lb. Macdonald & Sinclair, *History of Hereford Cattle*, p. 307.

30. W. Fream, 'Canadian Agriculture', *Journal of the Royal Agricultural Society of England*, Series 2, Vol. XXI (1885), pp. 377–464.
31. Johnny's exports to Jamaica were Cherry Boy (6351) and Lastspring (6517), sent out in 1881. MacDonald & Sinclair, *History of Hereford Cattle*, p. 350.
32. HRO A63/IV/56/4, JHA to CLA, 2 June 1879.
33. HRO A63/IV/21/15/3, Rev. Leigh Hoskyns to JHA, 20 April 1876.
34. *Ibid.*
35. HRO A63/IV/56/3, JHA to CLA, 26 April 1876.
36. *Ibid.*, 11 May 1876.
37. *Ibid.*, 12 May 1876.
38. *Ibid.*, 15 May 1876.
39. *Ibid.*
40. HRO A63/IV/21/15/3, Rev. Leigh Hoskyns to JHA, 25 May 1876.
41. *Ibid.*, 8 June 1876.
42. *Ibid.*, 15 June 1876.
43. HRO A63/IV/23/26, sale catalogue for Harewood, 14 July 1876.
44. HRO A63/IV/56/3, JHA to CLA, 20 July 1876.
45. *Hereford Times*, 9 December 1876, p. 6.
46. HRO A63/IV/21/15/3, Rev. Leigh Hoskyns to JHA, 31 January 1877.
47. HRO A63/IV/21/15/2, Anna Hoskyns to JHA, 13 February 1877.
48. HRO A63/IV/23/25, sale catalogue for Harewood, 24 March 1877. From the dining room Johnny bought two cane-seated chairs for 8*s*, a six-fold screen for £2 2*s* and a handsomely carved fire screen with plate-glass panels for £3 3*s*. From the drawing room, which Chandos had used as his library, Johnny purchased a very handsome Chinese cabinet with ten drawers for £5 5*s* and a music stool and stand for £1 14*s*. From the small drawing room, he bought a backgammon board and two alabaster jugs for £1 11*s*, and an oak box for 6*s*, making a total sum of £29 4*s* 6*d*. I am grateful to Mary's descendants for making family papers available.
49. *Agricultural Gazette*, 9 April 1877, p. 356, obituary to Chandos Wren Hoskyns.
50. HRO A63/IV/56/4, JHA to CLA, 4 February 1878 and 2 June 1878.
51. *Ibid.*, 2 April 1879.
52. Perry, *British Farming in the Great Depression*, pp. 18–20.
53. HRO A63/IV/9/9, Richard Phelips to JA, 1 March 1850.
54. G. Murray, *Agricultural Depression: its Causes and Remedies* (London, Bemrose, 1879), p. 15.
55. Perry, *British Farming in the Great Depression*, p. 51.
56. C69/312. Johnny criticised high rail transport costs of produce in his evidence to the 1880 Royal Commission on Agriculture. H. Rider Haggard also criticised the discrepancy in the treatment of home and foreign produce by the railway companies in *Rural England* (London, Longmans, 1902), conclusions, Vol. II, p. 536, *passim*.
57. Perry, *British Farming in the Great Depression*, p. 142.
58. F.M.L. Thompson, *English Landed Society in the Nineteenth Century* (London, Routledge & Kegan Paul, 1963), p. 242.

59. Jones, 'The Evolution of High Farming', p. 59, refers to the variety of opinions about the start of the Great Depression – 1873, 1874, 1875 or 1879. He classifies the price fall of 1874–8 as the end of the Golden Age and 1879–83 as the onset of the Great Depression, particularly with regard to cereal farming.
60. HRO A63/IV/56/4, JHA to CLA, 17 April 1878.
61. HRO A63/IV/23/23, 'Catalogue of a valuable cellar of about two hundred and thirty dozen of old wines, the property of JH Arkwright Esq of Hampton Court, Herefordshire . . . 3rd June 1878
9 doz East India Sherry 1854, Crawford of Belfast Bottled 1862 Binned 1864 Reserve Price 60s
Port:
40 doz Vintage 1854 (Portal) Binned 1863 In 3 doz lots Reserve 37s
+4 doz ditto
+36 doz Port Vintage 1854, Northampton Binned 1861 Reserve 39s
+4 doz ditto
7 doz (more or less) Vintage 1851 (Hutchinson & Greenwell) Binned 1858 Reserve 48s
6 doz ditto, Vintage 1847 (Hutchinson & Greenwell) Binned 1858 Reserve 63s
Claret:
27 doz Chateau Lafite, 1862 (Barton & Guestier) bottled by Fennell, Binned 1866 Reserve 78s
+3 doz (more or less) ditto
3 doz Beycheville, 1862 (Barton & Guestier) Bottled by Fennell, Binned 1866 Reserve 48s
+4 doz (more or less) ditto
6 doz Leoville, 1858 (Barton & Guestier) Bottled by Fennell, Binned 1864 Reserve 90s
+2 doz (more or less) ditto
27 doz Chateau Lafite, 1858 (Barton & Guestier) Bottled by Fennell in 1861 Reserve 94s
+3 doz (more or less) ditto
3 doz Chateau Lafite, 1858 (Barton & Guestier) Bottled by Fennell, Binned 1863 Reserve 94s
+4 doz (more or less) ditto
6 doz Chateau Latour 1857 (Barton & Guestier) Bottled by Fennell, Binned 1866 Reserve 116s
+4 doz (more or less) ditto
6 doz Chateau Lafite 1848 (Barton & Guestier) Bottled by Fennell, Binned 1861 Reserve 147s
+2 doz (more or less) ditto
6 doz Chateau Margaux 1844 (Bell & Rennie) Binned 1862 Reserve 115s
+3 doz (more or less) ditto
7 doz Claret 1858 (Barton & Guestier) Bottled by Fennell, Binned 1864 Reserve 98s
+3 doz (more or less) ditto'.
62. To Lucy he wrote from the Ramsay Arms in Fettercairn: 'We have not slept a wink for two nights. A clock on the stairs wakes us every hour with a noise like a gong, two puppies yell all night & two cocks begin at 4 o'clock.' Fettercairn was very fashionable at the time, as Queen Victoria had tried to visit incognito with Prince Albert in 1861, after walking over Mt Keen nearby. A red sandstone turreted arch topped with delicate ironwork crosses and fuchsias was erected to commemorate the visit in 1864. Johnny wrote: 'I sleep in Princess Alice's room as occupied by her.' HRO A63/IV/56/4, JHA to CLA, 22 August 1879.

63. I am grateful to Jeremy Rex-Parker of Christie, Manson & Woods Ltd for providing me with archival details of this sale. Multiplied by the Bank of England's recommended figure of £44.76, in today's prices the sum realised is equivalent to £51,384.
64. HRO A63/III/72/1, Joseph Yates's Notes on Hampton Court.
65. Johnny is still remembered at Hereford's new hospital today, where his portrait is on display.
66. Johnny and Lucy played *Cavatina*, and in the second half, Mrs W. Chester-Master and Miss Master played duets from *Spanish Dances for the Pianoforte*. £20 was made. *Leominster News*, 22 June 1883 (no page numbers printed).
67. HRO A63/III/72/1, Joseph Yates's Notes on the Hampton Court Estate.
68. Perry, *British Farming in the Great Depression*, p. 56.
69. *Ibid.*, p. 36.
70. D. Cannadine, *The Decline and Fall of the British Aristocracy* (New Haven, Yale University Press, 1990), p. 92.
71. Thompson, *English Landed Society in the Nineteenth Century*, p. 308.
72. Johnny's findings were written up as part of the 'Report on Liver-rot' for the *Journal of the Royal Agricultural Society of England*, Series 2, Vol. XVII (1881), pp. 184–6.
73. *Ibid.*
74. *Ibid.*
75. G.E. Mingay, *Rural Life in Victorian England* (London, Book Club Associates, 1976), p. 45.
76. W. Hogg, 'Farm Prize Competition, 1909', *Journal of the Royal Agricultural Society of England*, Current Series, Vol. LXX (1909), pp. 269–310.
77. G.M. Robinson, 'Agricultural Depression 1870–1900', *Transactions of the Woolhope Naturalists' Field Club*, XLII (1976–8), pp. 259–78. Robinson claims no significant drop in hop acreage in Herefordshire. Figures printed by the RASE, however, show that by 1909 hop acreage in the county had fallen to 4,997 acres. Hogg, 'Farm Prize Competition, 1909', p. 309.
78. P. Horn, *Joseph Arch* (Kineton, Roundwood Press, 1971), Appendix 1.
79. HRO C69/312, Johnny's response to the Royal Commission on Agriculture. His was a picture that might have been envied elsewhere within the county. The estate of Guy's Hospital (in two tranches; just south of Hereford, and nearer to Ross-on-Wye, both south of Hampton Court) in Herefordshire, where there was a greater emphasis on arable cultivation, reported that rent remissions of 10 per cent were being granted after the disastrous harvest of 1879. Robinson, 'Agricultural Depression 1870–1900', pp. 259–73.
80. HRO E41/40 and E41/41, Hampton Court Estate Rent Ledgers 1867–76 and 1877–84.
81. *Ibid.*
82. Mingay, *Rural Life in Victorian England*, p. 44.
83. Murray, *Agricultural Depression: its Causes and Remedies*, pp. 9–10.
84. HRO A63/IV/20/3, CLA to JHA, 6 November 1880.
85. HRO A63/IV/56/5, JHA to CLA, 4 November 1880.
86. HRO A63/IV/20/3, CLA to JHA, 6 November 1880.
87. HRO A63/IV/56/5, JHA to CLA, 30 November 1880.

Chapter Nine: Algiers to Aberystwyth, pp. 128–138

1. HRO A63/IV/56/3, JHA to CLA, 17 May 1876.
2. HRO A63/IV/56/5, JHA to CLA, 11 February 1881.
3. For details of the customary journey from Dover to Algeria, see J. Murray *Algeria* (London, Murray, 1874). Murray's guide continues: 'A long extent of seaboard, rich

soil, boundless mineral wealth, a fine climate, magnificent scenery, the most favourable geographical position conceivable – all these ought to secure for it [Algeria] a brilliant future.'

4. HRO A63/IV/56/5, JHA to CLA, 14 February 1881.
5. HRO A63/IV/20/3, CLA to JHA, 14 February 1881.
6. For a full account of Ticehurst, see C. Mackenzie, *Psychiatry for the Rich, A History of Ticehurst Private Asylum* (London, Routledge, 1992). This has been used extensively for the account given here.
7. Wellcome Institute, Ticehurst Archive 6327/316a. George Blandford signed the admission form, 20 July 1873. Noverre had a large and fashionable practice near Park Lane. He was 'much beloved for his gentleness of character and the high professional standards by which all his opinions and actions were guided', *Medical Directory*, 1885.
8. Wellcome Institute, Ticehurst Archive 6327/316a.
9. Sir William Gull (1816–90) was a consulting physician at Guy's Hospital, London. As a result of the Prince of Wales's recovery, Gull was created baronet in January 1872 and Physician Extraordinary to Queen Victoria, becoming in 1887 Physician in Ordinary. Born the son of a barge-owner and wharfinger from Colchester, on his death in 1890, he left over £344,000 besides landed estates, *Dictionary of National Biography*.
10. Wellcome Institute, Ticehurst Archive 6379/19, Case Records 1873–7, Vol. 22, p. 5.
11. Of the fifteen people admitted to Ticehurst in 1873, only five stayed for more than two years. In all, 5 recovered, 5 died, 2 were moved, 1 was not improved (most probably Emily) and 2 were relieved. These calculations are made using the records for admissions to and discharges from Ticehurst. The list runs from the foundation of the asylum until 1917 only. Emily remained there until her death on 17 February 1927. Wellcome Institute, Ticehurst Archive 6286/3, 1845–81, Admission Nos 1–459.
12. For evidence of George's illness, see Johnny's letters to Lucy, HRO A63/IV/56/2–3.
13. At the by-election of 16 February, Thomas Blake of Ross was returned by a majority of eighty-five votes, the first Liberal Member for Leominster since 1852, demonstrating how the radical mood stirred by the labourers had taken hold in the north of the county. W. Williams, *Herefordshire Members 1213–1896* (Brecon, published privately, 1896).
14. HRO A63/IV/56/3, JHA to CLA, 1 May 1875.
15. HRO A63/IV/20/2, CLA to JHA, 17 May 1875. This was the 4th Earl, a captain in the Grenadier Guards who, according to *Burke's Peerage* (1888), 'died while on a shooting expedition in Abyssinia, 10th May 1875'. He was succeeded by his brother as 5th Earl.
16. HRO A63/IV/20/2, CLA to JHA, 23 June 1877.
17. *Ibid.*
18. HRO A63/IV/56/3, JHA to CLA, 2 August 1877.
19. HRO A63/IV/20/2, CLA to JHA, 1 November 1877.
20. *Ibid.*, 27 November 1877.
21. HRO A63/IV/56/3, JHA to CLA, 18 March 1875.
22. For background information on Algeria, see J. Redouane, 'La présence anglaise en algérie', *Revue de l'Occident Musulman et de la Méditerranée*, No. 38 (1984), p. 15, *passim*.
23. Accounts of sojourns in Algeria, such as Rev. Blakesley's *Four Months in Algeria*, and H. Walmsley's *Sketches of Algeria* were published, and Louis-Napoléon's visits to Algeria in 1860 and 1865 were given extensive coverage in the British press. Redouane, 'La présence anglaise en algérie', p. 15, *passim*.

24. Bodichon was a cousin of Florence Nightingale, and the feminist who had inspired Emily Davies to press for education for women. She had married, in 1857, French national Dr Bodichon and settled in Algeria. She was a co-founder with Davies of Girton College, Cambridge. P. Hirsch, *Barbara Leigh Smith Bodichon* (London, Chatto & Windus, 1998).
25. Redouane, 'La présence anglaise en algérie', p. 15, *passim.*
26. *Ibid.* The first reference to 'the Algerians' is made by Lucy to JHA in a letter of 26 June 1873, HRO A63/IV/20/2.
27. 'We are to have my first and I hope last dinner party next week. I rather hate it.' HRO A63/IV/21/3, Alice Arkwright to JHA, 4 March 1883. 'We have not been to any parties this year and so have escaped a great many introductions.' HRO A63/IV/21/3, Edwyn Arkwright to JHA, 1 April 1889.
28. For an illustrated description of gardening in Algiers by Edwyn, see *Garden*, 20 December 1902, pp. 428–30.
29. HRO A63/IV/20/5, CLA to JHA, 18 May 1897.
30. HRO A63/IV/21/3, Alice Arkwright to JHA, dated only April 1899.
31. *Ibid.*, Edwyn Arkwright to JHA, 12 July (JHA's birthday) 1899.
32. It is not clear exactly when Edwyn acquired Saidia, but Dick's 1876 visit might have been in part to assist Edwyn with the legal paperwork. Fanny certainly had a share in the investment, so it seems likely that Alice would have done, too.
33. The Algerian wine-growing industry benefited from France's broken relations with Italy in the late nineteenth century. In 1878, the vine area of Algeria had been 15,000 hectares. By 1903, this had spread, as Edwyn's article suggested, by over ten times, to cover 167,000 hectares. *Cambridge History of North Africa*, Vol. VI, *c.* 1870–*c.* 1905 (Cambridge, Cambridge University Press, 1985), Algeria, p. 159. The Algerians had benefited from the attack of phylloxera in France, wiping out nearly 2.5 million acres of vineyards by 1885. Algeria was never affected by this aphid that had entered France on imported North American vines between 1858 and 1963. F. Huggett, *The Land Question and European Society* (London, Thames & Hudson, 1975), p. 130.
34. HRO A63/IV/21/3, Edwyn Arkwright to JHA, 20 July 1885.
35. *Ibid.*, 18 February 1884.
36. The Presbyterian Church was founded by Sir Peter Coats of the spinning family. Redouane, 'La présence anglaise en algérie', p. 15, *passim.*
37. HRO A63/IV/21/8, Alice Arkwright to JHA (undated), April 1889.
38. Mrs R. Barrington, *The Life, Letters and Work of Frederic Leighton* (London, George Allen, 1906), Vol. I, pp. 298–9. Leighton to his mother 18 September 1857.
39. HRO A63/IV/56/5, JHA to CLA, 15 February 1881.
40. *Ibid.*, 27 March 1881.
41. E. Arkwright, 'In a Land of Sunshine', *Garden*, 20 December 1902, pp. 428–30. The collection was established in Algeria in part because of the absence of phylloxera.
42. HRO A63/IV/56/5, JHA to CLA, 8 March 1881.
43. *Ibid.*, 23 February 1881.
44. *Ibid.*, 23 February 1881.
45. *Ibid.*, 13 March 1881.
46. *Ibid.*, 2 April 1881.
47. *Ibid.*, 4 March 1881.
48. Private collection.
49. HRO A63/IV/56/5, JHA to CLA, 22 March 1881.

50. *Ibid.*, 19 March 1881.
51. HRO A63/IV/20/3, CLA to JHA, 19 February 1881.
52. *Ibid.*, 26 February–10 March 1881.
53. HRO A63/IV/21/14, illustrated letter JHA to Geraldine Arkwright, March 1881.
54. HRO A63/IV/20/3, CLA to JHA, 23 March 1881.
55. HRO A63/IV/56/5, JHA to CLA, 2 April 1881.
56. *Ibid.*, 6 April 1881.
57. *Ibid.*, 2 April 1881.
58. HRO A63/IV/20/3, CLA to JHA, dated only 'Monday' April 1881.
59. *Ibid.*, 6 April 1881.
60. *Ibid.*, 6 April 1881.
61. HRO A63/IV/56/5, JHA to CLA, 22 (no month) 1881, but probably April.
62. HRO A63/IV/20/3, CLA to JHA, 11 April 1881.
63. HRO A63/IV/56/5, JHA to CLA, 12 April 1881.
64. HRO A63/IV/21/5, Mary Bosanquet to JHA, dated only 11 July, but must refer to Willie Hill-James and belong in this period.
65. HRO A63/IV/56/5, JHA to CLA, undated November 1885 and 6 November 1885.
66. *La Gazette de Biarritz*, the newspaper of the period listed new arrivals each week. Description of the hotel from an advertisement for the Grand Hotel des Princes in the *Biarritz Association Letter*, 1909. Queen Victoria visited the resort in April 1889, Gladstone five times between 1891 and 1898, and Edward VII every year from 1906. Both Willie and Fanny are remembered in memorial brasses in the north-west corner of St Andrew's Church, Biarritz, which today is the town's museum. 'To the Glory of God and in loving memory of Frances Catherine the beloved wife of Lt Col W. Hill James who worshipped God in this Church for 20 years 1888–1908. "They shall be mine saith the Lord of hosts in that day when I make up my jewels" and of Lt Col William Hill James, late 31st Regt the loving husband of the above who worshipped in this Church for 26 years 1888–1914 "But go thou thy way till the end before thou shalt rest and stand in thy lot at the end of thy days."' They are buried in Hope-under-Dinmore churchyard.
67. HRO A63/IV/56/5, JHA to CLA, 25 August 1881.
68. HRO A63/IV/20/3, CLA to JHA, 24 August 1881 and 27 August 1881.
69. *Ibid.*, 5 May 1880.
70. Jack became a member of the Royal Horticultural Society, and a breeder of daffodils, sowing an average 4,000–5,000 per annum. He was a Fellow of the Linnaean Society from 1925 to 1953. In 1912 he crossed *Lychnis chalcedonica* with *Lychnis haageana* to produce the prize-winning, flame-coloured *Lychnis arkwrightii*. *Proceedings of the Linnean Society of London*, 1953–4, pp. 45–6.
71. HRO A53/IV/56/5, JHA to CLA, 13 July 1881.
72. HRO A63/IV/217, JSA to CLA, 19 February 1882, 'I know Chester-Master.'
73. Cecil Parker was the second son of the Earl of Macclesfield and had married in May 1870 Rosamond Longley, sister of Di's husband Henry Longley. He was therefore related to Johnny through marriage to Lucy's sister. Cecil's brother Algernon was also married to the Kenyon family, to whom Johnny was related through the marriage of his brother George. Jack's school friend, Gerald Parker, was a year older than him, having been born on 24 February 1871.
74. HRO A63/IV/20/2, JHA to CLA, 1 December undated, but visiting Jack in Clevedon.
75. HRO A63/IV/21/9, JSA to JHA, 4 March 1885.

76. HRO A63/IV/217, JSA to CLA, 5 November 1882.
77. HRO A63/IV/20/3, CLA to JHA, 6 September 1882.
78. HRO A63/III/72/1, Joseph Yates's Notes on Hampton Court.
79. HRO A63/IV/56/5, JHA to CLA, 26 October 1882.
80. Olive was called Katharine for a Bodenham cousin (now Mrs Streatfield) and Mary for Dick's wife Minnie, who had remained childless and was the other godmother. George and Lizzie's son Bernard was Olive's godfather.
81. HRO A63/IV/20/3, CLA to JHA, 8 December 1882.
82. HRO A63/IV/56/3, JHA to CLA, 12 May 1876.
83. HRO A63/IV/20/3, CLA to JHA, 20 July 1888.
84. One surviving letter from Simmie, after her departure, thanked Johnny for his gifts and added that 'the hot water jug & your nice warm scarf, not to mention its owner are often in my thoughts on extra cold days!'. This seems remarkably bold for a relationship that was merely a former employee to her employer – might it suggest that Simmie was more than just the governess to Johnny's children? If so, it is the only surviving suggestion of marital infidelity on Johnny's part. HRO A63/IV/177, Emmeline G. Simpson to JHA, 11 January 1888. She emigrated to 40 East 14th Street, New York.
85. HRO A63/IV/21/12, Evelyn Arkwright to JHA, 31 July 1890.
86. HRO A63/IV/20/3, CLA to JHA, 31 August 1885.
87. HRO A63/IV/220, Geraldine Arkwright to JSA, 26 January 1887.
88. HRO A63/IV/56/6, JHA to CLA, 13 June 1887.
89. HRO A63/IV/20/3, CLA to JHA, 27 August 1883.
90. HRO A63/IV/20/3, CLA to JHA, 14 December 1883.
91. Although the oldest of the Bodenham children were thirty years older than Pinkie, the youngest two girls, Florence and Augusta, were much closer in age.
92. HRO A63/IV/20/3, CLA to JHA, 5 April 1882.
93. 'Please send me two boxes of cavalry and one of infantry of those lead soldiers.' HRO A63/IV/21/9, JSA to JHA, dated 1883.
94. HRO A63/IV/56/6, JHA to CLA, 25 (no month) 1884, but Lucy mentions it in September 1884.
95. HRO A63/IV/20/3, CLA to JHA, 24 September 1884.
96. *Ibid.*, 1 December 1884.

Chapter Ten: Sized up, Seized up and Silenced, pp. 139–148

1. The survey was requested by Lord Derby in 1871.
2. J. Bateman, *The Great Landowners of Great Britain and Ireland* (4th edn, 1883 Victorian Library Edition, Leicester, Leicester University Press, 1971). Bateman was no relation of the family at Shobdon Court, but an Essex squire.
3. D. Cannadine, *The Decline and Fall of the British Aristocracy* (New Haven, Yale University Press, 1990), p. 55.
4. *Ibid.*, p. 17.
5. HRO A63/III/72/1, Joseph Yates's Notes on Hampton Court.
6. Bateman, *Great Landowners of Great Britain and Ireland*, p. 14.
7. HRO A63/III/72/1, Joseph Yates's Notes on Hampton Court.
8. H. Lake, *The Arkwrights in Harlow* (published privately, 1995), pp. 49–50.
9. F.M.L. Thompson, *English Landed Society in the Nineteenth Century* (London, Routledge & Kegan Paul, 1963), pp. 308–9.

10. Mutton imports in 1882 were only 181,000 cwt in chiefly boiled or tinned form. By 1899 3.5 million cwt of frozen carcasses were being imported. Imports of cheese rose by more than a third, butter doubled and wool more than doubled. R. Prothero, Lord Ernle, *English Farming Past and Present* (6th edn, London, Heinemann, 1961), p. 381.
11. G.M. Robinson, 'Agricultural Depression 1870–1900', *Transactions of the Woolhope Naturalists' Field Club*, XLII (1976–8), pp. 259–78. Fat stock prices fell by more than store prices. P.J. Perry noted falls of 20–40 per cent for beef in the 1876–8 to 1904–8 period, and falls of 8–12 per cent in store prices over the same period. P.J. Perry, *British Farming in The Great Depression 1870–1914* (Newton Abbot, David & Charles, 1994), pp. 45–7.
12. N. McCord, *British History 1815–1906* (Oxford, Oxford University Press, 1995), pp. 395–6; F. Huggett, *The Land Question and European Society* (London, Thames & Hudson, 1975), Chapter 11.
13. Agricultural production had represented 20 per cent of GNP in the late 1850s, but was just 6 per cent by the late 1890s. Agriculture had employed over 20 per cent of the population in 1851, but this was down to less than 10 per cent by 1901. Perry, *British Farming in the Great Depression*, p. 14.
14. Huggett, *The Land Question*, p. 130, *passim*.
15. *Ibid.*
16. D. Farnie, *The English Cotton Industry and the World Market 1815–1896* (Oxford, Clarendon, 1979), p. 41.
17. Not even hops could make up the shortfall this time. From peak acreage of 6,000 in 1878, hop growing was hit, like corn and beef, by foreign competition, developments in brewing technology and rising productivity in the industry. Herefordshire did fare better than other areas nationally, though, owing to the high quality of produce, and acreage held up well into the 1890s. Robinson, 'Agricultural Depression 1870–1900', pp. 259–78.
18. HRO C69/312, rents received and allowed on the Hampton Court estate.
19. HRO A63/II/304, Arkwright Estate Act declaration. Rent for 1886, £11,426.
20. HRO A63/III/72/1, Joseph Yates's Notes on Hampton Court.
21. HRO A63/IV/56/6, JHA to CLA, 3 October 1884.
22. R. Jeffries, *Hodge and his Masters* (Stroud, Alan Sutton, 1992 edn, first published 1880), Chapter III, 'A Man of Progress'.
23. As David Spring has made clear, this legislation protected the capital sum and not the landed estate, a significant shift in outlook. D. Spring, *The English Landed Estate in the Nineteenth Century: Its Administration* (Maryland, John Hopkins Press, 1963), p. 175.
24. Until this period, the Three Choirs Stewards, as county grandees, had dominated the programme and the running of the festival. However, after they failed to make these contributions, the conductor came to play an ever stronger role in the festival's organisation, and by 1897, the dominance of the conductor was established – yet another way in which the patricians were ceding leadership. A. Boden, *Three Choirs: A History of the Festival* (Stroud, Alan Sutton, 1992), p. 3.
25. Thompson, *English Landed Society in the Nineteenth Century*, p. 320.
26. I. Pfuell, *A History of Shobdon* (published privately, 1994), p. 98.
27. HRO A63/IV/56/6, JHA to CLA, 26 July 1884.
28. HRO A63/IV/20/3, CLA to JHA, 19 July 1884.
29. Perry, *British Farming in the Great Depression*, p. 78.
30. Thompson, *English Landed Society in the Nineteenth Century*, p. 318.

31. HRO A63/IV/20/3, CLA to JHA, 14 December 1883. A mother's contribution could be considerable. At Hampton Court, in the immediate aftermath of John's death, Tally paid three-fifths of the actual household consumption, half of the repairs and wear and tear, three-quarters of permanent repairs to the house and a third of the sundry costs. HRO A63/III/77.
32. A. Le Blonde, *True Tales of Mountain Adventure* (London, Fisher Unwin, 1906), pp. 98–105.
33. Cannadine, *Decline and Fall of the British Aristocracy*, p. 113.
34. The late Diana Uhlman of Croft Castle, Herefordshire, recalled Johnny's grandson David Arkwright showing her Johnny's G Guarneri del Gesù in pieces in a cardboard box. Damp had made it fall apart, but all its components were present. See Chapter Four, note 38.
35. HRO A63/IV/56/6, JHA to CLA, 6 November 1885. The instrument was featured in *Strad*, April 1955, pp. 414–15. See Chapter Four, note 38.
36. HRO A63/IV/178, Hart & Son to JHA, 25 April 1885, confirms receipt of his 'Strad' violin on loan to the International Inventions Exhibition at the Albert Hall. The letter notes that Johnny was approached because he had lent it before to the Historic Musical Instruments Exhibition at South Kensington in 1872. See also HRO A63/IV/23/6.
37. Letter of Sidney Arkwright's describing Johnny's feelings on parting with his Strad (private collection). HRO A63/IV/56/9, JHA to CLA, 26 April 1893. I am immensely grateful to Hugh Dodgson for his generosity in sharing his research into the provenance of this instrument, and to Odeyne Lovell Smith and Dr Joseph Manig-Sylvan. See p. 240, note 38.
38. Bye's horticultural accomplishments were acknowledged in the neighbourhood. In 1883 he judged at both the Bodenham Horticultural and Floral Show (founded in 1880), and the Leominster Horticultural and Floral Show. *Leominster News*, 24 and 31 August 1883.
39. HRO A63/IV/56/6, JHA to CLA, 20 March 1886.
40. I am grateful to Eric Turton for drawing my attention to this correspondence.
41. HRO A63/IV/56/6, JHA to CLA, 22 September 1886.
42. HRO A63/IV/21/3, Edwyn Arkwright to JHA, 3 January 1885.
43. The Coningsby Hospital had been founded in 1614 at the wish of one of Johnny's predecessors at Hampton Court, Sir Thomas Coningsby (1550–1625). 'Coningsby's Company of old Servitors' was intended to give refuge to 'a Chapleyne and eleven poore ould servitors that have been souldiers, marriners, or serving men'. The upkeep and £200 income of the company was vested in the ownership of Hampton Court. The original details of the foundation are located at the British Library, MSS Ro King's 47. For an account of the hospital and its history, see A.K. Beese, *Coningsby Hospital* (Hereford, Coningsby Trust, 1971).
44. HRO A63/III/72/1, Joseph Yates's Notes on Hampton Court, 14–16 October 1885. It raised £271 6*s* 6*d*.
45. J. MacDonald and J. Sinclair, *History of Hereford Cattle* (London, Vinton, 1909), p. 174.
46. *Ibid.*, p. 194.
47. Until 1832, the county had two seats, the city two, Leominster Borough two and Weobley two. W. Williams, *Herefordshire Members 1213–1896* (Brecon, published privately, 1896).
48. Cannadine, *Decline and Fall of the British Aristocracy*, p. 39.
49. North Herefordshire went to Thomas Duckham, south Herefordshire to Michael Biddulph and the city to Joseph Pulley. Williams, *Herefordshire Members*, pp. 70, 71 and 109.

50. P. Horn, *Joseph Arch* (Kineton, Roundwood Press, 1971), p. 182.
51. Thompson, *English Landed Society in the Nineteenth Century*, p. 276.
52. Cannadine, *Decline and Fall of the British Aristocracy*, p. 189. Their proportion had fallen from over half the Members.
53. *Ibid.*, pp. 157–8.
54. *Ibid.*, p. 157.

Chapter Eleven: Arkwrights Act, pp. 149–162

1. HRO A63/II/304/1–35, Arkwright Estate Act.
2. *Ibid.* and advice made 8 December 1886 by George B. Rashleigh, 5 Stone Buildings, Lincoln's Inn.
3. *Ibid.*
4. For confusion about the amount of Tally's jointure, see p. 237, note 45.
5. HRO A63/III/77, expenditure on the house, garden, stables, 1858–1905.
6. HRO A63/II/304/1, Arkwright Family General and Miscellaneous.
7. HRO A63/IV/20/3, CLA to JHA, 1 March 1887.
8. HRO A63/IV/56/6, JHA to CLA, Monday 2 (no month but unquestionably here) February 1887.
9. HRO A63/II/304/15, JHA to Harry Davenport, 15 February 1887.
10. HRO A63/II/304/29, Henry Longley to Harry Davenport, 16 February 1878.
11. HRO A63/IV/56/6, JHA to CLA, Monday 2 (no month but unquestionably here) February 1887.
12. *Ibid.*, 12 June 1887.
13. HRO A63/IV/56/1, JHA to CLA, 11 June 1866.
14. HRO A63/IV/20/3, CLA to JHA, 13 June 1887.
15. *Ibid.*, 14 June 1887.
16. *Ibid.*, 17 June 1887.
17. *Ibid.*, 23 June 1887. From 1888 honours were granted at New Year as well as on the Queen's official birthday. D. Cannadine, *Decline and Fall of the British Aristocracy* (New Haven, Yale University Press, 1990), p. 300.
18. HRO A63/IV/56/6, JHA to CLA, 17 June 1887.
19. *Ibid.*, 11 July 1887
20. HRO A63/II/304, Arkwright Family General and Miscellaneous. Arkwright Estate Act 50 and 51 VICT.
21. House of Lords Journals 119, 50 VICT.–51 VICT. (1887), p. 113. Arkwright Estate Act, 1887.
22. HRO A63/IV/56/6, JHA to CLA, 8 September 1887.
23. HRO A63/IV/218, Alfred Bye to JHA, 7 September 1887.
24. HRO A63/IV/177, JHA reference for Bye to unnamed person in Tunbridge Wells, 21 December 1890.
25. HRO A63/IV/56/6, JHA to CLA, 29 and 31 October 1887.
26. HRO A63/III/72/1, Joseph Yates's Notes on Hampton Court.
27. Cannadine, *Decline and Fall of the British Aristocracy*, p. 100.
28. HRO A63/IV/56/8, JHA to CLA, 10 June 1891.
29. HRO A63/IV/56/7, JHA to CLA, 6 June 1889.
30. For a full account of the silver wedding formalities, see *Hereford Journal*, 27 June 1891, p. 5.

31. *Ibid.*
32. Jack played a character called Hand and wrote and spoke the prologue. The stage manager was Earl Beauchamp also of Christ Church. HRO AM12/43.
33. HRO A63/IV/21/9, JSA to JHA, 15 May 1892.
34. HRO A63/IV/56/8, JHA to CLA, 8 March 1892.
35. In 1892, Johnny won with Spring Jack (calved 2 January 1888); in 1893, with Rose Cross 2nd; in 1895, with Happy Hampton; in 1896, the winner was Prince Bulbo, sired by Rose Cross 2nd; and at Manchester in 1897, he won first and show champion with Red Cross; finally, in 1898, he was again successful with Red Cross. RASE Show Catalogues 1892–8.
36. HRO A63/IV/56/8, JHA to CLA, 4 April 1891.
37. HRO A63/IV/56/9, JHA to CLA, 30 April 1893.
38. *Ibid.*, 27 June 1894.
39. HRO A63/IV/56/7, JHA to CLA, 22 June 1889.
40. *Ibid.*, 21 August 1889.
41. HRO A63/IV/56/11, JHA to CLA, 30 April 1898.
42. RASE Show Catalogue 1901, Cardiff.
43. The HPS performed Elgar's 'My Love dwelt in a Northern Land' in 1891, and gave the first performance of Elgar's 'Spanish Serenade', Opus 23 on 7 April 1893. E. Wulstan Atkins, *The Elgar-Atkins Friendship* (Newton Abbot, David & Charles, 1984), p. 26.
44. HRO A63/IV/56/8, JHA to CLA, 13 July 1891.
45. HRO A63/IV/56/7, JHA to CLA, dated just '21st' from Lily Hill, Bracknell.
46. In 1892, after a cache of silver was discovered at Stoke Prior and was designated Treasure Trove, Johnny claimed it, and after a second inquisition at Stoke, the jury found for Johnny. The value of the silver was set at £70–80. *Hereford Journal*, 15 October 1892, p. 5.
47. Royal Horticultural Society, *The Garden*, Floral Committee report, 30 April 1898. Johnny also served on the committee of the RHS's Rose Conference in July 1889 at the Society's Chiswick Gardens.
48. Royal Horticultural Society, *The Garden*, 7 May 1898.
49. HRO A63/IV/56/11, JHA to CLA, 1 May 1898. Moon made an illustration of the primrose, but it did not appear in the magazine.
50. HRO A63/III/75/3, order book for primrose plants and seed, 1897.
51. Johnny went at least annually to Llandrindod Wells from about 1890. The town, over the Welsh border in Radnorshire, was prized for its sulphur, saline and chalybeate springs, and by about 1895 was known as 'the hygienic capital of Wales' or the Montpelier of Great Britain, being over 700ft above sea level. By the same date it was estimated that over 50,000 visitors came annually, with August the most favoured month. The train brought most of them to the town which expanded rapidly and ultimately became the county town of Radnorshire. Details from a 'Guide to Llandrindod Wells' of *c.* 1895. See also I.E. Jones, 'Growth and Change in Llandrindod Wells since 1868', *Radnorshire Society Transactions*, Vol. XLV (1975).
52. HRO A63/IV/56/11, JHA to CLA, 12 May 1898.
53. HRO A63/IV/56/12, JHA to CLA, 18 April 1900.
54. The garden account book for 1898 included: potatoes, sprouts, swedes, carrots, artichoke, rhubarb, celery, campion, lettuce, tomatoes, chicory, parsley, apples (King of Pippin, Golden Pippin, Ribston and Trumpington) and pears (Vicar of Winkfield), savoys, broccoli, asparagus, cucumber, spinach, onions, seakale, beet, horseradish,

walnuts, filberts, salsify, parsnips, watercress, mint, broad beans, French beans and runner beans, radish, strawberries, gooseberries, cabbage, peas, cauliflowers, bayleaves, redcurrants, raspberries, cherries, marrows, apricots, peaches, black and white currants, melons, plums, greengages, black and white grapes, nectarines, mulberries, autumn raspberries, elderberries, and mushrooms. HRO A63/III/75/5.

55. Patent No. 25,164 awarded to Arkwright J.H., 29 November 1898. Patent No. 4181 awarded to Eckley H.A., 5 March 1900. Patents Records at the British Library, London.
56. HRO A63/IV/56/11, JHA to CLA, 21 June 1899. Two years later he was back at the Royal Show, this time at Cardiff, trading in trays on Stand 42.
57. William Carter was duly commissioned to paint Jack's father.
58. HRO A63/IV/20/4, JSA to JHA, 6 June 1893, misfiled among Lucy's letters to Johnny.
59. Godwin had been making tiles for over forty years, and in Withington since 1863. The firm had a strong reputation for quality, both in their imitations of medieval tiles and new designs. Unattributed, 'The Arkwright Tile', *Herefordshire County Life*, Vol. IV, No. 4, September 1981, p. 45. Business had boomed with the wave of church restorations carried out in the nineteenth century and as early as 1868 they were claiming to have supplied over 300 churches. Sir George Gilbert Scott 'invariably specified' Godwin's tiles, as indeed he had when he worked on the pavements in the east end of Hereford Cathedral in 1857.
60. *Hereford Times*, 15 July 1893, p. 6. Details that follow are taken from this account.
61. Hope's schoolmaster, Mr Noakes, observed in 1902 that during the past six years, out of an average attendance of 100 lads, fewer than a dozen remained in the parish, and those who did were for the most part 'dullards'. Increasingly, Hope's homes had no children of school age, the children of the elderly occupants having left for the cities. Mr W.E. Britten, the agent for various Herefordshire estates, 'knew of cases in which every one of the young men went to coal mines or brick manufactories, or to the Birmingham waterworks, and when once they had touched the "big shilling" they would not come back.' H. Rider Haggard was also told that the young left because in the cities they could earn more money with less Sunday work, and enjoyed light amusements and greater liberty. H. Rider Haggard, *Rural England* (London, Longmans, 1902), Vol. I, pp. 315–16.

Chapter Twelve: Parasites and Mousetraps, pp. 163–174

1. D. Cannadine, *Decline and Fall of the British Aristocracy* (New Haven, Yale University Press, 1990), p. 92, and R. Prothero, Lord Ernle, *English Farming Past and Present* (6th edn, London, Heinemann, 1961), p. 382.
2. These shifts were reflected in changes over England and Wales as a whole, where corn acreage shrank from 8,244,392 acres in 1871 to 5,886,052 in 1901. Over the same period, permanent pasture increased from 11,367,298 to 15,399,025. Prothero, *English Farming Past and Present*, p. 381.
3. P.J. Perry, *British Farming in the Great Depression 1870–1914* (Newton Abbot, David & Charles, 1974), p. 57.
4. W. Hogg, 'Farm Prize Competition, 1909', *Journal of the Royal Agricultural Society of England*, Vol. LXX (1909), p. 309.
5. Perry, *British Farming in the Great Depression*, p. 40.
6. A. March, *Historical Directory of Trade Unions* (London, Gower, 1984), Vol. 2, p. 287.
7. *Hereford Times*, 14 May 1892, p. 10.

8. *Ibid.*, reporting speech of Mr Henry Aucketill, the organising secretary of the English Land Restoration League at Yarpole. Wellington's words were quoted by Auchmuty in a letter to the *Hereford Times*, 16 July 1892, p. 16.
9. *Ibid.*, 23 July 1892, p. 2.
10. HRO C69/312, speech written by JHA, 1886 (or 1892, or perhaps reused in 1892 – his own addition of dates makes this unclear), though for which occasion is not recorded.
11. English Land Restoration League, *Among the Labourers with the Red Van* (London, 1891–7), January 1893, the report of activity in 1892.
12. Herefordshire sent up one representative of every contemporary political hue. In north Herefordshire (Leominster) the Tories were returned in the form of James Rankin; south Herefordshire (Ross) returned Michael Biddulph (Liberal Unionist); and Hereford City returned a Gladstonian Liberal, W.H. Grenfell of Maidenhead, Berkshire. W. Williams, *Herefordshire Members 1213–1896* (Brecon, published privately, 1896).
13. *Hereford Times*, 27 August 1892, p. 6.
14. H.A. Russell, 11th Duke of Bedford, *A Great Agricultural Estate* (London, Murray, 1897), p. 52.
15. *Hereford Times*, 14 May 1892, p. 10.
16. *Ibid.*
17. English Land Restoration League, *Among the Labourers with the Red Van*, January 1893, the report of activity in 1892, p. 6.
18. W. Hasbach, *A History of the English Agricultural Labourer* (London, King, 1908), p. 303. The depopulation of the countryside and the 'flight from the land' as it has been called, undoubtedly contributed to the failure of unions too. H. Rider Haggard was to note local concern about the fall in labourers in Herefordshire in 1902. At Hampton Court, Mr Stephens (sanitary inspector for Leominster Rural District Council) stated that labour was 'scarce, dear and uncertain'. Commenting on the good condition of the cottages, 'he added that if things went on as at present they would soon be too ample for the population'. H. Rider Haggard, *Rural England* (London, Longmans, 1902), Vol. I, pp. 295 and 304–5.
19. HRO A63/III/62/3, notes on Johnny's arrangements with Yates on his resignation. Yates, like Colley, did not enjoy a long retirement. He died on 31 August 1896.
20. Cannadine, *Decline and Fall of the British Aristocracy*, p. 93.
21. The Thorney estates were on the Bedford Levels. H.A. Russell, 11th Duke of Bedford, *A Great Agricultural Estate*, Chapter VI, p. 113, *passim*.
22. H. Lake, *The Arkwrights in Harlow* (published privately, 1995), p. 51.
23. HRO A63/IV/67/21, In Memoriam, Colonel Thomas William Chester-Master JP DL (1841–1914).
24. Cannadine, *Decline and Fall of the British Aristocracy*, p. 99.
25. *Hereford Times*, 23 July 1892, p. 2, Joseph Arch 'we must have parish councils. By conferring upon these councils the control of the charities and the administration of the Poor Law many of the vile abuses at present existing will be disposed of. These councils, too, must take over the matters of rating and education in the villages.'
26. HRO A63/IV/23/24, Lord Bateman's sale of trophies, pictures and porcelain held on 11, 13 and 14 April 1896.
27. In the 1890s, land commanded a purchase price of only 20–25 years' purchase as against a former norm of 30–40 years. Perry, *British Farming in the Great Depression*, p. 69, *passim*.

28. The Franco-Prussian War had led to the collapse of the Paris money market and many European financiers had made their base in London, making the city the undisputed capital market of the world. This contributed to the shift of status and glamour in Britain from the shires to the city. J. Harris, *Private Lives, Public Spirit* (Oxford, Oxford University Press, 1993), p. 5.
29. Cannadine, *Decline and Fall of the British Aristocracy*, p. 110.
30. *Ibid.*, p. 106.
31. W. Gilpin, *Observations on the River Wye* (Woodstock, Oxon, 1991, facsimile of 1782 publication).
32. HRO A63/IV/56/8, JHA to CLA, 6 March 1892.
33. HRO A63/IV/56/7, JHA to CLA, 5 September 1889.
34. HRO A63/IV/21/15/3, Rev. Leigh Hoskyns to JHA, 29 December 1895. Leigh had become rector of Aston Tyrrold in 1845. He was a Patron of Magdalen College, Oxford, Rural Dean of Wallingford from 1860, and Honorary Canon of Christ Church, Oxford from 1880.
35. HRO A63/IV/56/9, JHA to CLA, 27 July 1895.
36. Johnny was shooting at Knockando, Invereshie.
37. HRO A63/IV/56/9, JHA to CLA, 14 August 1895.
38. HRO A63/IV/21/9, JSA to JHA, 4 November 1895.
39. Cannadine, *Decline and Fall of the British Aristocracy*, p. 450.
40. The prize was instituted in 1810 by Sir Roger Newdigate of Arbury in Warwickshire. He stipulated that works should not exceed fifty lines and should be limited to the subjects of Greek or Roman architecture, sculpture or painting. These restrictions were felt to be too narrow, and after seventeen years they were widened by Newdigate's heir. Bodleian Library, Oxford.
41. HRO A63/IV/57/7, JSA to CLA, February 1895.
42. *Ibid.*, June 1895.
43. Other former Newdigate prizemen of repute included John Ruskin (for 'Salsetto and Elephanta' in 1839), Matthew Arnold ('Cromwell' in 1843) and Laurence Binyon ('Persephone' in 1890). Bodleian Library, Oxford.
44. Montezuma won his class at the 1897 Manchester RASE Show.
45. W.S. Gilbert, Selections from the Savoy Operas (Ware, Wordsworth Editions, 1994), 'Patience' Opera Comique, 23 April 1881.
46. HRO A63/IV/56/9, JHA to CLA, 3 April 1895.
47. HRO A63/IV/20/5, CLA to JHA, 22 May 1896.
48. *Ibid.*, 30 May 1896.
49. *Ibid.*, 3 February 1897.
50. *Ibid.*, 3 February 1897 and HRO A63/IV/58/1, various correspondence to Lucy. Richard Chester-Master to CLA, 31 March undated, but undoubtedly 1897 as Dick is on the point of leaving for Cape Town.
51. HRO A63/IV/56/10, JHA to CLA, 13 April 1897.
52. HRO A63/IV/20/5, CLA to JHA, 13 April 1897.
53. HRO A63/IV/21/11, W. Chester-Master to JHA, 14 April 1897.
54. *Ibid.*, 15 April 1897.
55. *Ibid.*, JHA to W. Chester-Master, 17 April 1897 (copy).
56. In May 1897 Jack was moving into a new flat in Queen Anne's Mansions, St James's Park, which he rented for £95 a year.
57. HRO A63/IV/57/7, JSA to CLA, 25 November 1897.

58. *Ibid.*, 28 May 1897.
59. *Ibid.*, undated.
60. *Ibid.*, 14 July 1897.

Chapter Thirteen: Land Loss at Home, Victory Abroad, pp. 175–192

1. D. MacCulloch, *Romantic Lochaber, Arisaig and Morar* (Edinburgh, Chambers, 1971). The house was enlarged and became a hotel in 1947, but unfortunately was burnt down in May 1950. An avenue of trees a quarter of a mile to the north is still known as Banquo's Walk.
2. Telegraph contents, Arthur Arkwright's account of Henry's recovery in *Harrovian* magazine (1897), p. 103.
3. Maud Bosanquet to unnamed correspondent, 28 August 1897, explains that Stanffer is 'Uncle Edwyn's German (or Swiss) servant'. By this date, Maud is also at the Hotel Royal, having been travelling on the Continent herself when news of the discovery of Henry's body came. Private collection.
4. Private collection. Copied here from the original, spelling errors included.
5. HRO AM12/93, postcard to CLA from JSA, undated, from Dijon (midnight) but from this trip.
6. W. Shakespeare, *Macbeth*, Act II, Scene i.
7. In 1892, the railway's first year, visitor figures had been estimated at 24,000 over the summer season. By 1899 it was to reach 39,000, rising to 80,000 in 1903. F. Loux, A. Ducroz and A. Pocachard, *Chamonix Autrefois; le Mont-Blanc et sa vallée* (Montmélian, Fontaine de Siloe, 1988).
8. *Hereford Times*, 4 September 1897, p. 8. No name was given by the newspaper for its correspondent, present at the time of the recovery of Henry's remains.
9. H.W. Longfellow, *The Poetical Works of Henry Wadsworth Longfellow* (London, Warne, 1878), p. 46, 'Excelsior'.
10. *Hereford Times*, 3 September 1892, p. 14.
11. HRO AM12/91, JSA to CLA, 28 August 1897.
12. HRO AM12/96, JSA to CLA, 29 August 1897.
13. The bearers were Joseph and Hubert Simond, Albert and Jules Tournier, the sons of the porters and guide who were killed with Henry, plus Alfred and Auguste Payot who had found the remains. *Harrovian* magazine, 1897, p. 102.
14. AM12/89, JSA to CLA, 31 August 1897.
15. HRO A63/IV/56/10, JHA to CLA, undated.
16. HRO A63/IV/21/6, Fanny Hill-James to JHA, dated only 23 September, but probably 1897.
17. *Hereford Times*, 28 August 1897, p. 8, and 27 May 1905, p. 6, claimed that Fanny introduced the wearing of bells on some of the Herefords.
18. HRO A63/IV/21/6, Fanny Hill-James to JHA, 14 September 1897.
19. *Essex County Chronicle*, 10 September 1897. Remarkably, the case survives today in a private collection.
20. HRO A63/IV/20/5, CLA to JHA, 28 March 1899.
21. HRO A63/IV/21/9, JSA to JHA, 8 February 1898.
22. *Ibid.*, 3 July 1898.
23. *Ibid.*, 22 May 1899.
24. *Ibid.*, 28 June 1899.

25. HRO AM12/120, Sheila Powell's notes. Jack was probably helped in attaining this position by his cousin John Longley, Henry and Di's only son, who had held the same position from 1895 to 1896. HRO AM12/120 also mentions that Jack was Private Secretary to Gerald Balfour while he was at the Board of Trade.
26. HRO A63/IV/56/11, JHA to CLA, dated only March 1899.
27. Hereford City Library Newspaper Cutting Book 3, p. 195, *Hereford Times*, 6 July 1935. Johnny had been the first President and Chairman of the Committee of the Hereford and West of England Rose Society, founded in 1867. After three years, the Society had run into financial difficulties and it reluctantly decided to dissolve. 'The Committee was just rising when Mr Arkwright who had been detained elsewhere, came into the room, called upon it to sit down again, and exhorted it to sit tight. Then with silver eloquence, backed perhaps with golden coinage, he brought them to a resolution to maintain this Society for the glory of the rose.'
28. In 1890, Lloyds had purchased Johnny's bank, the Worcester City and County Banking Company Ltd. The Worcester Bank operated from the building it had erected in Corn Square in 1866, to designs by Henry Day of Worcester. Lloyds TSB Bank still has its Leominster branch in this building. On entering the building, the name of the Worcester City and County Bank can still be seen carved on the keystone overhead.
29. D. Cannadine, *The Decline and Fall of the British Aristocracy* (New Haven, Yale University Press, 1990), p. 94.
30. HRO A63/IV/9/12, Lady Hoskyns to JA, dated only December 1848. As research by W. Rubinstein makes clear, the wealthy in Britain had disproportionately earned their fortunes in the cities in commerce and finance as merchants, bankers, shipowners, merchant bankers, and stock and insurance agents and brokers. To such men, the countryside and its way of life was alien. Relatively few families like the Arkwrights, Strutts and Peels, who made money in industry, invested heavily in land (many invested to a smaller extent – an extent too small to appear in Bateman's survey – such as the iron-masters, the Crawshays of Cyfarthfa, S. Wales). It is furthermore notable that these families began their enterprises in the countryside and so to them rural life was more familiar. Therefore, there was less resistance on their part to investment in land. W. Rubinstein, *Men of Property* (London, Croom Helm, 1981).
31. I am most grateful to Eric Turton for helping me to track down J.A. Daggs in the Worcestershire census of 1881, when he was described as a 24-year-old bank clerk. Kelly's Directory for 1895 lists him as the manager of Lloyds Bank.
32. HRO A63/IV/23/9, Sale's Account, 1899–1903. This document is a useful source for the development of the disentailment during this period.
33. *Ibid*.
34. Doubtless, Dick merited the promotion, but the 'small world' was probably at work as well. At this time, Sir Michael Hicks Beach, an old Gloucestershire friend of the Masters, was Chancellor of the Exchequer in the Salisbury government that had appointed Milner.
35. Milner's close circle at Government House included Lady Edward Cecil (ultimately Milner's wife), Major-General and Mrs Hanbury-Williams (he was Milner's Military Secretary), Ozzy Walrond (Milner's Private Secretary), and another ADC, Hugh Grosvenor, the future 2nd Duke of Westminster, known as Bend'Or. C. Headlam (ed.), *The Milner Papers South Africa 1897–1899* (London, Cassell, 1931), Vol. II, pp. 11–12.

36. Rimington's men were known as the 'Tigers', after the bands (in fact, leopard skin) that they wore around their hats which were otherwise indistinguishable from the broad-brimmed felt hats worn by the Boers. Source T. Pakenham, *The Boer War* (London, Sphere Books, 1991), p. 180.
37. D. Judd, *The Boer War* (London, Granada, 1977), p. 386, *passim*.
38. On 10 December, General Gatacre was defeated at Stormberg in the north of Cape Colony. The next day, Lieutenant-General Methuen was halted in his attempt to reach Kimberley in a battle at Magersfontein near the Modder river. On 15 December, Sir Redvers Buller was defeated in battle on the eastern front, at Colenso, south of Ladysmith. Pakenham, *The Boer War*, pp. 246–9.
39. J. Evelyn Wrench, *Alfred Lord Milner: The Man of No Illusions* (London, Eyre & Spottiswoode, 1958), p. 213.
40. Most satisfyingly for Jack, the hymn was sung at Christ Church over Christmas, to a tune composed by Basil Harwood (1858–1949), organist at the cathedral. The hymn was also used at St Michael's, Hereford, in October 1900.
41. HRO A63/IV/23/9, Sale's Account, 1899–1903.
42. HRO A63/II/304/32, agreement between JHA and JSA to pay off JHA's liabilities. George B. Rashleigh to JHA, February 1900.
43. HRO A63/IV/23/9, Sale's Account, 1899–1903.
44. *Ibid.*
45. *Ibid.*
46. *Ibid.*
47. L. March Phillips, *With Rimington* (London, Edward Arnold, 1901), pp. 65–71, for an account of Dick's ride to Kimberley.
48. Lucy quoted from the newspaper to Johnny on 3 April 1900. 'Meanwhile, Lieutenant Chester-Master, of Rimington's Scouts, had found a passage across the spruit unoccupied by the enemy, by which the remainder of Broadwood's force crossed and re-formed with great steadiness, notwithstanding all that had previously occurred.' HRO A63/IV/20/5, CLA to JHA, 3 April 1900.
49. *Ibid.*, 4 July 1900.
50. Headlam, *The Milner Papers*, Vol. II, p. 209. Sir Alfred Milner to Lady Edward Cecil, 16 January 1901.
51. In March 1901, Milner wrote to Dick at Clanwilliam to specify military details. Then he asked that Dick keep him 'informed from time to time of your personal plans. As long as you are in South Africa and not better engaged, my ADC'ship is always open to you. I should certainly not think of putting another man in your place while you were available, but it may be that if you still think of going home this year, it would not be worth your while to rejoin me. I should be sorry for that, but I should certainly not complain of it.' Bodleian Library, Milner Deposit 176, ff. 234–50, Sir Alfred Milner to Richard Chester-Master, 11 March 1901.
52. Cooke had won the Hereford by-election in 1893 against a Gladstonian Liberal, and held the seat in 1895 with a majority of 313 votes. W. Williams, *Herefordshire Members 1213–1896* (Brecon, published privately, 1896).
53. Henry C. Beddoe was Hereford Conservative Association's Chairman. He was also a solicitor, magistrate, County Treasurer and Alderman of Herefordshire Council.
54. HRO A63/IV/20/5, CLA to JHA, 23 September 1900.
55. Payment of MPs was introduced at a rate of £400 per annum in 1911.
56. HRO A63/IV/57/9, JSA to CLA, 29 January 1901.

57. E.A. Smith, *The House of Lords in British Politics and Society 1815–1911* (London, Longman, 1992).
58. HRO A63/IV/57/9, JSA to CLA, 14 February 1901.
59. *Ibid.*, 22 February 1901.
60. *Ibid.*, 5 March 1901.
61. The sixty-seven pages were published by Grant Richard and dedicated to Jack's old Eton tutor, E.C. Austen Leigh, who, as Jack explained to his mother, more than anyone else 'put poetry in my way at an impressionable age'. *Ibid.*, 18 May 1901. Jack had 250 copies printed, mostly to give away, but he hoped thereby to raise enough orders to get another 500 printed.
62. *Ibid.*, 3 July 1901. Such approval was the more gratifying as Kipling had experienced the war in South Africa at first hand, and had written for the Commander-in-Chief, Lord Roberts's morale-raising daily paper the *Friend*. Pakenham, *The Boer War*, pp. 375–6.
63. Between April's publication and August, Jack was reported as having gone into partnership with the publisher of the *Westminster Review*, R. Brimley Richards. This may explain the contemporary edition of the collected Talpa writings of Chandos Wren Hoskyns with an introduction by Jack. *Hereford Journal*, 27 July 1901, p. 4.
64. For analysis of these roles, see C. Palley, *The Constitutional History and Law of Southern Rhodesia 1888–1965* (Oxford, Clarendon, 1966), and C. Harding, *Frontier Patrols: a History of the British South Africa Police & Other Rhodesian Forces* (London, Bell & Sons, 1937), p. 181. The post was vacant due to the retirement of Colonel Nicholson DSO.
65. HRO A63/IV/20/5, CLA to JHA, 26 May 1901.
66. *Ibid.*, 23 May 1901.
67. HRO A63/IV/21/11, W. Chester-Master to JHA, 23 May 1901.
68. HRO A63/IV/20/5, CLA to JHA, 4 June 1901.
69. HRO A63/IV/56/12, JHA to CLA, 24 June 1901.
70. *Ibid.*, 25 June 1901.
71. Henry Longley had died on Christmas Day 1899. Lucy had gone to be with Di and wrote to Johnny on 29 December 1899. HRO A63/IV/20/5, CLA to JHA, 29 December 1899.
72. *Ibid.*, 26 June 1901.
73. 'Hampton Court, Leominster, the seat of Mr J.H. Arkwright' with photographs, *Country Life*, Vol. IX, 29 June 1901, pp. 836–42.
74. The announcement appeared in the *Hereford Journal* on 6 July 1901, p. 5, with a vague date of 'some time in August', and was confirmed as 13 August in the same paper on 20 July 1901.
75. HRO A63/IV/20/5, CLA to JHA, 29 June 1901.
76. HRO A63/IV/21/10, Geraldine Arkwright to JHA, dated only July 1901.
77. The Chester family had owned the manor of Almondsbury since 1569. N. Kingsley, *The Country Houses of Gloucestershire* (Cheltenham, Kingsley, 1989), Vol. I, p. 117.
78. HRO A63/IV/57/9, JSA to CLA, 25 July 1901.
79. HRO A63/IV/20/5, CLA to JHA, 30 July 1901.
80. *Hereford Times*, 17 August 1901, second sheet.
81. The staff at this time included Jane Edwards, Annie Reay, Ada Webb, Esther Pownall, R. Hobday, E. Apperley, Elvy Gatehouse, Gertrude Smith, Jerusha Pyefinch, William Childs, Frank Mycroft, J. Coupland, and George Rea. Census 1901.
82. Sir John Leigh Hoskyns lived a remarkably long life, from 4 February 1817 to 8 December 1911. He was the rector of St Michael's Church, Aston Tyrrold, for sixty-six

years in all. His longevity was surpassed by his wife Phyllis Emma (known as Emma), who was born on 13 August 1817 and died on 7 May 1914.

83. The Duchess of Teck sent 'Very best wishes to you both from us for much happiness', *Hereford Times*, 17 August 1901, second sheet. Milner's wife, Violet, described the Duchess as 'one of the most glorious tomboys ever seen; a first-rate horsewoman, she was really only at home in the saddle where her slight boyish figure looked its best. She managed to get a lot of hunting at the Cape because the MFH, Captain Chester-Master, admired her and would have lent her any horse she fancied out of the Governor's stables.' Lady Milner recalled an occasion (6 September 1899) when she herself was carried to her 'horror' over the hounds by her horse and Dick caught her bridle 'or I should have been running still'. V. Milner, *My Picture Gallery 1886–1901* (London, Murray, 1951).
84. Bend'Or, as the Duke was known, had been co-ADC to Milner with Dick in Cape Town before the outbreak of war. Pakenham, *The Boer War*, p. 60.
85. HRO A63/IV/23/9, Sale's Account, 1899–1903.
86. HRO A63/IV/58/3, letters on birth of Geraldine's son January–February 1903. Geraldine Chester-Master to Olive, 30 December 1901, filed among these letters.
87. HRO A63/IV/23/9, Sale's Account, 1899–1903.
88. HRO A63/IV/57/9, JSA to CLA, 7 September 1901.
89. *Ibid.*, 11 June 1901.
90. The announcement of Lord Bateman's death appeared in the *Hereford Journal* on 7 December 1901, p. 5.
91. The letters between Salisbury, Balfour and Johnny regarding the Lord Lieutenancy were included in a scrapbook, which remains in a private collection today.
92. The role of Lord Lieutenant had been created in 1557 to relieve the sheriff of his command of the militia of each shire. The Lord Lieutenant held frequent reviews of men, armour and munitions. G.M. Trevelyan, *Illustrated English Social History*, 4 Vols (Harmondsworth, Penguin Books, 1964), Vol. III, p. 167. At this period, the Lord Lieutenant was chiefly responsible for the appointment of Deputy Lieutenants and was expected to attend county events. The military responsibilities had been removed from the role, and he no longer chose magistrates. Nominations for the Bench were increasingly of professional and middle-class businessmen, although still subject to a £100 property qualification (until removed by the Liberals in 1906). Cannadine, *Decline and Fall of the British Aristocracy*, p. 155.
93. Although Johnny did not know it, younger Lords Lieutenant were preferred by Tory administrations, not because the job was especially demanding, but because it was hoped that they would survive a long time to perpetuate the Tory interest. Cannadine, *Decline and Fall*, p. 155.
94. File referring to JHA's Lord Lieutenancy, private collection.

Chapter Fourteen: Lord Looted, pp. 193–202

1. This and the letters of congratulation were all kept together in a scrapbook about Johnny's Lord Lieutenancy, which remains in a private collection.
2. Lord Llangattock to JHA, 31 December 1901. Llangattock was the father of Charles Rolls, the co-founder of Rolls Royce motors in 1906. This made Rolls Dick's first cousin. He was killed in 1910 in his early thirties, in a flying accident, the first British pilot to die in this way.
3. File on JHA's Lord Lieutenancy, private collection.

4. The specification for the uniform was a scarlet coatee with silver epaulettes and buttons and gold embroidery, blue trousers with silver lace at the outside seams (from beneath which should rear brass box swan-neck spurs), a crimson morocco leather belt and dress sword, and a waistplate bearing the royal cypher. This was topped off with a cocked hat in black silk with a magnificent plume of 'white swan feathers, drooping outwards, 10 inches long, with red feathers under them long enough to reach the end of the white ones; feathered stem 3 inches long'. File on JHA's Lord Lieutenancy, private collection.
5. The *Daily Express* was ignorant of the fact that the Arkwrights had, for some time, been esteemed neighbours of the Rodneys. Johnny's father had been asked in 1851 to be a trustee of the Berrington estate. HRO A63/IV/9/25, William Rodney to J. Arkwright, 12 December 1851. The *Express* further failed to note that a title was no guarantee of moral comportment. Lord Rodney, who had married a granddaughter of the Duke of Marlborough ten years before, had fallen in love with the governess of their four sons. Later in 1902, the Lord was to divorce his wife and marry the governess. The Berrington estate had been sold to Mr F. Cawley MP (of a Lancashire cotton family) in 1901. (I am grateful to Eric Turton for sharing his knowledge of the Berrington estate.) Johnny looked up the former inhabitants of Hampton Court who had been Lord Lieutenant. Since the position had been instituted in 1549, Lord Coningsby had been Lord Lieutenant in 1715, Charles Hanbury-Williams in 1741 and the Earl of Essex in 1802. File on Johnny's Lord Lieutenancy, private collection.
6. File on Johnny's Lord Lieutenancy, private collection.
7. HRO A63/IV/56/12, JHA to CLA, 12 June 1902.
8. HRO A63/IV/23/9, Sale's Account, 1899–1903, 11 February 1902.
9. HRO A63/IV/57/10, JSA to CLA, 7 May 1902.
10. HRO A63/IV/56/12, JHA to CLA, 4 June 1902.
11. HRO A63/IV/57/10, JSA to CLA, 3 June 1902.
12. *Ibid.*, 26 June 1902.
13. HRO A63/IV/23/9, Sale's Account, 1899–1903, 6 November 1902.
14. *Ibid.*, 28 January 1903.
15. *Ibid.*, 12 May 1903.
16. HRO A63/IV/58/3, letters on the birth of Geraldine's son January–February 1903. Signature illegible, from St Stephen's Club, Westminster, 30 January 1903.
17. HRO A63/IV/57/10, Richard Chester-Master to JSA, 29 January 1903.
18. *Hereford Times*, 11 January 1947, obituary of Lady Arkwright.
19. W.S. Gilbert, 'Princess Ida', first performed at the Savoy Theatre, 5 January 1884. W.S. Gilbert, *Selections from the Savoy Operas* (Ware, Wordsworth Editions, 1994).
20. HRO A63/IV/60/92–148, Geraldine Chester-Master to JSA, undated 1903.
21. *Ibid.*, 30 September 1903.
22. HRO A63/IV/57/10, JSA to CLA, 30 June 1903.
23. I am very grateful to Llewelyn Powell for confirming that the Powells were 'a Radnorshire farming family, just down from the hills!'. Tommy, a barrister on the Oxford circuit, went on to become Chairman of Herefordshire County Council in 1937, and as such he received Queen Mary on her visit to the city in 1937. He also laid the first stone of the County Hospital in Hereford. He would posthumously be remembered for his 'wise council and warm personality'. *Hereford Times*, 18 May 1940, obituary of Captain T.P.P. Powell.
24. HRO A63/IV/60/92–148, CLA to JSA, 16 August 1903.

25. For Lucy's obituary see *Hereford Times*, 27 February 1904, p. 10. This gives her birth date as 13 December 1839.
26. *Hereford Times*, 27 February 1904, p. 10.
27. *Ibid.*
28. HRO A63/IV/60/92–148, JHA to JSA, 6 December 1903. On 21 July 1904 Johnny wrote to Jack that Ashworth 'talks to me as if I was a baby in things close round about home which I have known from my cradle'. HRO A63/IV/60/158.
29. HRO A63/IV/22/13/1–30, Sir J. Cotterell to JHA, 31 March 1904.
30. HRO A63/IV/21/13, Olive Arkwright to JSA, undated.
31. HRO A63/IV/60/92–148, Evelyn Arkwright to JSA, 12 July 1904 (Johnny's birthday). More on the TPPP issue are at A63/IV/60/150–163.
32. Details of the sale are taken from the *Hereford Times*, 8 October 1904, p. 6, and from a surviving catalogue of the sale, private collection.
33. The breeding cows were taken from the families of Hampton Beauty, Curly, Gaylass, Gipsy, Ivington Lass, Lively, Oyster Girl and Pretty Maid. Sale catalogue, private collection.
34. Account of the sale, *Hereford Times*, 8 October 1904, p. 6.
35. File on JHA's Lord Lieutenancy, private collection.
36. Sir John had married, in 1896, Lady Evelyn Gordon Lennox, a daughter of the 7th Duke of Richmond and Gordon. Lady Evelyn was a good friend of Evelyn Arkwright, and her early death in 1922 at the age of 49 affected Evelyn greatly. Evelyn was to have a breakdown (to which the first real reference was made in July 1922) and spend much of her life in a nursing home at Barnwood, near Gloucester. Evelyn was not even mentioned in Tommy Powell's obituary. *Hereford Times*, 25 February 1922, obituary of Lady Evelyn Cotterell. I am also grateful to Evelyn's nephew, Llewelyn Powell, for his help with aspects of Powell family history.
37. S. Watts, *Mary Lilian Clegg Remembered* (published privately, 1992), p. 8. I am grateful to Mr A.D. Reiss for assistance with the Robinson family history.
38. *Hereford Times*, 27 May 1905, p. 6.
39. The date of 25 May is given in the probate registry, and in the report of Johnny's death in the *Hereford Times*, 27 May 1905. The inscription on the plate on Johnny's coffin was quoted as saying 'Died May 25th 1905' in the funeral report in the *Hereford Times* of 3 June 1905. Inexplicably, however, Johnny's tombstone at St Mary's, Hope, was inscribed with the date 24 May 1905.
40. *Hereford Times*, 27 May 1905, p. 6.
41. The report of the funeral appeared in the *Hereford Times*, 3 June 1905.

Chapter Fifteen: Letting and Going, pp. 203–213

1. D. Cannadine, *The Decline and Fall of the British Aristocracy* (New Haven, Yale University Press, 1990), p. 148.
2. On 30 July 1907, an indenture was drawn up for the payment of £5,599 14*s* 8*d* to each of Jack's sisters, a third of the £18,000 less the £1,170 duty (at 6.5 per cent) that Jack had paid on it.
3. Johnny's free estate comprised the former kennels at Whitecross in Hereford that were now cottages, the herd of deer in the park, horses and livestock, harnesses, carriages and the household contents at Hampton Court. He wrote to Sale to ascertain what his possessions were. HRO A63/II/304/1–35, JHA to Sale, 15 October 1904.

4. The estate was mortgaged to Thomas Rawle of 1 Bedford Row and Sir Alfred Cooper of 9 Henrietta Street.
5. HRO A63/IV/60/191–196, Richard Arkwright to JSA, 2 September 1905.
6. HRO A63/IV/60/201–203, W. Hill-James to JSA, 25 October 1905.
7. *Hereford Times*, 2 September 2005. This makes clear that the Hampton Court chapel organ had been lent to St Mary's until now, but it would be returned once the £350 sought had been raised. It was felt that this was an appropriate memorial to 'one who did so much for music in the county'.
8. Colonel Scudamore lived at Cap House, Pontrilas, in the south of the county. Twenty years older than Jack, he had been defeated in the Leominster election of 1886 by Sir James Rankin, ostensibly over the issue of Home Rule for Ireland. The Scudamores had been in Herefordshire for twenty-seven generations and 850 years. *Hereford Times*, 28 October 1905.
9. John was to die, aged 36, in the Second World War in an accident during training on HM Submarine *Untamed* in Kilbrannan Sound off Campbeltown (30 May 1943). The submarine bottomed during exercises and the entire crew were lost. *Untamed* was subsequently raised, the bodies recovered and buried at Dunoon. The submarine was reconditioned and relaunched, apparently without any hint of irony, as HMS *Vitality*. She saw out the war. A memorial window to John was inserted at All Saints' Church, Kinsham.
10. HRO A63/IV/60/262–324, JSA's earliest correspondence with the Atherleys dates from February 1908. They are first writing from Hampton Court on 2 April 1908.
11. Cannadine, *Decline and Fall of the British Aristocracy*, p. 357.
12. The Leveson-Gowers in Sutherland (he would stand just once more in 1910), the Manners in Leicestershire, the Egertons and Tollemaches in Cheshire, and the Sandwiches and de Ramsays in Huntingdonshire, all withdrew from politics after the 1906 election. Cannadine, *Decline and Fall of the British Aristocracy*, pp. 149–50.
13. In neighbouring Shropshire, for example, the gentry of some established families survived; Jack's old friend R.J. More of Linley, W.S. Kenyon-Slaney, G.R.C. Ormsby-Gore and W.C. Bridgeman were all returned. *Ibid.*, p. 146.
14. A.H. Matthews, *Fifty Years of Agricultural Politics: The History of the Central Chamber of Agriculture, 1865–1915*, p. 341.
15. Cannadine, *Decline and Fall of the British Aristocracy*, p. 451.
16. B. Tuchman, *The Proud Tower* (London, Papermac, 1997), p. 369.
17. E.A. Smith, *The House of Lords in British Politics and Society 1815–1911* (London, Longman, 1992).
18. The 1906 Education Bill intended to undo the Tories' Act of 1902. Under the Plural Voting Bill the Liberals aimed to end the rights of those owners of land in more than one constituency to vote in all constituencies where they held a stake.
19. Tuchman, *The Proud Tower*, p. 377.
20. Imports of grain had more than doubled from just over 30 million cwt per year in 1870 to just under 70 million cwt in 1900. P.J. Perry, *British Farming in The Great Depression 1870–1914* (Newton Abbot, David & Charles, 1974), p. 52.
21. Jack was secretary to the parliamentary committee that opposed Lloyd George's 1909 budget. HRO AM12/120, Sheila Powell's notes.
22. A Development Tax raised a ha'penny in the pound from the added value realised from the sale of land where the new value was solely due to the effort and expenditure of the community; 20 per cent was to be charged on Increment Value; 2*s* in the pound were to be taken from the enhanced value of a property when it reverted to the owner at

the end of a lease; and finally a Mineral Rights Duty was imposed at 1*s* in the pound. F. Owen, *Tempestuous Journey: Lloyd George His Life and Times* (London, Hutchinson, London, 1954), p. 168.

23. Owen, *Tempestuous Journey*, p. 171.
24. HRO A63/IV/60/333–393, correspondence between JSA and Ashworth's widow, November 1908. Jack undertook to give Ashworth's widow £100 a year for five years, to which Stephanie added £25 for three years. Olive wrote from Biarritz offering £3 for three years.
25. HRO A63/IV/60/333–393, Stephanie Arkwright to JSA, 2 October 1909.
26. Owen, *Tempestuous Journey*, p. 183.
27. Smith, *The House of Lords in British Politics and Society*, p. 175.
28. In 1922 Willoughby de Broke would have to part with his estate at Compton Verney in Warwickshire.
29. Cannadine, *Decline and Fall of the British Aristocracy*, p. 256.
30. A.T.Q. Stewart, *The Ulster Crisis: Resistance to Home Rule 1912–14* (London, Faber, 1967), p. 57.
31. For Grange House, bids got to £800 but it was withdrawn, although it was sold within days to Quaker Mr Theodore Nield. Other notable sales were Priory House (£380), 36 and 38 Etnam Street (£870 to Mr James Castle, one of the occupants), the White Lion Inn (£1,875 to S.R. Taylor), Pinsley Mill (withdrawn at £1,200) and Marsh Mill (£1,200 to Mr Page). HRO E41/1–4 O/L334, register of property bought to add to the estate and of property sold. Grange Court's future is today once again under question. The Court is the property of Herefordshire Council and Leominster Town Council would like to purchase it, but the value sought by the County Council is believed to be around £400,000 and the Town Council could only afford £80,000. *Hereford Times*, 28 April 2005, p. 13.
32. HRO E41/1–4, register of property bought to add to the estate and of property sold. The auctioneers were Messrs A. & D. Edwards.
33. This trend helped to restore the class of yeoman farmer, the old owner-occupier who had been made almost extinct as estates had mushroomed in the eighteenth century. Thomas Parker bought Sidnall Farm, Pencombe (254 acres) for £2,900; George Bemand acquired New House Farm, Pencombe (134 acres) for £2,290; the family of George Bishop acquired Bank House – the farmhouse only and not the land – for £345; Benjamin Jones acquired Mill Farm, Pencombe (173 acres) with further portions for £3,250; and William Amos bought Heath Farm, Little Cowarne (26 acres) for £420. HRO E41/1–4. The purchases by tenants are confirmed by comparison of purchasers with a valuation of the estate made the previous year for land tax.
34. As correspondence in the press in 1911 showed, 'an estate of 10,000 acres produced £10,000 gross, from which was deducted £5,000 for maintenance and mortgages, leaving only £5,000 net for keeping up position. If half the estate was sold at twenty-seven years' purchase, that would realize £135,000, of which £62,000 could be put to paying off debts and charges, and the remaining £73,000 could be invested at 4 per cent. The result was an investment income of £2,900 a year, plus a net rental of £3,750 (being £5,000 gross minus £1,250 for expenses), totalling £6,650, or £1,650 more than before.' *Estates Gazette*, 14 January 1911, quoted in Cannadine, *Decline and Fall of the British Aristocracy*, p. 130.
35. O. Wilde, *The Works of Oscar Wilde* (London, Spring Books, 1963), *The Importance of Being Earnest*, Act I, p. 151.

36. Cannadine, *Decline and Fall of the British Aristocracy*, p. 91.
37. *Ibid.*
38. *Ibid.*, p. 103.
39. HRO A63/IV/60/437–566; these letters of March 1911 are all filed together.
40. *Ibid.*, Frederick Arkwright to JSA, 4 April 1911.
41. Cannadine, *Decline and Fall of the British Aristocracy*, p. 454.
42. HRO A63/IV/60/437–566; these letters of April 1911 are all filed together.
43. Edwyn and Alice both died (he 3 September 1922 and she 27 July 1918) and were buried in their adopted country, Algeria. In 1924, the priest of the English church in Algiers, Godfrey Guy, wrote to Jack to confirm that a marble tablet had been erected to Edwyn's memory in the church. It read: 'He took a prominent part in the foundation and erection of this Church – was a regular attendant at, and assisted often in the conduct of its services and for many years superintended the training of the choir. He was a lover of all things beautiful and left behind him the memory of a blameless life.' Edwyn and Alice were, he confirmed, buried in the churchyard, a child's grave between them. HRO AM12/79.
44. HRO A63/IV/60/437–566, Stephen Robinson to JSA, 2 May 1911.
45. HRO E41/1–4, valuation of the estate for Land Tax in 1910. For the Railway Inn and 6 acres of land, Chilman was paying an annual rent of £32 in 1910.
46. Jack was true to his word, and John became tenant of the home farm at Kinsham in 1929. I am very grateful to the late John Chilman and to Phyllis Chilman for recalling their memories of Jack and Stephanie, and of life as an Arkwright tenant at Kinsham.
47. *The Times*, 20 June 1911, p. 17e.
48. Timber sales were not included in these figures.
49. The farms sold off from Kinsham included The Leen and Lowe Farms (over 500 acres), which were home to one of the oldest and finest Hereford herds (the dispersal of which occurred on 10 October the following year), Stapleton Castle Farm (454 acres), Upper Broadheath Farm (147 acres), Lower Broadheath Farm (237 acres), Hill Farm (239 acres), Rodd Farm (468 acres), and Strangworth Farm (196 acres). *The Times*, 27 July 1911, p. 4d.
50. HRO A63/220/483, JSA copy of letter to tenants, June 1911.

Epilogue, pp. 214–226

1. The conveyance of Hampton Court to Richard Arkwright was dated 7 July 1810. HRO A63/II/305/11B.
2. D. Cannadine, *The Decline and Fall of the British Aristocracy* (New Haven, Yale University Press, 1990), p. 111.
3. HRO K38/F/52/100, sale of Hampton Court, *Hereford Times*, 15 June 1912.
4. I am very grateful to Mrs Rachel Harding, Mrs Burrell's niece, for sharing with me her memories of Hampton Court at this time.
5. See W. Rubinstein, *Men of Property* (London, Croom Helm, 1981) for the importance of geographical spread of wealth in Britain in the nineteenth century and up until 1914.
6. *The Times*, 2 March 1912, p. 6e.
7. Jack continued to be involved with politics in London between his resignation and the outbreak of war, particularly in the Ulster debate. After Milner entered the fray in support of the Unionists, it was suggested in early 1914 that a covenant be drawn up for supporters to sign (as it had been in the province itself) to offer an alternative to the increasing civil

disobedience arising from frustration. Milner asked Jack to keep the list of signatories at the Westminster offices set up for the purpose – the 'Lord High Keeper of the List', as Jack referred to himself in correspondence with Milner (Bodleian Library, Milner deposit 41, ff. 47–50, JSA to Lord Milner, 9 March 1914). Prior to the launch of the covenant in the newspapers, support was garnered from public figures including Lord Balfour, the Duke of Portland, Lord Roberts and Rudyard Kipling. Jack secured the support of Sir Edward Elgar. Besides his long acquaintance with Johnny through the HPS, the composer had signed Jack's nomination paper for the December 1910 election and had given Jack the use of Plas Gwyn, his home in Hereford, as his campaign base while Elgar (then working on his Second Symphony) had gone up to London. J.N. Mocre, *Edward Elgar: A Creative Life* (Oxford, Oxford University Press, 1984), p. 664, for Alice Elgar's diary entry, 2 March 1914.

8. Cannadine, *Decline and Fall of the British Aristocracy*, p. 97.
9. Duchess of Devonshire, *Chatsworth* (Derby, Derbyshire Countryside, 2000), p. 60, and the Duke and Duchess of Devonshire, *The Changing Fortunes of Chatsworth in the Twentieth Century*, illustrated lecture at the Institute of Historical Research, 27 January 2004.
10. Peel's decision was his personal reaction to all that he had seen first hand of famine there in 1817, when he had been Chief Secretary for Ireland. N. McCord, *British History 1815–1906* (Oxford, Oxford University Press, 1995), p. 165.
11. HRO A63/IV/67/21, In Memoriam for Colonel Thomas William Chester-Master JP DL, 15 May 1841–14 November 1914.
12. National Army Museum Ref 25853, *A Brief History of the KRRC* (1912).
13. Gloucestershire Record Office D/37/1/86, Maynard Colchester-Wemyss to the King of Siam, 23 December 1915. The 13th Battalion was part of the 111th Brigade (Barnes) of 37th Division (Gleichen) until 6 July 1916 when it became part of 34th Division, III Corps, Fourth Army, until 21 August 1916 when it rejoined the 37th. Regimental History, National Archive WO95/2533. Dick's battalion embarked for France on 30 July 1915. Geraldine's letter to Jack undated, but probably from spring 1915, described Dick as 'glued to his regiment in Bucks. Very busy & billetted on some old maids and a bachelor brother'. HRO A63/IV/16/385. Dick took command of the battalion on 9 July. National Archive WO95/2533.
14. This combined role commanding his battalion and occasionally the whole brigade meant that while the battalion could recover between front-line duties, Dick could not. Dick's battalion was noted for its fighting at Beaucourt (23 November 1916), Monchy-le-Preux (9 April 1917) and Gavrelle (22–9 April 1917). In the month before 21 May 1917 the battalion won a bar to a Military Cross, a Military Cross, a Croix de Guerre, eighteen Military Medals, and Dick and three others were mentioned in dispatches. The bar that Dick added to his DSO was awarded to him on 22 June by First Army Commander General Horne. For the Regimental Diary see National Archive WO95/2533.
15. HRO A63/IV/61/308–477, Stephanie Arkwright to JSA, 6 September 1917.
16. *Ibid.*, Geraldine Chester-Master to JSA, undated. Milner wrote, on 5 September 1917: 'I had a great affection for him, as well as a great respect for his fine qualities both as a man and as a soldier. His death is a very great blow to me personally.' *King's Royal Rifle Corps Chronicle*, Obituary Notices, p. 295.
17. HRO A63/IV/61/308–477, Stephanie Arkwright to JSA, 7 September 1917. Jack offered to help, but Geraldine felt that the Chester-Masters ought to pay Billy's school fees. Geraldine Chester-Master to JSA, 11 September 1917, HRO A63/IV/16/394.

18. Dick's obituary appeared in KRRC Chronicle Committee *King's Royal Rifle Corps Chronicle* (London, John Murray, 1920), pp. 294–9 and Harrow School, *Harrow Memorials of the Great War* (London, Philip Lee Warner, 1918–21), Vol. V.
19. HRO A63/IV/61/308–477, Geraldine Chester-Master to JSA, undated. Ozzy was in communication with Jack when he worked for Milner. He wrote to him on 3 April 1917: 'I am so glad you are lending my old chief a hand. I see Richard Chester-Master still when he comes over. He had a warmish time in this late scrap with the Bosche.' HRO A63/IV/61/345.
20. The grave of Brigadier-General R.C. MacLaclain DSO of the Rifle Brigade, was also relocated to the Hospice Cemetery. In the end around 250 British casualties were buried at Locre Hospice Cemetery, which is approximately 10km south-west of Ypres. Dick's grave is Plot II, Row C, Grave 8. For visiting this area, see P. Reed, *Battleground Europe – Walking the Salient* (Barnsley, Pen & Sword, 1999), p. 141, which mentions Dick's grave.
21. HRO A63/IV/61/405, Cyril Chester-Master to JSA, 30 September 1917.
22. Oddly filed at HRO A63/IV/20/2 and 20/3, i.e. among Lucy's letters to JHA. This would have been a blow to young Billy in particular who, as Geraldine acknowledged to Jack in 1917, 'simply adores Knole. His face flattens out into a full moon with satisfaction when he goes there.' HRO A63/IV/61/395.
23. Details of Knole Park and Abbey House from N. Kingsley, *The Country Houses of Gloucestershire* (Cheltenham, Kingsley, 1989), Vol. I, pp. 44 and 117, and Vol. II, p. 44.
24. HRO AK97/5, scrapbook, p. 97.
25. Hereford City Library, Newscuttings Book VI, p. 112.
26. *Hereford Times*, 15 September 1934. There were some misgivings that Jack was an atheist. A good friend of Jack's son David at Cambridge, the poet Patric Dickinson recalled that 'It had pleased me in Professor Housman's lecture "The Name and Nature of Poetry" (1933) when he suggested that atheists might have the most objective approach to judging the literary quality of hymns. David's father was so ardently objective an atheist that he felt he ought to write hymns, and did so.' P. Dickinson, *The Good Minute* (London, Gollancz, 1965), p. 113. I am most grateful to Mrs Dickinson for bringing my attention to this.
27. The poem was published as part of a collection by Jack, entitled *The Supreme Sacrifice and Other Poems in Time of War* (London, Skeffington, 1919). It was illustrated by, among others, Bruce Bairnsfather and L. Raven-Hill. The volume was dedicated to Alfred, Lord Milner. Jack had been an Assistant Private Secretary to Milner since November 1916 (Milner was in the War Cabinet from December 1916 to April 1918). See Bodleian Library, Milner Deposit 46, f. 252, JSA to Lord Milner, 14 November 1919, 'My Dear Chief . . .'. Jack was to be knighted in the New Year's Honours 1934. In his role as Chief Steward for Hereford he appropriately bestowed the Freedom of the City on Poet Laureate, John Masefield.
28. Cannadine, *Decline and Fall of the British Aristocracy*, pp. 116–17.
29. Consternation at the loss of the nation's great houses grew, as portrayed by Evelyn Waugh in *Decline and Fall of the British Aristocracy* (London, Chapman and Hall, 1928).
30. Cannadine, *Decline and Fall of the British Aristocracy*, p. 119. Drayton Manor was destroyed in 1926. G. Worsley, *England's Lost Houses* (London, Aurum Press, 2002). For some, the sales were fortuitous. In 1923, the trustees of Sir James Croft, 11th Baronet (being then a minor) were able to buy back Croft Castle in Herefordshire from the Kevill-Davis family. However, a complicated line of ownership ensued before the National Trust finally took over the freehold in 1957. The National Trust, *Croft Castle* (London, National Trust, 1995), p. 12.

31. *The Times*, 30 March 1927, p. 9g.
32. J. Cornforth, 'Uncertain Future of Sutton Scarsdale', *Country Life*, 16 April 1970, p. 850. Cannadine, *Decline and Fall of the British Aristocracy*, p. 119. Sutton also featured in BBC TV's 2003 series *Restoration*.
33. H. Lake, *The Arkwrights and Harlow* (published privately, 1955), p. 55.
34. Lake, *The Arkwrights and Harlow*, pp. 43–51.
35. Fifteen beds were installed in the music room, fifteen in the library, the mess in the Coningsby Hall; the billiard room was given over to the nurses' meals and the little room next to the chapel became the surgery. Nancy Burrell to JSA, 18 November, no year given. On 5 April 1917 she wrote that she now had fifty-five in the hospital: 'The dining room with 16 beds, and 7 in the room on the left half way up the front stairs, and 1 man in each of the other wards.' HRO A63/IV/61/347.
36. Cannadine, *Decline and Fall of the British Aristocracy*, p. 644. Giles Worsley in *England's Lost Houses*, pp. 16–22, rightly pointed out that the tide of public opinion had turned against the destruction of country houses by the mid-1950s, and that by the time of the V&A Museum's 1974 exhibition on 'The Destruction of the Country House', the battle 'had largely been won'.
37. For illustrations of several of Herefordshire's lost houses, see the *Hereford Times*, 8 July 1999, p. 7.
38. The Harewood estate is today owned by the Duchy of Cornwall. The Prince of Wales has been granted planning permission to build a house similar to Tally's home on the former site. *Hereford Times*, 15 October 2004.
39. I. Pfuell, *A History of Shobdon* (published privately, 1994), p. 113.
40. Worsley, *England's Lost Houses*, p. 187.
41. Wrotham's survival is the more remarkable because it was gutted by fire, but was restored in 1883. L. Lambton, *The Daily Telegraph*, 'Property', 17 May 2003, p. 2.
42. T. Lloyd, *Lost Houses of Wales* (London, Save, 1986).
43. Thoby Priory's sale catalogue can be seen at Essex County Record Office at B551. Hatfield was originally built for Agnes's ancestor Colonel John Tyrell by John Johnson (1732–1814) in 1791. N. Briggs, *John Johnson* (Essex County Record Office, 1991). The catalogue for the Hatfield sale by auction on 2 October 1917 is also at Essex County Record Office at A76.
44. *Essex County Chronicle*, 12 May 1916, p. 7. Hatfield was sold to Mr and Mrs Reed-Scott. I am grateful to Charlotte Ryder and Jim Stanton for their help with details about Hatfield.
45. In considering this point, it should be noted that not all newly monied men in the nineteenth century had put their wealth into acres. Even in the middle of the century, non-landed wealth-holders outnumbered those who held estates. Rubinstein, *Men of Property*, pp. 210–15.
46. R.S. Fitton, *The Arkwrights, Spinners of Fortune* (Manchester, Manchester University Press, 1989), p. 228.
47. D. Farnie, *The English Cotton Industry and the World Market 1815–1896* (Oxford, Clarendon, 1979), pp. 6–8.
48. *Ibid*., p. 127.
49. *Ibid*., p. 81.
50. F.M.L. Thompson, 'The Second Agricultural Revolution, 1815–1880', *Economic History Review*, Series 2, Vol. XXI, 1968, p. 71.
51. Farnie, *The English Cotton Industry*, p. 176.

52. *Ibid.*, p. 14.
53. In the first half of the nineteenth century, of the most wealthy in Britain, those not holding land were an insignificant percentage of the wealthy class. Until around 1880, more than half of all the really wealthy men in Britain (those with over £½ million) owned land, but from that date, non-landed income becomes increasingly important. Rubinstein, *Men of Property*, pp. 193–206.
54. When Jack had failed to get into Oxford at the first attempt, Johnny spluttered in his indignant letter to Lucy: 'I am beginning to think that there is something rotten in the state of Eton as so many people say – disgusting all round – He had better go sheepfarming to Australia.' HRO A63/IV/56/8, JHA to CLA, 28 August 1891.
55. Rubinstein, *Men of Property*, p. 220, *passim*.
56. Rubinstein notes that the Peels also showed this more middle-class tendency of dividing their fortune between their children. In this they more closely resembled the non-landed wealth-holders of the period who, as a result, moved over time from stately home to villa. Rubinstein, *Men of Property*, p. 135.
57. Johnny and John Heathcoat Amory were friends, as Johnny's correspondence makes clear. In particular, Johnny and Lucy often went to Scotland in August with the Amorys in the 1870s and early 1880s. When Lucy was in London prior to Johnny's trip to Algiers in 1881, and having problems with her move, she was getting sympathy from the Amorys who had a new house in town. During Johnny's journey, when he reached Marseille, he thought it hilarious that someone, seeing luggage marked JHA, ran over to greet John Heathcoat Amory but was stopped in mid-effusion on finding that it belonged instead to John Hungerford Arkwright. There was also some physical resemblance between the two bearded men. It is interesting to consider that the National Trust's most high-profile acquisition in recent years, Tyntesfield, was built on the fortune made by the Gibbs family in transporting across the Atlantic the guano that Chandos had made so popular as fertiliser. In many ways, then, Tyntesfield is built on the ruins of houses like Harewood, Foxley or Shobdon Court.
58. Some of this one-third reduction was not difficult. For example, nursemaids were not required by 1901. Censuses 1861 and 1901.
59. This weakness is shown by the doubts that Henry Longley had about Johnny's record of interest received on investments, and he demonstrated poor negotiating skills with Ticehurst about the fees for Emily's care. Instead of asking what the fees were, Johnny opened negotiations with Ticehurst by stating Emily's annual income and saying that he hoped that would cover her expenses. HRO A63/IV/69/5.
60. G. Robinson, 'Agricultural Depression, 1870–1890', *Transactions of the Woolhope Naturalist's Field Club*, XLII (1976–8), p. 273.
61. E.L. Jones and E.J.T. Collins, 'Sectoral Advance in English Agriculture, 1850–80', *Agricultural History Review*, Vol. XV (1967), p. 72.
62. H. Rider Haggard, *Rural England* (London, Longmans, 1902). Herefordshire is profiled in Vol. I, pp. 287–322. Conclusions in Vol. II, pp. 536–57.

Sources and Bibliography

Archive Sources

The Bodleian Library, Oxford University, Milner Deposit
Carmarthenshire Record Office, Campbell/Cawdor Collection
Essex Record Office D/Dar, B551, A76, Collection of Joseph Arkwright, and particulars of Thoby Priory and Hatfield Place
Eton College Archive
Gloucestershire Record Office, D37/1, Letters written by Maynard Colchester-Wemyss to the King of Siam, Rama VI, 1915–17; D674a and b, Chester-Master biography.
Harrow School Archive
Herefordshire Record Office (HRO), The Arkwright Collection, particularly A63, C69, E41 and AM12
Public Record Office of Northern Ireland, T2541, Papers of Lord Abercorn
National Archive, Kew, MAF 66/28–35, Lands Improvement Company Loans 1861–79; MAF 68, Agricultural Census: Herefordshire – county No. 17, and Hope-under-Dinmore Parish No. 177; Regimental Diary of KRRC, WO95/2533
National Army Museum, Records of the King's Royal Rifle Corps
Wellcome Institute, Ticehurst Archive 6327/316a, 1845–81, Admission Nos 1–459

Books

Arch, J., *Joseph Arch: The Story of his Life, Told by Himself*, London, Hutchinson & Co., 1898

Ashley-Cooper, F.S., *Eton and Harrow at the Wicket*, London, St James, 1922

Atkins, E.W., *The Elgar-Atkins Friendship*, Newton Abbot, David & Charles, 1984

Baines, E., *History of the Cotton Manufacture in Great Britain*, London, Fisher, 1835

Bateman, J., *The Great Landowners of Great Britain and Ireland*, 4th edn, 1883 Victorian Library Edition, Leicester, Leicester University Press, 1971

Beale, C., *Hampton Court, Herefordshire*, published privately, 2000

Beese, A.K., *Coningsby Hospital*, Hereford, Coningsby Trust, 1971

Boden, A., *Three Choirs: A History of the Festival*, Stroud, Alan Sutton, 1992

Bovill, E.W., *The England of Nimrod and Surtees 1815–1854*, Oxford, Oxford University Press, 1959
Brooks, D., *'The Age of Upheaval', Edwardian politics, 1899–1914*, Manchester, Manchester University Press, 1995
Cannadine, D., *The Decline and Fall of the British Aristocracy*, New Haven, Yale University Press, 1990
Channing, F.A., *The Truth about the Agricultural Depression; an Economic Study of the Evidence of the Royal Commission*, London, Longmans, 1897
Charles Cox, J. and Cox, Henry F., *The Rise of the Farm Labourer. A Series of Articles Reprinted from the* Examiner *1872–3 Illustrative of Certain Political Aspects of the Agricultural Labour Movement*, London, Dallow, 1874
Davies, E., *The Higher Education of Women 1866*, London, Hambledon Press, 1997
Devonshire, Duke and Duchess of, *The Changing Fortunes of Chatsworth in the Twentieth Century*, illustrated lecture at the Institute of Historical Research, 27 January 2004
Dickinson, P., *The Good Minute*, London, Gollancz, 1965
English Land Restoration League, *Among the Labourers with the Red Van*, London, ELRL, 1897
Farnie, D., *The English Cotton Industry and the World Market 1815–1896*, Oxford, Clarendon, 1979
Fitton, R.S., *The Arkwrights, Spinners of Fortune*, Manchester, Manchester University Press, 1989
Fletcher, S., *Victorian Girls: Lord Lyttelton's Daughters*, London, Hambledon Press, 1997
Foreman, S., *Loaves and Fishes – an Illustrated History of the Ministry of Agriculture, Fisheries and Food 1889–1989*, London, HMSO, 1989
Gilbert, W.S., *Selections from the Savoy Operas*, Ware, Wordsworth Editions, 1994
Gilpin, W., *Observations on the River Wye*, Woodstock, Oxon, 1991, facsimile of 1782 publication
Harding, C., *Frontier Patrols: a History of the British South Africa Police, & Other Rhodesian Forces*, London, Bell & Sons, 1937
Hardy, A.E.G. (ed.), *Gathorne Hardy: A Memoir*, 2 vols, London, Longmans, 1910
Harris, J., *Private Lives, Public Spirit*, Oxford, Oxford University Press, 1993
Hasbach, W., *A History of the English Agricultural Labourer*, London, King, 1908
Headlam, C. (ed.), *The Milner Papers*, 2 vols, London, Cassell, 1931
Hirsch, P., *Barbara Leigh Smith Bodichon*, London, Chatto & Windus, 1998
Horn, P., *Joseph Arch*, Kineton, Roundwood Press, 1971
Hoskyns, C.W., *Talpa: The Chronicles of A Clay Farm*, London, Brimley Johnson, 1903
Huggett, F., *The Land Question and European Society*, London, Thames & Hudson, 1975

Jeffries, R., *Hodge and his Masters*, Stroud, Alan Sutton, 1992
Jenkins, M., *White Death*, London, Fourth Estate, 2000
Jenkins, S., *England's Thousand Best Houses*, London, Allen Lane, 2003
Jewell, C.A., *Victorian Farming*, Winchester, Shurlock, 1975
Jones, E.L., 'The Changing Basis of English Agricultural Prosperity, 1853–73', *The Agricultural History Review*, Vol. X, 1962
——, 'The Evolution of High Farming 1815–1865 with special reference to Herefordshire', Oxford, D.Phil. thesis, 1962
——, 'Industrial Capital and Landed Investment: the Arkwrights in Herefordshire, 1809–43', *Land, Labour and Population in the Industrial Revolution: Essays Presented to J.D. Chambers*, edited by E.L. Jones and G.E. Mingay, London, Arnold, 1967
Judd, D., *The Boer War*, London, Granada Publishing, 1977
Kingsley, N., *The Country Houses of Gloucestershire*, Cheltenham, Kingsley, 1989
Lake, H., *The Arkwrights in Harlow*, published privately, 1995
Le Blonde, A., *True Tales of Mountain Adventure*, London, Fisher Unwin, 1906
Lees-Milne, J., *The Bachelor Duke*, London, John Murray, 1998
Lloyd, T., *Lost Houses of Wales*, London, Save, 1986
Longford, E., *Wellington: Pillar of State*, London, Weidenfeld & Nicholson, 1972
Loux, F., Ducroz, A. and Pocachard, A., *Chamonix Autrefois; le Mont-Blanc et sa vallée*, Montmélian, Fontaine de Siloe, 1988
Lysons, Rev. D., *History of the Origin and Progress of the Meeting of the Three Choirs of Gloucester, Worcester and Hereford*, Gloucester, 1812
McCord, N., *British History 1815–1906*, Oxford, Oxford University Press, 1995
MacCulloch, D., *Romantic Lochaber, Arisaig and Morar*, Edinburgh, Chambers, 1971
MacDonald, J. and Sinclair, J., *History of Hereford Cattle*, London, Vinton & Co., 1909, reprinted 1968 for the Hereford Herd Book Society
Mackenzie, C., *Psychiatry for the Rich, A History of Ticehurst Private Asylum*, London, Routledge, 1992
Mansfield, N., *English Farmworkers and Local Patriotism, 1900–1930*, Aldershot, Ashgate, 2001
March, A., *Historical Directory of Trade Unions*, 2 vols, London, Gower, 1984
March Phillips, L., *With Rimington*, London, Edward Arnold, 1901
Matthews, A.H., *Fifty Years of Agricultural Politics: The History of the Central Chamber of Agriculture 1865–1915*, London, King & Sons, 1915
Milner, V., *My Picture Gallery 1886–1901*, London, Murray, 1951
Mingay, G.E., *Rural Life in Victorian England*, London, Book Club Associates, 1976
Mocre, J.N., *Edward Elgar: A Creative Life*, Oxford, Oxford University Press, 1984
Moule, H.C.G., *Memories of a Vicarage*, London, Religious Tract Society, 1913
Murray, G., *Agricultural Depression: its Causes and Remedies*, London, Bemrose, 1879

Murray, J., *Algeria*, London, Murray, 1874
Owen, F., *Tempestuous Journey: Lloyd George His Life and Times*, London, Hutchinson, 1954
Pakenham, T., *The Boer War*, London, Sphere Books, 1991
Palley, C., *The Constitutional History and Law of Southern Rhodesia 1888–1965*, Oxford, Clarendon, 1966
Perry, P.J., *British Farming in the Great Depression 1870–1914*, Newton Abbot, David & Charles, 1974
Pfuell, I., *A History of Shobdon*, published privately, 1994
Prothero, Lord Ernle R., *English Farming Past and Present*, 6th edn, London, Heinemann, 1961
Reed, P., *Battleground Europe – Walking the Salient*, Barnsley, Pen & Sword, 1999
Rider Haggard, H., *Rural England*, London, Longmans, 1902
Rubinstein, W., *Men of Property*, London, Croom Helm, 1981
Ruskin, J., *Sesame and Lilies*, London, George Allen, 1905
Russell, H.A., 11th Duke of Bedford, *A Great Agricultural Estate*, London, Murray, 1897
Selley, E., *Village Trade Unions in Two Centuries*, London, George Allen & Unwin, 1919
Shaw, W., *The Three Choirs Festival*, Worcester and London, Baylis & Son, 1954
Smith, E.A., *The House of Lords in British Politics and Society 1815–1911*, London, Longman, 1992
Spring, D., *The English Landed Estate in the Nineteenth Century: Its Administration*, Maryland, John Hopkins Press, 1963
Stewart, A.T.Q., *The Ulster Crisis: Resistance to Home Rule 1912–14*, London, Faber, 1967
Thompson, F.M.L., *English Landed Society in the Nineteenth Century*, London, Routledge & Kegan Paul, 1963
Titchener-Barret, R., *Eton v Harrow at Lord's since 1805*, London, Quiller Press, 1996
Trevelyan, G.M., *Illustrated English Social History*, London, Penguin, 1964
Trollope, A., *Hunting Sketches*, London, Chapman & Hall, 1865
——, *Framley Parsonage*, London, Lane, 1903
——, *The Last Chronicle of Barset*, Oxford, Oxford University Press, 1989
——, *Can You Forgive Her?* London, Wordsworth Editions, 1996
Tuchman, B., *The Proud Tower*, London, Papermac, 1997
Turton, E., *Leominster*, Stroud, Chalford, 1996
Waugh, E., *Decline and Fall*, London, Chapman and Hall, 1928
Wilde, O., *The Works of Oscar Wilde*, London, Spring Books, 1963
Williams, W., *Herefordshire Members 1213–1896*, Brecon, published privately, 1896
Woodward, L., *The Age of Reform 1815–1870*, London, Book Club Associates, 1979
Worsley, G., *England's Lost Houses*, London, Aurum Press, 2003
Wrench, J. Evelyn, *Alfred Lord Milner: The Man of No Illusions*, London, Eyre & Spottiswoode, 1958

Journals

Agricultural Gazette
Agricultural History Review
Country Life
Daily Telegraph
Economic History Review
Essex County Chronicle
Farmer's Magazine
Financial Times
Garden
Garden History
La Gazette de Biarritz
Harrovian
Hereford Journal
Hereford Times
Herefordshire Country Life
Historical Journal
House of Lords' Journals
Journal of the Royal Agricultural Society of England
King's Royal Rifle Corps Chronicle
Leominster News
Radnorshire Society Transactions
Revue de l'Occident Musulman et de la Méditerranée
Shrewsbury Chronicle
Strad
Sunday Times
The Times
Transactions of the Woolhope Naturalists' Field Club

Index

Abbey, The, Cirencester, Gloucestershire 167, 217
Abel, John 28
Aberystwyth, Wales 138, 142
Acreocracy of England, The (Bateman) 139
Adforton, Herefordshire 116
agricultural census 45–6
agricultural depression 9, 140, 142, 148, 203, 215, 222, 224, 226
Agricultural Gazette 44, 121
agricultural machinery 42, 47, 49, 51
agricultural prices *see* prices
agricultural rents 47, 114; *see also* Hampton Court estate rents
agricultural trades-unionism: barriers to 101; propagation of 109, 215; *see also* Tolpuddle Martyrs and National Agricultural Labourers' Union
Ailesbury, Lord 210
Aix-la-Chapelle, France 63
Akenfield (Blythe) 2
Algiers/Algeria 118, 128, 130–2, 146, 161
Alleyne, Rebecca 144, 190, 219
Alnwick, Northumberland 7
anti-landlordism 10, 139, 202, 212
Arch, Joseph: at Hampton Court 50; NALU 109–10, 111, 147, 162, 164, 168, 186, 205
archery: bow meetings 5; at Johnny's twenty-first 17
Argentina 123
Arkwright, Alice: inheritance from father 43; visit to Mary 65; in Chamonix 86, 176; move to Llanforda Hall, Oswestry 87; twenty-first birthday 93; in Algiers 118, 128, 131; London house 128; hospital in Algiers 131; on death of Gerald Arkwright 181; on sale of Hampton Court 211; on purchase of Kinsham 212; *Plate 11*
Arkwright, Anne (wife of Rev. Joseph) 17
Arkwright, Arthur: carnations 19; at Eton 31; at Dover 62; visit to Emily 66; reaction to Johnny's engagement 71–2; trustee to Lucy's jointure 78, 151–2; marriage 95; children 137, 138; Thoby Priory 153; in Chamonix 175–9; sons in South Africa 181, 183; at Johnny's funeral 201; on sale of Hampton Court 210–11; suicide 221
Arkwright, Augusta 62
Arkwright, Bernard George 57
Arkwright, Caroline (Scudamore Stanhope): Johnny's twenty-first 16, 18; proposal from Berkeley 20, 31; 1857 season 29–31; character 31; income on marriage to Berkeley 32; 1858 wedding 33–5, 75; riding 67; reaction to Johnny's engagement 71; at Johnny's funeral 201; *Plate 5*
Arkwright, Cecil John 57
Arkwright, Charles: theatre trip 35; inheritance from father 43; visit to Emily 66; in London 99; in North Africa 129; fits 129; on sale of Hampton Court 210; *Plate 11*
Arkwright, Charles (of Dunstall) 3, 32, 219
Arkwright Collection of Papers 2, 10
Arkwright, Cyril 181, 184
Arkwright, David Lyndon 212, 262 n34

Arkwright, Edwyn: at Harrow 28, 31; visit to Emily 66; curacy 67; character 67; engagement 67–8; chaplain of Hampton Court Palace 68; tea party 70; in Algiers 118, 128, 131; farming 131–2; church and hospital in Algiers 131; Algiers hoteliers ruined 146; on sale of Hampton Court 211
Arkwright, Emily: scarlatina 28; inheritance from father 43; depression 65; reaction to Johnny's engagement 71; Ticehurst asylum, Sussex 129–30; *Plate 11*
Arkwright Estate Act, 1887 9, 149–53, 154, 182–3
Arkwright, Evelyn (Wee): birth 128; letters to Jack 135; education 137–8; cricketing 137; portrait by Tayler 153; discovery of primrose 159; jubilee 173; marriage to TPPP 197–9; relationship with father 197; effect of mother's death 198; wedding 201
Arkwright family motto 63
Arkwright, Fanny (wife of Robert) 19
Arkwright, Frances (Fanny or Banny): poetry book 55–6; care of mother 62; relationship with Johnny 62–3; music 64; care of Mary 64; care of Emily 65; birthday 67; Mont Blanc 86; Llanforda Hall, Oswestry 87; Algiers 128, 131; sick nurse 129; engagement 133; wedding 134–5; Tor Castle 175; Chamonix 175–9; at Johnny's funeral 201; on sale of Hampton Court 211; *Plate 11*
Arkwright, Frederic 69, 129
Arkwright, Frederic Charles 144, 190, 211, 219
Arkwright, George MP, of Sutton Scarsdale 21–4
Arkwright, Rev. George: at tutor's 16; geraniums 19; to Oxford 20–1; career 21; from Oriel 25; Boat Race and Covent Garden 27; father's health 28; on unrequited love 30; marriage to Lizzie 56–7; family 57; on Johnny's engagement 71; Johnny and Lucy's return from honeymoon 84; reaction to Jack's birth 97; speech about labourers 106; fits and death 129–30; son Sidney 152
Arkwright, Gerald 181
Arkwright, Geraldine (Pinkie): birth 128; pudding 128; eyes 133; letter from Algeria 133; letters to Jack 135; cuts a tooth 137; education 137–8; staying at Sherfield 160; in love 170–4; looks 171; Tor Castle 175; excitement at Dick's return 188, 189; tired of shopping 189; at Hampton Court with Dick 190; wedding 190–1; birth of son 196; verdict on Stephanie 197; warns Jack off giving up politics 197; mother's death 198; loss of two children 199; Dick's death 216–17; *Plate 25*
Arkwright, Godfrey 17, 71
Arkwright, Godfrey of Parndon Hall 167, 220
Arkwright, Harold 94
Arkwright, Henry: ferns 19; Valentine cards 20; father's health 28; Captain of Harrow cricket XI 31; up to Cambridge 32; with 84th Regt at Dover 62; reaction to Johnny's engagement 71; taking charge at Johnny's wedding 79, 83; ADC to Lord Lieutenant of Ireland 84; letter from Switzerland 85; death on Mont Blanc 86; memorials to 87; recovery of body and burial 175–9; *Plate 14*
Arkwright, Rev. Henry, Vicar of Bodenham 81, 102, 106, 112, 138, 156, 161
Arkwright, John: inheritance of Hampton Court 3, 5; management of estate 4; marriage 4; commissioning of Joseph Paxton 5; role in Herefordshire life 5, 29, 32; feelings for Herefordshire 15; delight in family 18; rejection of proposal to Carey 20; loans to aristocracy 21; pocket money for children 21; role in local politics 22–3; relationship with his heir 26; love of riding 18, 28; attitude to illness 28; land purchases 28; charitable nature 29, 36; repairs to coach 31; dowry

for Carey 32; death 36; expansion of estate 38; free trader 42; High Farming 42; will 42–3, 90, 223; involvement in Hoskyns affairs 45, 118; *Plate 4*
Arkwright, John Hungerford (Johnny): position in society 1, 5–6, 8; character 6, 25, 63, 69, 157 173, 180, 194, 198, 201–2, 224; role in Three Choirs Festival 6, 118, 143–4; finances at Oxford 14, 21; ignorance of farming 16; roses 19, 55, 77, 93, 180, 190; potential candidate for Leominster 23–8, 43, 147, 194; relationship with his father 26, 43; trip to Ireland 31; 1857 tour of Continent 32; High Farming 42, 47; inheritance 42–3, 149, 169, 224; RASE work 45, 87, 90, 120–1, 123–4, 153–4, 158, 205, 224; Hereford cattle 46, 52–3, 115, 117, 146, 158, 179, 195, 198–200, 253 n29; sale of land 47; paternalism towards tenants 47, 156, 161, 224, labourers 52, 107, 156, 161, 224, and family 54, 62, 118–19; investment in machinery 47; loans to improve estate 47–8, 90, 114, 223; experiments on estate 48; financial situation 48–9, 90, 94, 119, 130, 142, 145, 150, 169, 179, 191; foundation of employment agency 52, 107; attitude to investment in estate 53, 224; poetry 55; invitations to 57; beard 57; hunting 57–9, 60–1, 91–2, 127, 136, 201; High Sheriff 61; relationship with Fanny 62; depression 63, 65; music 63, 79, 123, 127, 145, 158; engagement 70; Lucy's first visit to Hampton Court as his fiancée 73; women as stronger sex 76; reading during sermon 77; in Chamonix 86; as husband 88–9, 156, 157; poor financial acumen 91, 152, 224; foreign honeymoon 92; reaction to Lucy's pregnancy 96–7; on Jack's birth 98–9; as father 99, 135, 136–7, 138, 171, 172, 197, 199, 199; attitude to labourers 106–7, 110–11; embroilment in Harewood affairs 118–20, 223; journey to Algiers 128–32; letters from Algiers 132–4; reliance on Lucy 142, 152, 198; Arkwright Act 149–54; silver wedding 156; cultivation of primrose 159; invention of fruit trays 159–60; on landownership by all 164–5; Board of Christ's Hospital 169; feelings on recovery of Henry's body 179; relationship with Jack 179, 182, 191, 198; mortgaging estate 182–3, 196; visit to Knole 188; Lord Lieutenancy 191–4, 200; first grandson 196; death 201; memorials 204; *Plates 6, 10, 11, 13, 17, 19, 26*
Arkwright, John of Parndon Hall 167, 220
Arkwright, John Richard Stephen 204, 207, 211, 219, 275 n9
Arkwright, John Stanhope (Jack): 6; birth 97; as baby 99; as child 122, 130; prep school 135, 138; Eton 135–6; gardener 135, 136; delicate health 135, 138, 180, 207–8, 214; school holidays 137; playing fives 151; provision for in Estate Act 154; to Oxford 157; acting 157; twenty-first birthday 160–2; politics 160, 162, 180, 197; interest in estate affairs 169, 179, 191, 195; Newdigate Prize for poetry 169–70; patent and commercial law 173; on Geraldine and Dick 173–4; Chamonix 175–8; called to Bar 179; Boer War poetry 181–2, 187; mortgaging estate 182–3, 207, 210; as Hereford's MP 185–7, 203, 205, 208, 214; trustee of Geraldine's jointure 190; godfather to Geraldine's son 196; in love with Stephanie 196–7; engagement 197; inheritance from his father 203; wedding 204; birth of son 204; secretary to the committee opposing 1909 Budget 207; estate office difficulties 207; defence of Ashworth 207; move to Kinsham Court 207, 210, 212; sales on estate 210; care of staff 212; final letter to tenants 213; personal secretary to Milner 216; 'The Supreme Sacrifice' 218; participation in Haggard's survey 226; *Plates 17, 23*

Arkwright, Rev. Joseph 3, 17, 31, 59–60, 93, 140
Arkwright, Loftus 59, 61, 122
Arkwright, Loftus Joseph 140, 167, 220
Arkwright, Mary (Bosanquet): Johnny's twenty-first 16, 18; sending seeds to brothers 19; 1857 season 29–31; poetry 55; marriage 61, 75; pregnancies 64–5; reaction to Johnny's engagement 71; Johnny and Lucy's return from honeymoon 84; attachment to Harewood 118–19; home at Tanhurst, Dorking 127; opinion of Hill-James 134; at Johnny's funeral 201; on sale of Hampton Court, 211
Arkwright, Olive: birth 136, 139; papa's girl 137; Kate Greenaway paper in nursery 138; mother's death 198; at Hampton Court with father 201
Arkwright, Peter 3, 17, 69, 93, 221
Arkwright, Richard 94
Arkwright, Richard (Dick), MP: ferns 19; unrequited love 30; playwright 35; marriage 61; visit to Emily 66; election as Leominster MP 69, 92; childless 95; London home 99; trip to Algiers 118; resignation as MP 129; Arkwright Act 153; estate Trustee 154; drinking 155; at Tor Castle 175; at Johnny's funeral 201; Johnny's jewellery 204; on purchase of Kinsham 212; *Plate 16*
Arkwright, Richard, the younger: career 3; wealth 3; investments 3, 40–1, 221; supervision of Hampton Court estate 4, 38; 'tradesman' 5; portrait by Joseph Wright of Derby 34; financial acumen 91, 224; movement out of cotton 221
Arkwright, Captain Richard 219
Arkwright, Sir Richard: spinning 3, 225; portrait by Joseph Wright of Derby 34; use of water power 40–1; provision for spinning workforce 52; on the family's origins 95; factory workers 101; patents 173; contribution to urban growth 221
Arkwright, Robert 3, 17, 24, 30
Arkwright, Sarah (Tally, née Hoskyns): marriage to John Arkwright 4; family 4; role as mother 29, 62, 65, 68, 71, 93; inheritance from her husband 42; jointure 42, 150; encouraging Chandos's influence on Johnny 45; work at Hope School 52; fiftieth birthday 54; laying first stone of Pencombe church 57; concern about Johnny's hunting 61; illness 62; reaction to Johnny's engagement 73; at Harewood 83; Henry's death 86, 93; pension for families in Chamonix 87; move to Llanforda Hall, Oswestry 87; death 93; endowment of Hampton Home 107; *Plate 12*
Arkwright, Sidney 152, 212
Arkwright, Wilfred 94
Arkwright, Willie, of Sutton Scarsdale 131, 136, 219
Arundel, West Sussex 7
Ashworth, Harry 167, 179, 182–3, 196, 198, 201, 207, 212
Aston Tyrrold, Oxfordshire 21, 169
Asquith, Herbert 208
Atherley, Major and Mrs Evelyn 204
Auchmuty, Rev. Arthur 164–7
Aucketill, Henry 166
Auckland, Lord 37
Austen, Jane 233 n16
Australia 108, 117, 123, 126, 133, 134
avalanche on Mont Blanc, 1866 86, 144

Badham, John, labourer 103
Bailey, Sir Joseph MP 17, 109, 110, 117
Balfour, Arthur 186, 200, 204, 205, 210, 278 n7
Ballard, W. 156
Balmat, Jacques 86
Barton, Dr, of Leominster 136
Bateman Arms, Shobdon, Herefordshire 166
Bateman, John 139
Bateman, Lord: speech at Johnny's twenty-first 17; model farming 49; 69; mortgages 144; clash with ELRL 166; selling silver etc. 168; death of 191–2, 220

Index

Bateman Hanbury, Hon. and Rev. Arthur 69, 81, 151, 201
Bath and West of England Agricultural Society 42, 117
Batson, T., of Kynaston, Herefordshire 51
Beaufort, Duke of 114, 168
Beaulieu, Hampshire 7
Bedford, Duke of 116, 166, 167
Bemand, George, tenant 126
Benbow, John, tenant 110
Berrington Hall, Herefordshire 114, 144 194
Bethell, William, labourer 103
Bevan, Edward, labourer 111
Bevan, William, gardener 212
Biarritz, France 135, 259 n66
Biddulph, Michael MP 109
Birmingham 100, 104, 108, 109, 116, 180, 195
Blandford, George Fielding 129
Blandings Castle 8
Blenheim Palace, Oxfordshire 7, 145
Blythe, Ronald 2
Bodenham, Herefordshire: 1852 election 23; Fishing Club 29; parish 39, 140, 165; Arkwrights of 62, 70, 138; wedding festivities, 81; schoolchildren 84, 135; Labourers' Improvement Society 106; population 109
Bodenham Court, Hampton Court 142
Bodichon, Barbara Smith 130
Boer War 171, 181, 183–4, 187, 208
Borth, Cardiganshire 138
Bosanquet, Maud 65
Bosanquet, Samuel Courthope (Courthope) 61, 65, 75, 84, 120, 203
Bosanquet, Samuel Ronald (Ronald) 65, 169, 173, 211, 217, 220
Bosanquet, Vivian 65
Bosbury, Herefordshire 29, 35
Bossons, Glacier des, Chamonix, France 85, 86, 177
Boughton, Francis 29
Bowles, William of Shrewsbury 48
Bradshaw, William 140
Brampton Bryan, Herefordshire 102, 104, 108, 127, 139
Brassington, Mr, tenant 112, 142
Brideshead Revisited (Waugh) 1, 8
Bright, John 139
Brisco, Sir Robert 49
Brislington asylum, Bristol 44, 236 n23
British Aristocracy, The Decline and Fall of the (Cannadine) 2
Brown, J.H. artist 17
Buckingham, Duke of, loan to by John Arkwright 21, 219
Bulawayo, Rhodesia 188, 189, 191
Bull, Mr, of Bear Farm, Weobley, Herefordshire 124
Burdett-Coutts, Angela 30, 57, 144
Burgess & Keys farm machinery 47
Burghope, Herefordshire 83
Burleigh, H.C., of Fairfield, Maine 117
Burley Gate, Herefordshire 58
Burlington Hotel, Cork St, London 30, 54
Burr, Higford D. 28
Burrell, Mrs Nancy 214, 220
Burrowes, Dr, in London 55
Burton Court, Herefordshire 234 n33, 240 n42
Butters, George, butler 122
Bye, Alfred, head gardener 138, 145, 155
Byford, Herefordshire 87
Byng, Francis 67, 68, 93
Byng, Lady Mary (Minnie, Dick Arkwright's wife) 61, 66, 93, 95, 175, 201, 221

Caird, James 41
Caldwall, Bonham: friend and bearer at John's funeral 37; trustee of estate 42, 47, 106, 154; relationship with Johnny 43, 90; death 156, 161; *Plate 8*
Caldwell, Jonah 140, 167
Cambridge University 5, 32, 60
Campbell, James 27
Campbell, John Frederick Vaughan 67–8
Campbell, Lady Muriel 67–8
Campbell-Bannerman, Henry 206
Canada 117, 123, 218
Cannadine, David 2, 6, 8
Cape Town, South Africa 171, 173
capital investment 142, 215, 222

Carlton Club, London 26, 120, 151, 172, 223
Carwardine, T.J. 146
Cawdor, 2nd Earl *see* Campbell, John Frederick Vaughan
Central Landowners' Association 205
Chamberlain, Joseph 109, 147, 148, 185, 187
Chamonix, France 86, 87, 88, 175, 176, 178, 204
Chandos-Pole-Gell, H. 158
Chaplin, Rt Hon. Henry MP 158, 205
Chatsworth, Derbyshire: 7; Johnny and George visit 19; death duties on 215
Cheltenham, Gloucestershire 217
Cheltenham Ladies' College 197, 243 n22
Chepstow Castle, Monmouthshire 29
Chester-Master, Andrew 217
Chester-Master, Cyril 217
Chester-Master, family of Cirencester 98, 135, 171, 217
Chester-Master, F.W. 98
Chester-Master, Georgina (née Rolls) 171, 217
Chester-Master, John Robert 199, 217
Chester-Master, Lettice 199, 217
Chester-Master, Richard C. (Dick): prep school with Jack 135; in love with Geraldine 170–4; ADC to Milner 181; Boer War heroism 183–4; Milner's opinion of him 184–5; roles in Rhodesia 187–8; marriage to Geraldine 188; return to London 189; return to Knole 189–90; at Hampton Court 190; birth of son 196; promotion to High Commissioner of Rhodesia 196; Chief Constable of Gloucestershire Constabulary 216; First World War service 216; death of 216; *Plates 24, 25*
Chester-Master, Colonel T.W.C. 167, 170, 172–3, 188, 201, 216
Chester-Master, William Alfred (Billy) 196, 217, 218
Chilman, Frank 190, 212
Chilman, John 212
Christ Church College, Oxford 19, 21, 24, 30, 69, 170
Christ's Hospital, London 29
Christie, Manson & Woods 122
Church of England clergy, alignment with landed class 102
cider as part of labourer's wages 102, 104, 112
Cirencester, Gloucestershire 167, 170, 172, 217
Clare, Mr T., Clerk of the Works 160, 201
Clayton, William Clayton 87
Clegg, Lily 201
Clive, Captain 200
Clowes, John 35, 75
Coats, Peter 200
Cobden, Richard 139
Cochrane, Hon. M.H., of Hillhurst Farm, Quebec 117
Colburn, Mr, of Bodenham 34–5
Cold Oak Farm, Hampton Court 156
Colley, Edward, agent 34–6, 38–40, 42, 47–8, 53, 64, 90, 97, 103, 107, 122, 149, 156; *Plate 7*
Colley, Henry, clerk at estate office 53, 63
Colley, James, gardener 103
Collings, Jesse, MP 109, 147, 186
Colwall, Herefordshire 218
Coningsby Hospital, Hereford 146
Conservative party: attitude to landowners 10
Cooke, W.R. 185
Corbet, Vincent 29
Corn Laws, repeal of (1846): 9, 22, 41–2, 47, 121, 141, 215, 223
Cornewall, Rev. Sir George 72, 139
Cornewall, Sir Velters 57, 59, 60, 61, 63, 72, 80, 91, 98, 171, 221; *Plate 13*
Cornewall Lewis, George 23
Corporation of the Sons of the Clergy 29
costume: at Carey's 1858 wedding 33; at John's 1858 funeral 36; at Mary's 1862 wedding 62; at Lucy's 1866 wedding; at Geraldine's 1905 wedding
Cottenham, Countess of, 29
Cotterell, Sir Geers (3rd Bart) 144
Cotterell, Henry 72
Cotterell, Sir John (4th Bart) 199, 200
cotton industry 222
country houses: destruction of 1, 219, 220; exhibition about 7; letting of 204; as powerhouses 214–15; inseparable from estates 225; renewal of 225

Country Life 189
County Council 148, 197, 201
Couttet, Sylvain 86, 144, 177
Covent Garden, London, fire at 1856
Coventry, Earl of 116, 117, 135, 158, 193
Coward, Noël 1, 8
Cowarne Wood, Herefordshire 59
Credenhill Park, Herefordshire 58
Croft, Sir Herbert, MP 109
Cromford, Derbyshire 3, 52, 219, 221
Cronje, Piet 183–4
Croome Court, Worcestershire 116, 135, 193
Crosskill, Beverly, farm machinery 47
Cucklington, Wiltshire 16

Daggs, John 180–1, 182, 191, 195, 196, 201
Daggs, William 13–15
Daily Express 194
Darwall, Randle, clerk 251 n29
Darwin, Charles 54, 101
Dashwood, Lewis 127
Dashwood, Sophy 69, 70, 94
Davenport, Charlotte Lucy (Lucy): 69, 72; first visit to Hampton Court 73; jointure 79, 151; thanks to Henry 85; sex 88; management of Johnny 89, 135, 198; Hope school 92; pregnancy 92, 94–7; selling ferns at bazaar 122; music 123; understanding of rental issues 126–7; in London 128; third pregnancy 128; in Germany 129; sympathy for Johnny 130, 153; reaction to Fanny's engagement 133–4; love for Johnny 134, 188; Bodenham School 135; fourth pregnancy 136; as mother 138, 171, 176, 190, 191, 197, 198; affair at the bank 179; Geraldine's posting abroad 188; discussion of estate finances with Jack 195; death 198; *Plate 15*
Davenport, Charlotte Nest (Nest) 94–5
Davenport, George 69, 70, 72, 73 78, 80, 94, 127, 201
Davenport, Harry 69, 78, 79, 151–2
Davenport, John 69
Davenport, Mary 69, 74, 84, 129, 151, 201
Davies, Emily 76
Davies, John 126
Davies, Richard, labourer 103
Davis, Francis 28
death duties 168, 215, 216, 217, 218
Denmark 140
Derby, Lord 69
Devonshire, 'Bachelor' 6th Duke of, 19, 57
Devonshire, 9th Duke of 219
Devonshire, 11th Duke of 215
Dickens, Charles 46, 55
Dilke, Sir Charles, MP 104, 106
Dingestow, Monmouthshire 61, 221
Dinmore Hill 15–16, 83, 92, 159
Disraeli, Benjamin 69, 125, 208
Dixon, George, MP 108, 109
Docklow, Herefordshire 15
Donnington Hall, Herefordshire 30
Dorrell, Simon 12
Dorstone, Herefordshire 197
Downton Castle, Shropshire 29, 139
drainage 43, 45, 47–8, 90–1
Drake, Mrs, housekeeper at Bosbury 35
Droitwich Spa, Worcestershire 135, 144, 158, 200
Drynam, W. 115
Dudley, Earl of 114
Duncan, Charles, cashier 207
Dunstall, Staffordshire 3, 228 n14

Earl, Adams, of Lafayette, Indiana 117
Eastern Counties Labour Federation (ECLF) 165
Eastnor Castle, Herefordshire 139
Eckley, Henry 159
Eckley, Robert 156, 181; *Plate 19*
Edouart, Rev. Augustin 145–6
Edward VII, King *see* Prince of Wales
Edwards, Alfred & Dearman, auctioneers 200
Edwards, Edward 90
Edwards, Rev. W.E. 194
Edwards and Weaver, auctioneers 124
Elgar, Sir Edward 64, 158, 278 n7
Elgars of Worcester 64
Emsworth, Lord 8
enclosure 41

England's Gate Inn, Bodenham, Herefordshire 39, 59, 83, 106, 111
English Heritage 7, 219
English Land Restoration League (ELRL) 164–7
entailment of estates 42, 45, 95, 143, 169
Essex, Earl of, 3, 32, 228 n9
Essex Foxhounds 59
estate office 38–9, 41, 207
estate unity 18
Eton College 2, 5, 19, 31, 98, 135, 282 n54
Evelyn, Lyndon 209, 212, 213
Evelyn, Susan Grace (Grace) 209
'Excelsior' 85, 93, 176–7

fertilisation of the soil 41, 44, 47
Feversham, Earl of 158
Fiennes, Isabelle Twistleton Wykeham 30
First World War 209, 215–16, 222
Fishpools Farm, Hampton Court 90
Fitton, R.S. 3
Foley, Lady Emily 17
food, at Johnny's twenty-first 17, 230 n12; at Carey's wedding 34; Mary's wedding 61;
foot and mouth disease 226, 248 n103
Ford Farm, Hampton Court 48
foreign competition and imports 41, 222, 226
Foxley, Herefordshire 58, 69, 70, 71, 73, 77, 79, 81, 85, 127, 144, 220
Fraser, Hugh 173
Freeman, A.P., of Huntington, Massachusetts 117
Free Trade 22, 42, 44, 230 n11
Fritz 94
fruit trays 159–60; *Plate 20*

Gadd, Henry, head gardener 19, 29
gardens: at Hampton Court, new 12; Arkwright children 19; fernery 19; cutbacks 145, 155; staff 156, 212; primula Evelyn Arkwrightii 159; produce grown in 159, 264 n54; in Algeria 131–2
Gardner, Dr, of Algiers 131
Garnons, Herefordshire 58, 72, 87, 144, 199, 220
Garnstone, Herefordshire 89, 124, 220
Garstone, Harry, acting agent 207, 212
Gatehouse, Thomas, gardener 34
George V, King 209
Gilbert and Sullivan 170, 197
Gilbey, Newman 167
Glading, William, Master of Estate Works 36, 40
Gladstone, William Ewart 69, 92, 95, 100, 126, 128, 165, 258
Glanusk Park, Breconshire 117, 151
Gloucestershire 8, 114, 163
Golden Grove, Carmarthenshire 68
Good, J.B. 104–5
Gore Ouseley, Sir Frederick 63
Gosford Park 221
Grands Mulets, Chamonix, France 86, 175, 177
Grane, Rev. Mr and Mrs John Willis, Vicar of Hope 56, 93, 97
Grange House, Leominster: relocation of town hall 28–9; sale of 209
Grange, The, Much Wenlock, Shropshire 211
Great Witley, Worcestershire 114
Gredington, Hanmer, Flintshire 56, 221
Green, C.E. 140
Green, Thomas of Kinnersley, Herefordshire 124
Green Farm, Hampton Court 38, 39, 42, 47, 51, 52, 53, 83, 90, 107, 115, 146, 156, 158, 159, 160, 200
Greenhead, Nurse 65
Greta 94
Grey, Hon. Odeyne de 145
Grosvenor, Charlotte 90
Ground Game Act 126, 128, 142, 148
guano *see* fertilisation of the soil
Gull, Sir William 129
Gwysaney, Flintshire 35

Haggard, H. Rider 226, 230 n44
Hamilton, Duke of 145
Hammond, Margaret 29
Hampton Court, Herefordshire: purchase of 3; alterations to 4, 18, 40; today 11–12; sale of contents 11; grounds 15; visit

by Earl of Essex 32; ball in Coningsby Hall 35; chapel 86, 179; household under Lucy 87–9; staff 159, 190, 212, 224; schoolroom 137; nursery 138; unusual artefacts 150; Jack's twenty-first birthday celebrations 160–2; featured in *Country Life* 189; Johnny's absence from 202; sale of by Arkwrights 203, 214; letting of 204; sales since the Arkwrights 220; *Plates 1, 22*

Hampton Court, Herefordshire, estate: application of industrial principles 4; extent of 39, 79, 125, 139, 140, 157; rents 39–40, 47, 79, 90, 114, 118, 126, 128, 142, 150; improvements and repairs 40, 48, 90–1, 149; estate works 40–1; Trust 42, 149; value of stock and machinery on Johnny's inheritance 43; tenants' contribution to improvements 47, 142; book-keeping 49; hedging 50; provision and rental of labourers' cottages 51; holiday provision 52; tenants' livestock shows 53; sales of farms 90, 157, 210; hunt kennels 91, 115; dairy 107, 158; number and age of labourers 111, 114; deer 124; tenant farmers 15, 124, 125, 213; evidence to Richmond Commission 125; depression bites 142; labourers' wages 102, 110, 111, 113, 114, 142; jubilee celebrations 153; visit by ELRL 165; disentailment of 182; mortgages against 182, 191, 195, 209, 210; duty payable on Johnny's death 204; sales of Leominster properties 207

Hampton Court Palace, London 8, 68

Hampton Court Savings Bank 107, 113

Hampton Friendly Society 107

Hanbury Tracy, Charles 4–5

Harbin, Rev. Charles 16, 20–1

Hardy, Gathorne 27

Harewood Park, Ross-on-Wye, Herefordshire 4, 36, 44, 46, 50, 72, 75, 78, 81, 83, 87, 93, 95, 118, 119–20, 122, 130, 220, 223; *Plate 29*

Harley, Robert 139

Harlow, Essex 220

Harris, Dr Charles 218

Harrow School 5, 28, 31, 87, 171

Harrowby, Lord 156

Hart-Smith, Dr 201

Hatfield Place, Witham, Essex 221

Hawkshaw, Edward and Catherine 24–5, 37, 79, 98

Hearst, William Randolph 219

Heathcoat Amory, Sir John and Lady 122, 152, 224, 282 n57

hedgerow removal 45; repairs 50

Hellens, Herefordshire 185

Henhouse Farm, Hampton Court 42, 81, 90

Herbert, William 87

Hereford: demolition of Butcher's Row 28; railway 51; Whitecross Kennels 59, 91; decorations for Johnny's wedding 81; Cathedral 87, 143, 146, 188; 1868 election 92; Rose Show 97; annual cattle fair 116; new hospital 123, 198; Shirehorse Show 157;

Hereford & West of England Rose Society 180

Hereford cattle 11, 46, 52–3, 115–17, 121, 131, 146, 158, 162, 179, 197, 222

Hereford family: at Johnny's twenty-first 17; ownership of Hampton Court 220

Hereford Herd Book Society 53, 117, 197

Hereford Militia 34, 51, 81, 84, 161

Herefordshire: location 8; development of 10; economy 11, 39; population 11, 39; agriculture 40, 125; landownership 139–40; parliamentary representation 146–7; livestock figures 163; crop acreages 163

Herefordshire Agricultural and General Workers Union 164, 166

Herefordshire Agricultural Society 42

Herefordshire Domestic and General Farm Servants' Registration Society 52

Herefordshire Hounds 57–9, 91

Herefordshire Philharmonic Society (HPS) 63–4, 69, 95, 102, 157, 158–9, 180

Heygate, Captain and Mrs 90, 194

Heygate, Walter 212

Heywood, Major 112
Hicks-Beach, Sir Michael 136
High Farming 22, 41–2, 47, 49, 52
Hill Hole Farm, Hampton Court 42, 90
Hill House Farm, Hampton Court 47, 50, 126, 167
Hill-James, Captain William 133–5, 175, 194, 204, 211
Historic Houses Association 7
Hodge, the labourer 102
Hodges, Edward, tenant and wife 15–16
Holcombe, George 22
Holme Lacy, Herefordshire 19, 32, 58, 72, 212, 220
Holt, Mr, caterer 17
Home Rule for Ireland: patricians' last stand 7; Gladstone and 69; gun-running 208–9; Curragh 'mutiny' 209; sales of land to tenants 211; role in landed decline 215; famine 215
hop growing 67, 115, 122, 125, 163
Hope-under-Dinmore: toll-gate 15; school 36, 52, 92, 161, 167, 247 n69; schoolchildren 34, 36, 37, 97, 198; parish of 35, 39, 140, 165; church 36, 84, 92–3, 98, 122–3, 134, 142, 153, 188, 190, 198, 204, 224; Oak Inn 39; reading room and library 92; population 109; floods 123
Hoskyns, Catherine Wren (CWH's daughter by first marriage), married name Piggott 56, 73, 118, 120, 130, 223
Hoskyns, Chandos Wren: speech at Johnny's twenty-first 17; politics 22, 44; John's funeral 37; marriage to Theodosia Wren 43; ownership of Wroxall, Warwickshire 43; *Talpa* 43, 46; relationship with his father, Sir Hungerford 44–5; on estate management 45; RASE Councillor 45; toasted by Charles Dickens 46, 55; on expenditure on improvements 49; employment of Joseph Arch 50; music 63; in Italy 73, 83; MP for Hereford City 92, 95; on Tally's death 93; death of sons 95; land ownership by all 101; Harewood 119–20; death 120; obituary 121; anti-entail 143; need a fortune to run an estate 180; influence on Johnny 224; *Plate 9*
Hoskyns, Hungerford 44, 83, 95, 119
Hoskyns, Hungerford Chandos 95
Hoskyns, Sir Hungerford 4, 22, 33, 36, 37, 44, 62, 118, 146, 152
Hoskyns, Sir John Leigh (Leigh): care of George at Oxford 21; Carey's wedding 34; John's funeral 37; visit to Emily 66; baronetcy 95; financial worries 118; 120; dismay at change 169; Geraldine's wedding 190
Hoskyns, Lady 44, 62
House of Commons: landowners a minority in, 10, 147; changes in 186, 205; terrace 190; clashes over 1909 budget 206–7
House of Lords 114, 186, 194, 205–7, 208–9, 216
Humber parish, Herefordshire 165
Humphries of Pershore farm machinery 47
hunting 57–9, 61, 140, 181
Hussey farm machinery 42

Importance of Being Earnest, The (Wilde) 1, 170, 210
imports: of grain 123, 126, 222; of frozen meat 126, 140, 222; of dairy produce 140; dependency on 206
India 123, 222
Industrial Revolution 3, 76, 222, 225
Ireland *see* Home Rule
Ivens, John 50
Ivington, Herefordshire 28
Ivington Court, Herefordshire 124

Jacquet, Mr, caterer 17
Jamaica 117
Johns, Major 216
Jones, Edwin 126

Kentchurch Court, Herefordshire 58
Kenyon, Hon. Elizabeth (Lizzie) 56, 71, 79, 129–30, 134, 152, 212, 221

Kingsland, Herefordshire 164
King's Royal Rifle Corps, The 170, 216
Kinsham Court, Herefordshire 207, 209-210, 212, 213, 216
Kipling, Rudyard 187, 278 n7
Kitchen, Mrs, cook 34
Kitchener, Lord 184
Knightshayes, Devon 224
Knole, Almondsbury 135, 172, 188, 189–90, 191, 217

labourers' wages: at Hampton Court 50–2, 102–3, 110, 111, 114; discontent 100–1, 108; northern counties 102; debate in *Hereford Times* 102–4; in USA 105; Johnny's research into pay and conditions 110–11; hours of work 113
labourers: growing shortage of 50; emigration of 103, 104, 108, 112, 162, 165, 221; political rise of 147
Lambeth Palace, London 72
land: decline in importance of 9–10, 146, 222; loans against 9, 180, 183, 215; value 9, 144–5, 168, 222; Acts in Ireland 139, 141; Settled Land Act 143; taxes 206; sales of early twentieth century 214; barriers to sale of 223
landowners: role of 15, 41–2, 49, 53, 126, 127, 141, 142, 143, 148, 161, 180, 201; Ground Game Act 126; financial difficulties of 127; alternative sources of income 126; sized up 139–40, 168; demand for price protection 141; sale of outlying acres 144, 168, 210; inability to grasp nature of change 202; Home Rule as the last stand for 208; sales to tenants 210, 211, 213
landownership: extent 8; by all 101, 164; under attack 139, 142, 164, 165–6, 168, 206; survey of 139; decline of political influence 147, 169, 185, 205, 215; a luxury 226
Lands Improvement Company 47, 90, 114–15, 122, 142, 149, 150
Langford, Mr, gardener 55
Laurels, The, Herefordshire 204, 207
Lawrence, William, labourer 103
Ledbury, Herefordshire 29
Leigh, E.C. Austen 135, 271 n61
Leighton, Frederick 130
Leinthall, Sir Rowland 8
Leintwardine, Herefordshire 101, 104, 139, 164; *see also* North Herefordshire and South Shropshire Agricultural Labourers Improvement Society
Leominster: in 1854 13; MPs for 22–3, 27–8, 92, 100, 146, 194; sale of land at The Grange 28, 207; flower show 55; train from 80; Royal Oak 81; agricultural show 117; Priory restoration 145; tradespeople's presentation 156; Arkwright properties sold 207
Leominster Cricket Club 29
Leslie, Sir Henry 63, 64, 70, 95, 159
Lewis Thomas, E. 208
Lind, Jenny 74
Little Berkhamsted, Hertfordshire 35
livestock: earlier maturity of 41, 52–3; sickness in 123, 215; national figures 163; Herefordshire figures 163
Llandinabo, Herefordshire 120
Llandrindod Wells, Radnorshire 159, 195, 264 n51
Llanforda Hall, Oswestry 87, 92
Llangattock, Lord 171, 194
Lloyd George, David: attitude to landowners, 10; pro-Boer 185; 205; 1909 budget 206, 208; War Cabinet 216
Local Government Act 167
Locre, Hospice, Belgium 217
Longleat, Wiltshire 7
Longley, Diana 72, 74, 75, 88, 99, 128, 129, 136, 173, 189, 223
Longley, Sir Henry 72, 75, 78, 88, 93, 99, 122, 128, 137, 151–2, 153, 173, 223
Lonsdale, Lord 122
Lopes, Sir Massey 158
Lord Lieutenant 141–2, 194, 200
Lord's Cricket Ground, London 31
Lower Buckland Farm, Hampton Court 90
Lower Wickton Farm, Hampton Court 48, 90, 126

Lowndes Street, London 88, 89, 97, 128, 136, 153, 223
Lucas-Scudamore, Colonel Edward 204, 252 n6
Ludge, John 124
Ludlow, Shropshire 142
Lugg, River 14, 123, 172, 207, 214
Lynhales, Herefordshire 196, 212

Madresfield Court, Worcestershire 8
Magdalen College, Oxford 21
magistracy 141, 147
Manchester, Duke of 116
Mark Hall, Essex 3, 59, 60, 93, 122, 140, 220, 228 n14; *Plate 30*
Marlborough, Duke of 145, 168
Marlbrook Farm, Hampton Court 110, 167
Marsh Court Farm, Hampton Court 90
Marshall, Miss, governess 137
Maund Common, Hampton Court 111
Mechi, Joseph 41
Medlicott, Henry, tenant 142
Meredith, Jonathan, tenant 84
Merrett, Mr, caterer 17, 34
Merrick, Samuel, labourer 103
Middlemist, Robert, Harrow housemaster 28
Middleton, Lord 29
Miller, T.L. of Beecher, Illinois 117
Milne, David 49
Milner, Sir Alfred (later Lord) 181, 184–5, 187, 188, 191, 196, 212, 216, 280 n27; *Plate 24*
Mitchell, Mrs, housekeeper 34
Mitford, William 37, 56
Moccas Court, Herefordshire, 58, 91, 139, 221
model farms 49
Monmouth, Monmouthshire 51, 168, 171
Mont Blanc, France 85, 86, 144, 175, 177; Ancien Passage 86
Moore, Henry, of Fields Place and Chadnor, Herefordshire 124
Moreton, Lord 158
Morris, Mr and Mrs 81
Mortram, Henry, pyrotechnic artist 18
Moule, Rev. Henry 229 n30, 247 n71
Mount, The, Shropshire 94, 137
Munros of Novar, Scotland 145
Murray, Rev. David R. 102, 104, 105, 111

Naples, Italy 92
National Agricultural Labourers' Union 110, 111, 113, 125, 147, 164, 165
National Fair Trade League 141
National Trust 7, 224
Netherton, Herefordshire 120
Nettleship, Richard 177
Nevill, Lady Dorothy 204
New Domesday survey 139, 148, 166
New Hampton Farm, Hampton Court 90
New House Farm, Hampton Court 47, 90, 126
Newington, Samuel 129
Newton, parish of, Herefordshire 35
Newton Court, Hampton Court 50
New Zealand 108
Nice, France 92
Nicholson, Newark-on-Trent farm machinery 47
Nightingale, Florence 76
Noakes, Mr, schoolmaster 198
Normanby, Marquess of 21
Normanton Turville, Leicestershire 3, 60, 228 n14
North Herefordshire and South Shropshire Agricultural Labourers Improvement Society 101–2, 103, 104, 108, 109, 110, 111, 139, 223
Noverre, Arthur 66, 129
Nuttall, George 3

'O Valiant Hearts' 218
Oliver, Richard, tenant 111
Onibury, Shropshire 142
Ordnance Survey 140, 148
Oriel College, Oxford 21, 25, 69, 177
Oxford, Countess of, 17
Oxford University 5, 19, 20, 24, 98, 160

Paccard, Michel-Gabriel 86
Parker, Hon. Cecil 135, 158, 191
Parker, Gerald 135

Parker, William, tenant 110, 126
Parliament Bill 208
Parndon Hall, Essex 140, 167
Parr, Wilson 167
Paxton, Joseph: conservatory at Hampton Court 5; use of conservatory 19; *Plate 22*
Peel, Frederick 231 n34
Peel, Sir Robert 22, 121, 141, 167, 215, 219
Pencombe Court, Hampton Court 126
Pencombe parish: 39, 110; new church and rectory 57, 71, 97
Pencoyd, Herefordshire 120
Peploe, Daniel 37, 89, 220
Peru, imports of guano from 44
Peto, Sir Samuel Morton 130
Phelips, Richard and Caroline 37, 45, 54, 118, 121
picture sales 145
Pitt, John 126
political influence, loss of 141
political retreat by landowners 10, 185
Powell, Thomas, gamekeeper 29
Powell, Thomas Percy Prosser 197, 199
Powis, Earl of 114, 148
Powis Castle, Montgomeryshire 87, 114
Presteigne, Radnorshire 207
Price, John, Court House, Herefordshire 117
prices for agricultural produce: grain 42, 115, 121–3, 140, 163–4; meat 42, 140; sheep 124; cattle 140, 164; wool 164; general 142, 164, 167, 168
primula Evelyn Arkwrightii 159
Prince of Wales (King Edward VII) 88, 106, 121, 129, 147, 158, 186, 195, 196, 206, 208
Prossers, staff at Hampton Court 87
protectionism 141, 147, 215
Proudman, William 126
Pusey, Philip 41

Quain, Sir Richard 96

railway in Herefordshire 11
Railway Inn, Bodenham 212
Ramsden Estate Act 1885 149
Rancliffe, Lady 22
Ranfurly, Lord 129
Rankin, Sir James, MP 117
Rashleigh, George B. 149, 150–1, 183
rates on agricultural land 126, 169
Ravensworth, Earl of 158
Redmond, John 208
Redwood Farm, Hampton Court 47, 90
Reform Acts 10, 24, 92, 100, 141, 146, 206, 215–16
Reid, H. Dawson 109
Reynolds, Elizabeth 60
Rhodesia 185, 187, 196
Richmond Commission 125, 128
Ricketts, Anna Fane 44, 120
Ridley, Sir Matthew White 180, 185
Riley, Benjamin 165
Rimington's Guides/Tigers 181
Risbury parish, Herefordshire 39
Robinson, Stephanie (Jack's wife) 196–7, 201, 204, 207, 211, 212, 216
Robinson, Stephen 117, 196–7, 200, 212
Rodney, Lord 114, 144, 168, 194
Rogers, Aaron 117
Rogers, Thomas 124
Rouse-Boughton-Knight, Andrew 139
Rowberry Farm, Hampton Court 111
Rowcliffe, William 179, 182, 191, 196
Royal Agricultural Society of England, The: Johnny on Council 6, 45 64, 90, 135, 158, 205; 1836 foundation of 22; machinery at 42; role of 45; show at Worcester 46; labourers' cottage design 51; victories for Johnny with Hereford cattle 53, 158; show at Birmingham 116; show at Liverpool 116; show at Bristol 116; show at Carlisle 117; show at Windsor 121; investigation into livestock sickness 123; show at Newcastle-upon-Tyne 154; vice-presidents of 158; show at Maidstone and fruit trays 160; show at Cardiff 188
Royal Commission into the conditions in Agriculture 125
Ruskin, John 75, 88, 137
Russells, auctioneers 91
Ruth, biblical story of, from Ruth i.16–17 74

Sale, Thomas (senior), solicitor 28, 32, 42, 43, 224
Sale, W.T., solicitor 149–50, 153, 169, 179, 181, 182, 191, 194, 195, 196
Salisbury, Lord 169, 180, 185, 186 192, 193, 218–19
Sanders, Mr and Mrs James 92, 97
Saye and Sele, Rev. Lord 17, 34, 37, 168
Scott, Sir George Gilbert 145
Scudamore Stanhope, Berkeley: proposal to Caroline 19–20, 31; vicar of Bosbury 29; income on marriage 32; 1858 wedding 33–5, 75; trustee of estate 42, 47, 90, 154, 203; relationship with Johnny 43; poetry 56; at Byford 87; visits from Johnny's children 138; Geraldine's wedding 190; Johnny's funeral 201; on sale of Hampton Court 211; on purchase of Kinsham 212; *Plate 5*
selling up, attitudes to 143
Sessions, George, bailiff 115
shipping 140, 148, 163, 168, 210, 223
Shobdon, Herefordshire 17, 49, 81, 84, 151, 156, 166
Shobdon Court, Herefordshire 139, 144, 167, 220
shopping, London 88, 153, 189
Shorthorn cattle 117
Shropshire 8
Sidnall Farm, Hampton Court 110, 126
Simond, Michel 177, 178
Simpson, Emmeline G. (Simmie), governess 137
Sitwell, Sir Osbert 219
Somers, Earl 139
South Africa 171, 172, 175, 181, 187
South America 200
Spondon Hall, Derby 71
Stackpole Court, Pembrokeshire 67
Stanage Castle, Radnorshire 127
Stanffer, Edwyn's valet 175, 176, 178
Stanford Hall, Nottinghamshire 70, 127
Stanhope, Sir Edwyn, 19, 31–2, 37, 72
Stanhope, Rev. Lionel 198
Stocktonbury, Herefordshire 146
Stoke Edith, Herefordshire 58
Stoke Prior, Herefordshire 15, 39, 165
Stone Lodge Farm, Hampton Court 90, 115, 124
Stradivarius violin, the Arkwright (1732) 63, 145, 146
Strafford, 2nd Earl of 61
Strange, Thomas 101, 104, 105, 108, 109, 111
succession, lines of 61, 98; *see also* entail
Sutton Scarsdale, Derbyshire 3, 19, 219–20, 228 n14; *Plates 27, 28*

Talbot, Lord 116
Talpa: The Chronicles of A Clay Farm see Hoskyns, Chandos Wren
Tatlow, James, butler 29
Tayler, Edward, artist 153
Teck, Margaret, Duchess of 191
Tennyson, Alfred Lord 1
Thoby Priory, Essex 153, 181, 221
Thompson, F.M.L. 2
Three Choirs Festival: Johnny's role 6; Handel's *Ruth 74*; 1882 Hereford 143
Tintern Abbey, Monmouthshire 168
Toddington, Gloucestershire 4, 228 n19
Tolpuddle Martyrs 50, 101, 108; *see also* agricultural trades-unionism
Tompion stable clock 38, 235 n1
Tor Castle, Scotland 175, 176
Tournier, François and Joseph 177
Trades Union Congress 101
Trinity College, Cambridge 19, 158
Trollope, Anthony 9, 59–60, 74
Trumpet, The, Herefordshire 58
Tudge, William 116
Tufnell, Agnes (Arthur's wife) 94, 137, 138, 153, 184, 221
Tuke, Rev. F.H. 198, 201
Tulitt, Mr 98
Turner, Philip 117
Tyntesfield 7, 282 n57

Ullingswick, Herefordshire 110
United States of America 104–5, 108, 117, 121, 123, 146, 200, 219, 222, 223, 252–3 n29
Uphampton Farm, Shobdon, Herefordshire 49
urban growth 141, 205, 215, 220, 221, 222

Urwick, Mr 105
Van Kampen, Robert 12
Victoria and Albert Museum, London 7
Victoria, Princess 34
Victoria, Queen 7, 104, 106, 153, 169, 186, 208, 255 n62, 259 n66

Waghorn, Edward 12
Walrond, Ozzy 189, 217; *Plate 24*
Ward, L.H. 72
Waugh, Evelyn 1, 8
wealth, rise of non-landed 9, 148, 168, 210, 223
weather and agriculture 113, 123, 125, 142, 162–3, 202, 215
Webb, Richard 30
Wellington, Duke of 30
Westcar, Mr, of Creslow 116
Westminster, 1st Duke of 135
Westminster, Bend'Or, 2nd Duke of 191; *Plate 24*
Westminster Abbey 218
Westwood Hall, Staffordshire 69
Wharton, Herefordshire 15, 35, 39, 84
Wheeler, David 12
Whitehead, Charles 158
Whitfield Court, Herefordshire 200
Wickton parish, Herefordshire 39
Wigram, Sir James 18–19, 22, 30, 93
Wilde, Oscar 1, 10, 170, 210
Wilding, George, labourer 110
Willersley Castle, Cromford, Derbyshire: visits to 19, 55, 69; hampers from 30; death of Peter 93; death of Frederic 129; Fred's marriage 144; Geraldine's wedding 190; sale of land to tenants 211; sale of 219; *Plate 3*
Willoughby de Broke, Lord 203, 209
Wilson, Sir Jacob 148
Wiltshire 114, 163
Windsor, Berkshire: model farming on royal estate 49; Hereford cattle at 116
wines, sale of Hampton Court cellar 122
Winhart, Nicholas 86
Winsley Farm, Hampton Court 126
Winton de, Mr 59
Woburn Abbey, Bedfordshire 7, 121
Wodehouse, P.G. 8
women: role of in marriage 75–6, 88; education of 75–6; position in society 151
Wonastow, Monmouthshire 64, 71, 75, 78, 83, 85, 221
Wood, T., tenant Hampton Court 156
Woodhouse Farm, Hampton Court 39, 112, 142
Woodhouse, Richard 90
Woolaston Blake, Edith 173
Wootton Farm, Hampton Court 48, 61, 90
Worcester, 1863 RASE show at 46
Worcestershire 8, 163, 219
Wren, Sir Christopher 43
Wren, Theodosia 43, 44
Wright of Derby, Joseph, Arkwright portraits by 34, 219
Wrotham Park, Hertfordshire 61, 221
Wroxall, Warwickshire 43–5, 50, 95, 119, 180

Yates, Joseph, agent 34, 41, 51, 61, 139, 140, 149, 151, 156, 167
Yazor, Herefordshire 73, 75, 79
Ypres, Belgium: Third Battle of 216, 217; burial flag of 218

Acknowledgements

A decade of work has gone into assembling this account, and the list of those to whom I am indebted for generous help over those years is long. Those who have been particularly patient and indulgent in giving of their knowledge and lending from their bookshelves include:

Vivian Biggs who shared her research on Rev. Leigh Hoskyns of Aston Tyrrold;
Ronald Blythe for his generous endorsement of this work;
Anthony and Helen Bosanquet who were kindly collaborators, and are exemplary keepers and consolidators of family paraphernalia;
The late Anthea Brian of Bodenham who has shared a lifetime's accumulation of local historical knowledge;
David Cannadine who was astoundingly generous in giving of his time and advice;
Priscilla Chester-Master who shed some light on Sir Velters Cornewall and corroborated findings and suspicions about Dick and Geraldine;
Darrell Clarke of the Arkwright Society who has been an enthusiastic correspondent;
The late Lyle Eveille who shared her extensive knowledge of the work of John Ruskin;
Rev. John Hoskyns who permitted me to take photographs of family pictures;
Heather Hurley who first showed me the Harewood estate;
Gillian Linscott who pointed, like Saussure, up Mont Blanc from her sitting room in Hope-under-Dinmore;
The late Llewelyn Powell, who helped recover lost information about Evelyn;
Geoffrey Treasure who offered support, books and encouragement;
Dennis Turton who helped me to navigate a route through complicated legal documents and financial arrangements;
Eric Turton who unstintingly offered his own and Leominster museum's resources;
Sheila Weston who rose to the challenge of the Hoskyns' genealogy and kindly invited me to visit the private Harewood chapel with her;
Sue Wood who granted open access to private papers with tea laid on;
The staff of Hereford City and Leominster Libraries, and of the RASE archive at Stoneleigh and the National Army Museum, London.

Needless to say, the conclusions that I drew from the help of all of the above are my own, as are any errors that result.

I wish to mention particularly Sue Hubbard, the retired Senior Archivist at Herefordshire Record Office and HRO staff past and present, especially Mary Hirons, who was working to reclassify the Arkwright collection while I was under the haystack of brown boxes. We discussed many items and shared interpretations of the people and events about which we had both read. It was fruitful and enjoyable to compare our impressions, particularly for me, since so much of the rest of the research was done alone. Mary died in 1998, but her contribution to this book is remembered with gratitude.

Finally, I wish to record my ineffable thanks to my daughter Genevieve who postponed crawling until the week that the final typescript was submitted, and to my husband Edmond Beale, who has had to live with the Arkwrights for as long as he has me. Without his support this work would have been impossible; spending part of his honeymoon in Chamonix went beyond the vows he had just taken. His delight at the completion of this book can be surpassed only by my own.